The King Can Do No Wrong

Why are some autocrats more effective than others at retaining popular support even when their governments perform poorly? To develop insights into popular politics and governance across authoritarian regimes, this book stresses the importance of understanding autocratic blame games. Scott Williamson argues that how autocrats share power affects their ability to shift blame, such that they are less vulnerable to the public's grievances when they delegate decision-making powers to other political elites. He shows that this benefit of power-sharing influences when autocrats limit their control over decision-making, how much they repress, and whether their regimes provide accountability. He also argues that ruling monarchs are particularly well positioned among autocrats to protect their reputations by sharing power, which contributes to their surprising durability in the modern world. Drawing on extensive fieldwork in Jordan and cross-national analysis of autocracies, this book illustrates the important role of blame in the politics of authoritarian regimes.

SCOTT WILLIAMSON is an Associate Professor in the Department of Politics and International Relations and a Tutorial Fellow in Magdalen College at the University of Oxford. He received his PhD in political science from Stanford University.

The King Can Do No Wrong

Blame Games and Power Sharing in Authoritarian Regimes

SCOTT WILLIAMSON
University of Oxford

Shaftesbury Road, Cambridge CB2 8EA, United Kingdom

One Liberty Plaza, 20th Floor, New York, NY 10006, USA

477 Williamstown Road, Port Melbourne, VIC 3207, Australia

314–321, 3rd Floor, Plot 3, Splendor Forum, Jasola District Centre, New Delhi – 110025, India

103 Penang Road, #05–06/07, Visioncrest Commercial, Singapore 238467

Cambridge University Press is part of Cambridge University Press & Assessment, a department of the University of Cambridge.

We share the University's mission to contribute to society through the pursuit of education, learning and research at the highest international levels of excellence.

www.cambridge.org
Information on this title: www.cambridge.org/9781009484084

DOI: 10.1017/9781009484053

© Scott Williamson 2024

This publication is in copyright. Subject to statutory exception and to the provisions of relevant collective licensing agreements, no reproduction of any part may take place without the written permission of Cambridge University Press & Assessment.

When citing this work, please include a reference to the DOI 10.1017/9781009484053

First published 2024

A catalogue record for this publication is available from the British Library

Library of Congress Cataloging-in-Publication Data
Names: Williamson, Scott, 1990– author.
Title: The king can do no wrong : blame games and power sharing in authoritarian regimes / Scott Williamson, University of Oxford.
Description: Cambridge, United Kingdom ; New York, NY : Cambridge University Press, 2024. | Includes bibliographical references and index.
Identifiers: LCCN 2024011575 | ISBN 9781009484084 (hardback) | ISBN 9781009484053 (ebook)
Subjects: LCSH: Authoritarianism. | Delegation of powers. | Kings and rulers. | Presidents.
Classification: LCC JC480 .W544 2024 | DDC 321.9–dc23/eng/20240920
LC record available at https://lccn.loc.gov/2024011575

ISBN 978-1-009-48408-4 Hardback
ISBN 978-1-009-48406-0 Paperback

Cambridge University Press & Assessment has no responsibility for the persistence or accuracy of URLs for external or third-party internet websites referred to in this publication and does not guarantee that any content on such websites is, or will remain, accurate or appropriate.

For Bittoo

Contents

List of Figures	*page* x
List of Tables	xi
Acknowledgments	xiii

1	**Introduction**		1
	1.1	Governance and the Public in Authoritarian Regimes	6
	1.2	Attributions of Responsibility under Authoritarianism	12
	1.3	The King Can Do No Wrong	17
	1.4	Contributions of the Book	23
	1.5	Plan of the Book	33
2	**A Theory of Power Sharing and Attributions under Authoritarian Rule**		39
	2.1	Why Attributions Matter for Autocrats	40
	2.2	Attributions and Strategic Power Sharing	50
	2.3	The Royal Advantage	63
	2.4	Testable Implications	72
	2.5	What's Next	77
3	**Cross-National Evidence on Power Sharing and Attributions in Autocracies**		78
	3.1	Citizens Respond to Changes in the Credibility of Power Sharing	81
	3.2	Attributions, Power Sharing, and Governance in Autocracies	101
	3.3	Conclusion	112
	3.4	Appendix	113

vii

viii   *Contents*

4   The Jordanian Monarchy's Strategic Blame Games   114
    4.1   Background on the Hashemite Kingdom   116
    4.2   Decision-Making and Delegation in Jordan   121
    4.3   Strategic Delegation to Protect the Monarchy   131
    4.4   Conclusion   142
    4.5   Appendix   142

5   How Jordanians Attribute Responsibility   146
    5.1   What Elites and Activists Say   147
    5.2   Surveying Jordanian Public Opinion   150
    5.3   Evidence from a Facebook Ad Experiment   161
    5.4   Conclusion   169
    5.5   Appendix   170

6   Power Sharing and Attributions across Jordan's
    Modern History   173
    6.1   Different Threats and Divergent Power Sharing   175
    6.2   Power Sharing and Blame under King Hussein   178
    6.3   Power Sharing and Blame under King Abdullah   197
    6.4   Back to More Direct Royal Rule?   207
    6.5   Conclusion   209

7   How Jordan's Blame Games Influence Governance   213
    7.1   Limiting Repression   214
    7.2   The Failure of Anti-Monarchical Coordination   225
    7.3   Providing Limited Accountability   228
    7.4   Conclusion   233

8   The Royal Advantage in Power Sharing and Blame Shifting   236
    8.1   Variation in the Credibility of Delegation   239
    8.2   Variation in Expectations   256
    8.3   Variation in Escalation of Opposition   263
    8.4   Conclusion   274
    8.5   Appendix   275

9   Power Sharing, Blame, and the Collapse of Royal Regimes   277
    9.1   Which Monarchies Survived into the Modern World?   280
    9.2   The Collapse of Modern Monarchies   285
    9.3   Conclusion   299

Contents ix

10	**Conclusion**	301
	10.1 Popular Politics in Autocracies	303
	10.2 Autocracy and Democracy	311
	10.3 In Conclusion	315
	References	317
	Index	342

Figures

3.1 Google Trends comparison of Putin and Medvedev	*page* 91
3.2 Google Trends comparison of King Mohammed and prime ministers	95
4.1 Map of the Hashemite Kingdom of Jordan	117
4.2 Foreign and domestic policy articles with topic models	141
5.1 Perceptions of cabinet and parliamentary responsibility	152
5.2 Who is most responsible for...	153
5.3 Parliament's role in policymaking	158
5.4 Policy grievances and suitability of democracy	160
5.5 Facebook ad for the king	162
5.6 Facebook ad click rate results	166
6.1 Abdullah steps back from economic policymaking	203
6.2 Google Trends for King Abdullah and prime ministers in Jordan	206
7.1 Protests in Jordan occur frequently	217
7.2 Repeat prime ministers	220
7.3 Minister exits by year, 1947–2018	230
8.1 Monarchs are less threatened by other political elites	240
8.2 Ruling party or family representation in cabinets, 2000–2010	247
8.3 Citizens of Arab monarchies perceived parliaments to have more policy influence	252
8.4 Monarchs do not bind elites through partisan ties	254
8.5 Monarchies have multiple executives	256
8.6 Experimental results: Acceptability of delegation	260
8.7 Experimental results by regime type: Acceptability of delegation	261
8.8 Constitutions do not create an expectation of accountability for monarchs	262
8.9 Parliamentary responsibility by country	275

Tables

3.1 Relative attention on autocrats is higher when they share less power	*page* 85
3.2 Perceptions of power sharing condition the link between economic assessments and support for the autocrat	99
3.3 Autocrats repress more when they share power less credibly	104
3.4 Autocrats are more exposed to popular opposition when they share power less credibly	108
3.5 Autocrats replace elites less when they share power less credibly	111
3.6 Trends ratios shift as delegation becomes more or less credible	113
4.1 Topics from STM analysis	143
5.1 YouGov survey attribution questions	154
5.2 Perceptions of responsibility and support for national leader	156
5.3 Ad demographics – gender and age	163
5.4 Timeline and political context	164
5.5 Principal components	170
5.6 Domestic policy grievances and suitability of democracy	171
5.7 Foreign policy grievances and suitability of democracy	172
6.1 Temporal changes in threat and delegation	177
7.1 Most protests in Jordan are not repressed	218
7.2 Minister removals and public pressure	231
7.3 Minister removals are lowest during periods of less credible delegation	233
8.1 Perceptions of parliamentary responsibility	253
8.2 Regime survival during the Arab uprisings	265

8.3	Autocratic monarchs are less vulnerable to protests	273
8.4	Logit model for balance in YouGov experiment	276
9.1	Royal survival and parliamentary responsibility	282
9.2	More constrained monarchies experienced fewer regime changes, 1800–1940	284

Acknowledgments

This book owes much to many. First and foremost, I will always be deeply grateful for the willingness of numerous Jordanians to assist me with their time and knowledge over the span of multiple years, including the dozens of people who sat down for interviews, as well as several others who provided advice and logistical support. The project would not have been possible without their openness and generosity. I am also grateful for the Tunisians who agreed to speak with me about their experiences, for Intissar Samarat for arranging interviews, and for Le Centre d'Etudes Maghrébines à Tunis (CEMAT) for sponsoring my visit to the country in the summer of 2019.

The project began to take shape as a dissertation, but its seeds go back further, when I was an undergraduate at Indiana University. It was while studying Arabic in Irbid and Amman during the Arab Spring, and then writing a thesis under the supervision of Abdulkader Sinno, that several of the ideas in this book first began to emerge. Even after finishing the thesis, I could not put down the questions of why some people do not perceive their powerful dictators to be at fault and why ruling monarchies in particular have been so stable in the past several decades. At Stanford, these questions gradually coalesced into a dissertation, and during that process, I benefited immensely from the support of my committee: Kenneth Scheve and Lisa Blaydes as cochairs, and Beatriz Magaloni, David Laitin, and Jeremy Weinstein as committee members. I am grateful for their generosity with their time. They were always there to ask probing questions, to provide detailed feedback, and to point out weaknesses in my arguments and analysis. This book is significantly better because of their help, and I am thankful for their trust in encouraging me to follow my intuitions and interests.

Several other professors were supportive at various stages of the project. I am thankful that Avidit Acharya always tried to push me to think more theoretically, and I am especially appreciative of the feedback and advice I received over the years from A.Kadir Yildirim, Kristin Fabbe, Marwa Shalaby, Nathan Brown, and Paul Schuler. I am likewise grateful for the feedback I received from scholars at New York University Abu Dhabi during my postdoc there, including Abdul Noury, Robert Kubinec, and Romain Ferrali. At Bocconi University, I was lucky to have help planning a book conference, where I received invaluable feedback from Carl Henrik Knutsen, Ellen Lust, Jan Teorell, Kevin Arceneaux, Milan Svolik, and Miriam Golden, as well as my colleagues Lanny Martin and Livio Di Lonardo. Two of Bocconi's PhD students, Dirck de Kleer and Roxana Burciu, helpfully took notes on the discussion. I also benefited from a book conference arranged by the Project on Middle East Political Science, in which I was given incredibly useful comments from André Bank, Anne Meng, and Marc Lynch.

Many others gave helpful advice for how to navigate academia or how to think about the politics of authoritarian regimes, including Adeline Lo, Amaney Jamal, Anna Grzymala-Busse, Brett Carter, Claire Adida, Dominik Hangartner, Elizabeth Nugent, Erin Baggott Carter, Jens Hainmueller, Ora John Reuter, Lauren Prather, Melina Platas, Michael Miller, Natalie Letsa, Rebecca Morton, Rich Nielsen, Rory Truex, Sean Yom, and Shana Marshall.

The book received financial support from a number of sources, for which I am very thankful. At Stanford, these organizations included the Abbasi Program in Islamic Studies, the Center for African Studies, the Center on International Conflict and Negotiation, the Center for Human Rights and International Justice, the Europe Center, the Freeman Spogli Institute for International Studies, the Graduate Research Opportunity Fund, and the Institute for Research in the Social Sciences. I am also thankful for financial support from the National Science Foundation and the Project on Middle East Political Science, as well as the Dondena Centre at Bocconi University.

I have been lucky to benefit from friendships with a number of other academics over the years, many of whom commented on versions of the book, but perhaps more importantly helped me sustain the energy and optimism to write it. I will always be thankful to Aala Abdelgadir, Alexandra Blackman, Alexandra Siegal, Andrea Dillon, Ashley Fabrizio, Basma Fahoum, Caroline Abadeer, Christiana Parreira, Daniel Tavana, Kerim Can Kavakli, Jane Esberg, Jonathan Chu, Jordan Bernhardt, Lachlan McNamee, Lillian Frost, Lindsay

Acknowledgments xv

Hundley, Luis Rodriguez, Nandita Balakrishnan, Nathan Lee, Ruxi Zhang, Salma Mousa, Sasha de Vogel, Seth Werfel, Steve Monroe, Sharan Grewal, Steven Schaff, Thomas Ginn, Tongtong Zhang, Vincent Bauer, and William Marble.

Finally, I am incredibly fortunate to have supportive and loving family members who were always there for me through the ups and downs of graduate school, including my wife Renu Singh, my parents Pamela and Bruce Williamson, and my brothers Gregory and Jeffrey Williamson.

1 Introduction

Throughout 2010, the Hashemite Kingdom of Jordan experienced a surge of social mobilization fueled by frustrations with the country's stagnating economy and political life. Growing numbers of workers were engaged in demonstrations and strikes (Christophersen 2013), while political parties staged protests against the country's electoral law following parliamentary elections in that November. As Jordan moved into 2011, these political and economic frustrations coalesced into weekly protests attended by thousands of demonstrators. Coinciding with the region-wide eruption of the Arab Spring uprisings, the protests were geographically dispersed and attracted a broad cross section of Jordanian society, including social groups that constituted a key part of the ruling monarchy's support coalition (Ryan 2018).

Nonetheless, the protests never escalated into a direct threat to the power of Jordan's autocratic king, Abdullah II. Though a small, radical fringe of demonstrators criticized the monarch, their message failed to resonate. Instead, the vast majority of protesters – and the public more broadly – directed their anger toward the prime minister, cabinet, and parliament while asking for the king to step in and correct the country's problems. Abdullah responded by dismissing the cabinet a few weeks after the weekly protests began, while also promising that subsequent governments would pursue political and economic reforms. These moves were welcomed by many Jordanians, and after a few months, the demonstrations had dissipated without the regime using significant repression and without ever posing a serious challenge to the monarchy.

In nearby Egypt, protests triggered by similar economic and political grievances to those in Jordan followed a very different trajectory. Egypt had also experienced a rise in political activism in 2010. When the young Egyptian man Khaled Said was brutally beaten to death by two low-level police officers in June of that year, anger had spread rapidly around the country. A Facebook page entitled "We Are All Khaled

Said" soon attracted hundreds of thousands of followers, and the page used this attention to advocate for reforming Egypt's abusive security forces and tackling deeper structural problems related to poverty and corruption. As part of these efforts, the page made explicitly political demands on President Mubarak and his government. Though initially adopting a cautious approach that did not attack the autocratic president directly, the page linked Egypt's persistent problems to the regime's policies and advocated openly for term limits that would end Mubarak's thirty-year presidency (Alaimo 2015).

As the Arab Spring uprisings began to spread across the Middle East in January 2011, the "We Are All Khaled Said" page reacted by escalating its demands against President Mubarak. After Tunisia's president was overthrown in mid-January, the page's founder, Wael Ghonim, quickly began to encourage Egyptians to mobilize against their president for his role in perpetuating Egypt's many political and economic problems. It soon became clear that much of the country shared this opinion that the president was to blame for their grievances. Demonstrations began on Police Day and were ostensibly focused on police abuse, as well as frustrations with Egypt's stagnant economy and repressive politics. But this issue-based anger coalesced into direct challenges to the president. Chants of "*irhal!*" (leave!) spread rapidly among the hundreds of thousands of protesters, who demanded that Mubarak resign for the country to move forward. As with King Abdullah in Jordan, the president responded in part by dismissing his cabinet and promising to usher in reforms alongside a new government. But this move did little to satisfy the crowds. Mass mobilizations targeting the president persisted for more than two weeks, outlasting the regime's repression and eventually forcing Mubarak out of office amid joyous celebrations all over the country.

Similar divergences occurred across the region. In addition to Tunisia and Egypt, uprisings escalated in Libya, Yemen, and Syria, where demonstrators were determined to oust authoritarian presidents who had brutalized their people, crushed democratic aspirations, and looted their economies. Meanwhile, mass challenges to authoritarian rule barely materialized in the Middle East's many monarchies. Royal rulers such as Abdullah did face protest movements of their own, some of which were quite large, and some of which pushed for significant reforms in their political systems. Large protest movements emerged in the monarchies of Morocco, Kuwait, and Bahrain, while Saudi

Introduction 3

Arabia and Oman also experienced rare unrest. Yet only in Bahrain did a substantial part of the public eventually turn against the ruling monarch, and there only after the regime itself chose to escalate by turning to harsh repression against demonstrators calling for reforms (El Gamal 2014; Louer 2012). Across the monarchies, the vast majority of protesters called for holding elites accountable and implementing political and economic reforms that would leave the region's royals largely unscathed. This story repeated itself a decade later, when authoritarian presidents in Algeria and Sudan were overthrown by mass uprisings, whereas the Middle East's authoritarian kings continued to hang onto power while mostly avoiding serious popular opposition to their continuation on the throne.

Countries such as Jordan, Egypt, and most others in the Middle East are said to be governed by autocracies, or authoritarian regimes, because in such countries core civil liberties are absent and the most important political leaders are not selected through free elections. Sometimes these political leaders are monarchs, and in other cases, they may be presidents, party bosses, or military officers, but they share in common the acquisition of power without genuine electoral competition as well as the denial of political freedoms to the citizenry. However, despite the absence of free elections, popular politics can still be contentious and influential in these contexts, as during the Arab Spring uprisings. When the public makes their voices heard, why might anger focus on the autocrat in some cases, while targeting lower level officials in others? Existing research on authoritarian regimes emphasizes the importance of the regime's ability to repress and co-opt effectively to keep the masses from overthrowing the autocrat, but these explanations do not account all that well for the variation that occurred in the Middle East during this time. While some of the region's monarchies benefited from natural resource wealth that helped them to buy the public's loyalty, this advantage did not apply to Jordan or Morocco, where economic and social grievances closely resembled those of the Arab republics, and where kings were using similar co-optive strategies as presidents to distribute resources to their peoples (Blaydes 2010; Lust-Okar 2006; Owen 2012). In addition, the Arab republics all possessed extremely large coercive apparatuses, and arguably even more so than the monarchies, their police and security forces had extensive experience using violence against civilians.

What seemed to matter for the trajectory of protests in this moment was not so much the coercive and co-optive capacity of these regimes, but rather, the extent to which most demonstrators believed that the autocrats bore responsibility for their grievances. Protesters tended to blame their presidents but not monarchs for what was wrong in their countries; as a result, protesters in the republics wanted their presidents to be replaced, while protesters in the monarchies were more likely to be placated by the dismissal of ministers and parliaments. How is it possible that powerful autocrats, such as the Middle East's monarchs, might escape blame for their country's problems? After all, it may seem intuitive that the great powers of autocratic rulers would make them magnets for credit during good times but also focal points for blame when the people become dissatisfied. Influential academic work has assumed that authoritarian regimes struggle to avoid blame during moments of discontent (e.g., Weaver 1986), and this challenge often is apparent, as with the example of Egypt's Mubarak. Yet, in other cases such as Jordan, autocrats appear to be successful at shifting the public's attributions of responsibility for poor governance, convincing many of their citizens that they are not personally to blame and should therefore not be held accountable for the country's trials and tribulations. To the extent that enough people do not perceive the autocrat to be at fault, these powerful political figures should have less need to rely on repression to maintain control, and they should be less at risk of losing their power to mass uprisings like those of the Arab Spring.

How Mubarak and Abdullah responded to protests at this time also implies that autocrats recognize the importance of blame attributions and that they seek to shape these attributions strategically. As the depth of the public's anger became apparent across the Arab world, authoritarian rulers responded by trying to cast blame for their countries' problems on other political elites in their regimes. In Egypt, Jordan, and elsewhere, this approach was reflected in how rulers initially reacted to protests by dismissing their prime ministers and cabinets. Rotating these officials out of office constituted an attempt to convince the public that these officials bore responsibility for unpopular policy outcomes and were being held accountable for their mistakes. But this strategy worked better in some countries than others, strengthening Abdullah's political position in Jordan, while failing to protect Mubarak in Egypt.

Introduction 5

This book advances two arguments that contribute to the understanding of why some autocrats are more successful than others at evading blame and retaining popular support, both in the Arab world and more generally among authoritarian regimes. The first argument is that how citizens in these political systems attribute responsibility is influenced by how credibly autocrats share decision-making powers with other political elites. The more the autocrat monopolizes the policy process, the more likely they are to be blamed by the public when outcomes turn out poorly. Alternatively, the more they delegate decision-making to ministers, members of parliament, or bureaucrats, the less likely they are to be viewed as the principal culprit when the people become dissatisfied, and the less likely their popularity is to decline. Furthermore, because autocrats have some capacity to shape the nature of power-sharing arrangements in their regimes, they can act strategically to influence the public's attributions by delegating more or less credibly over time and across different policy issues. Whether autocrats choose to empower other elites or not will influence their exposure to blame and thus their vulnerability to protests, as well as the dynamics of repression and accountability in their regimes. Returning to the Arab world, the region's monarchies had typically granted their cabinets and parliaments more influence over decision-making prior to the Arab Spring; as a result, their citizens were more likely than individuals living in the republics to accept that these actors, and not the autocrat, were at fault for their grievances. Because of these dynamics, the monarchies also responded to unrest with less severe repression and were able to provide a modicum of political accountability when they removed cabinet ministers and other officials from their positions.

The second argument articulated by this book sheds light on *why* autocratic monarchs were better positioned than autocratic presidents to avoid blame by sharing power. I claim that this variation is rooted in different institutional features of monarchies and republics. Monarchies are defined by the institutionalization of hereditary succession within a specific royal family, which establishes rigid standards about who can be the monarch while creating flexible expectations about how the monarch is involved in decision-making. This situation contrasts with republics, where anyone could – in theory – become the president, and where the president is supposed to govern for, and be held accountable by, the people. I argue these differences mean that delegating power over the policy process is both safer for monarchs and more in line with norms about how responsibility is supposed to be attributed in the political system. These advantages increase the likelihood that a monarch will share power credibly with other political elites, and they also strengthen the effectiveness of this power sharing at protecting the monarch's reputation when governance turns out poorly. Again returning to the Arab world, the region's presidents delegated less credibly to minimize risks associated with internal challengers from their regimes; in addition, they struggled to overcome expectations that they would be deeply involved in decision-making and should therefore be held accountable for policy outcomes. Meanwhile, the region's monarchs had less reason to fear internal challenges from nonroyal elites to whom they delegated, and their delegation to these elites benefited from norms that emphasized the appropriateness of keeping the monarchy above the decision-making process. Thus, as discontent spread across the region, monarchs were less likely to absorb blame than their presidential counterparts, which facilitated their ability to outlast the unrest.

The book's arguments contribute to the understanding of why some autocrats are vulnerable to escalating opposition during periods of popular dissatisfaction, while others are able to maintain genuine support from much of the public even as their regimes perform poorly for extended periods of time. In exploring why monarchs are particularly well positioned to rely on delegation of decision-making responsibilities to protect their reputations, the book also sheds light on monarchy as an understudied but highly stable type of modern authoritarian rule. The remainder of this chapter discusses why it is important to study the factors that shape popular support for autocratic rulers, summarizes the primary arguments in more detail, and expands on how the book develops our understanding of the politics of authoritarian governance.

1.1 Governance and the Public in Authoritarian Regimes

Saddam Hussein was Iraq's president for more than two decades, from 1979 to 2003. From the beginning, his rule was defined by ironfisted brutality. Less than a week after he forced his predecessor to resign and assumed the presidency, Hussein convened an assembly of the ruling Ba'ath Party and proceeded to denounce dozens of its leading members as traitors. Hundreds of the party's elites were soon detained

1.1 Governance and the Public in Autocracies 7

and executed. In the years that followed, Hussein would subject tens of thousands more of his country's citizens to state violence, whether rebellious Kurds, protesting Shi'a, dissident Sunnis, or any political elite who might plausibly pose a threat to his dominance of the political system (Blaydes 2018). Ruling through fear and with no one to challenge him, Hussein's unconstrained power left him free to pursue what policies he wanted, often with disastrous results. Most egregiously, the Iran–Iraq War that he started devastated the country during the 1980s, his invasion of Kuwait only made the situation worse in the 1990s, and his nonchalant response to the threat of invasion by the United States in 2003 ultimately proved his undoing.

In many ways, the presidency of Saddam Hussein reflects common assumptions about what authoritarianism is and how it works. In this view, authoritarianism means governance through brutality by an unconstrained and unpopular dictator, which breeds instability and ultimately ends violently. This trajectory certainly captures the truth in some cases, but the reality of authoritarian politics is far more complex. As mentioned earlier, authoritarianism (which I will also refer to as autocracy) is defined by the lack of basic civil liberties and the absence of free and fair elections for key decision-makers in the executive and legislative branches, and this broad definition captures an immense amount of variation in both how these regimes govern and the outcomes their governance produces.

For example, while some autocracies are controlled by single parties as in China, many others are governed by hegemonic parties that maintain their power through unfair elections like Putin's regime in Russia, and still others are led by monarchs, military juntas, or charismatic strongmen (Geddes et al. 2014; Magaloni et al. 2013; Wahman et al. 2013). In terms of outcomes, there are autocracies like the Kuwaiti monarchy that have survived for decades, and their stability aligns with high levels of economic development and relatively liberal political spheres. There also exist autocracies like Saddam Hussein's Iraq or Syria under the al-Asad family, which hold onto power for long periods of time while persistently mismanaging their countries' economies and resorting to extreme violence against the public. Alternatively, many autocrats, as well as the regimes they lead, survive in power for only a handful of years (Geddes et al. 2014), and this instability often breeds dire social and economic consequences. For instance, prior to the emergence of dominance by the al-Asads, Syria experienced ten coups between 1950 and 1970 (Powell and Thyne 2011), as autocrats were repeatedly overthrown by their political rivals.

Understanding this variation across authoritarian regimes is not just useful as a scholarly exercise but remains highly relevant to the contemporary world. Temporarily, as dozens of new democracies emerged between the 1970s and the 1990s, authoritarianism seemed on its way to becoming a historical relic. But two decades later, this trend had reversed. Many authoritarian regimes survived this third wave of democratization and continue to thrive; furthermore, even some mature democracies have begun to decay and are struggling to maintain their system of competitive elections. By 2020, a majority of the world's political systems had become authoritarian again for the first time since 2001 (Luhrmann et al. 2020), illustrating the persistent relevance of authoritarianism to global politics.

The academic literature on authoritarianism has become increasingly sophisticated and provides a number of insights into variation across these regimes. An important component of this research focuses on institutional configurations within autocracies and their effects on governance. Saddam Hussein's brutal dominance of Iraq may reflect the archetype of a dictator for many people, but, in fact, autocrats – who I define as the most powerful individual in an authoritarian regime – often face significant political constraints from other institutions in their political systems (Magaloni 2008; Meng 2020). Institutions ranging from parliaments and cabinets to courts and the military can exercise political influence and limit the dominance of the autocrat. As one example, Mexican presidents under the Institutional Revolutionary Party (PRI) regime were constrained by their party and consistently left office after a single six-year term (Magaloni 2006). Research suggests that authoritarian regimes in which autocrats face more constraints on their power tend to perform better economically (Wright 2008), in part because policymaking is less capricious, corrupt, and unstable (North and Weingast 1989). Likewise, these regimes are also less repressive on average, perhaps because the autocrat has less capacity to direct the security forces for their own ends (Frantz et al. 2020).

Institutions also have implications for the stability of authoritarian rule, as they can help autocrats to manage potential threats to their power. In thinking about where challenges to autocrats come from, scholars distinguish between threats that autocrats face from other

1.1 Governance and the Public in Autocracies

political elites in their regimes and threats they face from below as the public mobilizes against them (Svolik 2012). Regarding the former, even the most powerful autocrats do not rule alone; instead, they depend on elite allies to both take and then keep power (Haber 2008). However, by virtue of their own influence in the political system, these elites are often well positioned to overthrow and replace the autocrat through a coup d'état (Magaloni 2008), and most autocrats do lose power in this way (Svolik 2012). As a result, surviving in office means figuring out how to share power with elites to incentivize their loyalty. Institutions such as legislatures, parties, and cabinets can play an important role here, especially if they are relatively strong (Meng 2020). For example, holding a seat in the legislature may give elites access to rents and status, as well as influence over policy decisions (Blaydes 2010; Gandhi 2008; Truex 2014). Institutions can also enable elites to monitor the autocrat more effectively, increasing the credibility of power-sharing arrangements by making it easier to observe if the autocrat is trying to seize more power for themselves (Boix and Svolik 2013).

Regarding threats from below, autocrats also need to take the public into account as they try to hold onto power. Mass uprisings can trigger their downfall directly (Kendall-Taylor and Frantz 2014), as illustrated by the Arab Spring uprisings or the string of Colour Revolutions before them. Despite the absence of free and fair elections, many autocrats also hold manipulated elections, and sometimes they miscalculate and get voted out of office. In addition, evidence of popular opposition to the autocrat can motivate efforts by elites to seize power themselves (Casper and Tyson 2014). As a result, if autocrats want to stay in power, they need to have strategies for controlling their countries' citizens. Institutions can be helpful here as well. Legislatures, parties, and elections provide opportunities for short-term payments through vote buying, as well as sustained financial rents via patronage (Lust-Okar 2006; Magaloni 2006; Ross 2001). Such institutions can also offer limited representation of constituents' policy preferences (Gandhi 2008; Malesky and Schuler 2011; Truex 2016), or responsiveness to citizens' complaints (Lueders 2022).

However, though it has long been recognized that "the people" matter for the stability of authoritarian regimes, research on popular support for these regimes is underdeveloped (Carter and Carter 2023; Przeworski 2023), and the literature has tended to privilege the politics of elites over the politics of the masses (Magaloni and Wallace 2008). It is often assumed that autocrats must be unpopular, that they use repression to keep the people under control, and that what support they have is based on material transactions and is therefore fundamentally unstable (Przeworski 2023). Certainly repression is a central component of controlling the public in authoritarian regimes (Albertus and Menaldo 2012; Bellin 2004; Blaydes 2018; Greitens 2016; Levitsky and Way 2010). Fear of repression understandably keeps most citizens of autocracies out of politics, and they often either lack well-formed political views or hide their beliefs as a result. Nonetheless, even though many people falsify their preferences in these contexts, it remains the case that their genuine attitudes and beliefs can matter a great deal for their countries' trajectories, particularly during moments when repressive or co-optive capacity are shaken by exogenous shocks or internal crises (Kuran 1991). At the same time, there is plenty of evidence to suggest that many autocrats are genuinely popular with their people for reasons that go well beyond the receipt of patronage from the regime (e.g., Frye et al. 2017; Huang et al. 2022). In fact, even Saddam Hussein appears to have benefited from substantial popular support during certain periods of his rule (Blaydes 2018). Yet, our understanding of popular politics in authoritarian regimes continues to be relatively underdeveloped, especially when compared to what is known about democracies. The masses remain a mechanistic actor in many theories of authoritarianism, with blackboxed preferences that say relatively little about how people think and act under autocratic rule (Williamson and Magaloni 2020).

One area in which this absence is visible is in understanding how people living under authoritarian regimes perceive the distribution of power in their political systems, and how these views shape the ways in which they think about responsibility and accountability. Generally speaking, people hold preferences for certain policies or outcomes to be provided by their governments and they want to reward political leaders who deliver while holding accountable those who fail to deliver. For this accountability to take place, the public needs to figure out who in the political system is responsible for decision-making and therefore who should receive credit for good outcomes or blame for bad ones (Hood 2014). These attributions of responsibility are highly relevant to most political leaders. Whether they receive credit or blame has

1.1 Governance and the Public in Autocracies

major implications for their popularity. As might be expected, receiving credit tends to increase public approval, while being blamed tends to decrease it even more (Weaver 1986). Attributions also have implications for collective action: When people have a clear target to blame, they are more likely to protest (Javeline 2003a, 2003b). In other words, how people assign attributions of responsibility for political and policy outcomes has implications for the intensity of opposition a leader is likely to face and whether that opposition escalates into mobilization. These dynamics should also be important for authoritarian regimes, but we know relatively little about how people attribute responsibility in these contexts.

Because the consequences of attributions can be so important for their ability to survive in office, political leaders tend to work hard at shaping how the public thinks about responsibility. Such efforts can be symbolic or rhetorical, but they can also spill over directly into how leaders structure decision-making processes or the implementation of policies (Hood 2011). While some research studies from autocratic contexts suggests that authoritarian regimes take attributions of credit and blame into account in how they approach policymaking (e.g., Cai 2008; Schuler 2020), the academic literature has largely overlooked whether and how autocrats strategically approach decision-making in an effort to manage the public's ideas about responsibility in the political system. This absence reflects another, broader issue with the study of authoritarian politics, where the focus on how regimes survive has overshadowed attention to how these regimes actually govern. It remains common to assume that the autocrat makes most important decisions, while other elites play somewhat marginal roles in steering the state's policies. These dynamics reflect an abstracted version of reality for many authoritarian regimes, but decision-making processes also remain highly complex in these political systems, and there is substantial variation in the extent to which autocrats dominate the policy process. Part of the reason for the muted focus on these issues can be explained by data scarcity, since the opacity of authoritarian regimes makes it difficult to study their internal politics rigorously with either qualitative or quantitative social science methods (Gandhi et al. 2020). In recent years, scholars have increasingly used creative solutions to acquire data on authoritarian governance, producing insights into topics ranging from bargaining between executive and legislative branches (Noble 2020) to the dynamics of lobbying (Lü et al. 2020).

12   *Introduction*

Nonetheless, there remains much to be learned in terms of how autocracies make decisions and govern the societies they control.

1.2 Attributions of Responsibility under Authoritarianism

This book addresses the political dynamics surrounding attributions of responsibility – how people assign credit and blame, and how political leaders try to manipulate this process – to advance our knowledge of both popular politics and governance under authoritarianism. The underlying assumption of this study is that people try to understand who is responsible for policy outcomes they like or dislike, because they care about holding political leaders accountable. Political leaders receive "credit" when responsibility is attributed to them for positive outcomes, and they receive "blame" when responsibility is attributed to them for negative outcomes. As discussed earlier, these attributions can have direct and large consequences for the intensity of opposition faced by political leaders. How, then, might autocrats try to manage the public's attributions of responsibility? In general, two classes of strategies are available to political leaders. The first involves the use of *messaging* to advance claims of credit or to deny being at fault, while the second focuses on using *institutions* to influence who wields actual responsibility for decision-making, thus directing attributions toward that person.

In an authoritarian context, messaging strategies – that is, propaganda – are undoubtedly important for shaping how the public thinks about responsibility. The high degree of control over the media makes it relatively easy for most autocrats to distribute their message, and this propaganda can often be effective at influencing mass attitudes (e.g., Adena et al. 2015; Carter and Carter 2023; Stockmann 2013; Williamson and Malik 2021). Researchers have shown how propaganda is used explicitly to grant credit to the autocrat while assigning blame to others. For instance, Rozenas and Stukal (2019) document how the Russian media attributes good economic outcomes to President Putin while attributing negative outcomes to lower-level government officials or foreign actors. Similarly, Lu (2014) finds that social reforms increase trust in the Chinese central government but not local governments, because the media credits the former but not the latter with good policy outcomes. Aytaç (2021) also demonstrates that President Erdogan in Turkey appears capable of minimizing the risks of

1.2 Attributions of Responsibility in Autocracies

blame for poor economic performance by using propaganda to change the country's political agenda.

This research has been important for understanding attributions of responsibility in authoritarian regimes, but propaganda is not the whole story for explaining how people think about politics in these contexts, including when it comes to attributing blame and credit. Consider again the example of Egypt's Mubarak, who tried to deflate the mass uprising in 2011 in part by suggesting that his ministers were the ones at fault, while also propagating the narrative of a "plot" against the country. Such claims were dismissed by the protesters, who perceived that, "ultimately in Egypt, the power lies with the president" (Al-Jazeera 2011). Propaganda is not always persuasive (Huang 2015), and it becomes less persuasive as its claims diverge more substantially from reality (Carter and Carter 2023; Rosenfeld 2018). When it comes to perceptions of responsibility, an authoritarian regime's messaging may assert consistently that the autocrat is not at fault, but these claims should be less likely to affect how the public attributes blame in cases where the autocrat does in fact dominate decision-making.

This book moves beyond messaging and propaganda to consider how the distribution of power across governance institutions affects the politics of attributions in autocracies. In this framework, political leaders face a trade-off in their ability to claim credit or avoid blame. This trade-off is shaped by the extent of their control over decision-making. The more direct their control, the more likely they are to receive credit when outcomes prove popular, but the more likely they are to attract blame when they turn out poorly instead. By contrast, when decision-making responsibilities are delegated to others or spread across multiple institutions, the political leader will be positioned less well to claim credit but will also be more insulated from blame. This trade-off occurs because people make attributions based, in part, on their perceptions of who held power over a decision and its implementation (Alicke 2000; Knobloch-Westerwick and Taylor 2008; Weiner 1985). Research from a variety of contexts supports this idea. Whether in experimental settings (Bartling and Fischbacher 2012), corporations (Boeker 1992), or politics at the local, national, and international levels (Boyne 2008; Ellis 1994; Gulzar and Pasquale 2017; Hobolt et al. 2012; Martin and Raffler 2021; Tavits 2007; Williamson 2024), individuals who exercise less control over decision-making are less likely to reap the credit but also more likely to avoid the blame for subsequent outcomes. As will be discussed further in the next chapter, research suggests that political leaders are more likely to prioritize blame avoidance over credit claiming when they face a trade-off between the two, and I argue that this emphasis on minimizing exposure to blame should be particularly relevant to autocrats. As a result, this book will focus more so on how people living under authoritarianism attribute blame and how autocrats try to avoid blame, though it will give some attention to credit claiming as well.

But is it actually possible for autocrats to use institutional strategies to shift blame away from themselves? The typical portrayal of authoritarian regimes as those in which autocrats are all-powerful and their regimes are highly centralized would suggest they should find it easy to claim credit but also extremely difficult to avoid blame (Weaver 1986). Thus, when outcomes turn out poorly and the public is aggrieved, the autocrat should have no choice but to rely on repression, since they will otherwise become the target of mass opposition. Perhaps for this reason, most existing research on institutional strategies for managing attributions of credit and blame has focused on democratic political systems (Baekkeskov and Rubin 2016). Democracies may seem like the natural environment in which to study these dynamics, given their free-wheeling elite politics and divided institutions that enable political games over credit claiming and blame shifting. Meanwhile, institutional strategies may seem less relevant to the politics of blame in authoritarian regimes.

In fact, numerous examples suggest that autocrats are often quite effective at evading blame through institutional strategies, such that it frequently falls instead on the political elites with whom they share power. President Putin of Russia provides one illustrative case, at least prior to his decision to invade Ukraine in 2022. Putin was long described as a "Teflon" politician, since his approval tended to remain higher than support for his party or other regime elites, even during periods of significant economic and political disruption (Volkov 2015). In part, this greater popularity almost certainly reflected the effects of propaganda, as well as some degree of preference falsification to avoid repression. But several scholars of Russian politics suggest that much of Putin's popular support during his first two decades in power was genuine (e.g. Frye et al. 2017). One reason for his success at sustaining high levels of public approval may have been his efforts to distance himself from decision-making for many issues that affected Russians

1.2 Attributions of Responsibility in Autocracies

in their daily lives. Ministers, members of parliament, and regional governors all held power over policymaking in an authoritarian system in which Putin was predominant but not omnipotent. In fact, the president would make a show of stepping in to "fix" problems created by lower-level officials after they were brought to his attention by disgruntled citizens.

Most modern autocracies are similar. The autocrat is powerful and capable of pushing through their preferences in most cases, but they do not fully control decision-making within the political system. Instead, decision-making powers are delegated to other political elites through their positions in ministries, the parliament, or the bureaucracy (Magaloni 2008; Meng 2020; Svolik 2012). One of the core claims of this book is that these power-sharing arrangements are observed by the public and then affect how citizens attribute responsibility. As the autocrat monopolizes power more fully, they will find it easier to convince the public they deserve credit, but harder to convince the public they should not be blamed. Alternatively, as power is shared more widely with other elites across the country's political institutions, making it more credible that the autocrat is not steering every major decision personally, the autocrat will receive less credit but will find it easier to persuade people they are not at fault when something goes wrong. Throughout the book, I will refer interchangeably to power sharing over policymaking as "delegation," reflecting the provision of decision-making powers to political elites other than the autocrat.

This relationship between delegation and attributions can help to answer the question of why some autocrats are more likely to become the targets of mass opposition than others during periods of discontent, as with the Arab Spring. Consider an authoritarian regime where the autocratic president delegates substantial decision-making powers to the prime minister. Particularly since repression makes protests risky in authoritarian regimes, people who believe the prime minister is more at fault for their grievances than the president are unlikely to take to the streets for a demonstration that openly targets the president. In addition, even people who believe the president is to blame may not be willing to join such a protest if they believe that many *other* citizens perceive the prime minister as responsible and will not turn out to protest against the president. Alternatively, if the autocratic president monopolizes power in such a way that their responsibility is clear for all to see, people should be more likely to want to protest against the president directly, and they should also be more likely to believe that their fellow citizens will join them in large numbers. In other words, the extent to which the autocrat shares decision-making powers with other elites should influence the likelihood that disgruntled citizens coordinate against them when expressing their anger publicly.

Because autocrats often have some ability to shape their country's political institutions (Magaloni 2006), another central claim of the book is that autocrats will strategically alter the credibility of power sharing with the public's attributions in mind. With regards to credibility, I am referring to how costly it would be for the autocrat to force through their own preferences in the decision-making process. As these costs increase because the powers of other elites make it harder for the autocrat to get their way, the public should perceive delegation to be more credible, and they should be more likely to accept the autocrat is not dominating all decisions and should not be blamed for poor outcomes. However, this increased credibility comes with a trade-off, as it may also improve the ability of elites to threaten and potentially replace the autocrat (Paine 2021, 2022). This increased coup risk can occur because more credible power sharing may strengthen the ability of elites to claim credit and win over the public, and because it increases their access to networks and resources that can be turned to their own benefit (Meng 2020). Thus, in deciding how credibly to share power over decision-making, autocrats will weigh the costs of potential blame against the risks of delegating too much influence to other elites. This trade-off implies that autocrats should be more likely to delegate decision-making powers credibly during time periods and for issue domains in which they are relatively more concerned about the consequences of being blamed by a dissatisfied public. By contrast, they should be more likely to rein in elites' decision-making influence and accept the risks of being blamed where threats from internal challenges become too great.

In cases where the autocrat fears becoming the target of public unrest and it is not too costly for the autocrat to delegate credibly, it should be possible for autocrats to share decision-making powers in a way that facilitates an equilibrium of regime stability. In this equilibrium, the autocrat delegates credibly to other political elites, who have the opportunity to influence policies and steer them toward their own preferences. If the public dislikes the policies, they blame and then mobilize against the elites instead of the autocrat, and the autocrat removes

1.3 The King Can Do No Wrong

the elites from their positions in response to the public's demands. By removing the elites and providing a modicum of accountability to the public, the autocrat may even strengthen their reputation and bolster their popular support. Thus, the elites get to set the policy, the public gets accountability if they are unhappy with the decision, and the autocrat is able to stay in power without resorting to extreme repression. This equilibrium also highlights how the relationship between attributions and institutions in authoritarian regimes can facilitate understanding of how decisions are made, when opposition does or does not escalate, and how limited accountability can function in these contexts.

1.3 The King Can Do No Wrong

The relationship I have described between attributions of responsibility and delegation of decision-making powers should apply to authoritarian regimes generally. But are certain autocrats more likely than others to benefit from delegation as a blame avoidance strategy? As explained earlier, sharing power over decision-making is not risk-free for autocrats, and delegating too much influence to other political elites may empower them to challenge the autocrat from within the regime. It follows that in contexts where delegation is less likely to strengthen elites dangerously, the autocrat should be able to share decision-making powers more credibly, and their reputation should be more protected from popular anger as a result.

At the same time, research on attributions suggests that the effectiveness of delegation as a blame avoidance strategy is constrained by norms about who is *supposed* to take responsibility for governance outcomes. People expect some leaders or institutions to be accountable for decision-making more than others, which may motivate them to blame these leaders for unpopular outcomes even in cases where the decisions were delegated credibly to others (Arceneaux 2006; Arceneaux and Stein 2006; Hood 2011). Consider the United States, where President Harry Truman popularized the saying that "the buck stops here," by which he meant that he was ultimately responsible for any outcome produced by the sprawling US government. Expectations about who is responsible can take root in a society through numerous channels. Constitutions often define the officials who are meant to be responsible for setting the policy agenda and accountable for the outcomes it produces. Likewise, schools often teach their students an idealized version of how their country's policy process operates and who is meant to make decisions. If those expectations fall on the position held by the autocrat, they should create a limiting factor on delegation's ability to facilitate blame avoidance. As a result, understanding how these norms vary across different types of authoritarian regimes can help to explain why some autocrats may be better positioned to protect their reputations by delegating decision-making powers to other political elites.

The second major argument of this book is that ruling monarchs possess advantages on both fronts compared to other autocratic rulers in the modern world. First, delegation is less costly for monarchs on average. And second, delegation also aligns more closely with norms about how responsibility should be attributed in the political system. As a result, delegation is both *safer* and *more effective* at shifting blame for monarchs. These advantages make them especially well-positioned to escape blame by sharing power with institutions such as cabinets and legislatures.

This book focuses on ruling monarchies, which refers to a type of authoritarian regime in which decision-making power is held by an autocrat – the monarch – who (1) is selected on the basis of hereditary succession to rule for life and (2) holds a royal title as part of a predefined royal family. This combination of institutionalized hereditary succession and royal titles reflects the standard approach to defining monarchy both in popular understanding and in the academic literature (Cheibub et al. 2010; Geddes et al. 2014; Gerring et al. 2021; Magaloni et al. 2013). Importantly, this definition does not include ceremonial monarchies where the ruling family has been stripped of decision-making power, often in democracies such as Spain's where the cabinet and parliament govern, but sometimes in other authoritarian regimes where the monarch becomes a figurehead. In short, for our purposes, the monarch must actually rule. This definition also excludes the relatively few authoritarian regimes – for instance, Syria and North Korea – in which hereditary succession does occur, but the autocrat continues to hold a nonroyal title linked to republican ideas and institutions. This distinction is important because it creates different formal rules about who can hold power legitimately, as well as different expectations about the autocrat's governance role.

For centuries, ruling monarchies were the most common type of regime in the world (Gerring et al. 2021). Gradually during the

1.3 The King Can Do No Wrong

nineteenth century and then more rapidly during the twentieth century, they were replaced by republican political systems – either democratic or authoritarian – or by democratic, constitutional monarchies in which monarchs no longer governed (Stepan et al. 2014). As of 2021, ruling monarchies continued to exist in ten countries: Bahrain, Brunei, Eswatini, Jordan, Kuwait, Morocco, Oman, Qatar, Saudi Arabia, and the United Arab Emirates. The monarch also still plays an influential governance role in Thailand's often-authoritarian political system, and the monarch of Bhutan could arguably still be classified as an autocrat. Since 1945, authoritarian monarchs also governed for some period of time in Afghanistan, Bhutan, Burundi, Cambodia, Egypt, Ethiopia, Iran, Iraq, Libya, the Maldives, Nepal, Tonga, and Yemen. While these lists are relatively short, they include some of the world's most politically and economically influential countries, several of which punch above their weight when considering their small populations.

The survival of these regimes well into the modern period reflects something of a puzzle. Writing in the late 1960s, the prominent political scientist Samuel Huntington predicted that ruling monarchs would struggle to manage the difficulties of modernization and would soon disappear, whether they were overthrown by revolution or relegated to the ceremonial status of constitutional monarchs (Huntington 1968). More than two decades later, the esteemed Middle East scholar Lisa Anderson (1991) observed that Huntington's prediction had not yet borne fruit, particularly in the Arab world. She argued instead that the centralized authority and flexible ideology of ruling monarchs actually made them effective modernizers, relative to other types of rulers. But Anderson also speculated that kings would struggle to manage demands for popular sovereignty in a democratic age. In the three decades since Anderson's article was published, however, only a single ruling monarchy – that of Nepal – has lost power following a challenge from its citizens. In fact, several datasets of authoritarian regimes indicate that monarchies have been the most stable type of autocracy in the modern period, surviving more than 40 years on average (Geddes et al. 2014; Magaloni et al. 2013; Cheibub et al. 2010).[1] Given this surprising resiliency, the practical importance of those states that continue

---

[1] See the chapter appendix for a plot of regime duration by authoritarian regime type across these three datasets.

to be governed by royal autocrats, and the fact that ruling monarchies have been the most common type of political system historically, understanding how these regimes govern and why they tend to be stable should be of general and academic interest. Nonetheless, monarchies have received relatively little attention from political scientists and other researchers (Gerring et al. 2021; Stepan et al. 2014).

If monarchs are better-positioned than other autocrats to avoid blame through delegation, they should be more effective at protecting their popular support, which should contribute to the greater stability of their regimes. I argue that this advantage occurs because of different political dynamics created by hereditary succession and popular sovereignty. As discussed earlier, hereditary succession is the principle that underlies leader selection in monarchies. By contrast, popular sovereignty – the idea that governments derive their power from the people they govern – is the key principle that informs leader selection in most modern political systems, whether they are authoritarian or democratic in actual practice (Murphy 2022). Why does this difference matter? Compared to popular sovereignty, hereditary succession lowers the costs of credible delegation by creating relative *rigidity* in the rules defining who should be the ruler, while contributing to relative *flexibility* in expectations about their decision-making responsibilities. As a result, monarchs can share power more credibly with less risk to themselves, and this delegation should also be relatively more effective at protecting them from blame.

To summarize the argument in more detail, hereditary succession means that only people within the royal family can become the monarch legally. As such, any nonroyal elite to whom the monarch delegates, and who wishes to become the autocrat themselves, will have to pursue the costly option of overthrowing the entire royal regime and replacing it with a completely new one. Of course, such coups have happened historically: for instance, military officers ousted kings in Egypt and Iraq and replaced them with republics in the 1950s. But these actions are highly risky and often end poorly for the perpetrators. On the other hand, when popular sovereignty is the principle of leader selection, any citizen of the country with enough support could in theory become the legitimate autocrat. Thus, any elite could use their influence to replace the autocrat without necessarily subverting the existing rules of the political system, which tends to be a less risky and less costly approach to ruler change, even in authoritarian

1.3 The King Can Do No Wrong 21

regimes (Lucardi 2019). In Tunisia, for instance, Ben Ali used his positions as interior minister and then prime minister to mount a bloodless constitutional coup against the aging autocrat President Bourguiba. Many other autocrats have been removed through similar means, or even through elections contested by their elite opponents (Geddes et al. 2014). As a result of these higher costs to challenging them, monarchs should be able to give other elites credible influence over the decision-making process without having to worry as much about the threat such delegation poses to their hold on power.

Regarding expectations of responsibility and the influence of those expectations on the effectiveness of delegation as a blame avoidance strategy, popular sovereignty implies that the ruler is meant to govern for the people and will lack a legitimate claim to govern if they lose the people's support. This expectation often applies to presidents specifically – the most common type of nonroyal autocrat – and it is often codified constitutionally. In Egypt, for example, the 2014 constitution states that the president "defends the interests of the people" (Constitution of Egypt, Article 139), while also noting that "The President of the Republic, jointly with the Cabinet, sets the general policy of the state and oversees its implementation as set out by the Constitution" (Constitution of Egypt, Article 150). In other words, the president is supposed to act on the public's desires by setting the state's policies. In contrast, hereditary succession has no such implications about the monarch's role in governance. The king is the rightful ruler whether they micromanage all policy decisions or make no policy decisions at all, merely because they are from the right family. In fact, monarchs often face an expectation that they will not be held accountable for decisions of the state, because the king, as the sovereign, can do no wrong. Instead, the cabinet ministers and parliament are supposed to be the institutions that represent the people and take responsibility for decision-making.

This idea of ministerial responsibility evolved out of the British experience with kingship in the seventeenth and eighteenth centuries as parliament wrestled with how to constrain the monarchy while also recognizing its sovereign role. Gradually, ministers took on more power so that they – and not the king or queen – would be responsible and therefore accountable for governance problems that arose (Bogdanor 1995). Ministerial responsibility quickly became the norm for constitutional monarchies, whose constitutions often stated

22 *Introduction*

explicitly that the king could do no wrong and that ministers would be accountable for the state's policies. In ruling monarchies, this principle does not mean the disappearance of the king's political role, as it eventually did in the United Kingdom. But it does suggest that an expectation exists by which the monarch is meant to be distant from many of the decisions of day-to-day governance, while the cabinet and parliament are meant to be responsible instead. Thus, delegation by monarchs should align more closely with the public's understanding of who is *supposed* to be blamed when things go wrong, making it a relatively more effective blame avoidance strategy for monarchs compared to other types of autocrats.

This argument is a relative argument about how authoritarian monarchies compare to other types of authoritarian regimes. Those other regimes are largely the product of the shift toward ideas and institutions of popular sovereignty that occurred in the past few centuries. Part of the monarch's delegation advantage is rooted in this shift, which led to the development of expectations about the separation of monarchs and responsibility for governance. In terms of scope conditions, then, the argument is most relevant to our understanding of politics more recently.

It is also important to emphasize that the argument does not imply that modern monarchs will never be blamed or will never face mass opposition. Neither does it mean that all monarchs will choose to delegate in the first place. Many royal rulers of the past few hundred years have decided to monopolize decision-making in their political systems – a dynamic that should help us to understand which monarchies collapsed and which monarchies survived into the modern world. Finally, the argument also does not mean that delegation by ruling monarchs equates to constitutional monarchy as it exists in the democracies of the United Kingdom or Sweden. Kings in Jordan, Morocco, and elsewhere are still autocrats with immense powers and substantial political influence. Nonetheless, this argument does suggest that autocratic monarchs who share power over the decision-making process should be relatively effective at protecting themselves from popular anger. This protection should reduce the likelihood of mass uprisings that seek to overthrow the autocrat, since the public will direct their fury at other political actors without demanding that the regime be overthrown entirely. In turn, this ability to shift blame should

1.4 Contributions of the Book

facilitate accountability, limit the need for repression, and indirectly reduce threats from other elites even further.

1.4 Contributions of the Book

1.4.1 Understanding Autocracies Generally

This book contributes to knowledge of authoritarian politics in several ways. First and most directly, the book sheds light on a universal political issue – how people attribute responsibility for governance – that has received relatively little attention in autocracies. To date, only a handful of existing studies speak to the relationship between attributions of responsibility and power sharing in these settings. Beazer and Reuter (2019) demonstrate that decentralization enables Russia's ruling party to mitigate electoral punishment for poor performance, while Rosenfeld (2018) shows that Russians are more likely to punish the ruling party for poor performance in regions where its political dominance is more pronounced. Both studies are consistent with the idea that more credible power sharing can facilitate blame avoidance in authoritarian contexts. Research on China (Cai 2008) and Vietnam (Schuler 2020) also suggests that autocrats consider blame in how they approach the policy process. While important, these studies do not directly address the autocrat's exposure to attributions, whether and why these effects may vary temporally, by issue, and across countries, or the manner in which concerns about blame shape strategic interactions between autocrats, other political elites, and the public. My book addresses each of these topics in turn.

The book shows that people living in authoritarian regimes hold relatively complex and nuanced views about how responsibility operates in their political systems. They do not inherently blame the autocrat for all that goes wrong, but neither do they accept the propaganda of the autocrat's infallibility. Instead, many people will attribute responsibility to other elites in important political and bureaucratic positions, recognizing that they often wield substantial influence over the direction of specific policies. At the same time, these attributions vary based on the extent of the autocrat's actual control over the decision-making process. I provide evidence that the more the autocrat concentrates power in their own hands, the more they attract credit but the more they also expose themselves to blame. By contrast, the more credibly they delegate, the less they are blamed at the expense of losing some credit. In other words, the public has some capacity to evaluate objectively how power operates in many authoritarian political systems, and attributions shift as the situation changes, with implications for the stability of these regimes during periods of crisis or poor governance. This dynamic illustrates the importance of engaging with public opinion in authoritarian settings with more complexity, moving beyond binary distinctions that emphasize support for and opposition to the regime, or the predominant focus on how people are bought off or made to fear the authorities.

Along these lines, the book contributes to understanding of "popular" autocrats. Political scientists have often debated whether certain autocrats really do have the high levels of public approval that they *appear* to have. Some have argued that preference falsification explains this apparent support, with many people hiding their true views because they fear repression. Others, however, have argued that many autocrats are genuinely popular. For instance, researchers have explored the extent to which President Putin's high approval ratings in Russia are "real" (e.g., Buckley et al. 2022; Frye et al. 2017), or whether trust in the top levels of the Chinese Communist Party is as robust as Chinese citizens report it to be (e.g., Huang et al. 2022; Robinson and Tannenberg 2019). While preference falsification is an issue in some authoritarian contexts (Blair et al. 2020), its effects are often relatively small (Shen and Truex 2021), and in many cases, popular autocrats seem to be the real deal (Guriev and Treisman 2020). Particularly given the resurgence of authoritarian regimes, understanding why autocrats can be successful at acquiring popular support should be important (Carter and Carter 2023). Nonetheless, theories of authoritarian politics continue to lag in this regard (Przeworski 2023). By demonstrating that autocrats can protect their reputations and retain support even during periods of poor governance by using delegation to shift blame onto other political elites, the theory and evidence shed light on one important strategy on which autocrats can rely to influence public opinion in their favor.

In exploring how autocrats strategically structure decision-making in their regimes to manage the public's attributions, the book also provides insights into the understudied policymaking processes of authoritarian regimes (Gandhi et al. 2020). I provide a theoretical

1.4 Contributions of the Book

framework for understanding why autocrats may be more or less likely to exercise control over certain policy domains. For instance, they should be more willing to take the blame for foreign policy or security issues, where credibly empowering elites is particularly threatening, and they should be more willing to delegate decision-making powers for controversial social issues or the economy, from which elites acquire less power and where the public is particularly likely to be dissatisfied. In discussing my evidence from a number of different cases, I also provide detailed portrayals of how decision-making occurs. Much of my research focuses on the Hashemite Kingdom of Jordan, and I show how ministers and even members of parliament exercise genuine influence over policy decisions and implementation, pushing the kingdom's policies toward their preferences. Though the king retains immense power and can usually find the means to force through his preferred policies, this approach is not costless, and so the palace often refrains from dictating policies in certain areas or at certain times. To understand how and why authoritarian regimes choose some policies over others, it is important to recognize the limitations of the autocrat's power and to pay attention to how responsibility is delegated within the political system.

The link between attributions of responsibility and decision-making also furthers our understanding of how and why autocrats share power with other political elites. First, power sharing can be conceptualized as giving elites access to rents or influence over policymaking, but much of the literature has focused on the former over the latter (e.g., Blaydes 2010; Lust-Okar 2006; Magaloni 2006; Reuter and Robertson 2015; Truex 2014). By showing when autocrats are more or less likely to delegate decision-making responsibility to their elite allies in the regime, the book builds on this literature to provide a clearer picture of how power sharing related to policymaking works.

Second, the existing literature on power sharing emphasizes that autocrats are motivated to cede influence to other elites as an incentive to maintain their loyalty. This research suggests that autocrats are more likely to share power when elites are stronger and can credibly threaten to overthrow them (Meng 2020; Svolik 2012), because in these cases the autocrat needs to placate them by providing a positive incentive in the form of rents or influence. At the same time, autocrats are unlikely to share power when elites are too powerful, because doing so strengthens their coercive power and may backfire by further incentivizing a coup (Paine 2021, 2022; Roessler 2011). In other words, power sharing occurs when elites are neither too weak nor too strong. My book adopts this view of power sharing as an incentive for elite loyalty that may simultaneously strengthen elite threats, but I also explore how the decision to share power may be influenced by threats to the autocrat from the public. In doing so, my argument suggests conditions under which autocrats may be willing to cede some of their own influence even when elites are not particularly strong and are unlikely to threaten them credibly. As long as the autocrat is concerned that the public may become dissatisfied with policy outcomes, that they may be blamed for the public's grievances, and that this anger may facilitate protests challenging them directly, the autocrat has reasons to involve other political elites in the decision-making process.

This implication is related to seminal work by Gandhi (2008), who also argues that autocrats are more likely to govern alongside elites in institutions like legislatures and parties when they need cooperation from society at large. However, the mechanisms driving this dynamic differ. In Gandhi's theory, the public is co-opted by these institutions, because political elites will use their positions to bargain over and advocate for policies that their constituencies want. However, though these institutions can facilitate bargaining over policy (Noble 2020) and help autocrats to learn about the public's preferences (Truex 2016), the autocrat does not necessarily need to share significant power with elites in these bodies for them to fulfill these roles. Furthermore, even where institutions like legislatures do help the regime to understand the public better, the repressive nature of authoritarian politics will still make it difficult to know what exactly the public wants (Kuran 1991; Wintrobe 1998), and the regime may still struggle to govern effectively enough to avoid the kinds of unpopular outcomes capable of triggering mass protests. It is this concern about the ability to satisfy the public that should motivate autocrats to give elites actual power over decision-making, since they can reduce the risks of being held personally responsible if and when the public becomes dissatisfied. Thus, the book contributes to understanding of how power-sharing arrangements are not just a function of elite politics within authoritarian regimes, but also relate directly to popular politics. The autocrat's decisions about how to share power are influenced by potential threats from the masses, and the public's perceptions of blame and credit are then affected by these decisions about how power is shared.

1.4 Contributions of the Book

The relationship between how decision-making processes are structured and how people attribute responsibility is relevant to the intensity of repression used by authoritarian regimes as well. Existing research indicates that "personalist" authoritarian regimes – that is, those in which power is more concentrated in the hands of the autocrat – are more likely to repress the public violently (Frantz et al. 2020). Blame dynamics may help to explain this pattern. Where the autocrat is so clearly dominant, grievances are more likely to target them directly and escalate into demands for their ouster. Because this discontent threatens them personally, the autocrat is likely to respond with force. By contrast, in authoritarian political systems where autocrats share power more widely, grievances are less likely to pose as much of a threat to the top of the regime, since blame is more likely to be focused on other political elites who also shape important policy decisions. In these cases, the autocrat has less reason to suppress the public's anger violently, and even large protests may be tolerated (Schwedler 2022). In fact, the autocrat may actually benefit from learning about this dissatisfaction, since it provides information that allows them to give the people some of what they want by holding accountable the elites deemed responsible for their grievances (Lorentzen 2013; Schuler 2020).

This discussion suggests one channel through which limited accountability can operate in authoritarian regimes. Because free and fair elections are considered to be such a crucial element for holding political leaders accountable (Grossman and Slough 2022), it may seem an oxymoron to think of accountable autocracies. Nonetheless, there are mechanisms by which government officials can be held accountable in authoritarian regimes. Accountability can be implemented from the top down, with lower-level officials removed for poor performance by their superiors. In China, for instance, local leaders are often removed if they fail to meet governance targets (Guo 2007). For this approach to function, the autocrat and other powerful elites must have some commitment to good governance as well as accurate information about local performance – both of which are rare, particularly in authoritarian settings – or accountability will break down. Returning to China, local leaders will manipulate economic statistics to influence their chances of promotion, making it harder for the central government to identify effective governance (Wallace 2014). Other research has focused on bottom-up pressures for accountability in authoritarian systems. Along these lines, Tsai (2007) shows how local communities can use social pressures and norms to hold officials accountable and ensure they deliver for the community. My argument about the relationship between power sharing and attributions suggests the possibility of a system of authoritarian accountability that combines both top-down and bottom-up elements. To the extent that power sharing occurs and elites who take part in decision-making are removed by the autocrat following expressions of popular dissatisfaction, these elites are being held accountable for their performance in office. This outcome resembles the well-known model of "fire-alarm" oversight defined by McCubbins and Schwartz (1984), whereby political leaders respond to problems identified by their constituents, which allows them to not only address the issue but also to receive credit for doing so. Of course, in such cases, only a limited version of accountability occurs, since the autocrat remains unaccountable themselves despite exercising more influence than anyone else over the political system (Fox and Jordan 2011).

Another implication of the book is to take seriously the idea that people think differently about different types of autocrats. Existing research has provided a number of insights into how authoritarian regimes structured around parties, militaries, monarchs, or strongmen differ from each other, with variation in the incentives they create for elites to remain loyal to the regime (Geddes 1999; Geddes et al. 2018); their ability to generate economic growth (Wright 2008); the likelihood they become involved in international conflict (Weeks 2012); and other important outcomes. This book expands on this literature by considering how popular politics may differ in these regimes because of variation in norms associated with the rulers who lead them. In my argument, popular sovereignty norms attached to most autocratic rulers create expectations that they should govern actively and be held accountable for the outcomes produced by their regimes, which may limit the effectiveness of institutional blame avoidance strategies that seek to shift blame by delegating responsibility to other political elites. Monarchs, however, are much less likely to face this problem, because they hold their positions on the basis of hereditary succession and are not expected to govern directly. As a result, they can avoid blame more effectively by delegating. It is possible to think of other ways in which norms attached to certain types of autocratic regimes and rulers may influence popular politics, and scholars would benefit from pursuing

1.4 Contributions of the Book

this line of inquiry further. For example, there is a widespread norm of civilian authority that may shape how people react to military governments. There are also expectations for some types of leaders but not others to be elected, which may influence how people evaluate whether their countries are democratic or not.

1.4.2 Understanding Autocratic Monarchies

In one of his last publications before his passing, the renowned political scientist Juan Linz called on the discipline to "think about monarchy more" (Stepan et al. 2014). Monarchies may appear anachronistic in this age of popular sovereignty and elections, but they continue to govern several states of global importance. Furthermore, the trajectory of monarchies can provide important insights into the nature of authoritarian governance as well as historical and contemporary pathways of democratization. By identifying ways in which monarchies differ systematically from other authoritarian regimes, we can gain better insights into the factors that drive variation in outcome across autocracies as a whole. This book takes seriously the idea that the study of monarchy matters, and it advances understanding of this regime type in several ways.

First and foremost, the book contributes to a debate about the surprising pattern of royal durability in the post-World War II period, whereby ruling monarchies have been the most stable and longest-lived type of authoritarian regime (Geddes et al. 2014; Magaloni et al. 2013). Some scholars have suggested that the stability of monarchies has little to do with monarchy itself, but can be explained by omitted variables that correlate with these regimes. Greater oil wealth and more protective foreign patrons reflect some of the most cited factors (e.g., Gause 1994; Gause and Yom 2012; Gause 2013; Luciani 1987), but other relevant variables include the small size of most modern monarchies (Jugl 2020), their more liberal approach to governance (Lust-Okar and Jamal 2002; Spinks et al. 2008), or more conservative and submissive political cultures (Sharabi 1988). While these factors may contribute to the stability of some monarchies, the durability advantage of monarchies remains when controlling for many of them in empirical studies (e.g., Menaldo 2012), which suggests there may be something about monarchy specifically that contributes to this pattern of royal resiliency.

An additional possibility is that the stability of monarchies can be explained by selection bias, such that we observe only the most durable monarchies surviving into the modern period but compare them to the full range of stable and unstable authoritarian regimes of other types. This explanation cannot be ruled out completely, but other academic work implies it is unlikely to explain the pattern fully. Anderson (1991) points out that most of the Middle East's monarchies – specifically, Egypt, Jordan, Libya, and many of the Gulf monarchies – are historical accidents that were not deeply rooted in the Arab world or Arab culture. Instead, they were established because of the notions of British imperialists.[2] Menaldo (2012) attempts to account for selection bias empirically by using an instrumental variable design in his study of instability in monarchies and nonmonarchies in the Arab world. Even with this design, he finds that the region's monarchies are still more stable than the nonmonarchies. Likewise, Gerring et al. (2021) show descriptively that monarchies were more durable than nonmonarchies between 1800 and 1920, suggesting that royal resiliency is not just a pattern of the modern period when monarchies are less common.

Other works have explored the sources of royal durability with compelling arguments that seem more likely to apply to a specific monarchy or set of monarchies. In his influential study of the Gulf monarchies, Herb (1999) argues that their reliance on exceptionally large families allows them to operate similarly to party regimes, by filling most government positions with royals and then working out agreements to share the benefits of ruling among the family. While this argument pertains well to these cases, and there is evidence that it applies historically as well (Kokkonen et al. 2021), it is less reflective of the majority of modern monarchies that survived for many decades, in which royal families were typically much smaller. Others have used specific cases to argue that monarchies possess ideological advantages over nonroyal autocracies, including more ideological flexibility (Anderson 2000), more durable legitimating symbols (Moore 1970), or stronger religious legitimacy (Daadaoui 2011; Lewis 2000; Menaldo 2012). While these arguments may also be plausible for some monarchies, it is

---

[2] Two exceptions are the monarchies of Morocco and Oman, whose dynasties have ruled for several centuries.

1.4 Contributions of the Book

not clear that monarchies in general differ from other authoritarian regimes in terms of these characteristics (Bank et al. 2015). For instance, Egypt's authoritarian presidents have displayed significant ideological flexibility by adopting elements of nationalism, Islamism, and socialism (Brand 2014); Arab presidents in countries such as Algeria and Tunisia can legitimate themselves with powerful historical memories of anti-colonial revolutions; and nearly all Arab autocrats – in monarchies and republics alike – invest substantial effort in leveraging state religious establishments to demonstrate their commitment to the Islamic faith (Brown 2017). As such, my argument helps to push back against the claim that kings possess some special cultural or traditional legitimacy that creates a loyal and submissive populace.

My argument builds on another set of studies that focus on hereditary succession's ability to stabilize royal regimes. The advantage of this focus is that it draws on the institutional feature that most clearly sets monarchies apart from other regime types. In particular, scholars have argued that hereditary succession facilitates more effective coordination among political elites over the question of who should rule when the present autocrat dies or retires (Brownlee 2007; Brownlee et al. 2015; Menaldo 2012; Tullock 1987). As long as most powerful elites agree that a member of the royal family should take charge, even those who dislike the monarchy have few incentives to abandon it. This coordination reduces the likelihood that the regime breaks down because of conflict fueled by the uncertainty over succession, and it also grants monarchs a longer time-horizon that reduces their incentives to engage in potentially destabilizing actions like expropriations (Knutsen and Fjelde 2013). These arguments are focused primarily on elite politics within monarchies. My study extends this work by showing how hereditary succession helps to limit mass opposition to the monarch by facilitating more credible delegation and shaping expectations about the monarch's distance from decision-making. In advancing this argument, the book provides an institutional explanation for the surprising durability of these authoritarian regimes, and it supports this argument with case-specific as well as cross-national data analysis that reinforces the generalizability of my claims.

These findings contribute to understanding of why, in our democratic age, ruling monarchs who inherit the throne often appear to be genuinely popular for extended periods of time. That being said,

I do not challenge the idea that the widespread appeal of popular sovereignty means that monarchs are unlikely to reverse their slow march toward extinction, at least for the foreseeable future. Despite the machinations of scattered monarchists in countries such as Iran, it is almost inconceivable now that a new royal family can be created or a monarchy established in lieu of a republic. Today's royals benefit from institutionalized hereditary succession only because they could already claim royal status in decades past – theirs is not a title that can be claimed from scratch by an ambitious presidential autocrat.

Despite the possibility of this regime type's eventual disappearance, studying monarchy remains especially relevant for understanding the politics of the contemporary Middle East. Nearly all ruling monarchies that continue to survive today are located in the region. Given the global influence of several of these states, there is significant interest among policymakers and academics in understanding why they have been stable and whether they are likely to remain so. My book suggests that monarchies that delegate less credibly – such as the Saudi monarchy – will be more vulnerable to crises that generate widespread societal discontent. Though he remains Crown Prince at the time of writing, Mohammed Bin Salman's attempts to centralize power in his own hands may have implications for the stability of Saudi Arabia's authoritarian regime. On the one hand, he appears to have been effective so far at using his prominent position and association with popular social reforms to claim credit and build his reputation with the Saudi people. On the other hand, if his governance proceeds poorly, he may find himself relatively vulnerable to blame and more likely to be targeted by the masses. By contrast, the participatory politics of parliaments in Kuwait, Jordan, and Morocco, combined with relatively influential cabinets that take responsibility for day-to-day governance, should continue to help the monarchs in these countries weather periods of discontent. Meanwhile, the monarchies of Qatar and Oman have in recent years taken small steps to delegate more credibly to legislatures and cabinets.

In several European monarchies, delegation of decision-making responsibilities to parliaments and ministers eventually resulted in transitions to democracy. For this reason, there is much to learn about authoritarian stability and democratic change by studying the historical transitions of monarchies as a regime type (Stepan et al. 2014). Whether some of the Middle East's monarchies follow the very gradual

1.5 Plan of the Book

path of democratization experienced by some of their European counterparts remains an open question (Herb 2004). Where my study contributes to this literature is in showing that monarchies that centralized power more fully in the hands of the crown were less stable and more likely to be overthrown in the 1800s and early 1900s. In other words, kings who governed eventually could do wrong by their people, and they were more likely to lose their thrones as a result. By contrast, those monarchs who shared some genuine power with other political elites were more likely to survive into the modern period, even if they eventually became ceremonial leaders.

1.5 Plan of the Book

In the following chapter, I discuss in greater detail how people attribute blame and why blame matters for powerful autocrats. I then describe my theoretical framework for understanding strategic interactions around power sharing and blame in authoritarian political systems, considering the incentives of the dictator, regime elites, and the public. This framework expands on the discussion in this chapter about the contexts in which autocrats will be more or less likely to delegate decision-making responsibilities to other elites to avoid blame, highlighting variation across issues and over time. I next discuss why ruling monarchs are better positioned than other autocrats to use this strategy because of how hereditary succession creates more rigidity around who can be king while implying more flexibility for how kings are involved in governance. The chapter concludes by highlighting key implications that will be tested in the empirical sections.

The empirical chapters are organized to follow the structure of the theory. They first provide evidence for my general argument about the relationships between power sharing, blame attributions, and governance in authoritarian regimes, drawing on cross-national evidence as well as several chapters about politics in the Hashemite Kingdom of Jordan. I then move to the argument about why monarchs specifically are *comparatively* better positioned to use delegation of decision-making responsibilities to protect their reputations and stabilize their regimes, again drawing on a mix of cross-national evidence and case studies.

Chapter 3 is the first to provide evidence consistent with the general theory. Here, I use cross-national data to assess the theory's key assumptions and implications, illustrating the extent to which the connections between power sharing and the public's attributions are relevant to authoritarian politics globally. The chapter begins by using Google Trends data from dozens of countries to provide evidence that the public recognizes variation in the balance of power between autocrats and their elite allies. I then provide further evidence of this dynamic by analyzing trends data surrounding institutional changes affecting the credibility of delegation in Russia and Morocco. The fact that the public's attention shifts toward autocrats as they become less constrained in the decision-making process suggests that their exposure to attributions will be shaped by how they share power. Next, survey data from dozens of authoritarian regimes in Asia and Africa indicates that individuals who perceive the economy to be performing poorly are much more likely to report negative attitudes toward the autocrat *if* they believe that the autocrat does not share power with other elites, consistent with greater exposure to blame affecting popular support for the autocrat. Cross-national data on authoritarian regimes then illustrates how the politics surrounding attributions can affect strategic interactions related to autocratic governance more broadly. I document that autocrats who tie their hands and empower other elites more credibly are less likely to rely on repression, less likely to become the targets of mass opposition during periods of public discontent, and more likely to rotate elites out of government positions in a manner that is consistent with limited accountability for poor performance.

After discussing these cross-national patterns, the book turns to an in-depth case study of the Hashemite Kingdom of Jordan. The four Jordan chapters are particularly important for providing a fine-grained assessment of how delegation shapes public opinion in authoritarian regimes, how autocrats and elites react strategically to the public's attributions of blame, and how these blame games play out over time. Jordan itself provides a useful case for several reasons. First, Jordan represents a typical case of authoritarian rule in many ways (Seawright and Gerring 2008). The country is governed by a powerful autocrat – the monarch – who nonetheless shares power with many other political elites. This power sharing is facilitated by institutions such as the legislature and elections. Repression occurs but it is not especially heavy-handed; instead, as with many modern autocracies (Treisman and Guriev 2022), the regime prioritizes persuasion and

1.5 *Plan of the Book* 35

co-optation. As a result, lessons from Jordan may be applicable to authoritarian politics more generally. Second, Jordan has experienced substantial variation in the credibility of power sharing over time, and it is a monarchy. These features allow for a detailed exploration of the theory's mechanisms. Finally, Jordan also serves as an interesting case of authoritarian durability, as the monarchy has held onto power for more than a century despite a consistently weak economy, relatively frequent internal upheavals, and a difficult regional environment. In part for these reasons, the country has featured prominently in several important works on the survival strategies used by authoritarian regimes (e.g., Brand 1995; Gandhi 2008; Jamal 2013; Lust-Okar 2006, 2009; Yom 2015).

My study of Jordan was informed by one year of fieldwork in the country, and it relies on a mix of qualitative and quantitative data. These data include just over 100 interviews with Jordanian political elites, including 3 former prime ministers, 3 former chiefs of the royal court, dozens of current and former ministers, senators, and members of parliament, and a number of bureaucrats, opposition activists, journalists, and political analysts. Interviews were semi-structured, with an emphasis on how responsibility for policy was delegated within the political system and how this delegation was perceived by the public, but they included specific questions tailored to the unique background of each individual as well. The data also include archival documents on Jordanian politics that I gathered at the National Archives of the United Kingdom; an original dataset of ministerial tenures between 1946 and 2017; text data scraped from the official websites of the Jordanian monarchy and parliament; and a variety of public opinion data including surveys, Google Trends, and a Facebook advertising experiment.

In Chapter 4, the first of the Jordan chapters, I discuss how the country's political system is structured to enable delegation of decision-making responsibilities to nonroyal elites and to propagate the idea of the monarchy's distance from policymaking. I first review the country's background and explain how power sharing functions in the political system. I then provide evidence that Jordan's kings have intentionally relied on delegation to the cabinet and parliament to minimize their exposure to popular anger, that they delegate more credibly for issues where blame is particularly relevant to their survival, and that they use school curricula to reinforce this strategy by propagating the monarchical norm that the king is removed from – and therefore not responsible for – the policy process.

Chapter 5 leverages my public opinion data to offer micro-level evidence that Jordanians' attributions of responsibility are affected by the extent to which the king empowers other elites to govern. My interviews with opposition-oriented political elites suggest that even these individuals often believe sincerely that the king is not to blame for the country's issues. Survey responses indicate that this attitude is more widely held among the public, with many Jordanians believing that ministers and parliamentarians bear responsibility for poor outcomes in the country. An original experiment using Facebook ads provides one of the first attempts in Jordan to estimate support for the monarch relative to support for the prime minister and parliament: it suggests that the king is more popular, as expected, and that the king's popularity does not fluctuate in response to controversial policy decisions that do reduce support for the other two institutions. In other words, many Jordanians do not attribute blame to the king when they are upset, which helps to sustain popular approval of the monarchy and thus the stability of the regime.

Chapter 6 explores variation in delegation and blame across the country's modern history to offer further support for the theory's expectation that autocrats share power strategically to shape attributions as their threat environment changes. In particular, I explore how Jordan's monarchs have reacted strategically over time to different confluences of pressure from the public and political elites. During periods where the potential for popular dissatisfaction with governance outcomes has been high, the kings have reacted by strengthening the independence of the cabinet and parliament while distancing themselves from decision-making. When they have faced less public pressure, they have been more willing to assert themselves over the policy process. Alongside these trends, I provide evidence that the public's attributions of blame have shifted in response to these changes, with the Hashemite monarchs more likely to become the target of popular anger when they have controlled decision-making more directly. This pattern reinforces the idea that kings do not inherently benefit from some special bond with the people but are also likely to attract blame when the structure of decision-making demonstrates clearly their responsibility for governance outcomes.

1.5 *Plan of the Book*

As the last of the Jordan chapters, Chapter 7 considers how broader governance issues in Jordan are shaped by the blame avoidance strategy of the Hashemite kings. I document how protest activity is common and rarely repressed, reflecting the fact that most protests do not target the monarchy and if anything allow the king to respond to popular discontent. In addition to permitting protests, I discuss how the monarchy has rarely repressed political elites as well. Instead, the kings' approach has been to give elites policy influence alongside access to rents, which incentivizes elites to be involved in governance and protect the king from blame. This approach also explains why opposition elites often play along with the monarchy's blame game even when they themselves believe the king is at fault for the country's problems. By agreeing to publicly blame political actors other than the king, the opposition can also gain access to the decision-making process and the benefits this access entails. As long as most of the public does not agree with the opposition that the king should be held responsible for what goes wrong, this bargain makes strategic sense. Yet, the opposition's public endorsement of the king's lack of responsibility may help to reinforce the public's belief in the king's innocence, undermining the likelihood that a disgruntled public coordinates against the monarchy. Finally, I use data on ministerial tenures to show that the kings provide some measure of accountability in the political system by removing prime ministers and cabinets as the public becomes less satisfied with governance outcomes.

Chapter 8 returns to a comparative approach to assess the second primary argument of the book: that ruling monarchs are better positioned than other autocrats to use delegation as a blame avoidance strategy. It does so by combining global cross-national evidence with comparisons of monarchies and republics in the Arab world specifically. First, I compare how authoritarian monarchs differ from other autocrats when it comes to involving elites in their countries' decision-making processes, showing evidence that delegation is safer for monarchs and that they tend to delegate more credibly. I then use observational and experimental survey data from the Arab world to show that this difference is perceived by citizens of these regimes, and that monarchs also benefit from lower expectations to involve themselves in governance. Global comparative data on constitutions reinforce this latter point, illustrating how monarchs are not typically expected to participate in governance or face accountability for their decisions, particularly when compared to other types of authoritarian rulers. Finally, I consider the implications of these arguments for the extended durability of monarchies. Analysis of cross-national instability data shows that monarchs are less likely than other autocrats to confront mass opposition during periods when the public is aggrieved, suggesting that their blame avoidance advantage benefits the persistence of the regime. I connect these patterns to the monarchies' greater resiliency during the Arab Spring, tracing how presidential autocrats in Egypt and Tunisia failed to shift blame effectively in the decade prior to the Arab Spring when compared to their royal counterparts in Jordan and Morocco.

In Chapter 9, I assess how the book's argument contributes to understanding of political change *within* monarchies. Despite the fact that most governments in the modern world transitioned from monarchy at some point in the past two centuries, there are few studies that attempt to understand why some monarchies survived and others did not (Stepan et al. 2014). First, I use historical cross-national data on monarchies extending back to the 1800s to demonstrate that more centralized monarchies were more likely to experience regime change in a democratizing world, consistent with these monarchs being more exposed to the public's anger. I then discuss case studies of Iran and Nepal to illustrate how monarchs who centralize decision-making powers in their own hands make themselves vulnerable to blame and opposition just as any other autocrat does.

Chapter 10 concludes the book with a discussion of further implications for the politics of authoritarian rule. In particular, I consider how different types of authoritarian regimes may reflect the structures of royal institutions in ways that allow autocrats to protect their reputations, and how the theory may provide insights into trajectories of democratization.

2 A Theory of Power Sharing and Attributions under Authoritarian Rule

When COVID-19 erupted globally in February 2020, political leaders around the world responded differently to the challenges presented by the outbreak. While some acted decisively to assert control over the pandemic response, others stepped back and allowed subordinate officials to make crucial public health decisions. This latter group included several autocrats. For instance, Russian President Vladimir Putin delegated decisions about lockdowns and other policies to the local authorities (Beliakova 2020; Khurshudyan 2020). Likewise, the president of Egypt and the monarchs of Jordan and Morocco empowered their cabinets to manage the pandemic, relegating to themselves symbolic duties largely removed from the specifics of the response (Alshoubaki and Harris 2021; Hamzawy and Brown 2020). This delegation underscores the extent to which many political leaders, including powerful autocrats, worry more about avoiding blame than claiming credit when they face a potential trade-off between the two. Delegation can reduce a political leader's ability to claim credit effectively for popular outcomes, such as a competent emergency response, but it can also protect their reputation if outcomes prove unpopular instead, as happened frequently during the pandemic (Hood 2011). For instance, after hastily announced COVID-related travel restrictions led to chaotic highways and a spike in deadly accidents in Morocco, it was Prime Minister al-Othmani, not King Mohammed, who stated publicly that he bore "full responsibility for the decision" (Mebtoul 2020).

Why is it that powerful and repressive autocrats would care about who the public holds responsible for outcomes they dislike? After all, citizens who criticize the autocrat publicly will often end up jailed, harassed, or worse. Furthermore, would the autocrat actually be able to shift blame by granting other elites some influence over decision-making, or would people simply assume that the politically-dominant autocrat was still the one telling everyone what to do behind the scenes? Finally, if it is the case that this strategy of delegation can be effective at shifting blame, under what conditions is it more likely to be used by the autocrat, and in what contexts is it more likely to work well? Existing research on authoritarian political systems has relatively little to say about these questions, because scholars have focused primarily on understanding how autocrats repress or buy off their people to keep them loyal (Gandhi and Lust 2009; Przeworski 2023). While these factors are certainly important for the survival of authoritarian regimes, they do not tell the whole story about why the public does or does not oppose autocratic rule. After all, many autocrats appear to be genuinely popular with their citizens for extended periods of time (Guriev and Treisman 2020b), even as the political systems they dominate fail to govern well. Understanding why autocrats can succeed at maintaining public support even when their regimes perform poorly would benefit from thinking about how people living in these political systems attribute responsibility for their grievances.

This chapter aims to answer these questions. It first builds upon the introduction to discuss why attributions matter to autocrats. It then develops a general theory about the politics of blame and delegation in authoritarian regimes, outlining why sharing decision-making powers can help autocrats to avoid blame, the circumstances in which they are more or less likely to delegate, and the consequences of these blame games for broader patterns of authoritarian governance. Finally, it elaborates on my argument about why autocratic monarchs are better-positioned than other types of authoritarian rulers to rely on this strategy successfully, thus contributing to their puzzling stability.

2.1 Why Attributions Matter for Autocrats

We are used to thinking about autocracies as repressive regimes in which political leaders care little about what their people want, since the potential for violence keeps the public subdued and submissive. This portrayal reflects reality better than not in many cases. As an extreme example, the Soviet Union under Stalin, particularly in the late 1930s, executed hundreds of thousands of people in the "Great Purge." Though the purge started as an attempt to cement control over the Communist Party, it expanded rapidly and swept up many people with only the most tangential connections to politics. Even innocuous statements of dissatisfaction, such as observing that "in Greece there

2.1 Why Attributions Matter for Autocrats

are many types of fruit, and in the USSR few," could result in political convictions with terrible repercussions (Davies 1997). Such violence created a climate of fear in the society, and that fear likely contributed to regime stability while driving the absence of visible popular politics outside of actions endorsed by the party. The Soviet purges reflect the more violent end of the authoritarian spectrum, but there are many other cases where harsh repression – or at least its potential – helps autocrats to keep the people silenced and under control.

But the existence of repression does not negate the relevance of public opinion to the politics of authoritarian regimes. Even with its extensive violence, the Soviet Union of the 1930s recognized the importance of understanding the public's true opinions to the best of its ability. Party informants at the local level were tasked with monitoring the mood of the people as objectively as possible, and the internal security apparatus likewise maintained a massive network of agents to observe and report on the public (Davies 1997). These practices continued for decades, even after the shift away from the extremes of Stalin's terror. Worries about the popular mood were not ill-founded; indeed, the Soviet Union eventually collapsed after a series of mass uprisings. Similar fates have befallen a number of other repressive autocrats and their regimes, ranging from al-Qadhafi in Libya to Chun Doo-hwan in South Korea. The problem for authoritarian rulers is that once their popular support falls low enough, it can take just a single, unpredictable spark to bring the masses into the streets and create a revolutionary threat that repression cannot contain (Kuran 1991). Furthermore, because repression causes people to hide their views, it can be extremely difficult to know how much support the autocrat and regime actually have, whether the government's policies are giving the people what they want, and whether a specific policy change or outcome may trigger unrest (Wintrobe 1998). As a result, uncertainty over the public mood is a persistent feature of authoritarian politics with which autocrats must contend (Truex 2016), such that a mass uprising capable of bringing down the regime can always be just around the corner.

Another important component of the public's role in authoritarian regimes is that visibly low popular support for the autocrat may embolden elites to try taking power for themselves. If a coup-plotter believes their attempt to overthrow the autocrat will incur backlash from an angry public, they may think twice about making their move.

A potential elite challenger may believe their attempt is much more likely to succeed if the autocrat is already being targeted by large protests that suggest a lack of political support from the masses. For this reason, coup attempts frequently follow large demonstrations and other forms of visible public unrest (Casper and Tyson 2014; Johnson and Thyne 2018). As two recent examples, the long-serving autocrats of Algeria and Sudan, Abdelaziz Bouteflika and Omar al-Bashir, were both forced from power by their countries' militaries following mass uprisings in 2019. Without these protests, it is unlikely either president would have been forced to resign by others within the regime.

Managing how the public attributes responsibility is an important aspect of dealing with these threats. As discussed in Chapter 1, attributions are directly relevant to popularity: Credit for good outcomes tends to increase popular support, whereas blame for bad outcomes tends to decrease it. As such, autocrats are more likely to sustain some level of public approval if they can steer credit toward themselves while casting blame elsewhere. Indeed, while autocrats whose economies perform well tend to hold onto power longer (Stockemer and Kailitz 2020; Wright et al. 2015), some persist more than might be expected while overseeing weak economies, whereas others who govern well still find themselves facing an angry public mobilizing against their rule. Performance alone does not determine the popularity of political leaders, because it matters how people attribute responsibility for the outcomes that occur. If a country is well-governed but no one credits the autocrat with its successes, their reputation may still sour; alternatively, if the country has struggled for some time but the autocrat attracts little blame for these failures, their popularity may continue to thrive.

Given the uncertainty that typically surrounds public opinion in these contexts, investing in blame avoidance strategies may also be particularly important for limiting the risks associated with eruptions of discontent. Reducing the autocrat's exposure to blame makes it less likely that the public's anger, when it does erupt, targets the autocrat personally. In addition, managing attributions carefully can also weaken the potential threat posed by other elites. If the autocrat is able to claim credit, or if blame is shifted successfully onto other elites, the autocrat's relative popularity should help to protect them against internal challenges. For these reasons, autocrats resemble other political leaders in the extent to which attributions of credit and blame matter for their political survival.

2.1 Why Attributions Matter for Autocrats

2.1.1 Does Blame or Credit Matter More?

It can be difficult to predict policy outcomes, as well as the public's reactions to them, so political leaders do not fully know beforehand whether a decision is likely to benefit or harm their reputation. At the same time, political leaders often face a trade-off between their ability to claim credit and their ability to avoid blame for future outcomes, as positioning one's self to maximize credit can create more exposure to blame, whereas maneuvering to avoid blame can undermine the likelihood of receiving credit. When considering this trade-off in the context of uncertainty over the popularity of policy decisions, do political leaders tend to prioritize credit claiming or blame avoidance? Research suggests that blame is relatively more important than credit for popular support, because loss aversion means that people tend to weigh losses more than gains and will therefore punish politicians for bad outcomes more than they reward them for good ones (Weaver 1986). As a result, politicians are usually thought to prioritize blame avoidance over credit claiming (Hood 2011).

This emphasis on blame should be particularly relevant to autocratic political leaders for two reasons. First, unlike their democratic counterparts, autocrats do not need to actively build a coalition that can win free and fair elections (Hyde and Marinov 2012), which usually requires majority or near-majority support relative to the opposition. Instead, they need to avoid the emergence of a coalition large enough to overthrow them in unfair elections or a mass uprising (Howard and Roessler 2006). Thus, to hold onto power, it is particularly important that their support does not fall below some critical threshold, and it is less important that they fight for every additional supporter they can find to acquire a majority. This goal suggests that, for most autocrats, it will be more relevant to play it safe by protecting what popularity they already have, rather than gambling for credit to build greater support. Second, the fact that autocrats need to worry about being overthrown at any moment, rather than every few years in a prespecified election, should further enhance the relative importance of blame over credit. As was discussed earlier, when preference falsification is common, even seemingly minor policy changes can provide the spark that triggers a sudden and unexpected explosion of unrest. Given this uncertainty, autocrats should have incentives to adopt a risk-averse approach that attempts to reduce their exposure to popular anger that could unseat

44 *Power Sharing and Attributions under Autocracy*

them at any time. Democratic politicians may want to limit their exposure to blame as elections come closer, but they may be more willing to take risks for credit claiming opportunities otherwise because they are unlikely to be removed from power outside of electoral competition. Thus, blame avoidance should be particularly relevant to the uncertain nature of authoritarian politics.

For these reasons, the book emphasizes blame avoidance more than credit claiming when considering how autocrats react strategically to the public's attributions. Though both will be discussed, the theoretical and empirical focus is on the strategic decisions about power sharing that autocrats make to limit their exposure to blame.

2.1.2 How Decision-Making Shapes Attributions

For autocrats focused on reducing their exposure to blame, the structure of decision-making in their regimes should have important consequences for how the public attributes responsibility for governance outcomes. Of course, the ways in which people decide who deserves blame or credit are complicated and prone to biases. As just one example, motivated reasoning rooted in partisan political attachments may reduce the likelihood that a dissatisfied individual blames political leaders from their own political party, even if that party is in power at the time (Malhotra and Kuo 2008). In general, however, a leader is more likely to be perceived as responsible for an outcome when they exercised control over the decision-making or implementation process that led to it (Alicke 2000; Knobloch-Westerwick and Taylor 2008; Weiner 1985). It follows that political leaders can claim credit more effectively when they were clearly the one in charge; alternatively, they can avoid blame more successfully when their control was limited and someone else made the call (Hood 2011). This dynamic suggests that a ruler can strengthen or disperse their decision-making responsibilities based on their objectives for claiming credit or avoiding blame. Indeed, this strategy has been recommended for centuries. Writing in the 1500s, Machiavelli famously observed that "Princes should delegate to others the enactment of unpopular measures and keep in their own hands the means of winning favors."

Academic research suggests this advice is worth taking. When power is dispersed so that more political actors have the ability to influence

2.1 Why Attributions Matter for Autocrats

a decision-making process, it becomes less clear who is in control and therefore responsible for the outcome, and so the public is less likely to blame incumbent political leaders. In their seminal study defining this principle of "clarity of responsibility," Powell and Whitten (1993) show that people tend to punish the incumbent government less for economic outcomes when the incumbent has less unified control over the policy process, as in cases where weak parties or a minority government gives the opposition an important say in decision-making. A substantial body of subsequent research reinforces their findings (Duch and Stevenson 2008). For example, Hobolt et al. (2012) demonstrate that weaker government cohesion reduces the link between economic performance and voting, and De Vries et al. (2011) show that clarity of responsibility shapes the likelihood that voters hold political leaders accountable for their performance on other issues beyond the economy. Some research on Russia also indicates that this dynamic applies to authoritarian contexts, with voters less likely to punish the ruling party for poor performance in regions it controls less directly (Beazer and Reuter 2019; Rosenfeld 2018).

Political leaders seem to understand the relationship between control and blame. As one example, Tavits (2007) provides evidence that politicians are more likely to rein in corrupt practices when they exercise more direct control over the political system, implying that they know this clarity of responsibility means they are likely to be blamed for corruption. In recognizing this relationship, political leaders also have the ability to shape attributions directly by delegating decision-making responsibilities to other actors and institutions. By ceding partial or even full control over an issue, they can redirect the public's attributions away from themselves. For instance, American presidents often delegate issues to specific secretaries in the cabinet, creating "lightning-rods" who will attract the blame if outcomes are unsatisfactory (Ellis 1994). The same strategy even works for corporate leaders when they delegate to subordinate managers (Boeker 1992). Experimental research suggests that delegation can help to shift blame effectively even when the public knows that the individual to whom responsibility was delegated has the same preferences as the individual doing the delegating (Bartling and Fischbacher 2012). On the flip side, political leaders are more likely to reap the credit for positive outcomes when institutions clearly concentrate responsibility in their hands (Gulzar and Pasquale 2017). As a result, those who care about credit may choose not to delegate, structuring decision-making processes so as to hold all responsibility themselves. By contrast, those who care more about avoiding blame should be more likely to structure the decision-making process so that responsibility is delegated to others and is not held fully by them.

In an authoritarian context, these patterns suggest that autocrats who monopolize decision-making more fully will be better positioned to claim credit but will also be more vulnerable to blame, whereas those who share power more broadly with other elites will be able to avoid blame more effectively but at the cost of giving up some credit. This variation in attributions in authoritarian regimes is made possible by the fact that power sharing in these contexts often involves the delegation of decision-making powers away from the autocrat (Meng 2020). Even when the autocrat remains politically dominant, prime ministers and the cabinet may be able to influence the policy agenda of the government and their specific ministries (Noble 2020); legislatures may be capable of shaping laws and extracting policy concessions from the autocrat (Gandhi 2008; Karmel 2021; Lü et al. 2020); courts may constrain executive powers (Moustafa 2014); and bureaucrats ranging from military officers to health officials may influence decisions within their domains (Svolik 2012; Truex 2020).

An important issue to address is that some political leaders will *claim* to have delegated decisions to protect themselves from blame, scapegoating other elites while still making most decisions personally behind the scenes. This issue is especially applicable to authoritarian regimes, where autocrats tend to hold significant power and accurate information can be difficult for the public to acquire. For example, Stalin was a famous micromanager who oversaw the smallest decisions (Khlevniuk 2016), even though the regime consistently claimed that policy failures were the result of lower-level officials making decisions on their own (Pisch 2016). For the purposes of this book, I am interested in actual decision-making processes and how the public both perceives and responds to them, rather than messaging and propaganda about the autocrat's role. Of course, the public will not have perfect information about how decisions have been made. Thus, when they consider who controlled a decision as they decide how to attribute blame, I argue that people will evaluate how *credible* it is that delegation occurred and that the autocrat did not personally make the decision in question. As delegation is perceived to be more credible,

2.1 Why Attributions Matter for Autocrats

people should be less likely to believe the autocrat directly shaped the decision, and they should be less likely to blame them as a result.

What, then, makes delegation more credible in an authoritarian context? I claim that credibility is influenced by whether the autocrat delegates in such a way that they would pay costs for subsequently trying to force their own preferences onto the decision-making process, rather than allowing the delegate to choose and implement the policy. The more costly it would be for the autocrat to overturn or ignore the influence of political elites with whom they have shared decision-making powers, the more credibly people will perceive delegation to be.

This approach to credibility is similar to how the literature on authoritarianism discusses the credibility of power-sharing arrangements more broadly. As scholars of authoritarian politics have long recognized, why would elites trust the promises of wealth and influence made by an autocrat who can step in and take it away at any time? The answer is that power sharing is more credible when it is done in a way that makes it easier for elites to push back against and impose costs on the autocrat for trying to renege (Meng et al. 2023). In particular, researchers have focused on the ability of institutions like parties, legislatures, and cabinets to enhance this credibility by providing elites with information about the autocrat's actions, making it easier to coordinate opposition to the autocrat, and providing access to important resources that can be used to challenge the autocrat – all of which should make it costlier for autocrats to ignore the power-sharing arrangements they have established (Magaloni 2008; Meng 2020; Svolik 2012).

This approach to credibility is also similar to how the literature on central banks talks about the credibility of political leaders delegating monetary policy to these institutions. Central banks face a similar problem to the one discussed earlier in authoritarian regimes: Why, if the government can simply take back the central bank's independence when it wants, would delegation to the bank ever be credible? Here, the answer is also that delegation becomes more credible as it becomes costlier to overturn because of institutional or political factors. For instance, regarding institutions, specifying central bank independence in the constitution creates additional hurdles for the government if they wish to change it, and attempting to amend the constitution may also increase the likelihood that the government loses political support (e.g., Driffill and Rotondi 2006). Regarding political factors, it may become costlier to revoke the bank's independence if doing so requires overcoming veto points that are known to be controlled by political actors who have different policy preferences toward the bank, and are therefore less likely to agree on the decision (e.g., Keefer and Stasavage 2003).

In similar ways, the institutional and political context of an authoritarian regime may affect the credibility of delegation by the autocrat to other political elites. First, formal institutions can reinforce the credibility of delegation by establishing clear rules about who has which responsibilities in the policy process, including the autocrat themselves. If the autocrat transgresses those rules, it becomes easier to identify the violation of delegation, which can impose costs on the autocrat by facilitating coordinated resistance by elites or the public (Magaloni 2008; Weingast 1997). For example, delegation to the legislature should be perceived as more credible when an autocrat shares power with a legislature that possesses several constitutionally-ascribed prerogatives pertaining to the policymaking process, such as the ability to vote on the government's formation, vote on laws, query ministers, and investigate other government officials. Even when the legislature is relatively weak politically, attempting to sidestep these powers and ignore its influence can create costs for the autocrat (Meng et al. 2023). Likewise, the constitutional requirement to elect the legislature increases the likelihood that legislators will have their own political interests and make their own political calculations, which may contradict the priorities of the autocrat and require negotiating over policy outcomes. The credibility of an elected legislature's influence over decision-making should therefore be higher compared to a legislature that is appointed by the autocrat directly and functions primarily as an advisory body with no legal right to approve or block laws. Similar dynamics may apply to cabinets, with ministers wielding more or less formal powers over their associated bureaucracies as well as state resources that can be used to constrain the autocrat's decision-making role. There is extensive variation in institutions and their ability to impose costs on the autocrat across authoritarian regimes (Meng 2020), and this variation should influence how the public perceives the decision-making powers of the autocrat and thus their attributions of credit and blame.

2.1 Why Attributions Matter for Autocrats

Importantly, however, informal political factors may also demonstrate to the public that the autocrat is likely to confront costs for overriding the influence of elites with whom he or she has shared decision-making powers. One set of political factors relates to who holds positions of influence within the regime and what their personal characteristics are. For instance, autocrats often have the power to appoint important officials such as the prime minister. The dictator may choose to delegate to a prime minister who possesses their own personal base of support from a political party or social group, or that dictator may choose to delegate to a weak technocrat who is completely dependent on them politically. Sharing decision-making powers with the former should be perceived as more credible delegation, since a prime minister with their own political support should be more capable of asserting their influence and creating costs for the dictator if they try to subvert their role. Likewise, some autocrats establish or inherit political parties that they lead, whose members are tied politically to the autocrat's fate. There is variation across authoritarian political parties, and some are able to constrain the dictator better than others. In general, however, autocrats who share power with individuals in their own party should be seen as delegating less credibly than those who give decision-making responsibilities to political elites from other organizations that do not align so closely with the autocrat's agenda. In the empirical chapters of the book, I will discuss specific examples of how the credibility of delegation varies due to institutional and political factors, and how this variation affects the public's attributions of responsibility.

To summarize, a political leader's exposure to blame is influenced by how much control they wield over a decision-making process, and this relationship should apply to authoritarian regimes as well. As a result, autocrats should be able to avoid blame by delegating responsibility to political elites active in institutions like the legislature and cabinet. That delegation should be perceived as more credible by the public when political and institutional factors would make it costlier for the autocrat to overturn it, and this more credible delegation should protect the autocrat more from blame. As I discuss next, these dynamics should influence how, why, and when autocrats share power over decision-making, as well as the degree of mass opposition that autocrats are likely to face when their regimes govern poorly.

50 *Power Sharing and Attributions under Autocracy*

2.2 Attributions and Strategic Power Sharing

This section develops a theory about the relationship between power sharing and attributions in authoritarian regimes. It first discusses the theory's key actors and assumptions, before outlining the strategic interactions that occur around decision-making. It also considers the implications of this theory for different equilibriums of authoritarian stability and governance.

2.2.1 The Actors and Their Interests

My theory considers three actors: the autocrat, the regime elites, and the citizens. A similar framework is common in many theories of authoritarianism (e.g., Blaydes 2010; Gandhi 2008; Geddes et al. 2018; Magaloni 2006; Svolik 2012; Truex 2016). It recognizes that dictators are important in these political systems but always require the support of elite actors to maintain power (Haber 2008), and it also recognizes a role for the public in shaping political outcomes, even if everyday citizens possess limited access to formal channels of political influence (Gandhi 2008; Magaloni 2006). In what follows, I briefly define the core interests of these actors.

The Autocrat
The autocrat, or dictator, is motivated primarily by a desire to hold onto power. This assumption is foundational for many studies of political leaders, including those in democracies (e.g., Mayhew 1974), as well as those in authoritarian regimes (e.g., Svolik 2012; Wintrobe 1998). It is not difficult to imagine why, particularly in authoritarian regimes, that political leaders would want to hold onto their position as long as possible. Autocrats often acquire immense wealth: those governing countries ranging from Morocco and Saudi Arabia to Russia and North Korea are thought to be some of the richest people in the world, with billions of dollars in assets. Furthermore, given that the riskiness of authoritarian politics likely attracts individuals who desire power for power's sake, it is probably the case that being dictator also provides these individuals with significant immaterial benefits that they will strongly resist giving up. As just one example, former President Saleh of Yemen could have retired quietly and with much wealth to Saudi Arabia after being ousted by a popular uprising in

2.2 Attributions and Strategic Power Sharing

2012; instead, he took a massive risk by returning to the country in a long shot bid to reclaim power just a few years later. The gamble failed, and Saleh was summarily executed by his previous opponents in 2017. In other words, dictators like being dictators, and they will often risk everything to stay where they are.

The Elites

Elites who participate in high-level authoritarian politics may wield less power than the autocrat, but they often exercise significant influence in the political system, and they can reap substantial benefits from their positions as a result (Bueno de Mesquita et al. 2003). In particular, I assume that elites are motivated by the desire to acquire financial rents, as well as the ability to push policies toward their own preferences.

Regarding the former, levels of corruption are high in many authoritarian regimes (Montinola and Jackman 2002). Individuals with the right connections and institutional positions can gain access to sweetheart business deals, and in some cases, they may engage in direct theft of public funds without significant fear of legal retribution. For instance, in China, serving as a legislator in the National People's Congress generates higher profits for one's business (Truex 2014). Members of parliament in Egypt likewise benefited from corrupt business dealings under the regime of Husni Mubarak (Blaydes 2010). And legislators and cabinet officials in Jordan also gain access to higher profits and other material goods due to their connections (Lust-Okar 2006). These dynamics are common to most authoritarian regimes.

At the same time, elites in these political systems often hold their own preferences about the policies their governments should enact. Returning to Jordan, political elites tried to push foreign policy in a pro- or anti-British direction during the early years of King Hussein's reign; later, they were divided over the country's stance toward Iraq. Likewise, Lü et al. (2020) demonstrate that parliamentarians in China interact with bureaucratic interest groups to form coalitions that pursue certain policy objectives, even for policy issues like education where the likelihood of attaining corrupt rents is low. In Russia, Noble (2020) also documents how elites within the executive branch compete over different policy preferences, and these disagreements can be strong enough to generate serious intra-executive disputes.

Thus, elites seek to use their positions to maximize their combined access to rents and influence over policy. At times, these goals may motivate them to attempt a coup d'ètat that overthrows the autocrat. Seizing power should imply even greater wealth and influence; as a result, elites may be tempted to make their move if they calculate that the benefits from success outweigh the likely-high costs of failure.

The Citizens
The literature on authoritarian regimes places less emphasis on the public's preferences, but it remains the case that citizens hold policy preferences and care about policy outcomes. If their preferences are not met, I assume that citizens want to hold accountable the actors responsible for their grievance. The empirical validity of this assumption is reflected in the extensive literature on retrospective voting in democracies, whereby vote choice is influenced strongly by individuals' evaluations of political leaders' performance in office (e.g., Healy and Malhotra 2013). It also aligns well with the substantial literature demonstrating that authoritarian regimes benefit from good economic performance (Zhao 2009) but are vulnerable to breakdown during periods of economic crisis (e.g., Geddes 1999; Magaloni 2006; Reuter and Gandhi 2011). Finally, previous scholarly work on authoritarian regimes has also assumed that citizens hold policy preferences, and that the failure to match these preferences shapes the public's willingness to mobilize against the regime (Gandhi 2008; Magaloni 2006; and Truex 2016).

When considering whether to mobilize, however, citizens must weigh their desire for accountability against the costs of repression. Public displays of opposition in these political systems can often lead to punishments ranging from lost economic opportunities to imprisonment and death (Blaydes 2018; Greitens 2016; Kuran 1991). As a result, even citizens who are extremely angry at the autocrat specifically, or the regime more generally, may hide their preferences if they feel that the costs associated with repression are too high to justify speaking out.

2.2.2 Key Assumptions

The theory rests on two key assumptions about how power sharing functions in authoritarian regimes, especially related to the delegation

2.2 Attributions and Strategic Power Sharing

of decision-making powers to other regime elites. I elaborate on these assumptions here.

The first is that power sharing creates both benefits and risks for autocrats. Providing other elites with access to rents or influence over decision-making is beneficial because these measures provide elites with positive incentives to remain loyal to the autocrat. These elites acquire greater wealth due to their positions, and they also have the opportunity to shift policies toward their own preferences. These positive incentives are emphasized by much of the authoritarianism literature that discusses why autocrats are willing to cede some power to others in the regime (e.g., Gandhi 2008; Meng 2020).

At the same time, sharing power also creates risks for autocrats *because* it empowers these elites, who may wish to replace the autocrat themselves (Paine 2021). For instance, allowing someone to take charge of the defense ministry gives them strong ties to the military and other security forces that could facilitate a coup (Roessler 2016). Likewise, appointing a vice president or prime minister may provide an alternative focal point around whom elites can coordinate their opposition to the autocrat (Meng 2020). Elites who wield greater power may also be better-positioned to claim credit for popular policies, building their reputations with the public and other political elites in a way that may strengthen their ability to challenge the autocrat.

What does this trade-off imply about the conditions under which power sharing occurs in authoritarian regimes? First, if elites are unable to threaten the autocrat credibly, there is less incentive for the autocrat to share power with them, so power sharing is more likely to occur when the elites have some capacity to oust the autocrat from power (Meng 2020; Svolik 2012). At the same time, because power sharing further strengthens the influence of these elites and bolsters their ability to move against the autocrat, power sharing is less likely to occur when it would heighten the risk of a coup to an unbearable level (Paine 2021). I follow this research in my approach by assuming that sharing decision-making powers does not only benefit autocrats by allowing them to evade blame and incentivize elite loyalty but also brings potential costs since it could heighten the risks of an internal challenge from within the regime. This cost constrains the extent to which autocrats will be willing to delegate.

The second assumption is that autocrats have some ability to delegate more or less credibly by choosing how they share power. This

54   *Power Sharing and Attributions under Autocracy*

assumption is important because it means that autocrats can act strategically to shape the public's attributions to protect their reputations. In some cases, the autocrat very clearly has the ability to decide whether or not to give other elites responsibility for a decision, and to influence whether that delegation is credible or not. For example, when appointing a prime minister, an autocratic king or president may define the issues that official can address. Likewise, as discussed previously, they may choose a dependent technocrat who will clearly be under their thumb, or, on the other end of the spectrum, the leader of an opposition political party capable of mobilizing protests against the autocrat if they become disgruntled. In other cases, institutional rules that define who is meant to be responsible for which decisions may be more difficult to adjust and thus harder to manipulate strategically. Because of their great powers, autocrats and their supporters often can change institutions to suit their needs (Magaloni 2006). That being said, even if an autocrat changes an institution for the specific purpose of limiting their exposure to blame or facilitating more effective credit claiming, the longer-term effects may be harder to foresee. Thus, while it is important for my argument that autocrats have the capacity to delegate more or less credibly by manipulating political or institutional factors that change the costs of overruling or ignoring elites with whom they have shared decision-making powers, it is also important to acknowledge that these choices may be messy or constrained by longer-term political processes.

2.2.3 A Simplified Theoretical Framework

Here I develop a simplified framework for understanding how attributions shape strategic interactions between an autocrat, regime elites, and the citizens with regards to a country's decision-making process. In this framework, the authoritarian regime implements a policy without knowing precisely how the public will respond. The first decision falls to the autocrat. In trying to maximize their chances of holding onto power, they must decide how to delegate to another political elite: either they can delegate with low credibility, in which case they possess more influence over the policy, or they delegate with high credibility, in which case the elite exercises greater influence over the decision. After the policy is set, the elite then has the opportunity to attempt a coup, which – if successful – allows them to replace the autocrat and take the

2.2 Attributions and Strategic Power Sharing

benefits of power for themselves. If the coup does not happen or fails, it falls to the citizens to either accept the policy or mobilize against the regime because of its decision. If the citizens accept, both the autocrat and the elite remain in their position. If the citizens mobilize, however, they have the chance to acquire accountability by removing either the autocrat or the elite from their position.

As discussed previously, I assume that more credible delegation strengthens the elite relative to the autocrat, which can heighten the likelihood of a successful coup. At the same time, more credible delegation should also lower the risks of a mass uprising that targets the autocrat. On the one hand, this trade-off suggests that autocrats should be more likely to delegate credibly as they become more concerned about the potential for popular unrest, whether because repression is unreliable or because there is a high likelihood that the regime will fail to give the citizens what they want. On the other hand, there may be times in which the elite is already so well-positioned to mount a coup that empowering them further will ensure that the autocrat faces an especially dangerous elite challenge. Thus, as the elite becomes more powerful, the autocrat should be less likely to delegate credibility to reduce the threat of an internal putsch, even if doing so increases the risk that they face mass opposition targeting them personally. In other words, credible delegation is most likely to occur when the autocrat feels threatened by the public and therefore values the ability to avoid blame more effectively, but also when the threat from the elite is not so high as to make delegation dangerous to pursue.

For the elite, more credible delegation by the autocrat means they gain more control over the policy decision. This scenario gives them a reason to remain loyal to the autocrat, since they can now set the policy closer to their own preference. However, by giving them access to resources and networks, it also increases the likelihood that they can launch a successful coup to become the autocrat themselves (Meng 2020). More credible delegation can be costly to the elite as well. If they choose a policy and the public is dissatisfied with it, they are more likely to be blamed and thus targeted by the public. Not only does this situation put them at risk of losing their position, but it also means they are likely to experience social opprobrium and damage to their reputation. In some cases, these costs may be compounded by further punishments as the autocrat seeks to scapegoat them, such that the elite can be exiled, jailed, or even executed for their failings. Under the Roman Emperor Commodus, for example, his adviser Cleander was blamed by the mob for severe food shortages, and Commodus ordered Cleander's execution in response. More recently, in contemporary China and Saudi Arabia, senior political insiders have been stripped of their power and thrown in prison as part of the dictator's efforts to show the public that they are committed to fighting corruption (Leber and Carothers 2017). If these blame costs are high enough, the elite will have strong incentives to avoid them, perhaps even by trying to take the autocrat's position for themselves. This dynamic implies that autocrats should attempt to minimize the costs that elites suffer for taking the blame, with the goal of reducing their incentives to launch a coup. Altogether, then, whether elites attempt to seize power will be shaped by the benefits of influencing policy, the likelihood that a coup would succeed, and the costs of being blamed, all three of which should increase with the credibility of delegation.

Once the policy has been chosen and the elite decides not to attempt a coup, the citizens face their own decision about whether – and against whom – to protest. I assume that first and foremost, the citizens want a policy to be chosen that matches their own preferences. If such a policy is chosen, the citizens will be satisfied and will have no incentive to mobilize. However, if the selected policy does not match their preferences, the citizens want to hold accountable the government actor responsible for this deviation. Since elections are less relevant to authoritarian politics, the citizens can respond with protests demanding the ouster of either the autocrat or the elite. Citizens who blame the autocrat most will receive the greatest benefit from ousting them, but will still derive some satisfaction from removing the elite, and vice versa for those who blame the elite most. In deciding whether to protest and whom to target, citizens weigh the benefits of accountability against the likelihood of experiencing repression and forcing the targeted actor from their position.

In making this choice, the public faces a coordination problem that is influenced by whether the autocrat delegates with high or low credibility. Coordination problems occur when individuals receive higher payoffs for participating in some action as the number of other participants increases (Chwe 2001). This logic often applies to protests in authoritarian regimes, since a larger number of demonstrators increases the likelihood that a protest succeeds, while lowering the

2.2 Attributions and Strategic Power Sharing

risks that any single demonstrator suffers from repression (Christensen and Garfias 2018). A key component of coordination problems is an individual's beliefs about whether *others* agree with their objectives and are likely to act on those beliefs, since the benefits of participation depend on whether those other people will also join (Armstrong et al. 2020; Huang and Cruz 2021). How does delegation shape the coordination problem for disgruntled citizens weighing whether to protest in an authoritarian regime? If the credibility of delegation is low and it is clear that the autocrat exercised significant influence over the decision-making process, more of the citizens should believe personally that the autocrat is most responsible and deserves to be blamed. Importantly, more of them should *also* believe that others blame the autocrat as well, because the autocrat's power is apparent for all to see. As a result, they should be simultaneously more invested in ousting the autocrat and more convinced that enough of the public will join them for the protest to succeed. Alternatively, as it becomes more credible that the autocrat's influence over the decision-making process was relatively low, fewer citizens should believe that the autocrat is most at fault for the outcome, and those who do still blame the autocrat should be less confident that enough people share their opinion. As a result, they should be more concerned that protesting against the autocrat will fail to draw large enough numbers to succeed and will leave them exposed to repression. Thus, they may be willing to settle for the second-best outcome by targeting the elite instead.

In other words, power-sharing arrangements that delegate responsibility credibly to other elites should reduce the likelihood that demonstrators coordinate against the autocrat, *even if* many people privately believe the autocrat is at fault. The autocrat may be able to reinforce this dynamic further by ensuring that the costs of repression for targeting them directly are higher than the costs of repression for targeting the elite. If red lines are drawn around criticizing the autocrat publicly, but protesters are generally allowed to mobilize against other political elites without facing more severe consequences, citizens considering whether to protest against the autocrat will need to be even more certain that the autocrat is at fault and that many others share this view. Thus, credible delegation of decision-making responsibilities can function in tandem with repression to reduce the likelihood of coordinated opposition against the autocrat.

2.2.4 What about Opposition Elites?

Some citizens who believe the autocrat is responsible for many of their political system's problems may be influential elites in their own right, whether as political activists, journalists, or leaders of political parties. These "opposition" elites face a similar calculus to other citizens who blame the autocrat privately, in deciding whether to voice their attributions publicly or go along with blaming other elites in the regime. However, the decisions of these individuals may have particularly important spillovers for the beliefs and actions of the public at large.

On the one hand, it may be worthwhile for these opposition elites to attribute blame to the dictator, because doing so may provide the visible signal of discontent that triggers a much broader mobilization by revealing to people that many others share their views. If the opposition elites miscalculate, however, and much of the public does not agree with them that the autocrat bears primary responsibility for their grievances, they open themselves up to being repressed without having accomplished anything. At the same time, these opposition elites may be able to find positions within the regime if they refrain from speaking out publicly against the autocrat and go along with the idea that other political elites are at fault for problematic outcomes. By joining the regime – whether as ministers, legislators, or bureaucrats – they may be able to push policies toward their preferences. Furthermore, by blaming other political elites for the country's problems instead of the autocrat, they may be able to facilitate the removal of these elites, contributing to limited accountability. This bargain may well be worthwhile if most of the public does not agree with their negative views of the dictator's responsibility. In cases where the autocrat has delegated more credibly, these elites may think it is unlikely they can stir up enough anger against the autocrat, and so they may go along with blaming other regime insiders even if they personally believe the autocrat bears actual responsibility.

However, in making this choice to refrain from blaming the autocrat publicly, opposition elites will likely reinforce the autocrat's ability to avoid blame. Ordinary citizens often look to political elites for cues that help them to interpret political developments. When deciding how to attribute blame for some problem in the political system, they may reasonably believe that elites affiliated with the opposition will be

2.2 Attributions and Strategic Power Sharing

particularly likely to speak out against the dictator if the dictator really is at fault. If these opposition elites blame someone else instead – for instance, a prime minister to whom responsibility has been delegated – it should send a strong signal that the autocrat does not deserve to be blamed, or at least that very few people in the society believe the autocrat is at fault. As a result, coordination around demands to hold the dictator accountable should become even harder. Thus, the co-optation of opposition elites into the regime may further bolster the ability of delegation to shift the public's attributions of responsibility away from the autocrat.

2.2.5 Power Sharing, Attributions, and Governance Outcomes

The interactions I have just described suggest different stylized scenarios in which authoritarian regimes may find themselves: one in which the autocrat monopolizes decision-making and retains power for an extended period of time; a second that implies ruler instability regardless of how the ruler shares decision-making powers; and a third in which the autocrat delegates credibly to other political elites, while stabilizing their hold on power. In all three cases, dictators weigh the threat of being blamed by the public, and their concern about a mass uprising has implications for how they share power with elite allies.

Low Credibility Delegation and Ruler Stability: In the first scenario, the dictator has little reason to fear that the public will mobilize, so they do not worry about being blamed if people become dissatisfied. They may share power to a limited extent if elites are powerful enough and need to be co-opted, but this power sharing may be oriented more toward financial rents than the delegation of decision-making responsibilities. Two reasons stand out for why the autocrat may not fear being blamed. First, they may be confident that they can satisfy the public's preferences well enough to avoid any popular mobilization, perhaps if they have substantial resource wealth or a long record of strong economic performance. In such an environment, the autocrat may not only be less worried about blame but may also want to position themselves to claim credit more effectively rather than risking that other elites will be able to do so. Second, the dictator may be sure of themselves because their use of repression is so heavy-handed as to make mass mobilization very unlikely, which may make them less concerned about how the public is attributing blame. Thus, in particularly violent regimes like North Korea, Iraq under Saddam Hussein, or the Soviet Union under Stalin, there is less incentive for the dictator to cede control over decision-making. To some extent, the ability to use repression in this way reflects a strategic calculation on the part of the dictator, suggesting that they can influence how costly it is for the public to mobilize. Yet this is only partially true: External constraints on repression can limit its use (Levitsky and Way 2010), as can historically or exogenously determined factors like the professionalization of the security forces or the capacity to invest in the coercive apparatus (Bellin 2004).

If the autocrat has little reason to fear being blamed and can keep elites loyal by distributing rents, they are likely to rule in a highly personalist fashion, often for an extended period of time (Svolik 2012). Yet, dictators in these authoritarian regimes should also be vulnerable to unexpected crises that simultaneously generate public anger, while weakening the dictator's ability to provide patronage or rely on repression. Because responsibility is concentrated in their hands, they will take the blame for the crisis, and they will also no longer be capable of avoiding its consequences without turning to extreme violence. Existing cross-national research illustrates these dynamics well. Personalist dictatorships, in which decision-making revolves almost entirely around the dictator, tend to be more violent and repressive than other types of authoritarian regimes (Davenport 2007; Frantz et al. 2020), and also more vulnerable to crises (Geddes 1999). Likewise, regimes with greater resource wealth are more likely to concentrate decision-making powers in the dictator's hands, with institutions like the legislature facilitating rent distribution more than policy influence (Wright 2008).

Potential Credible Delegation with Ruler Instability: In the second scenario, the dictator does have reasons to fear that an angry public could mobilize against them effectively, but the dictator also must contend with elites who pose a serious challenge to their hold on power. Thus, they may decide to delegate more or less credibly based on their evaluation of the relative risks associated with coups or popular uprisings, without necessarily managing either threat all that well. Whatever their decisions, this scenario is one in which the dictator is unlikely to hold onto power for long. Unless they possess significant luck or skill, they are likely to be removed by either the citizens or the elite at some point in the near future.

2.2 *Attributions and Strategic Power Sharing* 61

Many authoritarian regimes appear to reflect this scenario. The average dictator held onto power for approximately a decade in the post-World War II period. Many survived for much shorter periods of time than that, with one-fourth of them ruling for three years or less (Geddes et al. 2018). For instance, in Syria between 1946 and 1958, the country cycled through seven different presidents, all of whom faced a volatile citizenry and elites emboldened by repeated coups. Similar patterns have occurred in authoritarian political systems around the world, whether in Latin America, Africa, or Asia.

Credible Delegation and Ruler Stability: The third scenario is one in which the dictator delegates decision-making responsibility credibly to minimize their exposure to blame and reduce the likelihood of a popular uprising that targets them personally. Meanwhile, elites are not so powerful that delegation motivates coup attempts, and instead, they are kept loyal through their ability to shape policy and their access to rents. This scenario is also one of ruler and thus regime stability: Elites absorb the public's anger in exchange for greater power, the public gets to hold these elites accountable when they are dissatisfied with the government's policies, and the dictator is able to remain in their position. Such an outcome is most likely when the autocrat is not confident in their ability to provide policies that match the public's preferences. For instance, an autocrat may be more likely to cede responsibility in a country where economic prospects are consistently poor or at least uncertain, and thus public anger can be anticipated with some degree of regularity.

This scenario should be characterized by relatively influential elites who participate actively in the policy process, even to the extent that they can overrule the dictator on certain decisions. Many authoritarian regimes reflect this dynamic, both historically and in the modern period. European monarchs often depended heavily on powerful nobles and other advisers to determine and then implement the state's policies (Blaydes and Chaney 2013). In more recent years, though some authoritarian regimes have been defined by a high degree of personalization (Geddes 1999; Geddes et al. 2018), it is more common that autocrats have depended on elite allies to sustain their rule (Haber 2008; Magaloni 2008). These elites have often been given substantial responsibility to make policy in various domains (Gandhi et al. 2020).

In cases where elites are given meaningful decision-making responsibilities, the argument implies that the political system should also be characterized by high elite turnover in formal government positions. Because these elites take the blame when policies prove unpopular, they are removed by the dictator and replaced by someone else to satiate the public. In that sense, accountability should be more common in these regimes. However, as discussed previously, these removals should not commonly result in significant legal punishments or even banishment from the regime's inner circle, so as to minimize the costs associated with being blamed. Instead, elites may cycle in and out of office over the years, and in periods where they do not hold formal positions, they should still have access to networks that facilitate informal influence and the acquisition of wealth. Finally, these regimes may also be characterized by more frequent public mobilization. Insofar as the use of repression is strategic, the dictator has less need to rely on heavy-handed political violence. Because they are not the target of the public's anger, they do not need to keep mobilization in check. In fact, where elites are taking the blame for the government's policies, dictators may actually have incentives to permit protests as a means of keeping elites honest and focused on performing well (Lorentzen 2013; Schuler 2020).

To the extent that this scenario can reflect a stable equilibrium, one question that arises is why the public would not "learn" over time that this system benefits the autocrat. However, if citizens are not disgruntled with the autocrat, they may not care that the autocrat benefits from this arrangement. In addition, my argument does not assume a static distribution of power between the autocrat and elites, but rather the existence of some capacity for the autocrat to delegate more or less credibly as they anticipate increasing risks associated with being blamed for governance outcomes. If the dictator adjusts in this way, the public should observe these changes and then update their beliefs about who in the political system is responsible. Thus, stability occurs not because the public is being "duped," but because they are adjusting their own perceptions of how much the autocrat should be blamed based on actual changes in the political system.

Another question is whether citizens will become angry with the autocrat for repeatedly allowing elites to govern who subsequently fail at their jobs. Such an outcome seems plausible, in the same way that people may become disenchanted with their democracy if the government performs poorly regardless of who is elected. As will be discussed in subsequent chapters, trust in Jordanian prime ministers has

2.3 The Royal Advantage

experienced a secular decline in the past two decades as different holders of the office have consistently struggled to right the country's stagnant economy, and it is plausible that this distrust has spilled over into more negative attitudes toward the king. Yet, if it is credible that elites other than the autocrat are making important policy decisions, and if those elites are then held accountable for those decisions, it seems entirely possible that an autocrat may bleed support only slowly, particularly compared to the loss of approval they would experience if they monopolized power much more directly.

2.3 The Royal Advantage

Why might some autocrats be better positioned to protect their reputations by delegating credibly, and thus more likely to end up in the stable situation just described? First, recall that delegation becomes more costly for autocrats as it becomes more credible, because as elites find it easier to resist the autocrat's influence in the decision-making process, they should also have an easier time challenging the autocrat if they wish to do so. If certain types of autocrats tend to face a lower baseline level of threat from other elites with whom they share power, they should have more leeway than their peers to delegate credibly without triggering a challenge from these elites.

Second, the ability of delegation to shape the public's attributions is also affected by norms within a society about who is *meant* to be responsible for certain decisions (Hood 2011). Some institutions or leaders are expected to bear responsibility for decision-making (Arceneaux 2006; Arceneaux and Stein 2006), to the point that people attributing blame may ignore whether these actors delegated to someone else or may even blame them *for* delegating when they were supposed to be taking charge instead. If delegation aligns more closely with norms of responsibility for some types of autocrats than others, they should have an advantage in convincing the public that they are not to blame when they share power credibly with other political elites.

Among the various types of autocrats in the modern world, I argue that monarchs are better positioned on both fronts because of how they are supposed to be selected and what this selection process implies about how they are supposed to govern. As discussed in Chapter 1, monarchs are defined by the reliance on hereditary succession within a royal family to choose who rules. For most other authoritarian

64   *Power Sharing and Attributions under Autocracy*

regimes in the modern world, popular sovereignty serves as the principle that informs who has the right to govern, such that a legitimate ruler is one who is chosen by and represents the will of the people (Bendix 1978; O'Donnell 2007). I argue that the institutionalization of hereditary succession in monarchies makes it both safer and more effective for royal autocrats to use delegation as a blame avoidance strategy, compared to dictators who are selected – at least in theory – by the public.

Regarding the issue of elite challenges, hereditary succession reduces the pool of individuals with a legitimate claim to the throne, since nonroyal elites cannot become king. In nonmonarchies, any political elite – or even any citizen – can make a legitimate claim to power with enough popular support. Furthermore, institutional channels often exist to facilitate popular input in the selection process. On average, this difference should make it costlier for nonroyal elites to remove a king from power, giving the king more space to delegate credibly, but safely. In terms of delegation's effectiveness at influencing attributions of blame, hereditary succession implies nothing about the need for monarchs to involve themselves in governance and the policy process, whereas rulers selected on the basis of popular sovereignty are expected to make decisions for – and be held accountable by – the people. As a result, when monarchs claim they are not responsible because they have delegated, it aligns better with the public's expectations about who is meant to be responsible for policy decisions. Thus, relative to nonroyal autocrats – whether presidents, prime ministers, or military officers – monarchs should on average be able to delegate more credibly without fearing elite threats as much, and that delegation should also protect them from blame more effectively. As a result, monarchs should be less likely than other autocrats to become the target of popular opposition when the public is dissatisfied. I elaborate upon these advantages in the following sections.

2.3.1 Monarchs Can Delegate More Credibly, More Safely

For monarchies, the reliance on hereditary succession to choose the autocrat means that a relatively small number of people in a state can legitimately become the ruler: Only those born to the right (royal) family can become king or queen. In addition, monarchs are almost always expected to keep their positions for life (Gerring et al. 2021),

2.3 The Royal Advantage

and monarchies often specify a line of succession to the throne, following a rule such as primogeniture that requires succession by the monarch's eldest child (Kokkonen et al. 2022). These rules further restrict legitimate claims on power by limiting which royals can plausibly expect to become the monarch. As a result, there are few ways to overthrow a monarch without entirely upending the country's existing political institutions. A member of the royal family can launch a coup, oust the king, and then plausibly establish themselves as the ruling monarch afterward. Such coups happened frequently in the past, especially where primogeniture was not the norm (Kokkonen et al. 2022), and they have happened in the modern period as well; for instance, the Emir of Qatar was replaced in a palace coup orchestrated by his son, the crown prince, in 1995. But because most royal families are relatively small, they can often be managed effectively. Meanwhile, the vast majority of political elites do not have the option of replacing the king, because they are not members of the royal family. If they acquire enough power, they can sideline the monarch in the decision-making process and relegate them to near-ceremonial status. In Iraq, for instance, the powerful prime minister Nuri al-Said often dominated the young King Faisal II, until both were overthrown in a military coup in 1958. But monarchs in this situation may regain their power after a time. To truly become an autocrat in a democratic age where new royal families are not easily established, a nonroyal cannot just overthrow the monarch. Instead, they must also overthrow the monarchy, making themselves president or prime minister in a newly-created republic. Thus, in a monarchy, there are few channels consistent with the country's existing institutions through which the monarch can be replaced legitimately, particularly by those not in the royal family.

The situation is different in nonmonarchies, where popular sovereignty is almost universally the principle by which rulers are supposed to be chosen (O'Donnell 2007). Since sovereignty belongs to the people, the person who rules should be chosen by or at least representative of the popular will, and elections have become the dominant process through which this will is expressed. In theory, then, anyone can become a legitimate ruler if they have the support of the people. In practice, authoritarian regimes restrict the public's input. However, nearly all of these regimes still emphasize popular sovereignty and claim to govern as representatives of the people (Elkins and Melton 2014). In addition, most of these regimes do incorporate legal procedures for changing the ruler to reflect popular input, as mass elections with universal suffrage are now a common feature of authoritarian politics. As a result, nonroyal autocrats usually need to contend with the possibility that they can be replaced legitimately by almost any political elite who acquires a robust popular following. In fact, despite their unfair nature, elections in authoritarian regimes have resulted in the ouster of a number of autocrats. For example, the ruling party and its autocratic prime minister lost elections in Malaysia in 2018, following the creation of a new opposition coalition (Nadzri 2018), and Mexico's PRI lost the presidency in the country's 2000 elections after decades in power (Magaloni 2006). Other autocrats have been removed "legally" by voting procedures restricted to elites within a ruling coalition or mass party that is supposed to play a representative role. In other words, nonroyal authoritarian regimes frequently include channels consistent with the country's existing institutions through which the autocrat can be replaced legitimately.

Data from Geddes et al. (2014) demonstrate this difference between authoritarian monarchies and nonmonarchies. For the years in their dataset, between 1946 and 2010, a majority of nonroyal authoritarian regimes were controlled by an autocrat who was technically chosen through elections. Furthermore, 28 percent of nonroyal authoritarian regimes that collapsed during this period did so as a result of these elections. By contrast, no monarchs in the dataset were selected through elections, as would be expected by definition, and only one royal authoritarian regime collapsed due to parliamentary elections bringing the opposition to power, equivalent to eight percent of monarchical regime changes in the data. These patterns indicate how nonroyal autocrats are frequently removed from power by an electoral process that is entirely consistent with – and even a central component of – the country's existing institutions, whereas royal autocrats are almost always removed through an extra-institutional, forceful process.

For two reasons, these differences imply that political elites in monarchies will, on average, face relatively higher costs for attempting to replace the autocrat themselves. First, removing dictators via institutional means is less costly than trying to overthrow the dictator with force (Gandhi 2008; Lucardi 2019), because an outbreak of violence becomes more likely when acting extra-institutionally. That violence can quickly spiral out of control and consume the elites mounting

2.3 The Royal Advantage

the challenge against the autocrat, as demonstrated by the many coup plotters who have ended up dead or in jail in decades past.

The removal of Nikita Khrushchev from his position as First Secretary of the Communist Party of the Soviet Union illustrates how political elites moving against a dictator will often prefer to keep their challenge within the bounds of existing institutions to reduce the potential costs of their actions. In October 1964, Khrushchev was forced to resign his position as leader of the world's most powerful authoritarian state after it became clear in a meeting of the Presidium – the Soviet Union's executive body – that his opponents had enough votes to remove him legally. Two days following the resignation, members of the Presidium and the Central Committee of the Communist Party voted to affirm the resignation, and Khrushchev was replaced by Leonid Brezhnev, the second most powerful official in the party and state. Khrushchev's opponents felt strongly that "the appearance of a coup must not be created," and that "all must be done in good order, by 'democratically' resolving the issue...", and so they did not make their move until "solid majorities in both the Presidium and the Central Committee were known to favour Khrushchev's replacement" (Tompson 1991, 9). To accomplish this task, they lobbied hundreds of other Soviet officials for support. While they did fear retaliation from Khrushchev, participants in "normal" politics were no longer punished by violent purges as they had been in Stalin's day; in addition, pursuing the vote through proper institutional channels helped to legitimate the move in the eyes of the Soviet elite (Tompson 1991). By relying on votes rather than force, Khrushchev's opponents lowered the likelihood of violence and reduced the potential costs of their challenge.

Second, if force does become necessary to remove an autocrat, it should be less costly to do so when the challenger can step into the autocrat's position and maintain the political system as it is. Political elites and the public tend to become invested in the existing political system and will often resist changing it in drastic ways (Jost 2018; Jost et al. 2004), so a challenger is less likely to trigger backlash to their actions if they adhere to the country's institutions as much as possible. If a military leader launches a coup against a president, they may be acting illegally and with force, but they can adopt the title of president and defend their actions by citing popular support for their coup. They can also organize and run in an election to legitimize their position further (Grewal and Kureshi 2019). These options mean that coup leaders can replace the autocrat without overturning the entire political system and the principle of popular sovereignty that is supposed to inform leader selection. By contrast, in a modern monarchy, a coup leader outside the royal family cannot plausibly make themselves a king. If they wish to become the autocrat themselves, they must overthrow the monarchy, establish a republic, and make themselves president or prime minister in the new system. Certainly, if the monarchy has lost popular support, such an action may be possible. Particularly in the 1950s and 1960s, monarchies confronted growing republican sentiment that contributed to several successful coups that ousted royal families from power. But the contrast between restrictive rules about who can be the monarch and the ability of anyone to be a legitimate president or prime minister imply that coup leaders will need a higher level of dissatisfaction with the existing political system to mount their challenge without triggering potentially-costly backlash.

These arguments suggest that monarchs should be less threatened than other autocrats by elite challenges to their rule, since these challenges will come with higher costs on average for the challengers. Thus, monarchs should be able to delegate more credibly without dangerously increasing internal threats to their rule, because in comparison to popular sovereignty, hereditary succession restricts legitimate pathways to becoming the monarch and pushes elites to engage in costlier, riskier actions if they wish to seize power for themselves. Because they can delegate more credibly more safely, monarchs should be better positioned to rely on power sharing as a blame avoidance strategy.

2.3.2 Monarchs Are Not Expected to Govern and Be Accountable

As noted by Hood (2011, 75) in his seminal work on blame avoidance strategies, "the assumption that delegation can shield the delegator from blame may simply not be valid in all cultural or institutional settings." This assumption may be particularly vulnerable to circumstances where institutions clearly define who is supposed to be in charge; in these cases, the delegating leader may actually be blamed *for* ceding their control over these issues, because they are *meant* to be the one who takes action and bears responsibility. In other words, the public's expectations about how responsibility should be attributed will shape the effectiveness of delegation as a blame avoidance strategy.

2.3 The Royal Advantage

I argue that hereditary succession and popular sovereignty create different expectations for the roles of political leaders in their governments, and monarchs should find these expectations relatively more conducive to their ability to escape blame by empowering other political elites.

To understand why this difference occurs, first consider the fact that the principle of hereditary succession is silent about what monarchs are supposed to do in their political systems. The monarch has a right to the throne because of who they are, not because of the actions they take or how they govern. Whether the monarch wishes to make all decisions themselves or wants to refrain from participating in governance at all, they remain the legitimate monarch as long as they were born into the right family. As a result, the principle that underlies the selection of the ruler does not by itself create clear expectations of the monarch's responsibility for decision-making.

In fact, due to their position as the sovereign, monarchs frequently benefited from a norm that "the king could do no wrong" and should not be held accountable for problematic actions taken by the state they ruled. In Stuart England in the 1600s, "there was broad agreement ... that the king of England was accountable only to God, and therefore irresistible..." (Burgess 1996, 209). The English monarchs were still supposed to govern within certain legal limits, even if they possessed absolute discretionary powers over many issues, and disagreements over these bounds could lead to rebellion against the monarchy. The Stuart monarch Charles I was famously and controversially executed in 1649 during the English Civil War, which erupted in large part because of such disagreements. Nonetheless, despite this conflict, the norm accepted by most of society at this time was that the king was not supposed to be accountable to the people (Burgess 1996). In many other societies historically, monarchs were also associated with religion and divinity (Gerring et al. 2021), and this sacredness elevated them above accountability, at least in principle (Monod 2001).

As ideas of popular sovereignty gained increasing prominence from the seventeenth century onward, belief in the divine nature of monarchs gradually faded. Instead, monarchs shifted to become part of a contractual system of government between subjects and their rulers (Monod 2001). However, royal institutions evolved alongside this shift toward popular sovereignty, with a model emerging in which the monarch remained apart from the political realm and therefore free of

70   *Power Sharing and Attributions under Autocracy*

responsibility for outcomes produced by the government. This model developed in the United Kingdom during the eighteenth century as parliament increasingly constrained the monarchs' ability to govern after the Glorious Revolution. Following the ascension of George I to the throne in 1714, the monarch began to attend fewer and fewer cabinet meetings, which were instead presided over by the senior minister, who became known as the prime minister. This trend eventually resulted in a clear distinction between the monarch's status as the head of state and the prime minister's position as the head of government (Bogdanor 1995), with the latter, along with the cabinet and parliament, setting the majority of the state's policies. As this distinction developed, it became accepted that if the monarch "was not primarily responsible for the determination of policy, he or she ought not to be held responsible for the outcome" (Bogdanor 1995, 14). This norm of ministerial responsibility co-existed with – and in fact sustained – the principle that the king could do no wrong and could not be held accountable for illegal or ineffective governance decisions. As such, an expectation developed that the ministers and parliament would make decisions and be blamed for them if they turned out poorly, while the monarch would be protected from accountability. This model became a norm of constitutional monarchy, spreading to many other political systems. In nineteenth-century Prussia, for instance, Article 43 of the constitution stated that "The person of the king shall be inviolable," and Article 44 asserted that "The king's ministers shall be responsible." Likewise, Thailand's previous king, Bhumibol Adulyadej, claimed that the country's constitutional monarchy was defined by the "basic principle ... that the monarch can do no wrong," while the monarch refrained from directing day-to-day matters of governance (Hewison 1997).

In practice, of course, these expectations of responsibility in constitutional monarchies can reflect a significant variety of power-sharing arrangements between the monarch, the cabinet, and the parliament (Przeworski et al. 2012). Even if the ministers and parliament are supposed to be making decisions, it is not necessarily the case that the monarch is removed from the policy process entirely, or even at all. In the United Kingdom, the monarch continued to intervene in important policy decisions throughout the 1700s. It took at least a century for ministerial responsibility to become embedded so thoroughly that the monarch had almost no decision-making role (Bogdanor 1995; Cox 2011). In other cases, this division never developed at all, and

2.3 *The Royal Advantage*

the monarch governed formally through subservient ministers, while preserving the legal doctrine that the king could do no wrong. For example, the Prussian monarch Frederick William IV, during disputes over a new constitution, insisted on institutional arrangements that would allow him to control his ministers closely. He affirmed that "I want 'responsible ministers'. But first and foremost they should feel responsible to God, then to me, and only then to the chambers that our future constitution will give us" (Hahn 1977, 6). Frederick William had initially questioned the constitutional provision placing responsibility on the ministers rather than him as the monarch, but his cabinet overcame this opposition by persuading him that this meant only that his person would be inviolable, whereas the ministers took the fall for him (Hahn 1977). The resulting constitution sustained a highly centralized state dominated by the monarch until its collapse following World War I. In yet other cases, the division between the monarch's factual and legal responsibility has been more blurred. In contemporary Thailand, for instance, the previous king stated repeatedly that he did not involve himself in the daily administration of the country in line with the principles of constitutional monarchy; on the other hand, he often did review government policies and intervene in decision-making informally, such that it could be difficult to determine the extent of the monarchy's influence over policy (Hewison 1997).

Regardless of variation in the actual separation between monarchs and governance, the important point is that a norm of monarchical separation from responsibility and accountability – often spelled out explicitly in constitutions – was a common feature of monarchies historically. That norm persists in many countries today, and the expectation in these political systems is that responsibility for policymaking should fall on institutions like cabinets and legislatures. Importantly, granting responsibility to these other institutions allowed monarchies to integrate themselves with the growing dominance of popular sovereignty, since parliaments were elected and often influenced the composition of the cabinet. As bodies that represented the popular will, their theoretical control over decision-making gave the people a voice in governance, as well as the ability to secure accountability for outcomes they disliked. Meanwhile, the monarch retained their throne, even if they were not supposed to dominate or even participate in the policymaking process. In this context, monarchs who delegate responsibility to other elites are matching the expectations set for them by their political systems, and this alignment should reinforce the ability of delegation to protect them from blame.

In nonroyal autocracies today, an expected division between the autocrat and "responsible" institutions is much less plausible. When the autocrat is the chief executive in a republican or parliamentary political system, they are supposed to hold that position because they represent the people, which implies that they should govern in the public interest and be held accountable by the people when they fail to do so (Manin et al. 1999). In other words, their connection to popular sovereignty means that autocrats who are presidents or prime ministers face an expectation that they will represent the public and be responsible for the decision-making process in their countries. This expectation is often codified constitutionally. For instance, in Russia, the constitution charges the president with determining "the guidelines of the internal and foreign policies of the State" and gives them the duty to "represent the Russian Federation within the country and in international relations," alongside a host of other specific governance responsibilities. They are supposed to do so under the oath that they will "...faithfully serve the people," and they can be held accountable if they fail to do so, whether removed through universal elections or impeached for high treason or other "grave" crimes. Russia's authoritarian president, Vladimir Putin, does not allow himself to be subjected to genuine electoral competition, and his stranglehold over the legislature means impeachment is not viable; nonetheless, the expectation remains that Putin will govern actively and should, in theory, be held accountable for the outcomes produced by that governance. As will be discussed in more detail in Chapter 3, Putin has delegated to other elites, and research suggests this delegation can be effective at protecting him from blame. However, my argument suggests that expectations associated with his position should make that delegation less effective as a blame avoidance strategy compared to delegation of similar credibility by an autocratic monarch.

2.4 Testable Implications

To conclude this chapter, I elaborate upon the aspects of the theory that are most important to evaluate empirically. The remainder of the book considers evidence for these implications, which I test in a number of different contexts using various methodological approaches.

2.4 Testable Implications 73

I consider support for my general arguments about power sharing and attributions of responsibility in authoritarian regimes, as well as my argument about the royal advantage in avoiding blame by delegating to political elites.

2.4.1 Do Attributions Vary with the Credibility of Delegation?

First, it is important for the theory that citizens' attributions are shaped by the nature of power sharing between the autocrat and other political elites. Because of the great powers held by dictators in most authoritarian political systems, as well as the ubiquity of propaganda that seeks to alter the public's attributions, it is possible that citizens' views of responsibility do not respond to changes in the balance of power between autocrats and elites, but are instead relatively fixed or affected by other factors. If this static relationship is common, my theory would be less relevant to authoritarian politics.

Establishing this relationship is difficult in authoritarian settings because people often hide their true beliefs and many will be unwilling to blame the autocrat publicly. As a result, I study this expectation in two ways. First, at a most basic level, it should be the case that people in authoritarian regimes perceive the elites and institutions to which responsibility has been delegated as influential actors capable of determining policy decisions. If they are viewed primarily as powerless facades regardless of the extent to which they are involved in the policy process, then it is implausible that they would protect the dictator from blame, even if people criticize them publicly as a way to avoid the harsher penalties associated with attacking the dictator directly.

Second, I use a variety of qualitative and quantitative methods to evaluate whether attributions of blame and credit vary over time and across issues based on the credibility of power sharing. As the autocrat delegates less credibly, people should credit them more with successes but also blame them more for failures; alternatively, as they delegate more credibly, their reputations should be less affected by policy outcomes whether they are positive or negative.

2.4.2 Do Autocrats Share Power Strategically to Shape Attributions?

The second key part of the theory is that autocrats strategically delegate more or less credibly in part to manage the public's attributions of responsibility. I expect that autocrats will share decision-making powers more credibly as they become more concerned about the costs of being blamed by the masses, but also that this benefit is bounded by the cost of empowering elites too much and creating a dangerous threat within the regime.

I test these expectations in two ways. First, I consider temporal variation in threats to the autocrat. The prevalence of mass grievances may shift over time, perhaps because of changing circumstances in the global economy or the long run effects of domestic policies. For example, China's economy has grown rapidly for nearly two decades, providing consistent opportunities for political leaders to claim credit and perhaps incentivizing them to rein in delegation. On the other hand, some countries enter periods of economic stagnation or repeated crises that may prompt the autocrats to distance themselves more credibly from decision-making, since they know that grievances are likely to be higher. Likewise, the cohesiveness and strength of potential elite challengers to the dictator may also change over time, incentivizing dictators to delegate relatively more or less to keep these challenges under control.

Second, I look at variation across different policy issues. Certain policy domains are so sensitive that delegating control over them is especially risky for the dictator. This dynamic should have particular relevance to policy domains that involve control over coercive capacity, including command of the security forces, military, and intelligence agencies (Bellin 2004; Svolik 2012; Truex 2016). It should also apply to control of foreign policy since the backing of foreign powers can be a crucial factor for the success or failure of a coup (Thyne 2010). On the other hand, some policy areas require decisions that are likely to anger part of the public regardless of what is done, or they are difficult and unpredictable to manage and may lead to outcomes that anger a substantial number of people. For instance, economic and social policies often create clear winners and losers, and economic crises can occur even in well-governed countries. As a result, I expect autocrats to be more likely to maintain control over foreign policy and national security, while being more willing to credibly empower other elites to make decisions related to economic and social issues.

If my theory is relevant to authoritarian politics, it should also be the case that decisions about power sharing are made *intentionally*

2.4 Testable Implications 75

because of concerns about credit and blame, at least in part. There are several reasons that might plausibly motivate dictators' decisions about how to delegate policymaking responsibility, including their lack of time and technical expertise or their interest in using policy influence to co-opt elites. It is possible that any blame avoidance that occurs as a result of this delegation may be only an unintended side effect. As a result, I also look for evidence that autocrats consider the public's attributions when deciding how to share decision-making powers.

2.4.3 Do Strategic Interactions over Attributions Affect Governance?

Strategic delegation by the autocrat that is motivated by a desire to manage blame and credit should have spillover effects on governance more broadly. First, autocrats who monopolize decision-making should be more likely than those who delegate credibly to rely on repression when their regimes are confronted by popular mobilizations. Because these autocrats are more likely to be blamed and then targeted by the opposition, protests are more threatening to them, and therefore should be more likely to be put down forcefully. On the other hand, autocrats who delegate more credibly have less to fear from protests or other forms of political participation and may in fact benefit from them, since these expressions of discontent are more likely to target subordinate elites.

Second, the autocrat's approach to power sharing should have implications for their ability to hold onto power during periods in which the public becomes more aggrieved. Autocrats who monopolize decision-making powers should be more vulnerable to crises because they are more likely to be blamed for them, and the masses are more likely to coordinate around demands for their removal. In contrast, autocrats who share power more credibly should be less vulnerable to crises because they can shift blame effectively onto other political elites, who become the preferred target around which demonstrators coordinate.

Third, accountability should be higher in authoritarian regimes where autocrats share more power over decision-making. In practice, this suggests that elites will be rotated in and out of important government positions more often when delegation is more credible. In cases where the autocrat monopolizes power, they may rely on a handful of loyalist cronies to carry out their orders and should be unlikely to remove these individuals when the regime comes under pressure from a dissatisfied public. Alternatively, when elites have some distance from the autocrat to credibly exercise influence over policy decisions, the autocrat should be more likely to remove them from their positions after the public expresses discontent, thus providing a limited measure of accountability for their performance.

2.4.4 Do Monarchs Have a Delegation Advantage?

Finally, do monarchs possess an advantage in using delegation to avoid blame? I have argued that their advantage is rooted in two factors: first, that credible delegation is less costly to them, and second, that norms of responsibility in monarchies align more closely with power sharing by the monarch.

If the costs of delegation are lower for monarchs, it should be possible to observe that on average they share decision-making powers more credibly than other autocrats. They should be more willing to appoint cabinets that are not entirely dependent on them, and they should be more likely to give the legislature a say in the policy process. Furthermore, people living in these political systems should perceive these differences to be meaningful, if this more credible delegation has implications for how people attribute responsibility.

If norms of responsibility are more favorable toward monarchs, it should be possible to observe this pattern in two ways. First, these norms should be codified in the constitutions of these political systems, since constitutions both reflect and establish political norms in a society. Second, these codifications should be reflected in how people actually think about politics, with the public more likely to agree that monarchs are not supposed to take an active role in governance compared to other types of authoritarian rulers.

Finally, monarchs should be less threatened by popular opposition than their autocratic counterparts. Because they are better positioned to avoid blame, it should be the case that monarchs are less likely to be targeted by protesters when the public becomes dissatisfied, with anger directed at subordinate political elites instead.

2.5 What's Next

The following chapter uses short case studies as well as cross-national statistical analysis to assess the observable implications of my general theory about the relationship between attributions and power sharing in authoritarian regimes. I then move to my detailed case study of Jordan, using several chapters to provide a more fine-grained exploration of the general theory in a typical case. Finally, I shift toward tests of the monarchy argument, drawing on various sources to compare the ability of royal and nonroyal autocrats to protect their reputations by delegating decision-making powers within their regimes.

3 | Cross-National Evidence on Power Sharing and Attributions in Autocracies

In 2009, the Islamic Republic of Iran faced a major eruption of protests surrounding that year's presidential election, after the conservative president Mahmoud Ahmadinejad was announced to have been reelected with an outright majority of the votes. Many Iranians had expected one of the two reformist candidates to win, following growing anger at Ahmadinejad's uneven stewardship of the economy and foreign policy. Protests quickly spread from Tehran to much of the country, as tens of thousands of Iranians took to the streets in what became known as the Green Movement. The unrest persisted for months, lasting throughout the summer and into the fall.

Despite the scale of the uprising, Iran's actual autocrat, Supreme Leader Ali Khamenei, did not become the primary target of the demonstrators' anger. Some protesters chanted against the supreme leader, calling out "Death to the dictator" and "Khamenei is a murderer, His rule is null and void" (Daragahi 2019; Milani 2010). Yet, these refrains never dominated the movement, and they were heard most clearly once its strength had dissipated to the most radical demonstrators in the fall (Majd 2010). Instead, much of the anger was directed at President Ahmadinejad and his supporters for rigging the election, and most of the demands focused on civil rights and liberties, or economic grievances (Dabashi 2013; Kurzman 2012). In other words, those in the radical camp of the Green Movement who targeted Khamenei were only speaking for "a small minority of Iranians" (Majd 2010).

Why was the supreme leader able to avoid much of the demonstrators' anger at this moment? My theory suggests that the credibility of power sharing within the Iranian regime can help to explain the trajectory of the uprising. Though the supreme leader is undoubtedly powerful, substantial influence is exercised by the elected president, as well as the parliament and many other bureaucratic and religious institutions (Abrahamian 2008). The president in particular holds responsibility for much of the country's economic policy and has the

Cross-National Evidence on Power Sharing and Blame 79

capacity to shape foreign policy as well. Though the supreme leader may be able to block many policy initiatives if he desires to do so, policies have varied significantly across presidential administrations, and Iranians have possessed some capacity to use elections to hold presidents and members of parliament accountable for their governance (Keddie 2003; Maloney 2015). These dynamics of the political system appear to have helped the supreme leader protect his reputation. In fact, following the 2009 election, a majority of Iranians who supported the reformist candidate who lost the election still expressed the belief that the supreme leader did not have too much power and claimed to be satisfied with Iran's system of government (Kull et al. 2010). In other words, even many Iranians affiliated more with the opposition seemed to accept at the time that the supreme leader did not fully dominate decision-making and that other political elites held responsibility for outcomes produced by the policy process. As will be discussed in Chapter 9, this system differs markedly from the more centralized rule of the Iranian shah, who encountered escalating opposition to his governance that eventually resulted in the 1979 Iranian Revolution.

Do similar political dynamics extend to authoritarian regimes more generally as my theory expects? Do people living in these political systems respond to variation in power sharing as they decide how to attribute responsibility for policy outcomes? Do autocrats delegate strategically to avoid blame, claim credit, and protect their reputations? And to what extent do these strategic interactions around the public's attributions affect how autocrats choose to govern, as well as their vulnerability to mass uprisings such as the Green Movement? This chapter relies on cross-national statistical analysis of authoritarian regimes in the post-World War II world, along with short case studies of Russia and Morocco, to test several implications of my theory. The evidence suggests that autocrats are more exposed to the public's attributions when they dominate decision-making, that autocrats are more likely to delegate credibly when they have more reasons to be concerned about exposure to blame, and that autocrats who do share power in this way tend to be less repressive, less vulnerable to mass opposition during periods of poor performance, and more likely to provide accountability to their citizens.

Throughout this chapter, my cross-national analysis relies extensively on data from Varieties of Democracy (V-Dem), which provides broad coverage both geographically and temporally. I limit my analysis to the post-World War II period, with the data running from 1946 to 2020, and I include only country-years where V-Dem codes the regime as a closed autocracy or as an electoral autocracy. I am left with approximately 7,900 country-years, though my sample size fluctuates based on the inclusion of variables from other datasets in the analysis. I discuss these other data sources as they come up in the chapter.

V-Dem's "Presidentialism Index" provides my measure of the extent to which autocrats credibly delegate decision-making powers to other political elites. This index provides a useful measure because it aims to capture the extent to which there is "systematic concentration of political power in the hands of one individual who resists delegating all but the most trivial decision-making tasks," as defined by Bratton and Van de Walle (1997, 63). To construct the index, which ranges from 0 to 1, V-Dem aggregates a number of measures related to constraints on the executive's decision-making role, including whether the executive respects the constitution, must contend with oversight mechanisms, and faces an independent legislature, judiciary, and electoral management body. Since the presence of these features suggest that the executive would find it costlier to force their preferences onto the policy process, they provide a useful measure of how credible it is that the autocrat has in fact ceded some control over decision-making to other political elites. Higher values of the index indicate more concentrated power in the hands of the executive, and I also create a binary measure for authoritarian regimes that are above and below the mean index score.

At several points in the chapter, I am interested in exploring how the public attributes blame for grievances and how the costs of being blamed for these grievances shape the behavior of the autocrat and their regime. To proxy for grievances, I focus on both perceived and actual economic conditions in the country. While other issues may certainly trigger mass anger as well as blame avoidance behavior by the autocrat, frustrations with the economy often have a substantial influence on popular support for political leaders in democracies and autocracies alike. Economic voting is widespread where elections take place (Lewis-Beck and Stegmaier 2000), and economic crises have triggered mass mobilizations in many authoritarian regimes, ranging from Indonesia under Suharto to Egypt under Mubarak (Beissinger et al. 2015; Freedman 2005). At the same time, effective economic performance can be a boon for leaders attempting to maintain or

3.1 Citizens Recognize Changes in Power Sharing 81

win political support, whether in closed autocracies such as China or democracies such as the United States (Nadeau and Lewis-Beck 2001; Zhao 2009). As a result, political leaders have strong incentives to manage how the public perceives the economy and how people attribute responsibility for it, making the issue a useful one for my analysis.

The chapter proceeds as follows. I first show that citizens recognize and respond to variation in the credibility of delegation in ways that suggest autocrats will be more exposed to both credit and blame when they dominate decision-making more fully. To do so, I focus on cross-national data from Google Trends, case studies of Morocco and Russia, and cross-national survey data. The case studies also highlight how autocrats delegate strategically as threats from the public become relatively more or less important. I then document patterns suggesting that the relationship between power sharing and attributions influences dynamics of repression, mobilization, and accountability in authoritarian regimes.

3.1 Citizens Respond to Changes in the Credibility of Power Sharing

A key element of my theory is that the public's attributions of responsibility will vary based on the credibility of power sharing between the autocrat and other political elites. As political and institutional factors make it costlier for the autocrat to dominate the decision-making process, they should receive less credit but also less blame for policy outcomes; alternatively, as more power is concentrated in the hands of the autocrat, they should be more exposed to both credit and blame. However, it is possible that this relationship is not especially relevant to authoritarian politics. Political processes are notoriously opaque in many of these regimes, which may make it difficult for the public to recognize when the autocrat faces more constraints on their ability to control decision-making. At the same time, many people may assume the political process is theater and that the autocrat dominates all important decisions behind the scenes. As a result, attributions of responsibility may not follow variation in the credibility of power sharing under authoritarianism.

I evaluate this relationship in several ways. First, I assess if the public pays relatively more attention to the autocrat when they dominate decision-making more fully, and if they pay relatively more attention to political elites as the credibility of delegation strengthens. If people cannot recognize shifts in the balance of power between the autocrat and elites, it would be unlikely that power sharing arrangements influence attributions of responsibility substantially in these contexts. Using Google Trends data to measure the relative salience of autocrats and elites, I provide evidence both across and within countries that the public seeks out relatively more information about the autocrat as their decision-making powers increase, and relatively more information about political elites as they gain more power instead. If we assume that political leaders are more exposed to both credit and blame as the public pays more attention to them, this varying exposure to public attention would be consistent with variation in the credibility of power sharing affecting attributions of responsibility in autocracies. I then draw on survey data from global barometer surveys to provide more direct evidence that the extent of the autocrat's influence over decision-making has implications for their popular support during periods of poor governance. Specifically, when people perceive power sharing to be less credible, they are less likely to approve of the autocrat when they believe that economic performance has been poor. This result is consistent with autocrats who share less power losing more support because they are being blamed more by the public. Altogether, these findings suggest that the link between delegating responsibility and avoiding blame – so far studied primarily in democratic contexts – also applies to authoritarian regimes, despite the greater powers of autocrats and the lack of transparency in these political systems.

3.1.1 Cross-National Evidence from Google Trends

To test whether autocrats attract relatively more of the public's attention as they concentrate more power in their own hands, I first draw on an analysis of cross-national data collected from Google Trends, which provides a time series measure of search interest in specified topics. The trends capture interest in the topic as a proportion of searches for all topics in the relevant geographic entity and time period, allowing for standardized comparisons over time. If two or more topics are queried together, the trend values provide a comparison of search interest in the two topics in the specified time period. As a result, Google Trends has been increasingly used by political scientists seeking to measure

3.1 Citizens Recognize Changes in Power Sharing

salience across issues (e.g., Cunha et al. 2022; Mellon 2013; Scheitle 2011; Weeks and Southwell 2010). Because the trends are aggregated and behavioral, the tool is also helpful for studying politics in authoritarian regimes, since it is less susceptible to social desirability bias and does not put individuals at any risk (Gueorguiev and Schuler 2016; Koehler-Derrick 2013; Schuler 2020).

For this analysis, I compare search trends for a country's autocrat to search trends for that country's parliament. Nearly all modern authoritarian regimes include a legislature, and though these bodies are typically weaker than their democratic counterparts, they often provide an important arena through which elites other than the autocrat can acquire wealth or attain influence over decision-making (Gandhi et al. 2020; Williamson and Magaloni 2020). However, the extent of this influence varies greatly, with some authoritarian legislatures operating as little more than window dressing to ratify the autocrat's decisions and others operating as key players within the regime. To the extent that the public pays attention to the balance of power between the autocrat and elites in the legislature, the trends data should show that there is relatively more interest in the parliament compared to the autocrat in regimes where the parliament holds a more important decision-making role, and vice versa in regimes where power is concentrated more fully in the hands of the autocrat relative to the legislature.

Because Google Trends coverage began in 2004, I identified all country-years coded as authoritarian by V-Dem between 2004 and 2020. I then queried Google Trends for search interest in the country's autocrat and search interest in its parliament during the relevant years for which the autocrat was in power, querying searches only in the relevant country. Google Trends returns search results by month or by week, depending on the length of the searched period. The trend values for each week or month can range from 0 to 100, with 100 indicating the period with the highest search interest for the topic and all other values normalized to that period.[1] For instance, a trend value of fifty would indicate half as much search interest as the week or month with a value of 100, whereas a value of ten would indicate

---

[1] Because Google Trends records values of 0 as well as values of "<1" that are not amenable to the analysis, I replace them with 0.5. I also create an alternative where I replace 0 with 0.25 and <1 with 0.5.

one-tenth the search interest. Once I compiled the autocrat and parliament search trends, I created a yearly trend average. Compressing the trends data in this way allows me to analyze the correlation between my yearly V-Dem measure of the credibility of power sharing and the relative search interest in the autocrat and parliament. The data collection resulted in approximately 1,200 country-years of annual trend values in ninety countries.

To analyze search interest in the autocrat *relative* to search interest in the parliament, I create two outcome variables. The first is a ratio of the yearly search interest in the autocrat to the yearly search interest in the parliament. On average, the autocrat received 14.2 times as much search interest as the parliament.[2] The second is an indicator variable for years in which average interest in the parliament was *higher* than average interest in the autocrat, which occurred in approximately 10 percent of country-years. I expect the ratio outcome to be positively correlated with more decision-making dominance by the autocrat, and I expect the indicator to be negatively associated with more concentrated power.

I use OLS regression with standard errors clustered by country to analyze the correlation between the two outcomes and the V-Dem measure of concentrated power that proxies for how credibly decision-making powers are shared. The results are reported in Table 3.1. The first and fourth columns show results for the ratio and indicator outcomes respectively, without control variables and using the continuous version of the concentrated power variable. Moving from the minimum to the maximum on this measure implies an average increase of nearly thirteen for the ratio, equivalent to 0.79 standard deviations. It also implies a 39 percentage point reduction in the likelihood that the parliament received more search interest than the autocrat in a given year. The second and fifth columns incorporate control variables to account for other events that may explain search patterns. I include year dummies to account for expanding internet access over time, and I control for whether V-Dem codes the regime as a closed or open autocracy in a given year, since the latter are less likely to censor the internet heavily. In addition, I control for coup attempts,

---

[2] The standard deviation of the measure is 16.3, the minimum is 0.03, and the maximum is 121.

Table 3.1 *Relative attention on autocrats is higher when they share less power*

	(1) Ratio	(2) Ratio	(3) Ratio	(4) Indicator	(5) Indicator	(6) Indicator
Concentrated power (Cont.)	12.92**	11.38**		−0.39***	−0.37***	
	(3.97)	(4.08)		(0.10)	(0.10)	
Concentrated power (Binary)			5.74*			−0.14**
			(2.30)			(0.05)
Open autocracy		−1.71	−1.91		0.02	0.04
		(2.57)	(2.64)		(0.06)	(0.06)
Coup		11.28***	11.32***		−0.04[†]	−0.04[†]
		(3.37)	(3.38)		(0.02)	(0.02)
Presidential election		5.80***	5.77***		−0.06*	−0.07*
		(1.35)	(1.34)		(0.03)	(0.03)
Legislative election		−2.37*	−2.31*		0.04[†]	0.04*
		(0.94)	(0.97)		(0.02)	(0.02)
Constant	5.73*	5.37	9.56**	0.35***	0.38***	0.21**
	(2.48)	(3.61)	(3.11)	(0.08)	(0.11)	(0.08)
Year dummies		✓	✓		✓	✓
Observations	1,247	1,158	1,158	1,247	1,219	1,219
Clusters	90	88	88	90	88	88

[†]$p < 0.10$; * $p < 0.05$; ** $p < 0.01$; *** $p < 0.001$
OLS models with standard errors clustered by countries
Ratio outcome is ratio of mean autocrat trend in country-year
to mean parliament trend. Indicator outcome = 1 when mean
value of annual parliament trend exceeds mean value of autocrat trend.

presidential elections, and legislative elections, since these events drive large increases in search interest and often account for the week or month pegged to the maximum value of 100. Finally, the third and sixth columns use the binary version of the concentrated power variable. In all cases the substantively large relationship remains, indicating that more decision-making dominance for the autocrat is associated with the autocrat receiving more public attention relative to the parliament.

It is not possible to know exactly what motivates people to search for either the autocrat or the parliament in these contexts, nor is it possible to know whether those searches are driven by positive or negative feelings. However, the results suggest that people living in authoritarian regimes are capable of recognizing when the autocrat is relatively more or less relevant to decision-making compared to the legislature, and that they shift their attention accordingly. This nuanced approach to information seeking implies that shifts in the credibility of power sharing between the autocrat and elites can be recognized by the public and will thus be relevant to how they attribute blame or credit.

3.1.2 Case Studies of Russia and Morocco

I now extend the analysis of Google Trends by analyzing changes over time *within* two country cases: Russia and Morocco. The advantage of these cases is that I can identify precise moments in which the balance of power between the autocrat and other political elites clearly shifts. If attributions of responsibility are shaped by power-sharing arrangements in authoritarian regimes, these shifts should be recognized by everyday people living in these countries, such that they adjust how much attention they pay to the autocrat relative to these other elites. I first look at the swapping of the presidency that occurred in Russia between Vladimir Putin and Dmitry Medvedev, which involved Putin ceding greater power over decision-making to the latter before taking it back four years later, and I analyze whether Russians shifted their search interest around these changes. I then look at constitutional reforms in Morocco that expanded the prime minister's ability to push back against the monarchy in the decision-making process, and I assess whether Moroccans became more likely to pay attention to the prime minister as a result. In exploring these cases, I also discuss the strategic incentives for these rulers to have expanded or restrained their own

3.1 Citizens Recognize Changes in Power Sharing

powers over the decision-making process, considering whether they align with the expectations of the theory regarding threats from elites and the masses.

Russia

In the two decades that followed his winning of the Russian presidency in March 2000, Vladimir Putin became one of the world's most recognized and influential autocrats. Throughout his time in power, Putin appears to have maintained high approval ratings from the Russian public (Frye et al. 2017). This approval has fluctuated between near-universal and bare majority support (Treisman 2014), but even through the War in Ukraine, Putin seems to have successfully retained a meaningful degree of support from the public. Russia had experienced dramatic upheaval and debilitating turmoil in the 1990s following the collapse of the Soviet Union, and Putin's early presidency coincided with a degree of political, economic, and social restabilization. Nonetheless, the country has continued to struggle with a number of serious challenges under Putin's regime, and Russians have also expressed low opinions of the government's performance over the years. In light of Putin's apparent ability to retain popular support despite this disgruntlement, his regime has received some attention in the nascent literature on the politics of blame in authoritarian regimes. Reflecting the argument that delegating can deflect blame in authoritarian contexts, both Beazer and Reuter (2019) and Rosenfeld (2018) find evidence that Putin's party is punished less by the public in areas where its members wield less control over regional governments. However, there is less evidence regarding attributions toward Putin specifically, or discussion of when Putin has been more or less willing to tie his hands more credibly in the decision-making process. I address these issues here by focusing on Putin's decision to hand the presidency to a subordinate and serve as prime minister from 2008 to 2012.

While Putin's initial two terms had begun the process of consolidating an authoritarian republic, the novelty of the system meant that succession posed a tricky question for the political elites who dominated the regime. Constitutionally, Putin was only allowed to hold the presidency for two consecutive terms, but it was not clear who could take his place, while keeping the existing regime intact (Hanson 2011). One solution was for Putin to overturn the constitutional term limits and continue serving in the presidency. In 2007, as the succession question intensified, a number of influential Russian elites began to call on Putin – both publicly and privately – to follow this path (Goldman 2008). Yet, despite this apparent elite support, Putin declined. Instead, he endorsed one of his proteges and deputy prime ministers, Dmitry Medvedev, for president. Upon winning the endorsement of United Russia, the regime aligned party, Medvedev promised to appoint Putin as prime minister. Medvedev won an overwhelming victory in the presidential election, winning seventy percent of the votes in an unfair contest that was heavily manipulated in his favor. He fulfilled his pledge to appoint Putin as prime minister, and for the next four years the two men governed Russia in what many scholars termed a "tandemocracy" (Ryabov 2008).

This arrangement meaningfully reduced Putin's decision-making powers in the policy process, reflecting an increase in the credibility of delegation. Formally, the prime minister led the government and had responsibility for a number of policy domains, meaning that the position was in no way toothless. Informally, Putin continued to wield significant influence over United Russia and networks of officials within the state, including institutions in the security apparatus (Ryabov 2008). Nonetheless, the presidency was a more significant and powerful position formally: it held the ability to set Russian policy and especially foreign policy in general, the role of Commander in Chief, the right to appoint judges to the constitutional court, and the option to remove the prime minister (Hanson 2011). In other words, by stepping down from the presidency and accepting the prime minister role instead, Putin had significantly reduced his own power and given substantially more responsibility to an individual who – informally at least – remained his subordinate within Russia's authoritarian regime.

Why did Putin take this step? The question puzzled analysts at the time, and a clear answer remains lacking. As discussed earlier, Putin likely had the elite backing to change the constitution and secure a third term if he wished, but he chose not to take it. Some speculated that Putin wanted to minimize criticisms from the West if he openly discarded Russia's democratic institutions in this way, but such criticism probably would have been muted (Hanson 2011) and highly unlikely to affect Russia's internal politics in any significant fashion (Knight 2008). Others speculated that Putin had simply tired of holding office or wished to respect the country's democratic institutions

3.1 Citizens Recognize Changes in Power Sharing

(Ryabov 2008), but these possibilities did not match well with Putin's willingness to continue exercising power as prime minister and the series of steps he had already taken to hollow out Russian democracy.

Another possibility that reflects the argument about elite and popular threats outlined in Chapter 2 is that Putin gave greater power to Medvedev – despite the ability to carry on as president if he had wanted to do so – because public threats were becoming increasingly salient in Russian politics relative to threats from other political elites. There are several points that align with this explanation. First, Putin had consolidated control over the regime's political elites, to the point that many of them were clamoring for him to remain in the presidency. He dominated United Russia and maintained significant influence over the security apparatus. An internal challenge was unlikely to displace him. On the other hand, though his approval rating remained high, there were indications prior to the presidential election that the positive economic outcomes produced by the government in the previous seven years would not be sustainable for much longer. Writing around the time Medvedev became president, Hedlun (2008) noted that "there are solid grounds to worry about Russia's macroeconomic performance" that made it highly likely Russia would experience declining GDP in the years ahead. Prior to the presidential election, inflation and debt were rising, and there had been a noticeable decline in the growth of the country's oil output, on which so much economic progress had depended (Knight 2008). Other problems that Putin had never tackled successfully – or had made worse – also continued to fester, including extreme corruption, declining life expectancy, rising crime, and an ineffective healthcare system (Knight 2008). As these challenges accumulated, the public expressed growing dissatisfaction with the government, such that only 13 percent rated the national government's performance as "excellent" or "good" in April 2007 (Guadalupe 2007). Furthermore, opinion polling from the period just after the 2008 election suggests that many Russians had not wanted Putin to continue in the presidency. Nearly half opposed changing the constitution to allow a third term, compared to forty percent who supported it. Two-thirds did not want Putin to become president for life at this time. Likewise, a plurality (42 percent) wanted Medvedev – not Putin – to wield more influence over policy following the election, whereas only 18 percent said Putin should dominate and 30 percent said they should share power equally (Hale and Colton 2010). In other words, to the extent that Putin was attuned to these attitudes and conditions, he would have had good reason to believe that remaining in the presidency could result in rising dissatisfaction with him personally, which should have created strong incentives to limit his decision-making role in an effort to reduce his exposure to blame.

Did the decision to empower Medvedev help in this regard? Opinion polling indicates that Russians generally did perceive Putin's power to have lessened as a result of him giving up the presidency. According to a poll conducted by the Levada Center in 2008, approximately half of the public believed that Putin and Medvedev were sharing power, with the remainder split fairly evenly between perceptions that Putin or Medvedev were really running the show (Ryabov 2008). These results are reflected in the poll conducted just after the election by Hale and Colton (2010), who found that just over a third of respondents believed that Putin would wield the most policy influence, whereas the rest believed that policy would be influenced equally or dominated by Medvedev.

Analysis of data from Google Trends further reinforces the idea that Medvedev's presidency reduced the extent to which Russians perceived Putin as the dominant decision-maker, likely reducing his vulnerability to blame. I compare the search trends for Putin to those for Medvedev using a single query of Google Trends within Russia from January 1, 2004 to January 16, 2020, when Medvedev was shuffled out of his position as prime minister. As with the previous section, I then create a ratio of Putin's trend values to Medvedev's trend values. This ratio comparing search interest in Putin and Medvedev is displayed in Figure 3.1. Higher values indicate relatively more attention to Putin, whereas lower values indicate relatively less attention. The ratio shows a clear decline that starts with Medvedev's election in 2008. Prior to Medvedev's presidency, Putin received between ten and thirty times as much search interest, but this declined to a nearly equal interest at the height of Medvedev's presidency. When Putin ran for president in 2012 and then assumed the office once more, with Medvedev now becoming prime minister, Putin consistently started to receive more than ten times as much search interest as Medvedev. These results align with the expectation that Russians recognized the relatively greater decision-making powers of Medvedev during his presidency and shifted their attention accordingly. If we accept that attention can proxy for exposure to the public's attributions, this pattern has implications for

3.1 Citizens Recognize Changes in Power Sharing

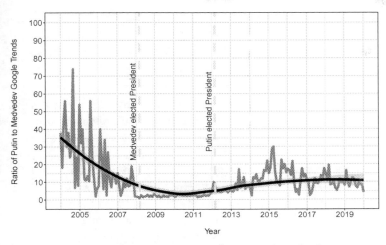

Figure 3.1 Google Trends comparison of Putin and Medvedev
Note: Figure displays a ratio of Putin's Google Trends to Medvedev's Google Trends from 2004 to the beginning of 2020. Higher values indicate relatively more search interest in Putin within Russia.

Putin's ability to shift blame during these different periods. In the chapter appendix, Table 3.6 shows these relationships formally using OLS regression with Newey-West standard errors to account for autocorrelation of the error terms. Structural break tests also align with these results, indicating breaks in the time series following the acquisition of the presidency by Medvedev and then Putin again.

Why did Putin take back the presidency and strengthen his decision-making role? Recall that the president's powers include the ability to remove the prime minister, meaning that Medvedev had the formal means to cut Putin out of the regime if he desired to do so. While Putin could likely tolerate four years with another individual wielding the powers of the presidency, another term may have proved too risky. Medvedev acquired real influence as the president, and he may have been increasingly well-positioned to appoint his own allies into important positions, steer financial resources into his hands, and generally undercut Putin's continued centrality to the regime. As a result, it seems plausible that Putin felt it was necessary to take back the presidency to avoid the possibility of a serious internal challenge to his rule.

As the theory would expect, however, reacquiring this more powerful position and reducing the credibility of delegation appears to have been costly for Putin, particularly as the performance of the Russian state continued to falter. Putin's approval rating declined in 2011 around the time that he announced he would run for president again in 2012, and it remained relatively low until 2014. Following Russia's seizure of Crimea, it spiked to nearly 90 percent, as Putin took credit for this immensely popular decision (Nadrelli et al. 2015). This popularity persisted for a time. Yet, by 2018, it had fallen off dramatically. With anger over low standards of living and economic reforms that raised the retirement age, anti-government protests erupted during Moscow City Council Elections in the summer of 2019 (Mackinnon and Standish 2019), and polling suggested that Putin's approval had fallen into the forties and even thirties (Fokht 2019). This popular discontent is consistent with Putin's reputation declining because he absorbed more blame for a series of unpopular policies and governance outcomes after he reacquired his more dominant position in the decision-making process.

Morocco

Morocco is a hereditary monarchy and one of the longest surviving authoritarian regimes in the world. The current king, Mohammed VI, acceded to the throne in 1999, following the death of his father. While the monarch has been politically dominant since independence from France in 1956, the kings have also shared power to varying degrees with a cabinet and parliament, and several well-organized parties have played an active role in the country's politics. With the cabinet and parliament involved in many issues of day-to-day governance, opposition has often focused on these institutions rather than the monarchy (Sater 2011).

Nonetheless, when the Arab Spring erupted in late 2010, Morocco was not immune, and mass demonstrations advocating for political reforms began to occur around the country (Madani et al. 2012). On February 20, 2011, between 150,000 and 200,000 Moroccans mobilized in more than fifty cities and towns around the country to express frustration with political and economic grievances (Madani et al. 2012). This mobilization spurred the emergence of the February 20 Movement, a confederation of youth activists supported by the opposition Islamist group Justice and Charity, as well as several small leftist parties (Radi 2017). Over the next several months, the movement organized frequent protests drawing tens of thousands of

3.1 Citizens Recognize Changes in Power Sharing

Moroccans into the streets, with demands focused on strengthening democratic institutions and addressing economic challenges including high unemployment and poverty rates (Radi 2017; Sater 2011). If the demonstrators had been united in anger against the king, it is plausible – given the scale of the mobilizations – that they could have posed a significant threat to the monarchy. Instead, the vast majority of protesters never called for the king to be overthrown, directing their anger instead toward other political elites. Nonetheless, many demonstrators did advocate explicitly for the monarchy's powers to be curtailed so that a more democratic Morocco could flourish (Madani et al. 2012), and King Mohammed certainly had strong reasons to be concerned about becoming the primary target of the protesters' ire.

Faced with this discontent, the king responded by backing institutional changes that would facilitate more credible delegation of policy responsibility to the cabinet and parliament, with the goal of shielding himself from the unrest (Monjib 2017). The king appointed a commission to revise the constitution, and the reforms were approved overwhelmingly in a popular referendum held in July 2011. Regarding the parliament, the body was given expanded responsibility for political, economic, and social policies, and MPs were granted the ability to initiate bills alongside the government. It also acquired stronger oversight abilities, including lower thresholds for censuring the government and its ministers and easier procedures for establishing fact-finding committees focused on the actions of the executive branch (Madani et al. 2012). The prime minister was empowered as well, through an important provision requiring the king to appoint a prime minister from the political party that wins the largest number of seats in parliament (Ottaway 2011). This change constrained the ability of the king to appoint a weak prime minister with no political base of their own who would be fully dependent on the palace. Notably, these changes were more relevant to issue domains less connected to coercive power, such as economic and social policy. Within the new constitutional framework, the king retained direct control over most national security and foreign policy matters, including sole discretion over military appointments, the position of supreme commander of the Royal Armed Forces, and the power to individually ratify most major treaties with foreign states (Madani et al. 2012). This issue-based distinction in the monarchy's explicit decision-making powers reflects the theory's expectations that autocrats will be more willing to share power over issues associated with frequent public discontent and less willing to delegate for issues that could facilitate more dangerous elite threats.

The constitutional reforms generated meaningful shifts in how the government and parliament shaped domestic policies, at least for several years. When parliamentary elections were held in November 2011, the largest share of seats was won by the Islamist Justice and Development Party (PJD), an opposition group that recognized the legitimacy of the monarchy but nonetheless butted heads frequently with the palace. Following the election, King Mohammed adhered to the new constitutional provisions by appointing Abdelilah Benkirane, the PJD's leader, as prime minister. Over the next five years, until elections in late 2016, Benkirane exercised more control over policy decisions than his predecessors, pursuing an ambitious if ultimately slow-moving program (Masbah 2013). Among other policy changes, the PJD-led government implemented privatization reforms, cut corporate taxes, increased government support for vulnerable groups, initiated major construction projects, and provided more scholarship support for students (Drhimeur 2018). While the monarchy was still able to constrain the party's governance (Monjib 2013), the PJD's institutional powers combined with its popular support enabled it to push back against the palace. For example, Benkirane publicly criticized members of the palace entourage a number of times (Masbah 2013), he openly stated that his relations with the king were "not always perfect," and he strongly defended his constitutional prerogatives (Monjib 2014). This relationship meant that "the consensus among many [Moroccans] is that Benkirane – and the PJD – have not been coopted by the King" (Fakir 2016), implying that the credibility of delegation had been enhanced significantly as a result of the post-2011 reforms.

To what extent did this more credible power sharing help to direct the public's attention away from the king during a period of heightened unrest and popular discontent across the Middle East? Figure 3.2 displays Google Trend results comparing search trends for King Mohammed to search trends for his prime ministers from January 1, 2004, to January 1, 2021. The figure shows a clear pattern in which the trend ratio declined substantially following the constitutional reforms and especially after Benkirane became prime minister in late 2011. Indeed, whereas King Mohammed tended to receive more than twenty times as much search interest as his prime ministers before Benkirane's appointment, he typically received between two

3.1 Citizens Recognize Changes in Power Sharing

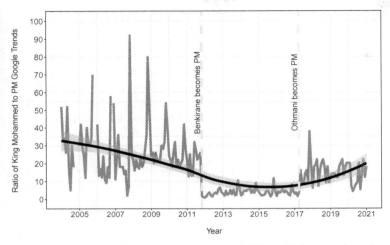

Figure 3.2 Google Trends comparison of King Mohammed and prime ministers

Note: Figure displays a ratio of King Mohammed's Google Trends to the Google Trends of his prime ministers from 2004 until the beginning of 2021. Higher values indicate relatively more search interest in King Mohammed within Morocco.

and ten times as much interest as Benkirane. This pattern indicates relatively more attention shifting toward the prime minister, suggesting that Moroccans recognized the change in power sharing, and implying that the king would have been less exposed to blame.

Yet, strengthening the decision-making abilities of the government and parliament also increased potential elite threats to the monarch. As was just mentioned earlier, the relationship between King Mohammed and Benkirane was often strained, with Benkirane willing to push for his policy objectives even when they conflicted with the preferences of the king (Monjib 2014). At times, these clashes were obviously threatening to the palace. For instance, the Minister of Justice, who was a member of the PJD, opened corruption investigations into two government officials with particularly close connections to the monarchy (Monjib 2012). Likewise, Benkirane forcefully asserted his right to oversee local elections, contesting the ability of the palace-controlled Interior Ministry to heavily influence the process (Monjib 2014). At the same time, Benkirane and the PJD were also using their strengthened policy influence to claim credit for popular policies and build their reputation with the public. Their approval ratings rose steadily through 2013 (Masbah 2013). By the time new parliamentary elections were held in 2016, they won the largest share of seats ever by a political party in Morocco, creating "an unwelcome surprise" for the regime (Monjib 2016). This changing power dynamic reflected a direct threat to the monarchy. As noted by Fakir (2016), Benkirane's "…popular appeal, in which he is admired and seems to have his own legitimacy independently of his relations with the palace, makes the monarchy nervous."

In response, King Mohammed sought to rein in delegation to the government. The formation of a new cabinet after the elections provided the monarch with his chance. Despite the PJD's unprecedented success in the elections, they had won only 125 seats out of 395, and so needed the support of several other parties. Behind the scenes, the palace leaned on these other parties to make demands of the PJD that Benkirane would find difficult to accept (Monjib 2017). This situation resulted in a stalemate of more than six months as Benkirane struggled to construct a new cabinet. The king eventually used this stalemate to justify appointing a new prime minister from the PJD, Saadeddine al-Othmani. Not only was al-Othmani a weaker and less effective politician, but his acceptance of the king's offer split the PJD internally between those who supported Benkirane's defiance and those who backed al-Othmani's compliance (Drhimeur 2018). In addition, al-Othmani's government was heavily dependent on Aziz Akhannouch, a billionaire friend of the king who led one of the parliament's smaller parties (Maghraoui 2018). As a result of these political factors demonstrating the weakness of al-Othmani's position relative to the palace, delegation to the government became significantly less credible, and we should expect that Moroccans recognized this change and shifted their attention back to the king.

Consistent with this expectation, Figure 3.2 shows an increase in the Google Trends ratio following al-Othmani's appointment as prime minister, with the king reaching twenty times as much search interest as the prime minister again by 2021. As with the Russia case, these results are shown formally in Table 3.6 in the appendix. This pattern suggests that in reducing the credibility of delegation to ward off the rising elite threat from Benkirane and the PJD, King Mohammed made himself more visible to the public and therefore more vulnerable to blame for popular grievances. Indeed, in the past several years,

3.1 Citizens Recognize Changes in Power Sharing

approval of the regime has faltered and further protests have erupted (Abouzzohour 2020). With the king more exposed to that anger, the regime's response has been to increasingly ramp up repression of the opposition (Abdel Ghafar 2021). The Morocco case illustrates how an autocrat may respond strategically to heightened threats from the masses by sharing power more credibly to protect themselves from blame, but also how the increasing salience of internal threats from other elites may constrain this strategy and facilitate a more repressive approach to governance.

3.1.3 Power Sharing and Support for Autocrats in Global Survey Data

The evidence from Google Trends, both cross-nationally and in the two case studies, suggests that citizens of authoritarian regimes recognize and respond to shifts in the credibility of power sharing over decision-making. As other elites gain more credible influence over policy decisions, the public seeks out more information about them relative to the autocrat. While this attention should affect the autocrat's exposure to the public's attributions of responsibility, Google Trends by itself does not provide direct evidence on this issue. To analyze whether these shifts have implications for the ability of autocrats to manage their popular support by claiming credit or avoiding blame, I turn to data from the Afro and Asian Barometers, which have implemented regular, high-quality surveys with nationally representative samples in a number of African and Asian countries respectively. The surveys extend from 2005 to 2016 and include tens of thousands of responses from thirty-six authoritarian regimes across the barometers.[3] Based on the inclusion of relevant questions, I draw this data from waves 5 and 6 of the Afro Barometer and waves 2 through 4 of the Asian Barometer.

My analysis focuses on the relationship between an individual's perceptions of poor economic performance by the government and their likelihood of expressing support for the autocrat. Specifically, I am interested in whether perceptions of poor economic performance are associated with a *larger* decline in support for the autocrat when the

---

[3] Authoritarian regimes were identified using Freedom House's coding of unfree and partly free countries in the year the survey was implemented.

individual also believes that the autocrat dominates the parliament in the decision-making process. In other words, I evaluate whether the perception of poor economic performance and the view that the autocrat does not delegate credibly interact to lower support for the autocrat. If such an interaction exists, it would be consistent with the argument that authoritarian rulers are less capable of avoiding blame when they do not credibly empower other political institutions and actors to influence the decision-making process. As discussed previously, focusing on perceptions of the economy in this analysis is particularly relevant because of the economy's importance to research on voter attributions in democracies (Anderson 2007; Healy and Malhotra 2013), and because economic grievances are so often cited for fueling opposition to authoritarian regimes (e.g., Geddes 1999; Magaloni 2006). Likewise, views of the legislature's influence relative to the autocrat provide a useful proxy for perceptions of power sharing, since legislatures are frequently cited as a key institution through which elites in authoritarian regimes can constrain the autocrat and influence decision-making (e.g., Boix and Svolik 2013; Gandhi et al. 2020; Opalo 2020).

To measure support for the autocrat, I rely on a question from both the Afro and Asian Barometers asking respondents whether they approve of the executive (the president or prime minister) on a four-point scale. To capture perceptions of economic performance, I use a question from the Afro Barometer that asks respondents to rate on a four-point scale how well the current government is managing the economy. Since this question is not available in the Asian Barometer, I use a question in these surveys that asks respondents to rate the overall economic condition of the country. Finally, both barometers include helpful questions about the autocrat's relationship with parliament, and whether the body is permitted to influence decision-making. The Afro Barometer asks respondents how often they believe the president ignores parliament, and the Asian Barometer asks them about the effectiveness of the legislature in keeping government leaders in check. For ease of interpretation, I recode all three of these variables as indicators taking values of 0 or 1, where 1 indicates approval of the executive, the perception that economic performance is bad, and the view that the autocrat dominates the legislature.

I use OLS regression to analyze the survey data. Standard errors are clustered by the country in which each survey was administered.

3.1 Citizens Recognize Changes in Power Sharing

Table 3.2 *Perceptions of power sharing condition the link between economic assessments and support for the autocrat*

	(1)	(2)	(3)	(4)
Poor economic	−0.27***	−0.20***	−0.20***	−0.19***
performance	(0.02)	(0.02)	(0.01)	(0.02)
Autocrat dominates	−0.19***	−0.13***	−0.12***	−0.09***
legislature	(0.03)	(0.03)	(0.03)	(0.02)
Performance ×	−0.08**	−0.07**	−0.08**	−0.10***
Dominance	(0.03)	(0.03)	(0.03)	(0.02)
Control variables		✓	✓	✓
Country dummies			✓	✓
Year dummies			✓	✓
Free to criticize				✓
Observations	78,521	64,833	64,833	47,722
Clusters	68	66	66	66

$\dagger p < 0.10$; $* p < 0.05$; $** p < 0.01$; $*** p < 0.001$
OLS models with standard errors clustered by country-year
Outcome is a binary variable for approving of the autocrat
Controls: Country democratic; legitimacy; protest; safety; trust parliament; internet user; democracy is best; free to criticize; gender; university; Christian.

The results are reported in Table 3.2. The first column shows the naive model in which only the three variables of interest are included. As might be expected, perceiving economic conditions to be poor and believing the autocrat dominates the legislature are both negatively correlated with support for the autocrat. For our purposes, the most important coefficient is for the interaction term. Consistent with the argument, the interaction is negative and statistically significant at 0.01. Substantively, the results indicate that individuals who dislike the country's economic performance are on average 26 percentage points less likely to approve of the executive when they do not believe the autocrat dominates the legislature, but are 34 percentage points less likely to approve of them when they do believe the legislature is subordinate. This difference of 8 percentage points – an increase in disapproval of approximately one-third – suggests that perceptions of power sharing in authoritarian regimes are associated with the extent to which individuals blame the autocrat for poor economic performance. This result is consistent with a meaningful blame avoidance advantage to delegation if it convinces more of the public that the autocrat is not solely responsible for decision-making.

While the possibility of omitted variable bias is present with this research design, I consider whether the findings are robust to control variables for the most plausible sources of endogeneity. First, supporting the executive, believing they control the political system, and assessing the economy negatively may all be correlated with other concerns about the regime and its performance. As a result, I control for respondents' assessments of whether their country is democratic, whether the government is legitimate, and the level of public safety. Second, trust in the legislature may relate to ideas about the legislature's policymaking role and may also correlate with support for the executive and views of the economy, so I control for self-reported trust in the legislature as an institution. These controls for legitimacy, performance, and trust in the parliament should also help to account for the possibility that individuals more cynical about the political system may say the parliament is weak, that they disapprove of the executive, and that the economy performs poorly. Third, individuals with more political knowledge may have a more accurate sense of the parliament's influence and more negative views of the executive and the economy in their countries. I therefore control for a history of protest activity and access to the internet. Fourth, in authoritarian regimes, respondents who care less about democracy may be more likely to support the executive, while also being more likely to answer survey questions in ways that paint their countries in a positive light – that is, that the legislature has a role and the economy is doing well. Respondents who do not feel they can speak freely about politics may also say the legislature is more influential, that they approve of the executive, and that the economy is good. As a result, I control for whether respondents think democracy is the best form of government and whether they feel free to criticize the government. I control for gender, university education, and Christian faith as demographic variables that affect many political attitudes and behaviors as well. Finally, to further assess robustness, I incorporate dummy variables for the country and year in which the survey was administered, to account for common shocks in a given year or time-invariant characteristics within each country.

These results are reported in the second and third columns of Table 3.2. In both models, the magnitude of the interaction term remains consistent. The coefficients for poor economic performance

3.2 Blame Games and Governance in Autocracies

and autocratic dominance decrease somewhat in magnitude, implying a larger substantive impact for the interaction. Finally, in column 4, I limit the analysis to respondents who said they felt free to criticize the government, since these individuals may be less likely to hide negative views of the autocrat if they blame them for poor economic performance. The magnitude of the interaction is larger among this group, at 10 percentage points, and though it is not shown here, the triple interaction is statistically significant ($p < 0.10$).

It remains possible that individuals who are disinclined to support the autocrat in the first place may be motivated to rate the economy poorly and more likely to believe the autocrat ignores the legislature. In addition, the survey data reflect perceptions of the autocrat's dominance over political elites in the legislature rather than their objective relationship in the decision-making process. However, as suggested by the Google Trends analysis previously, people living in authoritarian regimes are capable of recognizing shifts in power sharing between the autocrat and elites. Taken together, these results suggest that when autocrats delegate credibly and limit their influence over decision-making, they will be able to shape how their citizens attribute responsibility in a manner that protects their reputations more effectively from blame.

3.2 Attributions, Power Sharing, and Governance in Autocracies

The analysis discussed so far in this chapter provides evidence that the nature of power sharing in autocracies affects the public's attributions of responsibility. Consistent with the idea that more power attracts more credit but also more blame, the public pays greater attention to autocrats as they control decision-making more directly, and these assessments of how power is shared condition support for the autocrat when the regime is perceived to be performing poorly. The case studies of Russia and Morocco also suggest that autocrats are strategically more likely to prioritize the blame avoidance advantages of delegation as potential threats from the masses become more salient relative to threats from other elites. My theory suggests these dynamics have broader implications for governance in authoritarian regimes, including the extent to which autocrats engage in repression, the trajectory of opposition during periods of popular discontent, and the presence

3.2.1 Repression Is Higher Where Autocrats Share Less Power

Though authoritarian regimes tend to limit political freedoms and use violence against their people more often than democracies, there is substantial variation in the extent of repression that occurs within these political systems. Some authoritarian regimes repress even the slightest hint of opposition harshly, whereas others contend with active opposition parties and a relatively free press. A number of factors have been posited to explain this variation, with a more prominent political role for the military or the presence of instability thought to increase repression, and the existence of a ruling party capable of co-opting elites and the public thought to decrease it (Davenport 2007; Geddes et al. 2014). These arguments suggest that regimes in which the autocrat is more dominant should rely on repression more often, since these autocrats tend to have strong, personal relations with senior military leaders and often hollow out party institutions that may constrain their power. Empirical analysis supports this idea by showing that regimes in which the autocrat controls the military and ruling party more closely tend to be more repressive (Frantz et al. 2020).

How power sharing relates to blame and credit should have implications for the regime's reliance on repression as well. If the autocrat dominates decision-making, a public dissatisfied with governance outcomes is more likely to direct their anger toward the top of the regime. This situation makes any discontent more dangerous for the autocrat, which should prompt them to use repression more readily. On the other hand, if the autocrat shares power credibly by tying their own hands in the decision-making process and delegating responsibility to other elites, they are less likely to bear the brunt of the public's anger. As a result, discontent should be less threatening to them personally, and they should have less need to suppress it.

I test this expectation by analyzing the correlation between V-Dem's measure of concentrated autocratic power and three measures of regime repression. For my primary measure of repression, I rely on V-Dem's civil liberties index, which incorporates measures of how much the regime uses physical violence against its people, whether it

3.2 Blame Games and Governance in Autocracies

allows for organizing, expression, and other political freedoms, and whether it permits private liberties including the right to movement, religion, and property rights. For my two other measures of repression, I focus on the use of physical violence specifically, since this type of repression is most relevant to the autocrat's interest in suppressing public attributions of discontent. Here, I use V-Dem's measures of how much the regime relies on political killings and torture. The civil liberties variable ranges from 0 to 1, with 1 indicating greater respect for civil liberties. The killings and torture variables range from approximately −3.3 to 3.5, with higher values also indicating less repression.

I use three approaches to ensure that the analysis speaks to my blame game mechanism, as opposed to other arguments about the autocrat's personal control over the military and a ruling party making it easier for them to repress. First, the V-Dem variable that I am using to measure power sharing is focused on the existence of constraints on the executive that imply more credible limits on their decision-making powers, including legislative, judicial, electoral, and other institutional constraints. While these constraints likely correlate with the autocrat's control over coercive and party apparatuses, they speak more directly to the autocrat's role in decision-making for which the public may wish to attribute responsibility. Second, I control for the strength of the party and military in the regime relative to the autocrat, using V-Dem's ruling party dimension index and military dimension index. These controls give me some ability to account for these alternative mechanisms. Third, I extend existing findings by analyzing whether less power sharing is especially related to higher repression at moments when public discontent is likely to be high, and when dominant autocrats should be particularly worried about the costs of being blamed. To that end, I analyze whether there is an interaction between concentrated power and the occurrence of an economic crisis, with autocrats who share decision-making powers less credibly becoming even more repressive than their counterparts when the public is likely to be disgruntled about the regime's economic performance. I create an indicator variable for crisis that takes a value of 1 if a country experienced a decline in GDP of three percent or more in a given year.

The analysis uses OLS regression with standard errors clustered by country. Results are reported in Table 3.3. The first three columns include naive models analyzing the relationship between the binary

Table 3.3 *Autocrats repress more when they share power less credibly*

	Liberties respected (1)	Free from killings (2)	Free from torture (3)	Liberties respected (4)	Free from killings (5)	Free from torture (6)
Concentrated power	−0.19*** (0.02)	−0.76*** (0.17)	−0.87*** (0.13)	−0.16*** (0.02)	−0.59*** (0.17)	−0.72*** (0.15)
Economic crisis	0.00 (0.02)	0.04 (0.15)	0.02 (0.10)	0.01 (0.02)	0.17 (0.12)	0.08 (0.09)
Power × Crisis	−0.03 (0.02)	−0.36[†] (0.19)	−0.25* (0.13)	−0.03 (0.02)	−0.28[†] (0.16)	−0.15 (0.12)
GDP PC (Log)				0.02 (0.02)	0.40*** (0.11)	0.18[†] (0.10)
Open autocracy				0.11*** (0.02)	0.33* (0.16)	0.37** (0.13)
Protest lag				0.03 (0.02)	−0.22 (0.18)	−0.06 (0.16)
Coup attempt				0.01 (0.01)	0.01 (0.04)	0.06 (0.04)
Presidential election				0.01 (0.01)	0.04 (0.07)	0.02 (0.06)
Area				−0.00 (0.00)	−0.00 (0.00)	−0.00 (0.00)
Hereditary index				−0.01 (0.06)	0.72[†] (0.42)	0.98* (0.43)
Military index				0.01 (0.04)	−0.15 (0.29)	−0.21 (0.26)
Party index				−0.13** (0.05)	0.24 (0.41)	0.54[†] (0.31)
Constant	0.50*** (0.02)	0.17 (0.14)	−0.09 (0.11)	0.27* (0.11)	−3.24*** (0.79)	−0.57[†] (0.29)
Region dummies				✓	✓	✓
Year dummies				✓	✓	✓
Observations	6,518	6,518	6,518	5,254	5,254	5,254
Clusters	140	140	140	127	127	127

[†]$p < 0.10$; * $p < 0.05$; ** $p < 0.01$; *** $p < 0.001$
OLS models with standard errors clustered by countries.

3.2 Blame Games and Governance in Autocracies

measure of concentrated power, economic crisis, and their interaction with the civil liberties, killings, and torture outcomes respectively. For each of the three variables, there is a substantively large and statistically significant relationship between more concentrated power and less respect for civil liberties. In addition, the interaction provides some evidence that this link strengthens when the country's economy is struggling and discontent is likely to be high. The sign of the interaction indicates that regimes with more dominant autocrats become even more repressive in years of economic crisis, and the coefficient is significant for the killings ($p < 0.10$) and torture ($p < 0.05$) outcomes.

The fourth, fifth, and sixth columns add control variables to account for potential confounders. In addition to the ruling party and military indices mentioned earlier, I control for V-Dem's hereditary index, since ruling monarchies tend to respect civil liberties more than other autocracies (Spinks et al. 2008). I control for GDP per capita and the electoral openness of the regime as well, since wealthier, electoral autocracies may be less likely to rely on violence. To account for the relationship between political instability and repression, I control for protest activity in the previous year, using V-Dem's ordinal mobilization variable, as well as any documented coup attempts from Powell and Thyne (2011) and whether or not a presidential election occurs. I control for the country's area, since larger states may be less stable (Jugl 2020), and I include fixed effects for region and year. The relationship between the binary concentrated power variable and the three repression outcomes remains, providing strong evidence that autocrats who share power more credibly with other elites are less likely to rely on repression. In addition, the interactions continue to suggest that this repression difference becomes more pronounced during periods of economic crisis, though the coefficient loses significance for the torture outcome.

It is important to note that this sort of high-level analysis is unable to say whether the observed correlation occurs *because* autocrats who share power less credibly are more concerned about being blamed for the public's grievances and seek to repress those grievances as a result. However, the findings are consistent with the theory's expectation that autocrats who are more exposed to the anger of the masses should be more concerned with suppressing the public's ability to voice their grievances.

3.2.2 Discontent Escalates More Where Autocrats Share Less Power

If autocrats who dominate decision-making are more exposed to blame when the public is dissatisfied, they should also be more vulnerable to mass opposition during these periods. The heightened use of repression may make people less likely to express their beliefs about the autocrat's culpability, but it will not make these attributions disappear. As a result, when people become angry enough to take to the streets, they should be more likely to direct that anger at the autocrat specifically. By contrast, in cases where power sharing is more credible and many people blame other elites for their grievances, protests may occur with some regularity, but the demonstrators should be less likely to demand that the autocrat be overthrown or the regime changed as a whole. Since relatively more of them will believe sincerely that the autocrat is not at fault, fewer people will be willing to participate in protests against the autocrat, and coordination should be more likely to occur around less escalatory demands. These protests are also likely to be smaller on average, because the public is more likely to be divided about who should be blamed, depriving the protests of a clear focal point. When the autocrat is the only game in town, it will be clearer to the public who is at fault for their grievances, making it more likely that mass anger escalates into large-scale mobilizations targeting the top of the regime.

I test this implication of the theory by analyzing how concentrated power and economic crisis interact in their relationship with mass mobilizations in authoritarian regimes. Specifically, I expect that autocrats who share power less credibly will be more likely to confront major challenges to their rule during a period of economic crisis, when popular grievances are especially likely to be high. I use the same binary measure of concentrated power taken from V-Dem, as well as the same indicator for economic crisis from the previous sections. The analysis relies on three outcome variables. First, I use a measure of mass mobilization for V-Dem. I convert this measure into a dummy variable that takes a value of 1 for the highest level of mobilization, which states that "There have been many large-scale and small-scale events" in the relevant country-year. Second, I turn to the Nonviolent and Violent Campaigns and Outcomes (NAVCO) 2.1 dataset for their identification of mass movements between 1945 and 2013. They define these movements based on their articulation of "maximalist"

3.2 Blame Games and Governance in Autocracies

demands, their ability to mobilize at least 1,000 people in a given year, and their possession of organizational coherence that links different activities to each other. This definition fits well with my focus on major challenges to the autocrat's power, given the focus on maximalist demands and large-scale mobilization. Third, I also use an indicator variable for whether the autocrat was actually overthrown in a given year. I take this variable from Geddes et al. (2014), whose data extend from 1946 to 2010. Finally, as a robustness check, I create a fourth outcome variable from V-Dem that measures the occurrence of some protest mobilization in a given year, but not the highest level of mobilization. This variable allows me to analyze whether concentrated power and economic crisis interact to create more discontent overall, or whether they interact only to generate a higher probability of particularly threatening mass mobilizations as the theory would expect.

The results are displayed in Table 3.4. As in the previous section, the first three columns report the naive models interacting concentrated power and economic crisis for each of the three outcome variables. Consistent with the theory, autocrats who dominate decision-making face a larger increase in their likelihood of confronting mass opposition during periods of poor economic performance. The interaction is positive for all three outcomes and is statistically significant at $p < 0.05$ for the V-Dem and NAVCO indicators of mass mobilization.

Also as in the previous sections, the fourth through sixth columns incorporate control variables to contend with omitted variable bias related to wealth, the regime's openness, other forms of instability, and the autocrat's dependence on a dominant party, the military, or a ruling family. In addition, I include the killings variable to account for political repression, since the higher use of repression in regimes where the autocrat dominates decision-making may affect the likelihood of mass opposition. The models also include fixed effects for region and year. On balance, the interaction terms strengthen from the naive models, with the interaction also statistically significant for the GWF variable measuring the autocrat's removal from power, and with the magnitude of the interaction increasing for the V-Dem and GWF outcomes. The size of the interaction coefficients indicates a meaningful substantive relationship, with economic crisis 7–8 percentage points more likely to trigger mass opposition in regimes where power is concentrated in the autocrat's hands. Given the relative rarity of such uprisings in these contexts, this difference is substantial.

Table 3.4 *Autocrats are more exposed to popular opposition when they share power less credibly*

	V-Dem large protests (1)	NAVCO mass uprising (2)	GWF leader ousted (3)	V-Dem large protests (4)	NAVCO mass uprising (5)	GWF leader ousted (6)	V-Dem small protests (7)
Concentrated power	−0.04 (0.03)	−0.00 (0.03)	−0.04* (0.02)	−0.05 (0.04)	−0.06[†] (0.03)	−0.06*** (0.01)	0.04 (0.04)
Economic crisis	0.04[†] (0.02)	0.04 (0.04)	0.03 (0.03)	0.03 (0.02)	0.03 (0.03)	0.00 (0.03)	−0.03 (0.03)
Power × Crisis	0.07* (0.03)	0.10* (0.05)	0.04 (0.03)	0.08* (0.04)	0.08[†] (0.04)	0.07* (0.03)	−0.07[†] (0.04)
GDP PC (Log)				−0.01 (0.03)	−0.04[†] (0.02)	0.00 (0.01)	0.00 (0.03)
Free from killings				0.00 (0.02)	−0.05*** (0.01)	−0.00 (0.01)	−0.01 (0.02)
Open autocracy				−0.04 (0.04)	0.09** (0.03)	0.02[†] (0.01)	0.05 (0.04)
Protest lag				0.08*** (0.02)	0.09*** (0.03)	0.02[†] (0.01)	0.78*** (0.03)
Coup attempt				0.05** (0.02)	0.02[†] (0.01)	0.34*** (0.02)	−0.05* (0.02)
Presidential election				0.01 (0.02)	−0.01 (0.02)	0.17*** (0.03)	0.01 (0.02)
Area				0.00 (0.00)	0.00* (0.00)	0.00* (0.00)	−0.00 (0.00)
Hereditary index				−0.09 (0.06)	0.04 (0.09)	0.04 (0.04)	0.06 (0.08)
Military index				−0.05 (0.08)	0.06 (0.07)	0.04[†] (0.02)	0.04 (0.08)
Party index				−0.02 (0.07)	−0.13 (0.08)	0.02 (0.02)	−0.01 (0.07)
Constant	0.11*** (0.02)	0.18*** (0.02)	0.12*** (0.01)	0.06 (0.19)	0.17 (0.18)	−0.02 (0.08)	0.09 (0.19)
Region dummies				✓	✓	✓	✓
Year dummies				✓	✓	✓	✓
Observations	6,293	6,155	4,297	5,254	4,911	3,754	5,254
Clusters	138	140	112	127	127	106	127

[†] $p < 0.10$; * $p < 0.05$; ** $p < 0.01$; *** $p < 0.001$
OLS models with standard errors clustered by countries.

3.2 Blame Games and Governance in Autocracies

Finally, the seventh column runs the same model with the indicator variable for smaller protest activity occurring in that year. The negative coefficient on this interaction term suggests that smaller-scale protests increase more during economic crises in authoritarian regimes where power is less concentrated in the hands of the autocrat. This finding aligns with the theory, insofar as it suggests that people are mobilizing in these regimes to express their grievances, but less so in ways that escalate into a major challenge against the autocrat. Moreover, it suggests that autocrats who hold more power in their hands are not experiencing a larger upsurge in opposition generally during periods of poor economic performance, but are experiencing a higher increase in mass mobilizations specifically. This pattern is consistent with their greater exposure to blame for the public's grievances, as well as the facilitation of protest coordination that results.

3.2.3 Accountability Is Higher Where Autocrats Share More Power

If political elites are more likely to bear the brunt of the public's anger when they credibly exercise influence over decision-making, regimes that empower elites relatively more should be more capable of providing limited accountability to the public. Because people are not challenging the autocrat directly, the autocrat may feel less threatened by expressions of discontent and more willing to remove elites from their positions in response to popular demands. Since the influence wielded by these elites means they are likely to have shaped the policy decisions that frustrated the public, some measure of accountability is achieved. On the other hand, in regimes where autocrats dominate decision-making more fully, they should be more likely to surround themselves with dependent elites who are defined by their loyalty and commitment to implementing the autocrat's wishes. Because their influence over decision-making is less credible, these elites are less likely to shield the autocrat from blame, so the autocrat should be more likely to respond to popular discontent by doubling down on their loyalists instead of removing them to placate the public. As a result, we should observe different patterns of elite retention in authoritarian regimes based on the extent to which the autocrat shares decision-making powers.

110 *Cross-National Evidence on Power Sharing and Blame*

To evaluate this claim, I use cabinet data from WhoGov, which has compiled individual-level data on cabinet members in nearly every country from 1966 to 2018. Their cross-national dataset reports the retention rate for the cabinet, defined as the percentage of people in the cabinet who were also present in the cabinet the previous year. Using the binary measure of concentrated power from the previous sections, I analyze whether higher retention rates are indeed associated with autocrats who share power over decision-making less credibly. Using the V-Dem data on mobilization, I also explore whether this retention rate is even higher in these regimes during years in which protests of any size occurred. This finding would align with the idea that more credible power sharing is associated with greater account-ability, as autocrats are more likely to respond to popular discontent by removing elites to whom meaningful decision-making responsibilities have been delegated.

Results are reported in Table 3.5. The first column shows the rela-tionship with the binary concentrated power variable, and the second column adds the same control variables from the previous section. In both cases, the results suggest that autocrats who delegate less credibly keep a higher percentage of the same elites in the cabinet each year, with the coefficient indicating an average difference of 4 percentage points. Since the WhoGov data indicate that the average authoritarian cabinet consists of approximately twenty ministers during this period, the coefficient implies one additional minister is removed each year in regimes where the autocrat delegates more credibly.

The third and fourth columns interact concentrated power with the occurrence of at least some small-scale protest activity in that year. If the theory's implication about higher accountability is upheld, we should observe a positive interaction between the two variables, as the tendency for dominant autocrats to retain more of their cabinet becomes relatively stronger during moments of visible public discon-tent. The results support this expectation. With and without control variables, the interaction term is positive and statistically significant at $p < 0.10$, and the coefficient implies that protests are associated with a 5–6 percentage point increase of the retention rate for authoritarian regimes with more dominant autocrats compared to those with more delegation.

Previous research suggests that authoritarian regimes with domi-nant autocrats are more likely to circle the wagons during moments

3.2 Blame Games and Governance in Autocracies 111

Table 3.5 *Autocrats replace elites less when they share power less credibly*

	Cabinet retention rate (1)	Cabinet retention rate (2)	Cabinet retention rate (3)	Cabinet retention rate (4)
Concentrated power	0.03[†]	0.04**	−0.02	−0.01
	(0.02)	(0.02)	(0.03)	(0.02)
Protest			−0.13***	−0.02
			(0.03)	(0.03)
Power × Protest			0.06[†]	0.05[†]
			(0.03)	(0.03)
GDP PC (Log)		0.04***		0.01
		(0.01)		(0.01)
Economic crisis		−0.04**		−0.03*
		(0.01)		(0.01)
Free from killings		0.00		−0.00
		(0.00)		(0.01)
Open autocracy		0.02		0.02
		(0.02)		(0.02)
Protest lag		−0.07***		−0.09***
		(0.02)		(0.02)
Coup attempt		−0.11***		−0.12***
		(0.02)		(0.02)
Presidential election		−0.05**		−0.05**
		(0.02)		(0.02)
Area		−0.00		−0.00
		(0.00)		(0.00)
Hereditary index		0.02		0.06
		(0.06)		(0.06)
Military index		−0.06		−0.04
		(0.04)		(0.04)
Party index		0.13***		0.15***
		(0.04)		(0.04)
Constant	0.69***	−0.20**	0.80***	−0.02
	(0.02)	(0.07)	(0.02)	(0.08)
Region dummies		✓		✓
Year dummies		✓		✓
Observations	4,752	4,109	4,547	4,217
Clusters	143	124	138	127

[†] $p < 0.10$; * $p < 0.05$; ** $p < 0.01$; *** $p < 0.001$
OLS models with standard errors clustered by countries.

of unrest, as the small group of highly loyal elites stick by the autocrat on whom they depend (Geddes 1999). The findings here reflect this idea, suggesting that the autocrat is also more likely to respond to these moments by keeping their elite allies in place. On the other hand, when elites are better positioned to constrain the autocrat's influence over decision-making, they also appear to be more likely to cycle in and out of important cabinet positions. Perhaps somewhat paradoxically, their greater influence over policymaking is associated with a higher likelihood of being shuffled out of office. This lower retention likely occurs in part *because* their decisions actually matter, making it more likely that they attract the public's attention. As a result, when people become dissatisfied with the regime's performance, the autocrat can provide a measure of accountability by removing officials whom the public deems to be at fault.

3.3 Conclusion

The findings discussed in this chapter are consistent with an important role for blame and credit in the politics of authoritarian regimes, and they suggest that how autocrats share power affects their ability to protect their reputations and retain popular support. As illustrated by data from Google Trends, people appear to recognize when autocrats exercise more or less control over decision-making relative to other political elites, and they shift their attention accordingly. Survey responses from across Africa and Asia suggest that these perceptions about the extent of the autocrat's dominance also shape how much support the autocrat loses for poor economic conditions. And as highlighted by events in Russia and Morocco, this exposure to blame is reflected in when autocrats choose to share power more credibly, delegating at moments when public threats become more salient, and reining in elites when internal threats increase. These dynamics appear to have implications for broader patterns of governance in authoritarian regimes. Autocrats are more likely to repress the public in contexts where they are more likely to be blamed for popular grievances. At the same time, autocrats who delegate decision-making responsibility less credibly are particularly vulnerable to an escalation of opposition when their regimes perform poorly. They are also less likely to provide accountability by removing elites in response to these governance failures.

One limitation of cross-national analysis, however, is that it is difficult to provide strong evidence of the mechanisms underlying the

3.4 Appendix

results. While the evidence presented in this chapter is consistent with the expectations of the theory described in Chapter 2, it is not possible to demonstrate conclusively that blame and credit are influencing autocrats' decisions about how to share decision-making power, or that autocrats who delegate less credibly are more vulnerable to mass opposition *because* they are more exposed to blame for poor performance. The next four chapters address this limitation by providing a detailed exploration of the politics of delegation and blame in the Hashemite Kingdom of Jordan, leveraging both qualitative and quantitative data to provide more direct evidence within a specific case about the applicability of the theory to authoritarian politics. In particular, the chapters show how Jordan's monarchs have delegated strategically across issues and over time, ceding greater powers to other political elites where the costs of being blamed are likely to be highest. They also carefully explore how Jordanians attribute responsibility for their grievances and how these attributions are influenced by the monarchy's approach to power sharing.

3.4 Appendix

Table 3.6 *Trends ratios shift as delegation becomes more or less credible*

	(1)	(2)
Morocco		
PM Jettou	40.66***	
	(9.44)	
PM al-Fassi	22.94***	
	(2.20)	
PM al-Othmani	11.15***	
	(1.06)	
Russia		
Pres. Medvedev		−11.06***
		(1.56)
Constant	3.70***	13.66***
	(0.27)	(1.51)
Observations	205	193

$^{\dagger}p < 0.10$; $^{*} p < 0.05$; $^{**} p < 0.01$; $^{***} p < 0.001$
OLS models with Newey-West standard errors (lag 4).

4 The Jordanian Monarchy's Strategic Blame Games

When the Arab Spring triggered uprisings across the Middle East in late 2010 and early 2011, Jordan was not immune to the unrest. Thousands of protesters marched weekly to call for economic and political reforms to address social justice and facilitate democratization. As part of his response to this public pressure, King Abdullah released several personal essays that both defended the state's existing institutions and outlined his own vision for how the political system should be reformed. In his third essay, titled "Each Playing Our Part in a New Democracy," Abdullah described his view of the constitutional role given to each of Jordan's primary governing institutions. Regarding the parliament, Abdullah noted that "It is the solemn duty of Parliament to enact legislation in the best interest of the country, and also to hold the Government to account for its decisions." For the government (i.e., the cabinet), he claimed that "It is the responsibility of the government ... to formulate and implement a comprehensive programme of action to enhance the prosperity and security of all Jordanians," and that "The government must present its four-year programme to Parliament and is then held accountable for its implementation." For himself, Abdullah emphasized "my role as a unifying leader to prevent polarisation in our society and to protect Jordanian values," as well as his position as "Head of State and Commander-in-Chief of our Armed Forces" (Al-Hussein 2013). In other words, King Abdullah does not describe his position as one of close involvement in the country's policy process, at least beyond matters pertaining to national security and foreign affairs. Rather, it is the government and parliament that are meant to be responsible for managing the policies of the state.

King Abdullah's essay reflects an idealized version of Jordan's decision-making process, but its words are not just cheap talk meant to disguise the royal court's dominance of all policy decisions in Jordan. While the monarchy's de facto powers are greater than its de jure powers outlined in the constitution, Jordan's kings have delegated

114

substantial decision-making responsibility to the government, and to a lesser extent the parliament. Meanwhile, the monarchy – despite its significant powers – often keeps its distance from policymaking.

This chapter builds from the cross-national evidence discussed in Chapter 3 to provide a more detailed exploration of how power sharing related to decision-making occurs in a specific authoritarian regime. In doing so, it provides support for several aspects of the theory discussed in Chapter 2. After a brief historical overview of the kingdom, the chapter identifies how key assumptions of the theory apply to the Jordanian context. It shows that elites in Jordan do play a meaningful role in the policy process even while the monarch retains significant powers, and it discusses how this power sharing creates costs and risks for the king. It also illustrates how the king can adjust the credibility of power sharing over time. The chapter then explores whether delegation is used strategically to shape the public's attributions. I present evidence that the monarch delegates deliberately for the purpose of avoiding blame, that it attempts to reinforce this strategy by strengthening expectations about how responsibility is supposed to operate in the political system, and that it shares power more credibly with regards to social and economic issues where the costs of blame are more pronounced than the risks associated with challenges from other elites. The chapter focuses primarily on providing a general overview of the decision-making process in Jordan, while later chapters explore other aspects of how the theory applies to the Jordanian case. Chapter 5 evaluates how Jordanians attribute responsibility to actors within the political system, Chapter 6 takes a more historical view to consider how temporal variation aligns with the theory's expectations about power sharing and blame, and Chapter 7 analyzes how the monarchy's blame games influence governance dynamics related to repression, mobilization, and accountability.

As discussed in the Introduction, Jordan represents a typical case of authoritarian rule in many aspects, and as such, it should provide insights into the general applicability of the theory. The regime's status as a monarchy, in addition to variation in power sharing and threats from both the public and elites, also provides leverage with which to assess the core theoretical mechanisms underpinning the relationships between delegation and blame in an authoritarian setting. Thus, Jordan provides a useful case for exploring how the policy process

116 *The Jordanian Monarchy's Strategic Blame Games*

functions and how citizens evaluate responsibility for decision-making under autocracy.

This chapter, as well as the subsequent chapters on Jordan, relies on a variety of evidence from both qualitative and quantitative sources of data. As an important component of this data collection, I completed more than 100 interviews with political elites who have firsthand experience with Jordan's politics as well as its decision-making process. These elites include several former chiefs of the royal court, prime ministers, ministers, and members of parliament, as well as opposition activists, political analysts, and journalists. I draw on these interviews throughout the subsequent chapters, sometimes through direct quotes and at other times to fill in important background information without referencing the source directly. I explain the other Jordan data sources as they come up throughout these four chapters.

4.1 Background on the Hashemite Kingdom

Jordan was born as a political entity in the geopolitical upheaval that followed World War I. The Hashemites were the ruling family of the Hijaz in what is now Saudi Arabia, and they had helped the British war effort by leading a revolt against the Ottoman Empire in the Middle East. However, following the war, the United Kingdom backtracked on its promise to endorse the creation of a greater Hashemite Arab kingdom in the Levant and Arabian Peninsula. Abdullah bin al-Hussein, son of the Hashemite Sharif of Mecca, responded by moving with a small military force to lands east of the Jordan River, planning to press into Syria; instead, he ended up establishing an emirate with British support in 1921.

Situated between the emerging polities of Palestine, Syria, Iraq, and Saudi Arabia, as shown in Figure 4.1, the state was an awkward construction from the start. Despite its uncertain origins, however, Jordan became a fully fledged part of the post-Ottoman state system in the Middle East, first as a British mandate and then as an independent kingdom in 1946. Emir Abdullah (who became King Abdullah upon independence), consolidated Hashemite rule by mediating between the local tribes, providing them with jobs in the state's fledgling military and bureaucracy, and relying on British backing to resist foreign and domestic threats (Alon 2009). After his assassination in 1951, the throne passed to his son Talal, whose most important contribution was

4.1 Background on the Hashemite Kingdom

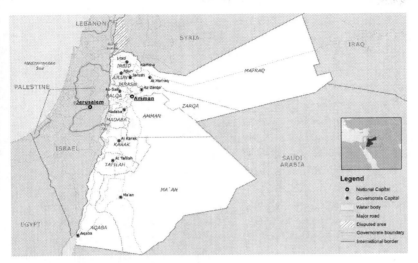

Figure 4.1 Map of the Hashemite Kingdom of Jordan
Note: Map of Jordan from the Joint Research Centre, ECHO, European Commission (2013). Licensed under the Creative Commons Attribution 4.0 International License.

to oversee the promulgation of a new constitution in 1952 that granted greater powers to the cabinet and parliament. Talal struggled with mental illness and was forced to abdicate by these institutions in 1952. His young son Hussein then became king at the age of sixteen, and he would govern the country for the next five decades, until his death from cancer in 1999. Hussein's son Abdullah became king following his father's death, a position he holds to this day. With the possible exception of Talal, Jordan's kings have ruled as powerful autocrats. However, they have also shared power consistently with other political elites, particularly in the cabinet, parliament, and bureaucracy.

Jordan is a small country that has a population of approximately ten million at the time of writing. Its geography left it with few natural economic benefits, and the labor rich but capital poor economy has struggled more often than not, relying heavily on remittances from Jordanians working abroad as well as foreign aid (Baylouny 2008). The government has played a key role in the economy since the state's foundation, though the economy was historically less controlled than those of Jordan's neighbors. However, the country has pursued neoliberal reforms since the 1990s, which have reduced the scope of its welfare system and generated political discontent.

Jordan's geography also left the country with a particularly challenging position in international affairs, though it has often leveraged that position successfully to exert surprising influence on global developments of major importance. This situation largely has to do with Jordan's close connection to Israel and Palestine. Jordan has fought two wars with Israel, first in 1948 and then in 1967. The two decades between these conflicts were scarred by repeated skirmishes between the Israeli military and Palestinian militants that brought significant suffering, especially to the Palestinian refugees caught in the crossfire. During this period, Jordan also governed the West Bank, before losing it to Israel in the 1967 war. Because of these conflicts, the country experienced two major waves of Palestinian refugees who dramatically restructured the kingdom's demographic balance. Today, a majority of the population has Palestinian roots. Tensions have often been high between Jordanians who trace their roots to tribal groups originally settled on the "East Bank" of the Jordan and those whose families came from Palestine. In 1970, the country fought a brief but violent civil war triggered by conflict between the Jordanian government and Palestinian nationalist groups, and its ethnic politics have been simultaneously taboo and fraught since that time (Reiter 2004). In the later part of King Hussein's reign, Jordan also played a key role in pushing for peace between Israel and its Arab neighbors. As a result of its centrality to geopolitical conflicts in the Middle East, Jordan after its independence was perceived as an important client state first by the United Kingdom and then by the United States, and that status persists until the present day.

The Hashemite family's consistent hold on power since the 1920s makes Jordan one of the longest-surviving authoritarian regimes in the modern world. This persistence comes in spite of Jordan's difficult economic and geopolitical situations (Ryan 2018), suggesting that the country can provide useful insights into the sources of authoritarian durability. At the same time, Jordan also boasts many features common to the universe of modern autocracies. These include governance through nominally democratic institutions such as a parliament, cabinet, judiciary, and constitution; the use of targeted rather than mass repression; strategic reliance on support from foreign patrons; and the sophisticated implementation of distributive politics to sustain loyalty to the regime.

A number of scholars have studied the monarchy's survival strategies, making Jordan an influential case in the study of authoritarian

4.1 Background on the Hashemite Kingdom

governance. This literature has focused primarily on how the regime has relied on distributive politics and foreign patrons to maintain its hold on power. Regarding distributive politics, scholars have studied the channels through which the regime has provided its supporters with material incentives to remain loyal. Historically, core constituencies of the monarchy – particularly East Bank tribes and rural communities – have been given special access to government jobs and other benefits in exchange for their loyalty (Tell 2013; Yom 2014). Beginning in the late 1980s, economic crisis and liberalization constrained the state's resources significantly, which made it more difficult to co-opt these groups. Lust-Okar (2006, 2009) and Kao (2015) show how the regime responded to this challenge by using legislative elections to facilitate competition between these constituencies over access to patronage. Members of parliament, elected primarily on the basis of tribal ties, use their positions to distribute jobs, healthcare, university admissions, and other perks from the government to their voters. The regime continues to rely more on East Bank Jordanians than Palestinian Jordanians for support, and the former are better able to access benefits from the state (El Muhtaseb 2013). However, this balance has shifted somewhat in the past two decades, as neoliberal economic policies have weakened the regime's relationship with its core East Bank constituencies (Yom 2014).

Regarding foreign patrons, Brand (1995) argues that the Jordanian monarchy formed its external alliances with states that could offer it the resources necessary to sustain spending on the military and contribute to modest economic growth, thereby securing its coercive power and warding off severe economic crises. Yom (2015) likewise suggests that foreign financial assistance, especially from the United States, has enabled the regime to finance patronage spending on its core constituencies. Relatedly, Jamal (2013) claims that public support for Jordan's monarchy is shaped by this relationship with the United States. The country's economic elites prefer a royal autocracy to democracy because they fear that a more democratic system of government would empower anti-American Islamists, who would then undermine the crucial economic relationship with the superpower. As a result, they continue to back the royal regime. There is little doubt that foreign patronage from the United States in particular has been a key contributor to the monarchy's stability, in large part because of the economic resources it funnels into the regime's hands. As I will discuss later in the chapter, this importance is reflected in how the monarchy has actively guarded its ability to control foreign policy and its relationships with foreign powers.

The regime has also been effective at making sure that the political opposition remains fragmented and unable to organize a unified front. Lust-Okar (2005), Lucas (2005), and Ryan (2018) document how the regime has used institutions and political reforms strategically to encourage these divisions. By offering limited – and often temporary – concessions on issues such as press freedom or the electoral law, the regime can dampen the intensity of opposition, making it more difficult for activists to mobilize meaningfully in the streets.

These arguments are complementary to the one outlined in this book. It is clear that patronage politics, foreign powers, and divisions within the opposition play a central role in Jordanian politics, accounting for much of its political economy while also contributing to the monarchy's durability. In fact, insights from these arguments are directly relevant to my own theory. For instance, the parliament's role in distributing economic resources to the public positions it to absorb blame when it fails to deliver satisfactorily. The importance of foreign support for the monarchy's survival is reflected in how the kings have been much less willing to delegate decision-making related to foreign policy, even if it means attracting blame for deeply unpopular decisions. And the monarch's strategic use of delegation facilitates divisions among its opponents by introducing multiple targets at which to be angry, thereby depriving the opposition of a clear focal point around which to organize. There are also outcomes in Jordanian politics that existing theories are less capable of explaining. While it is almost certainly true that foreign support and patronage distribution help the regime to reduce the likelihood of economic crises, it also remains the case that Jordan has experienced periods of deep economic pain and dysfunction in its modern history, which have triggered several bouts of mass unrest. Why has the monarchy not become the primary target of the opposition at these moments? Focusing on the politics of blame can help to address this question.

Existing work on Jordan also does not tend to focus on the country's policy process, and where it does, it typically ascribes a weak policymaking role to institutions other than the monarchy, such as the parliament (Karmel 2021). For example, in describing the logic of Jordan's parliamentary elections, Lust-Okar (2006) argues that "competition is not over policy making," because "many ... policy decisions

4.2 Decision-Making and Delegation in Jordan

are off-limits to parliamentarians..." Likewise, Ryan (2018) emphasizes the dominance of the monarchy when he notes that "Shifting some real power from the monarchy to parliament, the prime minister, and the cabinet would move reform beyond simply cleaner elections." In what follows, I do not disagree with the idea that parliamentary voting is motivated primarily by patronage, or that the king unquestionably possesses more power than the government and parliament. However, I do show how these dynamics coexist with a policymaking process in which institutions other than the monarchy exercise significant influence, with implications for how Jordanians attribute blame and how the monarchy is able to maintain relatively high levels of popular support.

4.2 Decision-Making and Delegation in Jordan

This section provides a general overview of the policymaking process in Jordan from 1952 to the present. I give background on the rules and principles of the 1952 constitution that formally structures the policy process, and I draw on my interviews about the reign of the late King Hussein and the current reign of King Abdullah to illustrate how Jordan's kings have shared power over decision-making, granting often substantial influence to the prime minister, cabinet, parliament, and bureaucracy despite also maintaining significant powers reflecting their status as dictators. I also discuss why this delegation can be costly for the kings to overturn and at times has facilitated elite threats to the monarchy. This discussion provides support for key assumptions of the theory by showing that delegation does occur, that the king has some influence over how this power is shared, and that these arrangements can be made relatively credible – despite the authoritarian context – by creating costs the king must absorb to force through his preferences.

4.2.1 Constitutional Provisions Surrounding Decision-Making

Formally, the Jordanian constitution divides decision-making authority between the monarchy, the government (which refers to the prime minister and his cabinet, also known as the Council of Ministers), and the parliament, though the document makes it clear that the king is

122 *The Jordanian Monarchy's Strategic Blame Games*

the pinnacle of the system and wields significant powers.[1] The document states that "The Legislative Power shall be vested in the National Assembly and the King," and that "The Executive Power shall be vested in the King, who shall exercise his powers through his ministers in accordance with the provisions of the present Constitution." Furthermore, not only is the king the head of state, the commander in chief of the armed forces, and the head of all branches of government, but he also has the right to appoint and dismiss the prime minister, senators, and a number of other important government officials, as well as the ability to dissolve the parliament. Furthermore, the king is constitutionally "immune from any liability and responsibility," meaning that the monarch can legally do no wrong.

This immunity is justified by the fact that the king, despite his great powers, is intended to play a limited role in matters of policy, with his influence running entirely through the government. The constitution grants the government "responsibility of administering all affairs of State, internal and external," and ministers are "responsible for the conduct of all matters pertaining to his Ministry." Legally, the king cannot simply issue orders: Every royal decree must be "countersigned by the Prime Minister and the Minister or Ministers concerned." In addition, the constitution notes explicitly that "Verbal or written orders of the King do not release ministers from their responsibilities," giving them incentive to resist illegal directives from the palace for which the king cannot be held personally accountable.

The constitution grants parliament a modest role in making policy: Legislation can be edited, approved, or rejected by the parliament, but it can only be proposed by the government or a group of at least ten representatives or senators, rather than individual members. This provision limits the ability of parliament to set the policy agenda, particularly because parties have almost always been weak in the body (Lust-Okar 2001), and because the king is under no obligation to appoint a prime minister from the largest party and in fact has only done so once in the country's history. However, the parliament's formal powers of oversight are more substantial, such that the government is "collectively responsible before the Chamber of Deputies in

---

[1] The full text of the constitution of Jordan, including recent amendments, can be seen here: www.refworld.org/pdfid/3ae6b53310.pdf.

4.2 Decision-Making and Delegation in Jordan 123

respect of the public policy of the State." To conduct this oversight, members of parliament (MPs) have the right to receive answers to any query directed at the government, and the body can withdraw confidence from individual ministers or the prime minister and his entire cabinet. These oversight abilities give parliament leverage over the policy process by enabling them to engage regularly with ministers over administrative and legislative issues, while also providing the body with a potential threat to strip ministers of their positions.

4.2.2 Decision-Making in Practice

The king has several points of de facto leverage over the policy process that are not clearly reflected in the constitution, or in King Abdullah's letter discussed in the opening of this chapter. First, officials – especially the prime ministers – are well aware that the king has the right to remove them from their positions. As one former prime minister stated in an interview, "you accept what he [the king] says or you resign," when disagreements emerge between the palace and the government on issues for which the king has decided he has important interests at stake. Second, the king meets weekly with the National Politics Council (NPC), which also typically includes the chief of the royal court, the heads of the intelligence agency and army, the prime minister, the interior and foreign ministers, and other advisers close to the king. This council focuses on issues considered to be of particular importance to the state. Though the prime minister has a say, interviews with Jordanian elites suggest that it is very much the king's council, and its decisions are almost always adopted by the government. One minister described implementing the NPC's proposals as follows: "we would discuss routine issues [in cabinet meetings] and then in the last few minutes, the prime minister would come with his pink file, and it would take five or ten minutes to pass ... ten decisions."

Particularly under King Abdullah, the monarchy also has access to a large, extra-constitutional bureaucracy within the royal court, similar to the presidential bureaucracy in the United States. These officials often work both publicly and behind the scenes to influence the government's policies. In addition, the palace oversees an extensive patronage network that can incentivize support for its positions. Finally, the king maintains a particularly tight relationship with Jordan's intelligence agency, the General Intelligence Directorate (GID), whose officers monitor the political system closely and can apply pressure on government officials if needed. For instance, it is widely believed that GID officers will lean on members of parliament for important votes and that they will smear in the press or at times rig elections to defeat those who challenge their directives (Obeidat 2014).

These tools mean that when the king really wants to throw his weight around to achieve some outcome, he has a good chance of making it happen – and this dynamic is well understood across the country. But the fact that the king possesses these powers does not imply that all decisions originate with the palace, or that the king's preferences are always reflected in policy outcomes. Instead, delegation still occurs in a meaningful way. The monarchy typically distances itself from the policy process, and its own actions – alongside other elements of the political system – can make this distance credible. Meanwhile, the government, and to a lesser extent the parliament, contribute substantially to the design and implementation of state policies. Other bureaucratic offices matter as well; for instance, despite the king's close relationship with the GID, the directorate's head can also wield significant influence independent of the monarchy and often takes a major role in setting policy (Bank and Schlumberger 2004). Lower-level bureaucratic officials beneath the ministers possess the ability to influence policy implementation too, and in some cases they can set policy themselves. While I will at times mention these types of officials, I focus predominantly on the cabinet and parliament, in large part because they are the institutions emphasized by the constitution for their role in decision-making.

Upon appointing a new prime minister, the king provides him publicly with a list of broad objectives for the government to pursue, such as improving public services and increasing government efficiency. For instance, in his letter of designation to Prime Minister Omar al-Razzaz on June 5, 2018, King Abdullah wrote, "I direct you, as you embark on this mission, to launch a comprehensive national awakening that empowers Jordanians to harness their energies and pursue their dreams; and meets their needs through quality services, fair taxation, an agile, efficient government team, and a social safety net that protects the vulnerable" (Al-Hussein 2018). In the remainder of the letter, the king outlined a broad set of "priorities and pillars" to guide the new prime minister, but specific policy proposals were absent from the document.

4.2 Decision-Making and Delegation in Jordan

This approach is typical: The details of how to achieve the broad goals articulated by the king are left primarily to the prime minister and his cabinet. A former prime minister, who served under King Hussein, denied that the king ever "interfered in the general issues," noting that, "He [the king] did not like to go into the details. He was a strategic man, not a technical man." A former minister of planning and international cooperation under King Abdullah described the relationship similarly, noting that, "The palace will not have a program for you. You have your own detailed program and it is your responsibility to achieve it. They will give you general guidelines, for example, what you need to do economically to enhance growth and youth employment. But how to do it, the specifics are absolutely the government's business." In my interviews, a number of other former government officials and outside observers assessed the dynamic between the government and the palace in similar terms. While the king sets the broader agenda, he leaves most of the details to the prime minister and his cabinet.

Within each government, the policy process depends heavily on the structure imposed by the prime minister. Some delegate to deputy prime ministers, granting them responsibility for broad issue areas such as the economy or relations with parliament. Some also give individual ministers significant independence, monitoring their decisions only when they touch on sensitive matters capable of weakening the government's popularity. Others insist on running a tight ship in which ministers interact with them frequently. In general, however, former ministers reported an ability to shape the policies of their ministries, as long as they accounted for the government's interests. One former minister asserted that "...you have a wide range of freedom to do whatever you want ... to achieve the goals and objectives of the ministry." Another summarized this position by observing that, "...there is a margin of freedom to take decisions, but you have to remember that you work through a team led by the prime minister. In technical work, the prime minister never interferes, and no other power, even the palace, interferes. But sometimes in public policy, there is intervention related to the government's mission." In other words, prime ministers and their cabinets are not mere figureheads; rather, they matter in important ways for the policies implemented by the Jordanian state.

This influence of prime ministers appears throughout Jordan's history. For instance, Wasfi al-Tell advanced ambitious economic reforms during his time in office, while others such as Taher al-Masri attempted to pursue democratic-oriented political changes. Under King Abdullah, some prime ministers – such as Ali Abu al-Ragheb and Samir al-Rifai – were defined by their interest in policies aimed at liberalizing the economy, while others, such as Abdelraouf al-Rawabdeh, pursued conservative policies that favored the state-dependent East Bank tribes (Robins 2004). Prime ministers have also been able to influence the direction of foreign policy, despite the monarchy's more involved approach on these issues. For example, when Abdul Karim Kabariti became prime minister in 1996, he used his time in office to push for regime change in Iraq (Ashton 2008). Kabariti's efforts came in the context of a long-running back and forth between Jordan's political elites over the wisdom of aligning with the Iraqi dictator. This division resembled earlier conflicts from the 1950s and 1960s, when elite factions fought to influence Jordan's stance toward Nasser's Egypt, and when changing prime ministers often meant a shift in this policy matter (Shlaim 2007).

Cabinet ministers can also exercise substantial influence over the direction of their ministries, pursuing policies they consider rewarding. In many of the more technical ministries that nonetheless address issues of economic and social importance – such as those focused on education, the environment, public sector employment, and energy – the ministers are often technocratic specialists with strong views about what constitutes good policy. For instance, a former minister of municipal affairs excitedly described efforts to restructure the debts of Jordan's dozens of municipalities. Likewise, a former minister of the environment with a background in environmental issues discussed pushing forward a major new law for waste management, while also focusing on smaller but still meaningful policies to promote awareness of environmental issues.

As noted earlier, parliament's influence over policies is more modest because of its limited constitutional prerogatives. These constraints are reinforced by the government's ability to pressure individual members of parliament to vote for its legislation. As other scholars have documented extensively (Kao 2015; Lust 2009; Lust and Hourani 2011), Jordan's electoral laws favor independent, tribal-backed candidates who win based on promises to distribute goods to their constituents, and especially government jobs. Because ministers control access to these jobs, they can freeze out members of parliament who challenge the government's positions, robbing them of the clientelistic successes

4.2 Decision-Making and Delegation in Jordan

they need to secure re-election. At times, elections for the lower house have also been rigged more directly to ensure the existence of a loyal legislature. The government holds less leverage over senators, who are appointed by the king; however, as former ministers and senior bureaucrats themselves, the senators can typically be relied upon to sympathize with the government's position.

Nonetheless, both representatives and senators have the opportunity to shape legislation, particularly when the government initially brings draft laws to the relevant parliamentary committees for review. For instance, a former minister of the environment recalled how members of parliament actually increased the fines for littering in draft legislation intended to strengthen environmental protections. A former senator proudly described securing funding for a new sewer system in her hometown. And a former representative described how he and his colleagues convinced the government to implement important changes to the electoral law by emphasizing how it benefited the government's interests. Some MPs have acquired such influence by forming policy-oriented blocs, of which the most successful was the Mubadara bloc that existed between 2013 and 2016. Led by then-MP Mustafa Hamarneh, the bloc grew to almost 20 percent of MPs at its peak and had some success at enforcing unified voting. This approach gave them enough strength to draw attention to their preferred reforms, including the provision of legal rights to the children of Jordanian women married to foreigners. Hamarneh explained the motivation for this controversial policy change by stating that it was "a matter of principle" that made Jordan "a better place for its citizens and all who live here" (Kayyali and Al-Wakeel 2015). The GID soon came to view this organization as a potential threat, it began to fragment under pressure, and Hamarneh was defeated in his 2016 election bid. Nonetheless, additional blocs formed in the subsequent parliament as well. Individual MPs are also able to secure a degree of policy influence through their participation in committees and their ability to question the government's ministers (Shalaby and Williamson 2023).

The extent of this activity appears in data collected by Al-Hayat Center, a Jordanian research institute, on parliamentary procedures in the country. In 2017, the first full year of the 18th parliament, the House of Representatives approved thirty seven laws, to which members of parliament made 1,762 proposed changes (Al-Hayat Center 2018). The representatives also submitted 1,055 questions to government ministries as part of their formal oversight role, to which the vast majority received the legally-required response (Shalaby and Williamson 2023). In other words, while representatives and senators lack the ability to set the agenda, their positions do enable them to contribute substantively to the laws on which they vote, even when the outcome of these votes is rarely in doubt.

In fact, the government almost never loses votes in the parliament in part *because* the government is forced to make meaningful efforts to satisfy the preferences of the representatives – the lack of lost votes is not just an indicator of legislative weakness. For instance, the minister of parliamentary affairs is responsible for making sure that MPs' needs are met by the government to ensure smooth passage of legislation. In some governments, the prime minister will even empower a specific deputy prime minister to make sure that these relations remain strong.

Thus, the policy process is not just a matter of the king asserting his preferences and forcing the government and parliament to follow through. While this dynamic does exist for certain policy domains, important policy decisions often originate within the cabinet, not the palace. The government must then take the preferences of dozens of legislators into account when it seeks to implement these decisions, and the legislators are frequently able to use their positions to extract concessions on policy matters.

4.2.3 The Costs and Credibility of Delegation

The formal rules of the political system in Jordan, combined with informal dynamics of elite and popular politics, mean that it can be costly for the monarchy to sidestep the decision-making influence of other political elites (Shalaby and Williamson 2023). Such costs make power sharing credible (Meng et al. 2023), and should therefore increase the likelihood that Jordanians do not hold the king fully responsible for outcomes produced by the political system. For example, when the king does try to overturn policy decisions of the cabinet and parliament, it can trigger elite opposition that is visible to the public and damaging to the monarchy. One high profile incident involved the resignation of former Prime Minister Awn al-Khasawneh, a respected judge who briefly headed the government from October 2011 to April 2012 during the height of the Arab Spring. When the king and prime minister clashed over the timing of elections, the prime minister refused

4.2 Decision-Making and Delegation in Jordan 129

to sign off on the king's request to accelerate the electoral timeline (Ryan 2018). The king waited until the prime minister was visiting Turkey, and then he asked the prime minister's deputy to sign a decision extending the parliamentary session for the purpose of discussing the draft election law. This maneuver so angered al-Khasawneh that he resigned while still in Turkey, faxing his resignation letter to the king (Al-Isawe 2012). This spat played out in public at a sensitive moment for the regime, particularly given al-Khasawneh's strong reputation with Jordan's reformists. With his resignation, tensions between the opposition and the palace increased (Black 2012).

Likewise, seeking to browbeat parliament into implementing unpopular policies can trigger public displays of elite discontent. When King Hussein decided that Jordan should pursue a peace treaty with Israel in the 1990s, he faced significant opposition to the plan in the legislature, and prominent members of parliament went on to organize protests, vote against the treaty, and then publicly lead efforts to resist normalization with Israel in the years that followed (Robins 2004; Schwedler 2003). Hussein felt that the strategic benefits were important enough for Hashemite rule to justify paying these additional costs, and so he used his substantial powers to make the treaty happen (Ashton 2008). In other cases, however, the monarchy does not get its preferred policy outcomes, because it does not wish to pay the costs associated with overruling the government and parliament. On social issues, for instance, the monarchy will at times sponsor liberalizing reforms that likely reflect the worldview of the Western-oriented king and queen. More typically, the monarchy cedes these issues to the government and parliament, even though it leads to the adoption of more conservative policies (Ryan and Schwedler 2004). For instance, one Jordanian scholar noted how "The monarchy is genuinely interested in the welfare of orphans, but we have a terrible law here ... there's the whole idea of not wanting to step on parliament's toes with the law," and as a result, "the monarchy does not push it [reforms] through."

As discussed in Chapter 2, empowering political elites through power sharing does not just make it more difficult for the autocrat to dominate decision-making, but can also increase the risks of an elite challenge from within the regime. This risk has been visible during certain periods of Jordanian history in which the cabinet and parliament have posed significant threats to the monarchy. In the 1950s and 1960s, powerful prime ministers posed a challenge to King Hussein's authority, and in one case mobilized parliament as well as mass opposition to directly challenge the king's dominance of the political system (Shlaim 2007). In more recent decades, following the return of parliamentary and party politics since 1989, the monarchy has worried that Islamist elites in particular will use the parliament to challenge the throne (Magid 2016). That delegation is costly for the monarchy to overturn – and may even embolden elite threats to the monarchy – reflects a key assumption of the theory, and it implies that delegation is more likely to be perceived as credible and not just cheap talk by at least some Jordanians.

Another important assumption of the theory is that dictators can strategically manipulate whether and how credibly they delegate responsibility for decision-making in the policy process. In Jordan, the formal institutional structure described earlier has been relatively fixed since the 1952 constitution. Yet, within this structure, the monarchs possess a series of strategies by which they can increase or decrease the credibility of their distance from policymaking by changing the costs they would pay to overturn decisions made by the government and parliament. The monarch can choose to appoint prime ministers who vary in their ability to assert their independence from the palace, with the kings sometimes appointing powerful prime ministers and at other times appointing weak and dependent figures. While the ability of the king to fire these prime ministers does not change, their willingness to visibly assert themselves relative to the king does shift, with implications for how much Jordanians are likely to assume the palace is dominating decision-making while these prime ministers are in office. Parliament's independence can also be strengthened or weakened by adjusting control of electoral outcomes, thereby affecting the credibility of the institution's influence over the policy process. Throughout Jordan's history, the fairness of its parliamentary elections has varied significantly, with some almost completely free and others manipulated heavily by the GID. More competitive elections have typically produced parliaments that are more assertive in the decision-making process. At other moments, the monarchy has closed the parliament, removing the body's policymaking influence but also its ability to shield the king from blame. More generally, Jordan is an authoritarian regime, in which institutions are particularly fluid. As such, the monarchy also retains substantial capacity to restructure institutions strategically based on the needs of the current moment. For instance, the kings can expand or contract the royal court and the extent to which it involves itself in setting policies, and they have at times backed changes to the constitution that affect their formal powers over the decision-making process.

In sum, decision-making powers in Jordan are shared in a manner that can impose visible costs on the monarchy for forcing its preferences through the political system. And though Jordan's existing institutions are sticky, the monarchs have the ability to shape the extent of these costs in ways that should influence delegation's perceived credibility, and thus its relative effectiveness at protecting them from blame. Chapter 6 will consider these dynamics in further detail by analyzing variations in delegation and blame attributions in Jordan over time.

4.3 Strategic Delegation to Protect the Monarchy

Delegation of policymaking responsibility to the cabinet and parliament can serve many purposes for the monarchy, including the facilitation of patronage distribution to different constituencies (Kao 2015; Lust-Okar 2006). However, evidence from my interviews with senior decision-makers suggests that the country's monarchs do delegate to the cabinet and parliament with the intentional goal of protecting themselves from blame. The benefits of blame avoidance are not just a by-product of delegation for the monarchy but reflect an important motivation for why power sharing takes place. This deliberateness is also reflected in how the monarchy seeks to propagate expectations among the public about how responsibility is meant to be held by the cabinet and parliament. Furthermore, Jordan's kings have been more likely to delegate credibly for policy matters pertaining to the economy and social issues, while openly exercising influence over the country's policies related to foreign affairs and national security. Insofar as the former issues have often generated substantial popular anger in Jordan, while delegation for the latter issues could heighten threats from Jordan's other political elites, this variation is consistent with the monarchy delegating strategically to take into account the costs of blame compared to the risks of elite threats across different issues. The following sections discuss each of these points in turn.

4.3.1 Intentional Blame Avoidance

Evaluating the intentions of political actors is difficult in any situation. Perhaps the most direct strategy for evaluating intentions is to ask decision-makers why they act the way they do, but this approach is often especially difficult in authoritarian regimes where information is more constrained and the actors themselves may be harder to access. While speaking with King Abdullah was not possible for a researcher in my position, I was able to acquire interviews with individuals who had held some of the country's most senior decision-making roles, including former prime ministers as well as chiefs of the royal court. The latter in particular work closely with the king to manage and protect the monarchy, giving them direct insights into the king's political calculations. It is possible, of course, that such politically savvy individuals would provide misleading answers to serve their own political agendas. However, an important component of my theory is the claim that blame avoidance helps to *motivate* the sharing of decision-making powers in autocracies and is not just a byproduct of other considerations. These interviews reflect the most feasible approach to evaluating this claim in the Jordanian context.

The interviews clearly point to blame avoidance as an important contribution to the monarchy's strategic calculus. All of the former prime ministers and chiefs of the royal court to whom I spoke explicitly described delegation from the palace to the government as a deliberate strategy to insulate the king from unpopular policy decisions while providing a mechanism for removing those whom the public blames instead. For instance, a former chief of the royal court who held the position under King Abdullah argued that the king shared decision-making powers because, "You need to protect the consensus on the Hashemite family," and "Unfortunately, any leader can start with the highest approval rating, and then it starts to go down in any country." Delegation helps to solve this problem for the king by "getting the executive branch to take the responsibility," thus insulating the king from blame. A former prime minister agreed, stating that, "The prime minister in Jordan is a bumper ... so that any differences are not directed to the throne itself, but to the prime minister."

Another prime minister also acknowledged that his role as the decision-maker was intended to protect the monarchy from the public's anger. In fact, this prime minister claimed to have resigned voluntarily

4.3 Strategic Delegation to Protect the Monarchy 133

because he felt pressure building over a series of unpopular decisions by his government, and he did not want it to explode against the king. Similarly, a former chief of the royal court under King Hussein described this strategy as the "Lampedusa formula," based on a quote from the novel *The Leopard*, in which it is famously said that "everything needs to change, so everything can stay the same." What this former chief meant by referencing this quote was that "if you want to maintain the king's stability, you have to get rid of prime ministers," because "when they change, the people are happy that you got rid of the culprit ... while the policy does not change." In other words, delegating responsibility to the cabinet means they absorb the public's attributions of blame for unpopular policies, and removing these officials then helps to assuage the public's anger by providing a degree of accountability.

Because prime ministers understand their role to be one of absorbing blame for the king, they are "obsessed with their image," according to a former minister of media affairs. They realize that once their popularity declines, the king will remove them to reduce the likelihood of public anger exploding against the regime more broadly. Because of this dynamic, prime ministers will be particularly likely to control ministers in their cabinet whose portfolios are most likely to attract public anger, and they often "go out of their way ... to win the support of the media," according to the same former minister of media affairs. These efforts include rumors of bribes paid to journalists for favorable coverage. However, despite these efforts to sustain their approval, over time the prime ministers all lose support. Since the initiation of regular opinion polling about the prime minister and cabinet in the 1990s, every Jordanian government has seen its approval drop after an initial honeymoon period. The consistency of this pattern illustrates why the former prime ministers and chiefs of the royal court are insistent that delegation to the government is needed to protect the monarchy from the negative effects of day-to-day governance and politics on the public's support for individual political leaders.

4.3.2 Propagating Expectations of Responsibility

Chapter 2 argued that monarchs have a blame avoidance advantage over other autocrats partly because delegation aligns with norms about how responsibility is *meant* to operate in the political system.

Monarchs are not expected to take an active role in decision-making or bear responsibility for policy outcomes, and so monarchs who choose to delegate credibly are more likely than other autocrats to avoid blame effectively. In Jordan, it is clear that the regime recognizes this advantage and seeks to reinforce it, actively propagating the idea that the king is not involved in day-to-day decision-making and therefore should not be held responsible for unpopular policies. These efforts explicitly portray Jordan as a constitutional monarchy similar to the United Kingdom, emphasizing the importance of the cabinet and parliament in the policy process while maintaining more ambiguity about the king's role. The visibility of this messaging aligns with the argument that the monarchy delegates in part as a deliberate strategy to protect itself from blame for the public's grievances.

This strategy is apparent in the king's own public pronouncements. For example, returning to the king's essay that opened this chapter, "Each Playing Our Part in a New Democracy," it is clear that he wishes to paint a picture of where responsibility for decision-making lies in the political system. In the essay, he states directly that it is the government's responsibility to develop a policy agenda that meets the needs of Jordanians, and that the government should be held accountable for its implementation. Meanwhile, he talks about his own role in the "Hashemite Constitutional Monarchy" as one that is fundamentally about guaranteeing the constitution and protecting national unity rather than engaging directly in policymaking. This emphasis on the decision-making responsibilities of Jordan's other institutions is a recurrent feature of the king's rhetoric.

To highlight further how the regime seeks to propagate the expectation that the cabinet and parliament should be held responsible for governance outcomes, I turn to social studies textbooks that have been used to educate schoolchildren about the country's political system as far back as the 1950s. These textbooks are available for researchers to access in a Textbook Museum located in the town of Salt. Since educational materials are often intended to influence how people view their political systems, they provide a useful material for insights into how governments want to be perceived (Brand 2014; Cantoni et al. 2017).

The social studies textbooks define Jordan as a hereditary monarchy, but one that is governed by a constitution as a democracy. This framework is said to differentiate Jordan from dictatorships, which

4.3 Strategic Delegation to Protect the Monarchy

are described as political systems governed by a single person. For instance, a sixth grade textbook for national civic education, published in 1999 and reprinted in 2002, categorizes countries as "states bound by a constitution" and "states with no constitution." The former category is defined as states that are "governed by the provisions of the constitution, of which examples include the Hashemite Kingdom of Jordan, the Lebanese Republic, the United Kingdom (Britain), the United States of America, and the French Republic," while the latter category is defined as states in which "power is concentrated in the hands of a single person, of which examples include Italy under Mussolini and Germany under Hitler." In other words, according to these books, Jordan is not a country where responsibility falls on one dominant political leader; rather, the country is governed as a constitutional monarchy just like the British model, with power spread across various governing bodies.

In how the textbooks talk about Jordan's institutions, this idea of the country as a constitutional monarchy is linked more explicitly to ideas about who holds responsibility for governance. They frequently emphasize that the political system consists of three branches – the government, the legislature, and the judiciary – that operate on the basis of a separation of powers. For instance, a diagram from a national civic education textbook, written in 1993 and reprinted in 2006, describes the relationship between the people, the legislature, the government, and the law as one in which the people elect their representatives to pass laws, the representatives monitor the government to make sure it properly implements the laws, and the laws then govern the people. There is no mention at all of the monarchy in this idealized description of the country's policymaking process.

The kings do feature prominently in these textbooks, but they are mentioned primarily for their historical accomplishments. Their governance role is kept ambiguous. For instance, a social education textbook for the fourth grade that was published in 1980 and reprinted in 1986 talks about the royal family's religious lineage and their commitment to Arab unity, before concluding with the statement that "today under the reign of His Majesty King Hussein, Jordan is enjoying security, progress, and prosperity." The book then launches into a description of the country's political system by noting that "The council of ministers helps the king govern the country ... and the council of ministers assumes responsibility for managing all of the internal and foreign policies of the state." In other words, the king's role is undefined, while emphasis is placed on the cabinet's responsibility for decision-making.

An earlier textbook titled "National Education," published in 1958, adopts a similar approach. After noting that the king "heads" the three branches of government, it includes only a single page listing his constitutional responsibilities, including his position as head of state that grants him immunity from accountability, his role in "certifying" laws, and his appointment powers for the cabinet and senate. The textbook then devotes five full pages to the cabinet, describing its formation, responsibilities, and composition, and devoting paragraphs to the duties of specific ministries including the ministries of finance, defense, public works, health, the interior, foreign affairs, the economy, and construction.

Discussions of parliament emphasize its role in representing the public in the policy process. For example, the 1986 social education textbook referenced earlier writes that "the voters have the right to present their problems to their representatives." Likewise, the 2006 national civic education textbook includes a discussion of indirect democracy, where it notes that direct democracy is infeasible and so "the people elect a number of individuals that they trust to represent them with good judgment." It links this description directly to Jordan's political system, implying that the parliament is intended to play this role.

By the time Jordanians graduate from high school, they will have been exposed repeatedly to textbooks describing the country as a constitutional monarchy. In part, this rhetoric is clearly intended to convince Jordanians that they are governed by a democracy, reflecting the importance of democratic norms for the legitimacy of authoritarian regimes (Williamson 2021). In other work, I discuss how modern monarchs attempt to convince their citizens that they govern democratically. However, it is also apparent that this rhetoric intends to instill ideas about how decisions are made in the political system and where responsibility for governance lies. They are not just focused on discussing elections and representation, but on painting a clear picture of the decision-making roles of the cabinet and parliament, while leaving the monarch's role much more ambiguous. Reinforcing the expectation of cabinet and parliamentary responsibility should strengthen the ability of delegation to shift blame away from the monarchy. The consistency and apparent deliberateness of the messaging further

4.3.3 Delegation across Issue Domains

Another indicator of the monarchy's intentional and strategic use of delegation as a blame avoidance strategy is the extent to which the monarchy's involvement in decision-making varies across issue domains. The kings have maintained close control over issues where delegation would be particularly likely to create powerful elite threats. Meanwhile, they have shared decision-making powers much more credibly for issues with a high potential to arouse mass opposition, where being blamed is especially likely to be costly. This logic is illustrated by the fact that both King Hussein and King Abdullah have maintained a tight grip on policy decisions related to foreign affairs and national security, delegating not at all or with low levels of credibility. On the other hand, they have typically given the cabinet and parliament substantial leeway to determine policies related to economic and social issues (Ryan and Schwedler 2004).

The difference between these issue domains is institutionalized. On the one hand, the king has a constitutionally-mandated role as Commander in Chief of the Armed Forces, and his formal position as Head of State likewise grants him duties in foreign policy. On the other hand, the constitution bars him from making policy decisions directly on most policy matters. This difference between issue domains is also reflected in actual practice. As one Jordanian analyst observed, King Abdullah "wants to see economic governments [and] he wants them to focus on economic issues." In contrast, a former chief of the royal court noted that Abdullah "believes he should take care of the army and foreign policy" to the extent that "many ministers don't think of the foreign minister as part of the cabinet, they think of him as part of the palace."

This pattern was even more pronounced during the reign of King Hussein. A former prime minister observed that King Hussein had a strong say in "foreign affairs and relations with other countries," but that "the internal affairs – social, economic, financial – were ... almost totally the responsibility of the cabinet." One of Hussein's biographers noted that the king "took only a superficial and intermittent interest in economic affairs, delegating them to the government, while he himself was much more directly involved with the army and with foreign relations" (Shlaim 2007, 175). The British embassy in Amman also observed in their 1964 annual report that Hussein's "preoccupation with military and foreign affairs has left neglected the intractable long-term problem of how to achieve or even approach economic viability" (TNA FO 371/180728). In fact, this particular gripe reflected a long-running complaint by British diplomats that King Hussein devoted far too much time to foreign affairs and national security, and too little to domestic governance.

Despite these British complaints, however, blame avoidance provided a powerful reason to delegate control over domestic issues. Though Jordan's economy has fared relatively well at times, particularly from the late 1970s to the early 1980s and during the early 2000s, the country's lack of resources, low initial levels of development, and difficult regional position have meant that the economy has struggled more often than not (Ashton 2008; Ryan 2018; Yom 2015). This near-constant level of low performance has provided few opportunities to claim credit for economic successes. At the same time, periodic economic crises have sparked severe political unrest. As a result, the monarchy faces few upsides and many potential downsides for closely controlling economic policy. Similarly, on social issues, the divide between conservative Islamists on one side and more orthodox Muslims and religious minorities on the other has sparked a number of political conflicts in countries around the Middle East, particularly since the Islamic revival beginning in the 1970s. By ceding more control over social policy to the government and parliament, the monarchy tries to distance itself for the purpose of minimizing blame when one of these camps becomes upset with the state's approach. In addition, delegating decision-making responsibilities over these economic and social issues is unlikely to significantly enhance the coercive powers of elites in ways that make it easier for them to challenge the monarchy. As a result, sharing power over these domains allows the kings to protect their reputation more effectively without unduly increasing their vulnerability to internal threats from other elites.

The strategic calculus has been different for issues of foreign affairs and national security. These issues are sensitive for all dictators because of how they touch on their ability to manage coercion (Truex 2016), but they have been especially important for Jordan's kings (Brand 1995). Since the founding of the state, the military, and later the

4.3 Strategic Delegation to Protect the Monarchy 139

intelligence apparatus and other security forces, have been the cornerstone of Hashemite support. Furthermore, King Hussein in particular faced down several potential military coups that were linked to other political elites in the country. In describing the king's preoccupation with the military at the expense of giving greater attention to the economy, Shlaim (2007, 175) noted that "The army was the key to the survival of the monarchy and ... it called for careful monitoring." Likewise, O'Connell (2011, xv) wrote that Hussein "knew where his strength lay, and he spent his whole life making sure that the army and the Bedouin tribes were behind him. They were his insurance policy, and those around him knew it."

Foreign affairs strongly influenced the loyalty of the military, as well as the reliability of the security forces and other political elites. King Hussein depended heavily on the United Kingdom and then the United States to provide financing and equipment for the military, which he used to bolster the loyalty of the troops and build a deterrent against both foreign invasion and domestic upheaval (Yom 2015), and Jordan remains heavily dependent on the United States for foreign aid today (Ryan 2018; Moore 2018). In the past, Jordan's neighbors also sought to use the Jordanian military and Jordanian political elites as part of their efforts to overthrow the monarchy. In the 1950s and 1960s, the radical Arab states, led by Egypt and its President Gamal Abdel Nasser, cultivated relationships with prime ministers and MPs, and they also attempted to recruit agents within the Jordanian military to mount a coup against the king. In both 1957 and 1958, for instance, King Hussein faced down coup plots with connections to Egypt (Robins 2004; O'Connell 2011). These states also supported radical political parties within Jordan that hoped to overthrow the regime, providing them with military training and weapons that were used to launch a series of bombings and assassinations in Amman in the late 1950s (Cohen 1980). Furthermore, Jordan has had to contend with the Arab–Israeli conflict, including large inflows of Palestinian refugees in 1948 and 1967 who substantially reshaped the country's domestic politics. For decades, King Hussein needed to maintain a careful balancing act between the Israeli government and Palestinian nationalists, since both posed a major threat to his regime and at times attempted to topple him directly (Shlaim 2007).

That is not to say that there are no costs to being blamed for policy decisions related to foreign affairs or security matters. Especially in the context of the Israeli–Palestinian conflict and dependency on the United States, the Jordanian public often responds negatively to their country's policies. As will be described in the next two chapters, the public recognizes the king's direct power over these domains, and discontent is more likely to be directed at the monarchy when it is motivated by policies related to these issues. However, the risks of elite threats are higher when delegating power over foreign affairs or security threats, and so the monarchy has been more willing to absorb the costs of being blamed for these issues.

To demonstrate more systematically the monarchy's tendency to hold onto foreign policy and national security decisions while delegating more credibly for most economic and social issues, I collected text data from the official websites of King Abdullah and the Jordanian parliament, which I then analyzed with quantitative methods for studying textual data. The data were taken from the news section of these websites, which post near-daily articles about the activities of their institutions. I collected the data in September 2017. The monarchy articles are posted in both English and Arabic, and they extend from 2002, early in King Abdullah's reign, until the date of collection. The parliament articles are posted in Arabic, and they extend from 2010 until the date of collection. Approximately 7,800 articles were scraped from the monarchy page in Arabic (6,000 of which were also posted in English), indicating a rate of more than one article per day. Approximately 2,800 were scraped from the parliament page, suggesting a rate of just under one per day. Given that all political leaders face serious time constraints, the frequency of the articles suggests that they should provide a reasonable proxy for the issues in which these institutions have been more or less involved.

I analyzed the data with Structural Topic Models (STM), an unsupervised method of identifying topics in a set of documents. More details about the analysis are provided in the chapter appendix. I used the models to estimate the percentage of articles that addressed foreign policy and security issues, domestic policy issues, or other (procedural and ceremonial) issues. Figure 4.2 shows these percentages for the monarchy and parliament, illustrating how King Abdullah focuses far more on foreign policy and security issues than domestic policy. More than two-thirds of the monarchy articles in both English and Arabic focus on the king's involvement in diplomacy, national security, or the Israeli–Palestinian conflict, while approximately a quarter of the

4.3 Strategic Delegation to Protect the Monarchy

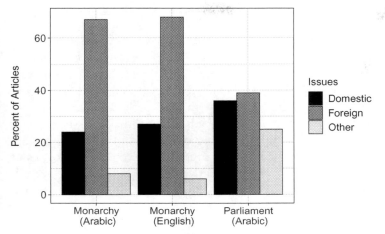

Figure 4.2 Foreign and domestic policy articles with topic models
Note: Aggregate percent of articles in topic models in which "domestic" and "foreign" issues predominate. See the chapter appendix for details on specific topics.

articles address domestic issues such as the economy or development. The story is different for the parliament, where domestic policy and foreign and security policy are evenly split at just under 40 percent of the articles.

It is possible that attention given to these issues on the institutions' websites does not accurately reflect their involvement in these domains. Perhaps the king wishes to present himself as removed from domestic affairs even while he controls all political decisions behind the scenes. Yet, the king's time is limited, and the articles analyzed here were posted nearly every day. It is possible that selection of the articles for the website is biased, but it is also the case that they draw on the king's actual activities from the day in question, suggesting that they do reflect something meaningful about the issues over which the king exercises greater control. The large magnitude of the difference should help to illustrate how Jordan's kings have been less willing to delegate for security and foreign policy issues that are particularly likely to strengthen threats from elites within their regime, and more willing to delegate for economic and social issues that have a high likelihood of angering the masses and for which blame avoidance is particularly important.

4.4 Conclusion

Since the establishment of the Hashemite state, Jordan's kings have ruled as autocrats but have shared power widely with other political elites, particularly in the cabinet and parliament. These institutions play an important role in the country's policy process, and they often steer specific policy decisions, while the monarch keeps his distance. As I have argued in this chapter, this decision-making structure is partly the result of a conscious strategy by Jordan's kings to protect themselves from blame for poor governance outcomes. Recognizing that policy outcomes will frequently be subpar or controversial, particularly with regards to economic and social issues, the kings have often delegated credibly to other political elites to help preserve their popular support.

In illustrating these dynamics of Jordanian politics, the chapter aligns with the observable implications about strategic delegation discussed in Chapter 2. It provides evidence that power sharing varies strategically across issues based on the potential costs of blame and the risks associated with elite threats, and it suggests that influencing attributions is a key motive in this case for why power sharing occurs. The chapter also offers support for important assumptions of the theory, illustrating how delegation occurs in a way that can be costly for the king to overturn, which should make delegation to the government and parliament more credible in the eyes of the public. At the same time, the king also has some capacity to influence the extent of this credibility by appointing prime ministers and other officials with more or less independence and by manipulating the institutional strength of the parliament.

Does this strategy actually have its intended effects? Do many Jordanians perceive institutions other than the king to be involved in and responsible for decision-making, such that they are less likely to blame the monarch for their grievances? Or is the king still seen as such a powerful actor that most Jordanians, at least privately, consider him to be responsible for most important governance outcomes in the country? The next chapter explores these questions by analyzing evidence about how Jordanians attribute responsibility.

4.5 Appendix

As with LDA topic models, topics from the STM models in my analysis reflect a probability mass function over words, such that each

Table 4.1 *Topics from STM analysis*

		Monarchy articles – English			
Topic 1: **12%**	Topic 2: **25%**	Topic 3: **22%**	Topic 4: **15%**	Topic 5: **21%**	Topic 6: **6%**
Domestic (Politics)	Foreign (Diplomacy)	Foreign (Palestine)	Domestic (Economic)	Foreign (Security)	Mix (Meetings)
will	region	palestinian	project	princ	minist
reform	countri	peac	will	royal	royal
nation	develop	effort	develop	hussein	court
govern	cooper	arab	sector	forc	prime
polit	two	support	educ	visit	attend
countri	meet	isra	plan	arm	meet
peopl	discuss	region	invest	receiv	chief
elect	econom	intern	govern	saudi	ambassador
challeng	bilater	iraq	provid	high	foreign
law	relat	stress	implement	militari	director
		Monarchy articles – Arabic			
Topic 1: **9%**	Topic 2: **27%**	Topic 3: **15%**	Topic 4: **24%**	Topic 5: **16%**	Topic 6: **8%**
Domestic (Economic)	Foreign (Diplomacy)	Domestic (Development)	Foreign (Palestine)	Foreign (Security)	Ceremonial (Religion)
aQtSad	rys	kwm	flsTyn	rys	aslam
astUmar	laQ	wTn	dwl	Qad	Qal
alm	bld	mwaTn	slam	msl	alm
QTa	smw	mafZ	rys	amn	allh

Table 4.1 *(cont.)*

Monarchy articles – Arabic					
Topic 1: **9%** Domestic (Economic)	Topic 2: **27%** Foreign (Diplomacy)	Topic 3: **15%** Domestic (Development)	Topic 4: **24%** Foreign (Palestine)	Topic 5: **16%** Foreign (Security)	Topic 6: **8%** Ceremonial (Religion)
dwl	ywm	mjls	jhwd	allh	dwl
Wrk	dwl	dktwr	mnTQ	ywm	slam
mjal	amyr	Kdm	lQa	haWm	dyn
KaS	zyar	mal	asrayl	wTn	syas
mnTQ	wzra	rys	akd	alA	mslm
tjar	mbaU	tlym	raQ	mjls	wTn

Parliament articles – Arabic					
Topic 1: **15%** Foreign (Security)	Topic 2: **17%** Domestic (Development)	Topic 3: **4%** Procedure (Names)	Topic 4: **19%** Domestic (Economic)	Topic 5: **24%** Foreign (Diplomacy)	Topic 6: **21%** Procedure (General)
wTn	dktwr	mmd	QTa	dwl	ljn
syas	alam	abw	ljn	rys	Qan
Qal	mdyr	amd	kwm	laQ	ajtma
amn	Qan	mSTfA	aQtSad	mnTQ	mWrw
jlal	rys	Kald	mal	mjal	rys
aslam	tlym	abrahym	Qal	flsTyn	nyab
rys	jam	mmwd	sya	mKtlf	mra
aSla	ljn	mwsA	Wrk	bld	ywm
kan	Kdm	allh	astUmar	akd	Warkan
arhab	atSal	iyn	zra	lQa	lsn

4.5 Appendix

topic features a certain probability for the appearance of each specific word (Grimmer and Stewart 2013; Roberts et al. 2019). In Jordan, for instance, a topic about the Arab–Israeli conflict might be expected to feature higher probabilities for words such as *Palestinian* and *peace*. These topics are constructed by the model based on the manner in which words cluster together in documents; however, one downside of these models is that the analyst must personally determine the number of topics for the model to discover. For this analysis, I set 6 topics after reading the documents and making my own determination about the number of topics that seemed to exist in the data, but the results are similar if setting a different number of topics.

I used the *stm* package to analyze the documents, stemming the Arabic documents with the package arabicStemR (Nielsen 2017). I removed standard stopwords and several extra stopwords for cleaner topics. For the monarchy topic model in English, I removed king, majesty, Abdullah, ii, said, also, al, Jordan, and bin. For the monarchy topic model in Arabic, I removed malak, Abdullah, jallal, jallalt, al-urdun, bin, and thani. For the parliament topic model in Arabic, I removed al-urdun, majlis, bin, nuwab, naib, barlaman, dowla, and malak. The ten most prominent stemmed words from the topics in the three models are displayed in Table 4.1. While the topic model assumes that each document is a mixture of topics, I can provide an overview of the issue domains that take up the most time of the monarchy and parliament by classifying each document to the topic that it features most prominently. I use this procedure to determine the percentages in Figure 4.2. The percentages for the six individual topics are displayed in Table 4.1.

5 | How Jordanians Attribute Responsibility

When Hani al-Mulki became prime minister of Jordan in 2016, he confronted a daunting economic situation defined by anemic growth and a skyrocketing debt-to-GDP ratio. Al-Mulki responded by pledging to pursue austerity, and in January 2018 his government passed a budget that helped to slow the rising debt by increasing taxes and reducing subsidies (Sowell 2018). Unsurprisingly, these policies proved unpopular, and small but persistent protests plagued the government throughout the first half of the year. When al-Mulki's cabinet proposed further tax hikes in May, the country erupted. Mass protests led by trade unions and opposition activists clogged the streets of Amman in the first week of June, and the demonstrators demanded that al-Mulki resign and the government withdraw the bill. After a week of unrest, the king dismissed the prime minister and replaced him with the popular education minister, Omar al-Razzaz. Yet the new prime minister faced the same problems as the old one: There was little doubt that Jordan would need additional revenues, even as the economy continued to stagnate. Bowing to these pressures, al-Razzaz eventually succeeded in raising taxes.

The June 2018 protests were one more iteration of unrest triggered by a decade of economic stagnation in Jordan. Did the king's reputation suffer irreparable harm in these years as a result of the dismal economic situation? Or did Jordan's successive governments absorb much of the blame, while the king's support remained relatively stable? This chapter addresses these questions by exploring whether power sharing by the monarchy shapes how Jordanians attribute responsibility for their grievances. Do they perceive ministers in the cabinet, along with members of parliament, as relevant decision-makers who should be credited with or blamed for important policy decisions? And do the public's attributions vary across issues based on the extent of the king's involvement in those domains, as the theory would expect?

146

5.1 What Elites and Activists Say

To study these questions, I first use my interviews to consider how opposition elites talk about the king privately, showing that they often absolve him of responsibility even when there are few strategic incentives to do so. This dynamic suggests that delegation can limit the king's exposure to blame even among Jordan's most politically-aware and opposition-inclined citizens. I then turn to polling data from an original survey with YouGov and nationally representative surveys from the Arab Barometer to illustrate that Jordanians generally attribute responsibility for policymaking to the government and parliament. This finding aligns with the theory's expectation that when credible delegation takes place, citizens of authoritarian regimes will perceive actors other than the autocrat as important contributors to the decision-making process. Using this same survey data, I also show evidence that is consistent with delegation helping the king to maintain his public approval, but more so for domestic policies than issues of foreign affairs or national security where the monarchy is more directly involved in determining policies. These patterns also reflect the theory's expectations that autocrats can protect their reputations by sharing power and that these advantages will be stronger as the credibility of this power sharing increases. I end the chapter by utilizing a novel Facebook advertising experiment to reinforce these findings with additional evidence that the king retains popular support and that delegation limits his exposure to blame.

5.1 What Elites and Activists Say

Conversations with Jordanian elites sympathetic to the country's reformist and opposition currents suggest that governing institutions outside the monarchy often absorb blame instead of the king. Even many of these politically sophisticated individuals frequently expressed the view that government officials, but not King Abdullah, were to blame for the continuation of the most problematic aspects of the political system and an inability to implement successful political and economic reforms. For instance, a charismatic member of parliament involved in one of Jordan's few opposition-oriented political parties voiced the belief that "the king is here as a reformist, and then there are powers pushing back who would lose everything in a democratic state." Another prominent opposition activist suggested that governing institutions outside the monarchy are unwilling to implement reforms

148 *How Jordanians Attribute Responsibility*

and that, as a result, "In many cases only the king, when he interferes, can change things." While criticizing the parliament for not conducting active oversight of the government, a scholar at a reform-oriented NGO argued that:

...if you look at political will, his majesty the king has tried to push the members of parliament to do more monitoring and oversight in different occasions. The political will is there. The king said just a few weeks ago at the university that students should pressure their members of parliament from the bottom up, while he works from the top down.

One opposition-oriented politician described how – when he was in government – his reform proposals had been blocked by the GID and other prominent conservatives in the government, who had gone to the king and pressured him to back away from the plans. Even one of the country's most critical opposition activists conceded that "The king maybe wants reform to happen," though he clarified that "he [the king] has a very different vision of what that means." That activist then partially absolved the king for not acting on whatever reformist inclinations he might have, blaming the GID for obstructing them. Said the activist: "The king can say what he wants [about reform], but the GID will say ... 'hell will break loose,' and so he will respond to the apparatus instead of pushing forward his mandate. He could order them to do something, but that's not what the relationship is." Another journalist who has been an outspoken proponent of press freedoms expressed the view that restrictions on these freedoms are the fault of governing institutions other than the monarchy, because "The palace has a more open mind than the government and parliament [on freedom of the press]."

What all of these comments share is a tendency to direct most of the blame at the government, parliament, and bureaucracy, while giving the king a pass. Of course, given the penalties for speaking out against the king, not all of these statements can be taken at face value. However, there was little incentive for these interview subjects to affirm the king's lack of responsibility. The interviews were anonymous, and they could have avoided mentioning the king at all. Yet such quotes came up frequently in the interviews, even among opposition-leaning figures like these.

That is not to say that everyone directed blame away from the king – critics of the monarchy definitely exist. As one notable said,

5.1 What Elites and Activists Say

"We have a law that can put you in jail for up to three years for saying something bad about the king ... I won't sit here and say he's wonderful, though, because he's not." Several interview subjects made similar comments, while stating directly that they held Abdullah responsible for the country's most difficult problems. Some of them felt that the public agreed with their view that delegation was meaningless and the palace controlled all. As they saw it, whenever anyone publicly attributed responsibility to the government and parliament, it was because they feared the costs of repression. One opposition politician who had served in parliament articulated this view wryly, stating that "If people are blaming the parliament, it's because they're scared. If you swear on God, you're forgiven the first time ... the second time they put you in prison for three months. But [if you swear] on the king, [you get] three years in prison [the first time]." Similarly, a notable known for their opposition views claimed that "The people know that the whole responsibility of what is happening in the country is due to the king and his way of ruling."

However, other leading opposition figures associated with activist circles expressed frustration because of their belief that much of the public views delegation to the government and parliament as genuine and attributes responsibility accordingly. A prominent activist claimed the following about the power-sharing relationship between the monarchy and these other institutions:

It's rhetoric and bullshit and people buy into it. The government is supposed to work on long-term policy ... But in fact the government is very low on the rungs of power. And the lower house of parliament, these guys are on the street. They are the ultimate pawns in the entire game ... It all serves the purpose to distract from what is happening ... And it works. People buy into it.

Another well-known opposition activist spoke similarly, stating that:

Usually, people who get involved in politics start by complaining about the mayor, and then the parliament, and then the government, and then the policies, and then the system, and then maybe they get to the king ... The problem in Jordan is that people think they are aware, but they are really not aware. They don't understand the political system. They complain about the government's policies, and then you ask who chose the government, and they don't want to accept that it's the king's fault.

One interpretation of this quote is that even though Jordanians understand that the king chooses the government, many of them also believe delegation is credible, and so they do not necessarily view the king as responsible for the government's policies.

The interview subjects cited here should have been some of the most likely elites in Jordan to claim that people merely blame the government because they are afraid of repression, not because they actually believe the government holds some responsibility for what occurs. Many of them are active in trying to build support for agendas that include substantially reforming the political system to reduce the king's powers, so they even had incentives to play up their popular support by dismissing the effectiveness of delegation as a blame avoidance strategy. The fact that many of them appear to believe instead that delegation influences the public's attributions suggests that the strategy may well be effective at accomplishing this goal.

5.2 Surveying Jordanian Public Opinion

This section draws on two opinion polls from Jordan. The first is an original, online survey that I conducted through the survey firm YouGov in the spring of 2018. The sample of 500 is not nationally representative, but it is intended to be representative of the country's urban population. Because these groups have traditionally been more opposed to the monarchy, they provide a useful sample for this project.[1] In addition, the online survey is less exposed to the government's fairly stringent censorship of survey questions, which allowed me to ask more detailed questions on these topics than might normally be conducted face-to-face or by telephone in the country (though still nothing about the king directly). Following a review of the YouGov results, I then turn to analysis of several questions from the nationally-representative Arab Barometer surveys in Jordan, which has a broader temporal coverage with four waves between 2006 and 2016.

---

[1] Among Jordanian respondents, the sample is 50 percent male and 50 percent female. Approximately 55 percent of respondents live in Amman, compared to 42 percent of the population at the time the survey was implemented. Approximately 66 percent of respondents were between the ages of 18 and 40, compared to approximately 60 percent of the adult population.

5.2 Surveying Jordanian Public Opinion

5.2.1 YouGov Survey

The survey implemented with YouGov was designed to probe whether the Jordanian public generally considers the government and parliament to be important contributors to the policy process, or whether these institutions are viewed as relatively powerless figureheads next to the royal court.[2] I also explore whether these attributions of responsibility vary by issue area in a way that aligns with the credibility of delegation from the palace, such that the government and parliament are less likely to be perceived as responsible for issues related to national security and foreign policy. In addition, I use a proxy of support for the monarchy to provide evidence consistent with the expectation that Jordanians who perceive the government and parliament to be more responsible for policy decisions are more supportive of the king.

The survey first asked respondents to rate the extent to which they believed the government and parliament to be responsible for several important policy domains, with ten equal to full responsibility and one equal to no responsibility.[3] The average ratings for each domain are displayed in Figure 5.1. Two patterns are apparent, both of which are consistent with theoretical expectations. First, in general, the averages are fairly high, suggesting that Jordanians do perceive these institutions to be meaningful actors in the policy process. For the government, the average is 8.7 for taxes and subsidies, 8.6 for economic development, and 8.1 for education, whereas for parliament they are 8.1 for taxes and subsidies, 7.6 for development, and 7.3 for education. Second, for both the government and parliament, the averages are lower for foreign and military affairs than economic and social affairs, with the exception of women's rights. The average response for foreign affairs is 7.8 for the government and 6.6 for the parliament, and the average for military affairs is 7.4 for the government and 6.7 for the parliament. These differences align with the credibility of delegation from

---

[2] I limit the sample to the 439 citizens for the results presented here, but the results are the same when including all 500 residents.

[3] Exact wording: "On a scale of 1 to 10, where 1 equals no responsibility and 10 equals full responsibility, please tell us how much you consider the prime minister and his cabinet/parliament to be responsible for state policies related to the following issues." Grid 1: Taxes and Subsidies, Education, Military Affairs. Grid 2: Women's Rights, Foreign Affairs, Economic Development.

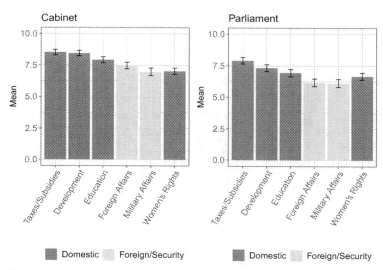

Figure 5.1 Perceptions of cabinet and parliamentary responsibility
Notes: Figure displays mean rating of cabinet and parliamentary responsibility for each policy domain on a ten point scale among Jordanian respondents in the YouGov survey.

the monarchy across these various domains, insofar as King Abdullah has been relatively less involved in domestic policy issues.

Next, respondents were prompted with three unpopular policy outcomes and asked to identify the political actor most responsible for them.[4] Respondents were asked to attribute responsibility for recent tax increases and subsidy cuts (which had been implemented one month prior to the survey), high youth unemployment, and maintaining relations with Israel. For all three questions, respondents could blame the government (specified as the prime minister and his cabinet), the parliament, or the United States. For the two economic policies, they could also blame the IMF, and for the Israel outcome, they could also blame the Jordanian security agencies. In addition, respondents could choose to answer that none of the above were most responsible, or that they did not know. These latter options were intended to provide an indirect method for assessing whether many Jordanians believe the monarchy to be responsible for these outcomes. If the king was the

---

[4] Exact wording of question: "Who is most responsible for..."

5.2 Surveying Jordanian Public Opinion

obvious choice to be blamed, then many respondents should have gravitated toward these answers, which provided a safe outlet for signaling this belief.

The results are displayed in Figure 5.2. The combined percentage answering don't know or none was not the highest choice for any of the three questions. Respondents were most likely to blame the government for the subsidy cuts and tax increases, at 42 percent. The next most popular choice was the IMF, at 28 percent, and then

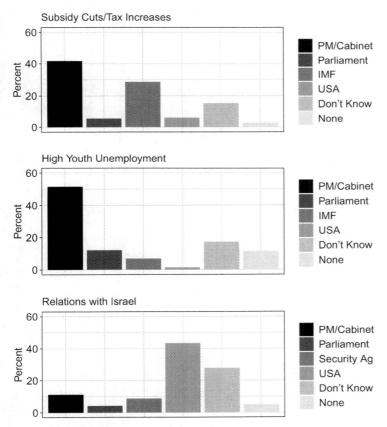

Figure 5.2 Who is most responsible for...
Note: Figure displays percent of respondents in YouGov survey identifying the relevant institution (prime minister and cabinet; parliament; IMF; security agencies; USA; don't know; or none) as being "most responsible" for the labeled policy.

154   How Jordanians Attribute Responsibility

Table 5.1 *YouGov survey attribution questions*

	Strongly agree	Agree	Neither	Disagree	Strongly disagree
PM leads government, is responsible for mistakes.	34%	35%	21%	6%	3%
Economy would improve with more competent PM.	35%	34%	19%	5%	7%
Ministers accountable for policies of their ministries.	51%	33%	14%	1%	1%
MPs could improve policies, but they do not try.	40%	36%	15%	4%	6%

none/don't know, at 18 percent. For high youth unemployment, 51 percent chose the government, followed by 28 percent for none/don't know. And for relations with Israel, 43 percent selected the United States, with 33 percent choosing none/don't know. These responses suggest that delegating economic policies to the government does direct blame away from the king, insofar as many Jordanians are willing to attribute responsibility to the government even when given the option to indicate safely that the king is at fault. Furthermore, the fact that the government received a low percentage of responses for the Israel question, and that this question also demonstrated a slightly higher percentage saying none/don't know, provides support for the claim that shifting blame to other domestic institutions is harder for issues such as Israel and Palestine, where the monarchy exerts more control.[5]

Table 5.1 reports results for an additional set of questions meant to gauge the extent to which Jordanians consider the prime minister, ministers, and parliament to be consequential political actors who hold responsibility for poor policy outcomes. First, approximately 70 percent of respondents agreed with statements that "the prime minister leads Jordan's government, and he is responsible whenever the government makes a serious mistake," and "Jordan's economic situation would improve if the country had a more competent prime minister."

---

[5] However, as indicated by the high percentage of respondents choosing the United States on this question, redirecting blame toward foreigners can provide another option in some cases.

5.2 *Surveying Jordanian Public Opinion* 155

These percentages are inconsistent with a widespread view of the prime minister as little more than a mouthpiece for the king; instead, they suggest that the public attributes responsibility for poor outcomes to the prime minister.

Likewise, more than 80 percent of respondents also agreed that "government ministers in Jordan should be held accountable for the policies of their ministries," suggesting that ministers are not viewed as mere figureheads but rather as officials who are responsible for what their ministries do. The last survey question addresses parliament. A common refrain among Jordanian political analysts is that the public holds parliament responsible for policy failures because even though the institution has the ability to wield significant political power and check unpopular actions taken by the government, it decides to pursue its own parochial interests instead. To gauge whether this view is widely held, I asked respondents whether they agreed with the statement that "members of parliament in Jordan have the ability to improve policies and hold the government accountable, but they do not try hard enough to represent their constituents effectively." More than 75 percent of respondents agreed.

The preceding questions provide evidence that Jordanians hold the government and parliament responsible for unpopular policy outcomes. However, it is possible that the public does not distinguish between these actors and the monarchy but perceives the regime as a unitary actor. In this case, they would simultaneously attribute blame to the king. To evaluate whether blame directed at the government and parliament protects the monarchy, I assess whether Jordanians who attribute more responsibility to these institutions are more likely to show higher levels of agreement with a statement that proxies for supporting the king. This statement was "a just national leader can protect common people like me from a corrupt political system." Though indirect, it provides a reasonable proxy in the Jordanian context because there are no figures other than the king whom it could be referencing, and because the king presents himself in this way.[6]

For the independent variable of attributing more responsibility to the government and parliament for unpopular policies, I constructed

---

[6] A Jordanian political analyst expressed surprise that the question could be asked because they thought it was clearly referencing the king. Approximately 70 percent of respondents agreed or strongly agreed with the statement.

Table 5.2 *Perceptions of responsibility and support for national leader*

	National leader scale	National leader scale	National leader binary	National leader binary
Responsibility Index	0.093***	0.090***	0.032***	0.028***
	(0.017)	(0.017)	(0.007)	(0.008)
Controls		✓		✓
Observations	439	439	439	439

*** $p < 0.001$, ** $p < 0.01$, * $p < 0.05$, † <0.10

Controls include: Age, Gender, Income, Marital and Employment Status, Amman Resident.

an index from the questions in the previous two subsections using principal components analysis (PCA).[7] The index has a high degree of reliability, with a Cronbach's alpha of 0.88. If blaming the government and parliament does not protect the king, this index should be negatively correlated or uncorrelated with the proxy for support of the monarchy. However, if the index is positively correlated with support for the monarchy, it would be consistent with a dynamic in which blame directed at these other institutions permits the king to keep his reputation intact, or perhaps even improve it at their expense.

The results are displayed in Table 5.2. The first column shows the bivariate relationship between the index and the scalar outcome for the monarchy proxy. The second column includes demographic control variables from the YouGov survey, including age, gender, income, residency in Amman, and marital and employment status, that likely correlate with attitudes toward the monarchy and other political actors. The third and fourth columns show the same specifications, with a binary construction for the dependent variable. The models demonstrate a strong, positive relationship between viewing the government and parliament as more responsible for unpopular policy outcomes and expressing more faith in the ability of a just, national leader who can defend the people against a corrupt political system. In all four columns, the coefficients are statistically significant at 0.001. The relationship is substantively meaningful as well: A one standard

---

[7] The index was constructed with questions from Figures 5.1 and 5.2 and Table 5.1. See the Appendix for additional details.

5.2 Surveying Jordanian Public Opinion

deviation increase in the index is associated with a one-quarter standard deviation increase in agreement with the dependent variable. This analysis does not rule out the possibility of reverse causation or omitted variable bias; however, this pattern is consistent with delegation from the palace helping to protect the king's reputation.

5.2.2 Arab Barometer Survey

I now turn to the nationally representative Arab Barometer to provide further evidence that Jordanians attribute decision-making responsibility to institutions other than the palace and that these attributions help to protect the king from blame. First, I use a question from waves 1 (2006) and 2 (2010), in which respondents were asked to evaluate parliament's role in determining economic, social, and foreign policies.[8] As in the YouGov survey, Jordanian respondents appeared to attribute meaningful responsibility to the parliament. Results are displayed in Figure 5.3. A majority of respondents said that parliament played a big or medium role in all three policy domains. However, consistent with variation in the credibility of delegation across issue domains, these percentages were lowest for foreign policy, with just over 50 percent of respondents answering in this way. For economic and social issues, more than 60 percent of respondents believed that parliament had a big or medium role in shaping policy decisions in both waves of the survey.

Data from waves 3 (2012) and 4 (2016) also provide an additional, indirect test of delegation's ability to protect the king from blame. Because of restrictions on asking survey questions about the monarchy in Jordan, the Arab Barometer does not ask directly about King Abdullah or royal rule more generally. As a result, to acquire a proxy indicative of such support, I exploit the fact that a more democratic Jordan would mean even greater responsibility for the government and parliament, whereas a less democratic Jordan would mean more direct policymaking responsibility in the hands of the king and royal court. In talking about the public's frustration with parliament, an editor at a major Jordanian newspaper highlighted this dynamic, noting that "At least half [of the public] would say we don't need a parliament [at

---

[8] Exact wording: "To what extent do you think Parliament has a role in deciding the following policies: economic policy, social policy, foreign policy."

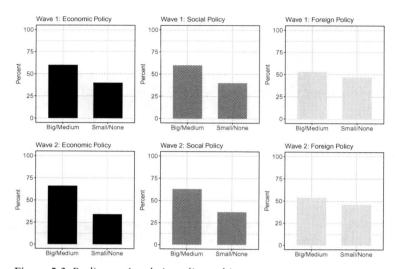

Figure 5.3 Parliament's role in policymaking
Note: Figure displays percent of respondents from waves 1 and 2 of the Arab Barometer who perceive parliament to play a "big" or "medium" role in the labeled policy domains as opposed to a "small" role or none at all.

all]. They would say they want a benign dictatorship with the king as tribal chief." I therefore use respondents' answers to a question about whether democracy is suitable for Jordan to gauge whether they prefer the king to exercise greater control over policy, or if they prefer the government and parliament to exercise greater control. If they believe democracy to be less suitable for Jordan, it is plausible to assume they would support more direct rule by the king, and if they believe democracy to be more suitable for Jordan, it should imply support for more policy influence in the hands of the government and parliament.

Next, I use a variety of questions in which respondents evaluate the state's performance and policy positions to measure the intensity of their grievances with state policy. I examine questions related to both domestic policy and foreign/national security policy. For domestic policy, respondents were asked about the government's economic performance, as well as the state of the economy more generally. In addition, they were asked to rate the government's performance on employment, inequality, healthcare, prices, education, and limiting corruption. For foreign/national security policy, respondents were asked about the government's performance on security matters and their

5.2 *Surveying Jordanian Public Opinion* 159

level of concern about terrorism in the country. They were also asked whether they support a two state solution to the Israeli–Palestinian conflict (which is the government's position), whether they support the treaty with Israel, whether they want weaker security and economic relations with Israel, and whether they want weaker economic relations with the United States.

I then analyze the relationship between higher grievances and views of democracy's suitability for Jordan to assess whether frustrated respondents are more likely to blame the king or the government and parliament. If Jordanians with stronger grievances view democracy as less suitable for their country, it would imply that they blame the government and parliament for the country's problems and want the king to rule more directly as a result. Furthermore, if these relationships are indicative of blame attributions, they should be more pronounced for the domestic policy issues compared to the foreign and security policy issues, since the monarchy more openly determines Jordan's policies in these latter issue domains.

I include some controls in the regression models to account for the most obvious concerns with omitted variable bias. First, results could be driven by a general preference for authoritarian government rather than views of the relative responsibility of different governing institutions. I therefore control for whether respondents view democracy as the best form of government in the abstract, as well as their self-reported willingness to trust others. I control for urban residency as a rough proxy to account for political differences between Jordanians of Palestinian and East Bank descent, and I control for education, internet usage, and self-reported confusion with politics to control for political knowledge. I also control for age. However, the results are the same when no control variables are included, and they are robust to model specifications with a number of additional controls as well.

The results for the domestic policies are shown in the left panel of Figure 5.4, and the results for the foreign and security policies are shown in the figure's right panel. Each coefficient reflects a different model in which suitability of democracy in Jordan is regressed on attitudes toward the relevant state policy.[9] For the domestic policies, there

---

[9] See the Appendix for tables showing the number of observations for each model and the Arab Barometer waves from which data are taken for each model. Control variables not shown.

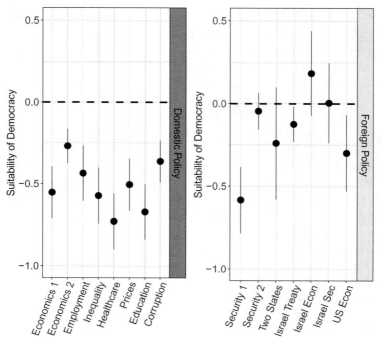

Figure 5.4 Policy grievances and suitability of democracy
Note: Each coefficient is taken from a different model in which perceived suitability of democracy is regressed on attitudes toward the relevant policy. The left panel includes domestic policies, while the right panel includes foreign and security policies. Models also include control variables not shown. Negative coefficients indicate that stronger dissatisfaction with state policies is associated with weaker beliefs of democracy's suitability for Jordan. Responses are from waves 3 and 4 of the Arab Barometer.

is a consistent and strong relationship between expressing greater dissatisfaction with state policies and viewing democracy as less suitable for Jordan. The coefficients for all of these policy variables are negative and statistically significant at 0.001. This pattern is consistent with the "democratic" institutions of the government and parliament absorbing blame for these frustrations rather than the monarchy, such that openly autocratic rule by the king would be preferred by individuals who hold these grievances more strongly.

On the other hand, the pattern for the foreign and national security policies is much less pronounced. Two of the coefficients are

5.3 Evidence from a Facebook Ad Experiment

statistically significant at 0.05, and one is statistically significant at 0.01. Two other coefficients are negative but statistically insignificant, and the remaining two coefficients are positive. This inconsistency between the domestic and foreign/security issues aligns with the fact that the king delegates much less credibly for policies related to the latter. As a result, he should absorb more blame for their unpopularity.

5.3 Evidence from a Facebook Ad Experiment

I now turn to a Facebook advertisement experiment to acquire a more direct – though still relative – measure of support for King Abdullah. I implemented the experiment in three waves to provide temporal variation and validation for the measure, and I aligned these waves with specific political events and nationally representative opinion polling to strengthen external validity.[10] The results provide experimental evidence that King Abdullah is relatively more popular than the prime minister and parliament, which would be expected if Jordanians differentiate between these actors when they attribute responsibility and do not express anger at the regime uniformly. It also provides suggestive but nonexperimental evidence that King Abdullah's approval did not decline following a controversial decision to raise taxes, but instead remained steady or increased over the course of the three waves, whereas approval of the government and parliament decreased at this time. This pattern is consistent with power sharing helping the king to mitigate his exposure to blame for tax increases.

5.3.1 Design

Facebook advertisements reach a broad segment of the public in many countries. This coverage includes Jordan, where advertising on all Facebook platforms had – at the time the study was implemented – the potential to reach more than 3,000,000 individuals out of a population of approximately 10,000,000. Furthermore, Facebook advertisements are relatively cheap, making them accessible to researchers. Facebook's advertising platform also includes a split test feature, which allows advertisers to measure the effectiveness of their ads experimentally. The

---

[10] The study was approved by Stanford IRB (protocol 44188).

Figure 5.5 Facebook ad for the king
Note: Figure displays the "king" ad placed on Facebook to measure support for the king. The "prime minister" and "parliament" ads were identical except for the text identifying the relevant institution and its website.

advertisers create two or more versions of an advertisement, and Facebook then assigns the ads to randomly constructed, nonoverlapping treatment groups.[11]

I created ads associated with three of Jordan's governing institutions – the king, the prime minister, and the parliament. Each ad asked viewers to click on it for the purpose of demonstrating support for the respective institution. The ads were designed to be identical except for the name of the institution (see Figure 5.5).[12] Viewers interested in additional information about the ads could click on a tab to see the sponsoring Facebook page, which I designed to state clearly that the ads were being used for research purposes.[13] For my target audience, the split test included Facebook users living in Jordan who had Arabic as their profile language and who were using a desktop or laptop. This audience consisted of tens of thousands of individual profiles with some probability of viewing one of the ads.

By comparing the click rates for the different ads, I argue that it is possible to develop a measure of popular support for the king *relative* to popular support for the prime minister and parliament at that time. It is almost certain that some Jordanians clicked on the ads for reasons other than showing support – for example, out of curiosity. However, as long as these other factors are distributed evenly across the three political actors, random assignment of the ads means that it

---

[11] For more information, see Facebook's explanation here: www.facebook.com/business/help/1738164643098669
[12] When users clicked on the ad, they were then redirected to the official website of the monarchy, the prime ministry, or the parliament.
[13] Data on the page indicate only a handful of page views during the time of running the ads, meaning that the results could not be confounded by potential participants figuring out the purpose of the study.

5.3 Evidence from a Facebook Ad Experiment

Table 5.3 *Ad demographics – gender and age*

	N	Male	Female	18–24	25–34	35–44	45–54	55–64	65+
Wave 1	84,272	66%	33%	35%	31%	16%	11%	5%	3%
Wave 2	82,160	63%	36%	34%	29%	17%	11%	5%	3%
Wave 3	84,352	63%	37%	35%	30%	18%	11%	4%	2%

should be possible to interpret the click rates as a measure of relative support among the large population of Facebook-active Jordanians. In addition, the Center for Strategic Studies (CSS) at the University of Jordan implements regular opinion polling in Jordan about public support for the prime minister, his cabinet, and the parliament. These polls have been conducted since the 1990s, and the regime views them as an important metric for evaluating the performance of the government and parliament, suggesting that they can be trusted as a reliable measure. As a result, I attempt to provide a rough estimate of actual support for the king by benchmarking the relative results from the ads to this opinion polling data.

The first wave of the split test was active from June 12, 2018, to June 16, 2018. The ads reached 84,272 Facebook profiles in the specified target audience, and they received a total of 1,799 clicks (2.1%). The second wave was active from September 26, 2018, to September 30, 2018. The ads reached 82,160 profiles, and they were clicked on by 1,311 individuals (1.6%). Finally, the third wave was active from July 22, 2019 to July 26, 2019. The ads reached 84,352 profiles and were clicked on by 2,142 individuals (2.5%). These click rates are fairly high, as marketing data suggest that the average click rate across industries was approximately 0.9% around the time of the study.[14] Gender and age breakdowns of the profiles that viewed the ads in each of the three waves can be seen in Table 5.3. The sample is skewed toward male and younger Jordanians. Note that it is possible for the same profiles to be included in the different waves.

The political context in which the ads ran relates to the anecdote about Prime Minister Hani al-Mulki mentioned at the start of the chapter, and it has important implications for the experiment

---

[14] See: www.wordstream.com/blog/ws/2017/02/28/facebook-advertising-benchmarks.

164   *How Jordanians Attribute Responsibility*

Table 5.4 *Timeline and political context*

Wave 1	
May 30:	Protests begin over proposed income tax law.
June 4:	Hani al-Mulki resigns as prime minister; replaced by Omar al-Razzaz.
June 7:	Omar al-Razzaz withdraws tax bill.
June 12–June 16:	Wave 1 of Facebook Study
June 26–July 2:	CSS poll on approval of al-Razzaz government.
Wave 2	
Sept. 25:	Al-Razzaz government sends similar tax bill to parliament.
Sept. 24–Sept. 30:	CSS poll on approval of al-Razzaz government.
Sept. 26–Sept. 30:	Wave 2 of Facebook study.
Wave 3	
Jun. 11–Jun. 16:	CSS poll on approval of al-Razzaz government.
Jul. 22–Jul. 26:	Wave 3 of Facebook study.

(see Table 5.4 for a concise timeline). In late May and early June 2018, mass protests erupted in Jordan against a proposal to increase income taxes. Due to the magnitude and persistence of the protests, King Abdullah dissolved the government of al-Mulki, who had taken the lead on negotiating the reforms and became a focal point of blame for the demonstrators. The king then appointed the Minister of Education, Omar al-Razzaz, as the new prime minister. Al-Razzaz was popular as a minister, and he had a reputation for being both honest and inclined toward reformist currents. He withdrew the proposed tax bill three days after his appointment. The first wave of the study was conducted during this period. However, despite the dismissal of al-Mulki, Jordan continued to find itself in a difficult place financially, and it could not abandon the efforts to reform the tax code. Al-Razzaz and his government eventually conceded that a similar tax bill would need to be introduced, and they sent a draft to the parliament on September 25, to the apparent dismay of much of the public (Al-Khalidi 2018). The second wave was run at this moment in an effort to analyze whether blame for the reintroduced tax bill was being attributed to the new prime minister, or whether it was being attributed to the king. Finally, as a further check on the validity of the click rates as a measure of

5.3 Evidence from a Facebook Ad Experiment

relative approval, I ran the experiment for a third time approximately one year after al-Razzaz's appointment.

I expected that click rates for the prime minister and parliament would be lower than the click rate for the king, which would align with the claim that the king is *relatively* more popular than these other political elites. I also expected that the click rates for the prime minister and parliament would decline relative to the click rate for the king across the first and second wave of the study, if these former institutions were absorbing blame for the reintroduction of the unpopular tax bill in September 2018. Furthermore, I expected that benchmarking the levels of relative support to actual opinion polling would imply meaningful public approval of the king across the three waves, suggesting that he has been successful at mitigating his exposure to blame for the country's decade of poor economic performance. To be clear about the study's design, it allows for a causally-identified test of this first expectation regarding *relative* support for the king, but not for the latter two expectations, where I am comparing results between experiments over time and incorporating descriptive survey data in the analysis.

5.3.2 Results

The results from the three waves are displayed in Figure 5.6, where the y-axis shows the click rate for the parliament and prime minister relative to the click rate for the king ad, which has been standardized at 1.[15] The results show that the parliament was the least supported actor in all three waves, whereas the prime minister was the most supported in the first wave and the king was the most supported in the second and third waves following a steep, relative decline in the click rate for the prime minister ad.

---

[15] The baseline click rates were as follows: In the first wave, the click rate for the king ad was 2.07 percent, the click rate for the parliament ad was 1.57 percent, and the click rate for the prime minister ad was 2.87 percent. In the second wave, the click rate for the king ad was 2.3 percent, the click rate for the parliament ad was 0.9 percent, and the click rate for the prime minister ad was 1.7 percent. Finally, in the third wave, the overall click rate increased by approximately 1 percent point for each ad, with the relative patterns mirroring the second wave: The click rate for the king ad was 3.5 percent, the click rate for the parliament ad was 1.9 percent, and the click rate for the prime minister ad was 2.5 percent.

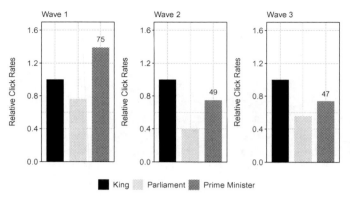

Figure 5.6 Facebook ad click rate results
Note: Figure displays click rates for king ads relative to parliament and prime minister ads in waves 1, 2, and 3 of the Facebook ad experiment. Numbers above the prime minister bar are the percentage of Jordanians approving of the prime minister at the time each wave of the experiment was implemented.

Nationally representative polling about support for the prime minister as he took office helps to benchmark the results against actual public attitudes. According to a poll conducted by CSS between June 26 and July 2, 2018, initial public support for al-Razzaz as the prime minister was significant, with 69 percent of respondents stating they had confidence in his ability to perform effectively going forward, and 81 percent of respondents stating they had been optimistic about his appointment when the king first announced it in early June. Given that wave 1 of the ad experiment ran from June 12 to June 16, one week after al-Razzaz's appointment and ten days before the implementation of the CSS survey, his support during the experiment can be pegged between 70 and 80 percent with a reasonable degree of confidence.

In the same poll, CSS asked about satisfaction with the performance of the parliament. 31 percent of respondents said they were satisfied with parliament at least to some extent, and 19 percent said they were satisfied to a large or medium extent. These responses suggest support for the parliament at the time of the experiment can be pegged between 20 and 30 percent. If we assume that differences in click rates track to differences in public opinion linearly, we can calculate a rough estimate of popular support for King Abdullah between 40 and 50 percent at the

5.3 Evidence from a Facebook Ad Experiment 167

time the first wave was implemented.[16] Given that many democratic leaders struggle to maintain similar approval ratings after just a few years of governance, not to mention the fact that the experiment had been conducted after public anger in Jordan resulted in the country's largest demonstrations in years, this estimate suggests the king maintained fairly widespread public approval two decades after coming to power.

Comparing waves 1 and 2 also provides support for the king's ability to protect himself from blame by delegating contentious policies to the government and parliament. After three months of al-Razzaz's government, the prime minister ad no longer achieved a higher click rate than the king ad. These changes in relative click rates suggest that the popularity of al-Razzaz and the parliament, but not the king, may have been harmed by the decision to bring back the tax bill.[17] Conveniently, the second CSS survey on al-Razzaz and his government was conducted at the same time as wave 2 of the experiment, and it reinforces this interpretation of the experiment. The poll shows that confidence in al-Razzaz had fallen to 49 percent of the public. This poll did not ask about the parliament, making it more difficult to benchmark. However, given that the click rate for the king ad was higher than the click rate for the prime minister ad, the results of the poll suggest that King Abdullah's support may have increased slightly over this time period, while the prime minister's support decreased.

The validity of using the split test as a relative measure of support is further reinforced by the results from wave 3. In June 2019, one year after al-Razzaz's appointment, CSS implemented another nationally representative survey that showed the prime minister's approval rating had stabilized and remained at 47 percent. The fact that the ratio of the king and prime minister ads remained nearly identical in waves 2 and 3, and that support for the prime minister did not change, is consistent with the ads offering a reasonable proxy for relative approval of these institutions.

There are four alternative explanations about the relative click rates that would be problematic for my conclusion that the results indicate relatively higher and more stable support for the king. First, the click

---

[16] See the Appendix for a discussion of this calculation.
[17] The popularity of the prime minister and parliament may also have declined due to other decisions made by these institutions in the intervening months.

rates could be random and unrelated to actual support, even in relative terms. Second, the high click rate for the prime minister in the first wave could have resulted from relatively higher curiosity because of his recent appointment. Third, clicks on the king ad could have been driven by fear that noncompliance with the ad's request for support would somehow result in sanctioning by the regime. Fourth, Jordanians may also have been more likely to expect that they would receive a reward for clicking on the king ad. However, I do not believe that any of these explanations are consistent with the results, particularly when observed in the context of the opinion polling.

If the click rates were truly random, it seems unlikely that the parliament would have the lowest click rate in all three waves, and that the relative click rate for al-Razzaz would align with his initially sky-high approval rating and subsequent decline in support. While curiosity may explain some of the higher click rate for the new prime minister ad in the first round, again the opinion polling about initial attitudes toward his appointment suggests that this explanation is unlikely to account for the results fully. Likewise, fear of coercion seems unlikely to explain clicks on the king ad because (1) the king ad did not even achieve the highest click rate in the first wave and because (2) Jordan's political system does not operate in this way. While the regime relies on an effective coercive apparatus, part of its effectiveness stems from its known reliance on targeted rather than indiscriminate repression. It does not seem plausible that Jordanians would see an ad on Facebook and believe their loyalty was being tested based on whether they affirmatively clicked on the ad to show support or not. For similar reasons, it does not appear likely that the pattern can be explained by a stronger hope for receiving patronage as a result of clicking on the king ad. Again, the king ad did not receive the highest click rate in the first wave. In addition, while extensive patronage does flow from the royal court, substantial research on Jordan shows how patronage also comes regularly from the government and parliament.

As a result, I argue that the experiment indicates relatively high and persistent levels of public approval for King Abdullah, despite his long rule and poor performance by the Jordanian government during much of that time. Furthermore, the changes in relative click rates between waves 1 and 2, though not causally-identified, align with the claim that delegating responsibility for these unpopular policies can help to sustain the king's approval by directing blame to the prime minister

5.4 Conclusion 169

and parliament instead. These findings offer additional support for the argument that Jordanians perceive the government and parliament as responsible for policy, which helps to protect the reputation of the king.

5.4 Conclusion

This chapter relies on interviews and public opinion data to provide evidence that the strategy of sharing power over decision-making is effective at protecting the reputation of the Jordanian monarchy. The findings suggest that Jordanian public opinion is nuanced, such that the public attributes more or less responsibility based on the extent to which different political actors and institutions are involved in the policymaking process. The public is not naive; they do not assign no responsibility to the king, but neither do they blame him for everything that occurs in the political system. Jordanians perceive the government and parliament to play an important role in setting policies in addition to the monarchy, and these perceptions appear to align with less blame directed at the king. As expected by the theory, however, these perceptions also vary across issue areas, with Jordanians less likely to attribute responsibility to the government and parliament for issues where the king takes a more direct role in decision-making.

This chapter and Chapter 4 take a relatively static view of power sharing and attributions in Jordan. However, the credibility of delegation by the monarchy has varied throughout the country's history, with the kings sometimes taking a more active role in decision-making and at other times sharing decision-making powers more credibly with others in the regime. Does the monarchy's vulnerability to opposition change over time as the monarch becomes more or less involved in the policy process, as the theory would expect? Or, is support for the monarchy relatively unchanging, which might suggest that delegation has relatively little effect on attitudes toward the king? Furthermore, does the king act strategically in response to these attributions, attempting to change the credibility of delegation over time as the nature of public and elite threats to the monarchy shifts? The following chapter builds on the evidence presented so far by exploring the causes and consequences of this variation for the monarchy's decisions about how to share power and its ability to retain popular support.

5.5 Appendix

5.5.1 YouGov Principal Components Analysis

Table 5.5 lists the principal components from the analysis used to construct the independent variable for Table 5.2 in the chapter. The PCA uses responses to questions from Figures 5.1, 5.2 and Table 5.1. The questions have high internal consistency with a Cronbach's Alpha of 0.88.

5.5.2 Regression Results from Figure 5.4

Table 5.6 displays the coefficients for the domestic issues, and Table 5.7 shows the coefficients for the foreign policy and national security issues. The dependent variable (suitability of democracy) is displayed in the first row for each table, whereas the independent variables (policy attitudes) are shown in the columns.

Table 5.5 *Principal components*

Component	Eigenvalue	Proportion
Component 1	6.49	0.34
Component 2	2.34	0.12
Component 3	1.27	0.07
Component 4	1.05	0.06
Component 5	1.00	0.05
Component 6	0.76	0.04
Component 7	0.71	0.04
Component 8	0.70	0.04
Component 9	0.67	0.04
Component 10	0.63	0.03
Component 11	0.56	0.03
Component 12	0.48	0.03
Component 13	0.44	0.02
Component 14	0.43	0.02
Component 15	0.37	0.02
Component 16	0.33	0.02
Component 17	0.29	0.02
Component 18	0.27	0.01
Component 19	0.22	0.01

Table 5.6 *Domestic policy grievances and suitability of democracy*

	Economic 1	Economics 2	Employment	Inequality	Healthcare	Prices	Education	Corruption
Suitability of	−0.55***	−0.27***	−0.44***	−0.57***	−0.73***	−0.51***	−0.67***	−0.36***
democracy	(0.08)	(0.05)	(0.09)	(0.09)	(0.09)	(0.08)	(0.09)	(0.07)
Controls	✓	✓	✓	✓	✓	✓	✓	✓
Wave 3		✓						✓
Wave 4	✓	✓	✓	✓	✓	✓	✓	✓
Observations	1,128	2,659	1,136	1,128	1,143	1,137	1,139	2,578

*** $p < 0.001$, ** $p < 0.01$, * $p < 0.05$, † <0.10

Controls include: Democracy Best, Urban, Age, Education, Internet Use, Trusting, Confused by Politics.

172

How Jordanians Attribute Responsibility

Table 5.7 Foreign policy grievances and suitability of democracy

	Security 1	Security 2	Two states	Israel treaty	Israel econ	Israel sec	US econ
Suitability of	−0.58***	−0.05	−0.24	−0.12*	0.18	0.00	−0.30*
democracy	(0.10)	(0.06)	(0.17)	(0.05)	(0.13)	(0.12)	(0.12)
Controls	✓	✓	✓	✓	✓	✓	✓
Wave 3		✓		✓	✓	✓	✓
Wave 4	✓		✓				✓
Observations	1,134	1,141	1,120	1,393	1,522	1,522	2,665

*** $p < 0.001$, ** $p < 0.01$, * $p < 0.05$, † <0.10
Controls include: Democracy Best, Urban, Age, Education, Internet Use, Trusting, Confused by Politics.

5.5.3 Estimating Support for the King in Wave 1

To calculate a rough estimate of popular support for the king, I performed the following calculations:

- The CSS poll conducted just prior to wave 1 of the Facebook experiment suggests an estimated difference of 50 percentage points in the popularity of the prime minister and parliament.
- The Facebook experiment returned a click rate difference of 1.3 percentage points for the prime minister and the parliament.
- Assuming linearity, a 1 percentage point difference in public opinion polling would indicate a 0.026 percentage point difference in the click rate.
- The click rate difference between the monarchy and prime minister ads was 0.8 in the first wave.
- This suggests an estimated 45 percent approval rating for the monarchy.

6 | Power Sharing and Attributions across Jordan's Modern History

When rising debt and years of economic mismanagement forced Jordan to implement IMF-backed austerity reforms in 1989, the price increases were so severe that the country's standard of living dropped precipitously in just a few months (Harrigan et al. 2006). Unsurprisingly, this sudden decline shocked and angered Jordanians, triggering the largest protests witnessed by the country in at least twenty years. Yet, despite the scale of this April Uprising, King Hussein never became the target of the unrest. Between 1986 and 1989, as economic prospects worsened, Hussein had "virtually switched off from domestic politics" (Robins 2004, 157), and many Jordanians appeared to believe the government, and not the monarch, was responsible for what had gone wrong (Ryan 1998). Rather than calling for the king to be overthrown, protesters asked him to intervene in defense of their interests. One tribal chief articulated these views succinctly, while speaking directly to Hussein in a public gathering, saying "Abu Abdullah, where have you been all these days? We missed you ... Your prime minister is a thief, your ministers are no good" (Shlaim 2007, 482). King Hussein promptly replaced the government and promised political reforms, after which the protests died down (Lucas 2003). In subsequent months, Hussein followed through with the promised changes to the political system. With the country likely to need years of unpopular economic adjustment policies, the king backed reforms that strengthened parliament's role in the policy process, increasing the credibility of delegation in ways that could help him to keep his distance from future public dissatisfaction.

This chapter builds on the findings of Chapters 4 and 5 to show how both power sharing and blame have varied over time throughout the country's history. In line with the theoretical framework described in Chapter 2, Jordan's kings have been more likely to delegate credibly to the cabinet and parliament in contexts where the costs of being blamed are especially relevant to their survival in office. During time periods when it is more likely that the public will be aggrieved, the country's kings have strategically reinforced the credibility of their distance from the policymaking process. On the other hand, when the kings have had less reason to fear popular grievances and could benefit much more from credit claiming, they have strengthened their grip over decision-making.

I also provide evidence that Jordanians' attributions of blame for unpopular outcomes have varied in response to these changes in the policy process. As the kings have become more involved in decision-making, they have also exposed themselves to greater blame and direct opposition from the masses; however, when the kings have taken steps to delegate more credibly, their popularity has been less likely to suffer as a result of unpopular governance outcomes. In illustrating these patterns, the chapter underscores further how the Jordanian monarchy uses delegation strategically to protect its popular support by shaping the public's attributions of responsibility. These shifts in blame attributions also help to account for two sets of alternative explanations to my argument. The first is that Jordanians blame institutions other than the king because they fear repression by the state. The second is that Jordanians blame the king but do not say so because they support the monarchy for other reasons. For instance, in an unstable neighborhood, Jordanians value the stability of the Hashemite monarchy, and for this reason, they may be unwilling to challenge the king even if they believe he is responsible for other poor governance outcomes. Both of these dynamics are certainly relevant to Jordanian politics, but if they accounted fully for how Jordanians attribute blame, we would be much less likely to observe the variation in public opposition to the monarchy that I document in this chapter.

The chapter proceeds by reviewing historical periods in Jordan from 1952 until the present. I describe five periods in the country's history in which the general threat environment for the monarchy differed, providing variation that is useful for assessing the extent to which attributions have influenced the regime's decision-making process. For each period, I describe the type and intensity of threats faced by the kings, and I show how their subsequent decisions about delegation are consistent with the strategic logic emphasized by the theory. I also provide evidence that indicates the kings' exposure to blame has fluctuated alongside these changes in delegation.

6.1 Different Threats and Divergent Power Sharing

I draw on a variety of evidence to establish these patterns. Hundreds of archival documents collected from the National Archives of the United Kingdom are particularly important. These documents include British diplomatic reports from their embassy in Amman about Jordan's political developments between the early 1950s and the late 1980s. The British had their biases; in particular, they preferred for Hussein to remain on the throne and had a strong dislike for his Nasserist and leftist opponents. However, this reporting was classified at the time, and it focused primarily on analyzing the kingdom's political trajectory for use by policymakers back in London, with frequent assessments of the king's popular support and internal dynamics within the regime. As a result, the documents provide a particularly insightful source of information on delegation and attributions over time. The chapter also relies on secondary source literature, my interviews with Jordanian political elites, further analysis of the text data referenced in Chapter 4, and internet search data from Google Trends.

6.1 Different Threats and Divergent Power Sharing

In analyzing temporal variation in power sharing and attributions, I divide Jordan's modern history into five periods, beginning in 1952 with the promulgation of the constitution and the ascension of King Hussein to the throne and extending until 2020 and the outbreak of the COVID-19 pandemic. For each period, I assess the threat environment facing the monarchy, considering the potential for mass opposition as well as the likelihood of being challenged by other political elites. I then evaluate the credibility of power-sharing arrangements related to decision-making to ascertain whether shifts in the threat environment align with changes to delegation as the theory would predict.

I describe the threat environment by drawing on objective indicators alongside subjective assessments of Jordanian history. Regarding the likelihood of popular dissatisfaction and mass opposition, I consider economic performance as well as the frequency of incidents indicating substantial discontent. In terms of internal threats to the kings from other political elites, I look at the occurrence of coup attempts in addition to attempts to undermine the privileged position of the monarchy.

To determine the credibility of power sharing, I follow Chapter 5 in focusing primarily on the monarchy's relationship with the cabinet and

176   *Power Sharing and Blame in Jordan Over Time*

the parliament. As discussed before, there are other power centers in Jordanian politics to which the king delegates decision-making powers (Bank and Schlumberger 2004), and I will discuss some of them in the pages that follow. However, the primary emphasis will remain on the cabinet and parliament as the two institutions that are formally tasked with governance. Assessing how credibly these institutions are able to make decisions independent of the king is not always obvious, but clear shifts have occurred over time in Jordanian history. For the cabinet, I analyze whether the prime minister held their own power base separate from the monarchy as well as an established record of acting independently. For example, some prime ministers came from powerful tribes or were well-known for their reformist tendencies, whereas others were conservative stalwarts who openly advertised their dependency on the king. I also consider the extent to which the royal court is known to have intervened in general policy matters at different time periods. For the parliament, I focus first on whether the parliament was allowed to operate at all, and then whether the monarchy allowed relatively clean elections to proceed, resulting in a more independently-minded parliament willing to challenge both the government and the palace. More powerful prime ministers and emboldened parliaments should make it costlier for the king to force their own policy preferences onto the decision-making process, increasing the credibility of delegation and leaving them less exposed to the public's attributions. I draw on various data sources to draw these conclusions.

Table 6.1 summarizes the five historical periods, listing the assessments of threats and the credibility of delegation. The first period captures the early years of King Hussein's reign, from 1952 to 1971, as he struggled to consolidate his power. This period was marked by major governance challenges as well as substantial opposition to the monarchy from a restive public and powerful political elites alike. In these circumstances, the king oscillated between delegating to strong prime ministers capable of insulating the monarchy from popular anger and weaker prime ministers whom he could control more easily. By 1972, King Hussein had succeeded in crushing mass opposition and cowing other elites in the regime. For the next decade, Jordan also experienced an economic boom. As the theory would expect, King Hussein dominated decision-making during this period more than at any other time of his reign, closing the parliament and making policy with a small circle of close advisers. The economic boom turned into

Table 6.1 *Temporal changes in threat and delegation*

		Public and Elite Threats					Delegation by Monarchy		
(1) Period	(2) Years	(3) Avg. GDP PC growth %	(4) Instability per year	(5) Major crises	(6) Coup attempts	(7) Level of threat	(8) Cabinet influence	(9) Parliament influence	(10) Delegation credibility
1: Hussein	1952–1971	1.2	3.5	2	2	Public: High Elites: High	Mix of strong and weak PMs	Controlled elections	Medium
2: Hussein	1972–1985	11.9	0.1	0	0	Public: Low Elites: Low	Royal court dominates	Parliament dissolved	Low
3: Hussein	1986–1998	0.5	0.6	2	0	Public: High Elites: Low	Most PMs are strong	Cleaner elections	High
4: Abdullah	1999–2009	7.8	0.1	0	0	Public: Low Elites: Medium	Royal court dominates	Controlled elections	Low
5: Abdullah	2010–2020	1.7	7.8	1	0	Public: High Elites: Low	Mix of strong and weak PMs; But active royal court	Cleaner elections	Medium

GDP data are from Gleditsch (2002) from 1952 to 1964, and from the World Bank from 1965 to 2019.

Instability Per Year uses counts of events from Banks. These data end in 2014. Major crises are self-coded.

Note that Banks appears to significantly undercount incidents of unrest during the late 1980s and early to mid 1990s.

178 *Power Sharing and Blame in Jordan Over Time*

an economic bust in the late 1980s, triggering another period of rowdy popular politics. During these last years of his rule, again as the theory would predict, King Hussein responded to this heightened unrest by granting the parliament an expanded role in the policy process and stepping back from his more direct control over decision-making.

Following his father's death, King Abdullah came to power in 1999. The economy was gaining consistently again and there was an outpouring of public sympathy for the monarchy, reducing the need for the king to be concerned about his exposure to blame. At the same time, King Abdullah had weaker ties to many of the country's political elites compared to his father, and he faced potential competitors for the throne, indicating a more threatening environment from within the regime. As the theory might expect, these shifts were matched by the new king taking a much more active role in decision-making, expanding the role of the royal court and keeping parliament largely at bay. However, the threat environment transformed once again following the global financial crisis of 2007–2008 and the eruption of the Arab Spring uprisings a few years later. With popular grievances rising, the king acted as the theory would expect by appointing some prime ministers with more independence from the palace, backing reforms to strengthen parliament, and limiting his involvement in policymaking.

The remainder of the chapter explores each of these periods in more detail, discussing how decision-making operated and how it shifted alongside the changing threat environments. I also show evidence that Kings Hussein and Abdullah became relatively more or less exposed to blame for the public's grievances depending on the extent of their involvement in the policy process.

6.2 Power Sharing and Blame under King Hussein

6.2.1 Period 1: A Balancing Act (1952–1971)

When King Hussein came to the throne in 1952, he was only a teenager. Not only did his youth and inexperience pose problems in their own right, but the monarchy's control over the political system was far from complete at this time. Hussein's father Talal had just been deposed by the parliament on account of his mental health issues, and the constitution promulgated prior to Hussein's ascension had established a constitutional monarchy in which the king was meant to share

6.2 Power Sharing and Blame under King Hussein

significant powers with – if not be dominated by – the cabinet and the parliament (Rath 1994).

As he attempted to consolidate his position, Hussein faced a series of political and economic crises that generated mass grievances among the public, while also motivating other political elites to challenge the power of the monarchy. Economic growth was inconsistent, and Jordan's acquisition of the West Bank in the 1948 war with Israel complicated domestic affairs severely. The country's development and infrastructure were strained by the rapid population increase, and many Palestinian refugees did not feel any desire to be governed by the Hashemite monarchy (Cohen 1980). Israel contributed to this complication by frequently attacking Palestinian targets over the Jordanian border, which angered the public, while making Jordan's military forces look weak. The rising tide of Arab nationalism had also begun to threaten governments across the region following the Free Officers Coup in Egypt in 1952. Because of Jordan's close ties to the British, the Jordanian monarchy became a preferred target of Nasser's by the mid-1950s, posing a major challenge to the young king. Anti-British and anti-royal propaganda pushed by Egyptian radio resonated with many Jordanians, especially those in the West Bank and of Palestinian descent. At the same time, Nasser and his allies were cultivating assets in the Jordanian military and political elite with the goal of destroying the monarchy from the inside.

Resembling the second scenario described in Chapter 2, in which an autocrat must juggle severe threats from both the public and other political elites, the young king responded to these challenges by oscillating between governments that were either strong enough to demonstrate their independence and deflect some of the public's anger or weak enough not to pose a major threat to the palace. As mass opposition became more salient, the king appointed stronger prime ministers; alternatively, as he became more concerned about elite challengers, he installed loyalist cabinets. These shifts reflect the theory's expectations that autocrats will share power over decision-making more credibly when they have more reason to worry about being targeted by an angry public, but also that this dynamic is constrained by the risks inherent in giving other political elites too much power.

Hussein's first choice of prime minister was Fawzi al-Mulki, a political outsider who could be controlled by the palace relatively easily (Robins 2004). Within a year, however, his inexperience had created a

180 *Power Sharing and Blame in Jordan Over Time*

number of problems and became a political liability for Hussein. As the king faced mounting pressure from the public, al-Mulki was replaced by a series of experienced prime ministers who had been active under Hussein's grandfather. Though loyal to the monarchy, they were established operatives with their own political capital, which gave them the capacity to manage the country's political system with a strong hand of their own (Robins 2004).

Despite their relative independence from the palace, these governments proved ineffective at dealing with the rise of mass politics in Jordan, which was intimately connected to surging anti-British sentiment among the public. Hussein recognized the importance of British protection for his regime, and so he continued to do what he could to push his governments toward a pro-British foreign policy, which included joining the pro-British Baghdad Pact. The king's desire was known by the Jordanian public, and it conflicted with their strongly-held anti-colonial, anti-British attitudes. As a result, the British embassy's annual report in 1956 observed that Hussein's efforts to push for the Baghdad Pact meant that "...the King, and indeed the monarchy itself, became targets of criticism on the ground that they were obstacles to the attainment of nationalist goals" (TNA FO 371/127876). Mass protests followed, and Hussein's government refused to join the pact. Hussein responded by appointing Hazza al-Majali as prime minister, a more forceful personality than his predecessors who also came from an important tribe. The king hoped that Majali could push through the policy, while absorbing the public's anger (Shlaim 2007). Instead, he was unable to deal with the riots and resigned after just one week in office. In the face of this popular pressure, Hussein appointed Samir al-Rifai to be the next prime minister. Al-Rifai was a stronger political figure who had previously served as prime minister three separate times. He possessed an established political network that allowed him to restore order but also enabled him to enforce his will on the king.

Al-Rifai's power was useful for deflecting the public's anger, but it also threatened Hussein, illustrating the costs of credible delegation for the monarchy. The British embassy observed that "at present, the dominant feature of the situation is the tension between King Hussein and the Government of Samir Rifai. The King distrusts his Prime Minister and ... probably believes Samir is working at least as much for the Egyptians and Saudis as for the Hashemite cause..." (TNA FO 437/12). Partly in response to his declining political position, the

6.2 Power Sharing and Blame under King Hussein

king took the drastic step of firing the British commander of Jordan's army, Glubb Pasha, which would help him to build his popularity by establishing his credibility as a nationalist. As news about the dismissal broke, the British reported that Hussein became "a national hero instantaneously" (TNA FO 437/12). The decision even won Hussein plaudits from the Jordanian Communist Party (JCP), which among Jordan's political organizations held "the most negative attitude toward the king" (Cohen 1980, 237). Indicative of the extent to which Hussein's broader public support depended on his decision-making role, the JCP was "prepared to judge that regime in the light of its policies." As such, Hussein's dismissal of Glubb Pasha "earned him considerable praise both in the party's publications and from its members in the House of Representatives in Amman" (Cohen 1980, 72).

With his reputation restored and the public threat momentarily quashed, Hussein felt more secure in pursuing his desire to "rid himself of a Prime Minister who wished to govern" (TNA FO 371/127876), and so he forced al-Rifai to resign. Consistent with the expectation that autocrats will delegate less credibly when avoiding blame becomes less important, the new prime minister was Said al-Mufti, who the British described as "a bibulous nonentity whose chief attribute was a desire to avoid responsibility and who was thus well fitted to occupy the role of non-governing Prime Minister for which he had been cast by the King" (TNA FO 371/127876).

However, the king's popularity proved ephemeral. The gains associated with Glubb's expulsion were undermined just weeks later when Hussein met with the British-aligned King Faisal of Iraq, while refusing to meet with the revolutionary Syrian prime minister. These actions convinced the public that the king still wished to join the Baghdad Pact, undermining his support once again. Writing at the time, the British claimed it was "probable that if he had accepted this invitation [to meet with the Syrian prime minister] his popularity in Jordan would have remained high" (TNA FO 437/12). Following this shift, the opposition groups returned to attacking the king directly for his decisions in foreign affairs and national security. For instance, the JCP "resumed its attack on him and his administration ... accusing the army of committing atrocities in the rural areas, and even hinting at concessions that the Hashemite regime was making to Israel" (Cohen 1980, 237).

Facing this pressure, Hussein allowed parliamentary elections to proceed freely in 1956, and a number of political parties performed well. The king then appointed Suleiman al-Nabulsi as prime minister, whose National Socialist Party had won the largest share of seats in the elections (Rath 1994). With party and parliamentary backing for his government, al-Nabulsi was a political force to be reckoned with and could demonstrate clearly his independence from the king. This appointment initially seemed to benefit Hussein by helping to reduce public pressure related to anti-colonial and anti-Israeli grievances. In particular, having al-Nabulsi at the helm appears to have mitigated the potential for substantial unrest when Israel, the United Kingdom, and France attacked Egypt in October 1956, since al-Nabulsi was visibly steering the government's response (TNA FO 371/127876).

Al-Nabulsi and his government subsequently negotiated the end of their country's defense treaty with the United Kingdom, winning popular acclaim. However, the government's ability to claim credit for this success created serious dangers for Hussein, highlighting one of the potential costs of delegating (Shlaim 2007). Buoyed by the public's approval, "Nabulsi concluded that the King could not afford to do without him, and started behaving accordingly" (TNA FO 371/134006). What followed was a sequence of policy decisions by the government that contradicted the king's wishes, including some that were designed deliberately to weaken and perhaps end the king's power in the country. For example, on April 2, 1957, the cabinet established diplomatic relations with the Soviet Union (Robins 2004). According to the British, Hussein "radically opposed the decision," but "did not feel strong enough to do anything but acquiesce." Next, the government, "clearly wishing to undermine the King's position further," dismissed four senior officials in the bureaucracy, including a general in charge of domestic security whose loyalty to the monarchy "was one of the most valuable cards in the King's hands." On April 10, they took further steps to constrain the king, firing another twenty-five officials known for their commitment to Hussein (TNA FO 371/134006).

By this point, it was clear that empowering the cabinet and parliament to this extent had created a major threat to the monarchy's survival. Hussein responded by using his prerogative to dismiss al-Nabulsi and the government in April 1957, despite knowing that this move risked triggering a direct challenge from his elite opponents. Indeed, three days after the dismissal, Hussein was forced to stare down a coup attempt involving the Army Chief of Staff, Ali Abu Nuwar, who was ideologically oriented toward al-Nabulsi's

6.2 *Power Sharing and Blame under King Hussein* 183

pan-Arab leftism. Soon after, a "Patriotic Congress" formed in the West Bank challenging the monarchy's authority, and among its members were twenty-three MPs from al-Nabulsi's camp. Following these developments, Hussein declared martial law to break the strength of the opposition (Robins 2004). Political parties were banned, and hundreds of partisans from the Communist Party and other opposition organizations were arrested and given long prison sentences (Cohen 1980). Unrest continued over the next year, and the sense of crisis worsened when the Iraqi monarchy, ruled by Hussein's cousin Faisal, was overthrown by a coup in 1958 (Tal 1995). The Qawmiyun Party and other groups launched a campaign of sabotage and terrorism in this period, backed by Syria and the new revolutionary regime in Iraq (Cohen 1980), and a coup plot involving twenty-two officers was uncovered as well, also with Egyptian involvement. Yet, the heightened use of repression gradually restored order, weakening the organized political parties and purging the security forces of disloyal officers.

To pursue these unpopular policies, Hussein relied on two strongman prime ministers both serving for their fifth time in office: first, Ibrahim Hashem from April 1957 to May 1958, and then Samir al-Rifai once more until May 1959. These prime ministers and their cabinets could maintain order, while keeping blame away from the king, in large part because the public knew they had their own policy agendas as well as the strength to enforce their will on Hussein when disagreements arose. As the British noted about al-Rifai's government at the time, this dynamic had "value in keeping the King to that extent above politics," so that "Samir's unpopularity acts as a sort of lightning-conductor for the Monarchy" (TNA FO 371/151040).

By the early 1960s, however, Robins (2004) notes that "the chronic instability experienced by Jordan in the previous decade was at an end." This shift resulted from four important changes. First, the loyalty of the coercive apparatus was now more assured, following the failed coup plots and subsequent purges in the years prior. Second, the heightened repression of 1957 and 1958 had succeeded in breaking the country's organized political parties, forcing them underground and depriving them of many of their most committed activists (Cohen 1980). Third, both of these developments were reinforced by the tarnishing of Nasser's reputation and the declining allure of Arab nationalism following the breakdown of the United Arab Republic in 1961 (Robins 2004). Nasser no longer focused as much effort on overthrowing the Hashemite monarchy; instead, his efforts were aimed much more strongly at the civil war in Yemen. In fact there was a rapprochement between Egypt and Jordan for some years during this period, which gained Hussein "unprecedented popularity" and allowed him to "sleep more soundly in his bed at night" (Shlaim 2007, 204). Finally, Jordan's economy also grew at a more rapid pace during these years.

These changes reduced the potential for mass opposition, lowering the costs of being blamed by the public for their grievances. In line with this change and consistent with the theory's expectations, King Hussein chose to reduce the credibility of delegation and become more active in decision-making. Indeed, as it became clear that the likelihood of mass opposition has decreased significantly, the king began to chafe at the constraints imposed by these relatively independent prime ministers. As the British noted in 1959, "there are strains and creakings while Samir is in office," some of which developed out of fears within the palace that al-Rifai sought to diminish Hussein's role. For instance, Queen Zein was said by the British to feel "that Samir was trying to build himself up at the King's expense as a sort of dictator or Mayor of the Palace" (TNA FO 437/12). Al-Rifai was soon fired. Reflecting on the king's decision in a private conversation with the British ambassador, al-Rifai alleged that his removal occurred because the king "thought the time had come to try to rule the country more directly, through a more pliable Prime Minister" (TNA FO 437/12).

This prediction proved accurate. Over the next few years, King Hussein dominated a series of relatively weaker prime ministers who were less willing to impose their will on Hussein. The first was Hazza al-Majali, under whose government it was "more nakedly a palace regime" (TNA FO 371/151040). As mentioned earlier, al-Majali came from a powerful tribal family that dominated the military, and so he had some political base independent of the palace to call his own. However, his previous one-week stint as prime minister that had ended disastrously, combined with his "genial" personality, created a political reputation of dependence on the king. As a result, delegation to his government was less credible and less likely to shift blame effectively. Observing the government's effects on public opinion, the British claimed that Jordanians' anger became more likely to "strike King Hussein as the real master" (TNA FO 371/151040).

6.2 *Power Sharing and Blame under King Hussein* 185

Al-Majali was assassinated by Syrian intelligence officers in 1960, and for a time there was speculation that al-Rifai would again return to be prime minister. Yet, "the call never came," because Hussein "seemed unwilling to accept the role cast for him in Samir's concept of constitutional rule" (TNA FO 437/10). Instead, al-Majali was replaced by Bahjat al-Talhouni, who was even more dependent on the monarchy than his predecessor. As stated by the British, al-Talhouni "seldom opens his mouth publicly without making it clear that responsibility for his actions, and even for his words, lies with his master [the king]." Notably, this attempt by Hussein to take a more active role in governance occurred as it became clear that there was little chance of major public unrest. According to the British, there was "little danger of imminent collapse" at the time. Instead, it was noted that "with a good season ... and an absence of external threat, the country may well ... make some progress in spite of its Government" (TNA FO 437/12).

However, al-Talhouni's administration was perceived as corrupt and ineffective, and some of the public's growing anger began to be directed publicly at the king as the real master of a dependent government. According to the British, Hussein's noticeable control of this cabinet meant that he was "acting as his own Prime Minister with all the disadvantages, and especially the odium, that this entails." More directly, the British wrote that "This emphasis on personal rule has undoubtedly lost him [Hussein] popularity; and towards the end of the year it was becoming much more common to hear Jordanians blaming, not the Government or the Palace entourage, but the King himself for their ills" (TNA FO 371/164080). Likewise, another British report from this period noted that "We now hear much more frequently the criticism that the King himself is responsible because a Government of sycophants who leave in his hands all the real power is, in fact, the kind of Government he wants" (TNA FO 437/12).

Hussein responded to these rising grievances by dismissing al-Talhouni in January 1962 and appointing Wasfi al-Tell, a dynamic reformist who was "the nearest that Jordan came to producing a man of genuinely national stature..." (Robins 2004, 106). Al-Tell demonstrated his independence from the monarchy by virtue of his strong personality and ambitious policy agenda. He was "one of the few ... who would go a long way to impress his views on Hussein, at the risk of displeasing him" (Susser 1994, 37). The king gave him leeway to implement major domestic reforms, which al-Tell pursued with gusto. These included the removal of more than 700 bureaucrats suspected of corruption and poor performance, the professionalization of the foreign and civil services, the establishment of a Central Bank, and the initiation of a 356 million dollar five-year investment program aimed at jump-starting economic growth (Robins 2004).

Al-Tell's demonstrated independence resulted in the public again directing their attributions of responsibility more strongly at the prime minister, which helped to protect the king from blame. The British noted that the shift to al-Tell was "a healthy one" because Hussein's "reputation suffered badly when he was held primarily responsible for the misfeasances and nonfeasances of a corrupt and supine administration" (TNA FO 371/170263). Notably, these changes were not just related to grumbling and complaints among the public, but also to more serious threats against the king's life. During al-Tell's premiership, the British wrote in their diplomatic reporting that "...during the last few months, the country has been disturbed by far fewer and far feebler reports of the King's impending assassination" (TNA FO 437/12).

Al-Tell governed for over a year, but his strength engendered fears in some quarters that he was "deliberately encouraging the King's known taste for foreign adventure with a view to destroying the Hashemite dynasty and replacing it by a republic of which he seeks to be the first President" (TNA FO 437/12). These fears were almost certainly unfounded – al-Tell was a Hashemite loyalist – but they are illustrative of the extent to which the king still needed to worry that a particularly strong prime minister could use his control over the policy process to undermine the monarchy. Al-Tell's policies soon became unpopular with the public, however, and he was removed in 1963 after a surge in public unrest. Al-Rifai was briefly brought back into office to deal with these difficulties. Yet, once Hussein decided that "the fabric of the country was not so badly damaged as to need Samir's firm but desperately unpopular hand to hold it together," the British observed that he "had no hesitation in ditching him in favour of the more acceptable and amendable Sherif Hussein," who was a relative of the king and more easily controlled by the palace (TNA FO 437/12).

Within a year, however, the king began to clash with the prime minister because of disagreements over foreign policy. King Hussein had started to pursue a rapprochement with President Nasser of Egypt,

6.2 Power Sharing and Blame under King Hussein

who had long funded attempts to overthrow the Jordanian monarchy – Hussein saw the rapprochement as a chance to end this threat to his rule. This move was resisted by conservatives in the regime, including the prime minister, because of their distrust of the Egyptian president. They noticeably "dragged their feet where possible and made no secret of their belief that the country was being delivered to Nasser." Frustrated by this resistance, Hussein dismissed his relative and appointed Bahjat al-Talhouni as prime minister again, since he could be "relied upon to forward the King's pro-Egyptian policy without arguing" (TNA FO 437/12). Al-Talhouni remained in office for six months, until Wasfi al-Tell was once more brought back to serve as prime minister for approximately two years, until 1967. Al-Tell's more independent government successfully "eased the pressure on the King" (TNA FO 371/186547) that had increased once more when the weaker al-Talhouni was prime minister.

After the relative calm of the early 1960s, the disaster of the 1967 war with Israel dramatically heightened threats to Hussein's rule. Jordan and its Arab allies were defeated in a matter of days, and Israel seized control of the West Bank in the process. The West Bank was crucial for Jordan's economy, accounting for a substantial portion of its GDP, and the loss of the territory sent the economy into a tailspin. The defeat also triggered a new wave of refugees, while generating substantial popular anger at the regime. Support surged for Palestinian fedayeen movements whose aim seemed to be toppling the monarchy, in large part because the king himself was viewed as increasingly ineffective and at fault in dealing with the Israeli threat (Ashton 2008). Following the war, the fedayeen worked to establish their own pseudo-state within Jordan as their power grew at the expense of the monarchy.

Hussein also faced mounting pressures from elites within the regime during this period. Most threateningly, his control over the military appeared to waver. The army and air force had lost almost all of their equipment in the defeat, and morale collapsed to the point that "the bastion of the kingdom's security was on the verge of revolt and the king was losing his grip on this pillar of his support" (O'Connell 2011, 77). This problem was worsened by the military's anger at the king for not striking back at the fedayeen as their hold on the country strengthened and they became increasingly brazen in their assertions of authority (Ashton 2008; O'Connell 2011).

Political elites began to resist the king's authority as well. For instance, following the war, Bahjat al-Talhouni was again prime minister from 1967 to 1969 and from 1969 to 1970. Even this formerly-pliant loyalist began to assert himself in ways that potentially threatened the palace. At one point, following the king's condemnation of the fedayeen, al-Talhouni issued a more ambiguous statement, which "the fedayeen and their supporters interpreted as a repudiation of the King's strictures on them and a tacit invitation for them to continue their work" (TNA FO 437/12). There was speculation that Hussein would fire al-Talhouni as a result, yet the statement had dramatically increased his popular support. As a result, Hussein "apparently decided he would have to tolerate this disregard of his instructions." Said the British looking back at al-Talhouni's administration in 1969, "It may be asked whether the King in October 1967 had misjudged the character of the man and did not suspect that he would in the latter stages of his Premiership aspire to attain a position which some judged challenged that of the monarchy itself..." (TNA FO 437/12). Even Hussein's intelligence chief began to hedge his bets by making overtures to the fedayeen (O'Connell 2011).

In other words, following the war, Hussein was in a bind, trapped between acute pressure from both the public and his ostensible elite allies. As the British described it, the king faced "growing discontent among the refugees, the army, and Palestinians at the King's lack of success so far in getting back anything of what he lost" (TNA FO 437/10). Hussein responded by taking charge of the situation directly. The king publicly "accepted personal responsibility for the losses Jordan had suffered" in the war (O'Connell 2011, 62), and he took it upon himself to win back concessions through diplomacy. He also focused heavily on receiving shipments of weapons from the Americans to retain the loyalty of the army. Furthermore, he appointed relatively weak prime ministers during this period in an attempt to manage the possibility of a revolt from within his own government. These prime ministers included the previously submissive al-Talhouni and also Abdelmounim al-Rifai, "a rather weak politician" (Shlaim 2007, 322). Given the fedayeen's apparent goal of establishing their own state in Jordan, Hussein likely judged that a popular uprising was inevitable, and he focused on maintaining tight control over other political elites.

6.2 Power Sharing and Blame under King Hussein

After making a number of concessions to the fedayeen as part of a successful attempt to help them overextend themselves, the king moved decisively against them. He declared a military government, concentrating power more fully in his hands, and then ordered the military to confront the guerrillas in an uncertain contest for control over the country (Robins 2004). Thus Jordan entered its short but bloody civil war, now known as Black September. Several thousand people were killed in the brief but intense conflict, but by the end in July 1971, opposition to the Hashemites had been crushed (Ashton 2008). Facing significant threats from both the masses and elites, Hussein gambled on centralizing control and facing down the popular uprising with force.

These political dynamics in Jordan between 1952 and 1971 illustrate several key expectations of the book's theory. First, when Hussein took an active role in policymaking, his positions often won him great acclaim or triggered widespread opposition against the monarchy directly. Hussein did not hold some special legitimacy with the Jordanian public but instead saw his reputation shift based on the policies for which he was perceived to be responsible. However, Hussein could also protect himself from the vagaries of public opinion by delegating more credibly to other political elites, appointing strong prime ministers who could demonstrate their independence from the palace. In these cases, unpopular policies implemented by the government would not generate as much ire directed at the king, indicating that Jordanians were not reflexively blaming the regime as a whole. Hussein appears to have responded strategically to this variation in attributions by delegating more or less credibly as the potential for public anger shifted, in line with the theory's expectations. Finally, when Hussein did gamble on centralized control during periods of mass discontent, these were the moments when his regime pursued the most intensive repression against the opposition, as the king resorted to crushing those attacking the monarchy's rule directly.

6.2.2 Period 2: A Secure King (1972–1985)

The outcome of Black September transformed the threat environment in Jordan, with repression destroying mass opposition to the monarchy, and allowing the king to reassert his control over political and military elites. Though Palestinian nationalism did not disappear as a

190   *Power Sharing and Blame in Jordan Over Time*

motivating force of opposition, a majority of Palestinians in Jordan appeared to have acquiesced to the regime by the mid 1970s (TNA FCO 93/664). In addition, Nasser died in 1970, and with him went the revolutionary wave of Arab nationalism that had repeatedly fueled opposition movements in the country. As the British put it, "Nasserism, once the main threat to the regime, has died with its founder: The last tattered photograph has now vanished from the small shops" (TNA FCO 93/664). This development also meant that Jordan faced fewer threats from abroad. Dictators interested only in their own survival, and not in overthrowing their Hashemite neighbor, soon consolidated control in Syria and Iraq. Israel increasingly recognized Hussein as a friend. As a result, Jordan was no longer surrounded by foes who had sought to destabilize the country's domestic politics with the goal of ousting the monarchy. The combination of Black September and Nasser's death reduced the need for Hussein to worry about challenges from the masses.

This secure position was reinforced by another development during this period: Jordan experienced an economic boom fueled by the rise in oil prices that began with the 1973 oil crisis. Friendly oil states – especially Saudi Arabia – sent significant aid to Jordan. A massive number of Jordanians began working in the Gulf, with 40 percent of the labor force located abroad by the beginning of the 1980s. From these jobs, they sent a steady flow of remittances back home. Throughout the 1970s, approximately one-half of the government's budget originated in foreign income sources (Baylouny 2008). These rents fueled high levels of economic growth, a drop in unemployment, and the expansion of the state bureaucracy, with jobs in the civil service rising from 27,000 in 1970 to 74,000 in 1985 (Robins 2004). As shown in Table 6.1, per capita GDP also expanded rapidly during this period. The government used the windfall to expand the welfare state, creating subsidies for basic goods such as rice and sugar as well as other programs to direct benefits toward state employees and members of the security apparatus in particular (Andoni and Schwedler 1996; Baylouny 2008). In this context, Hussein had less reason to fear the costs of being blamed, since there were fewer grievances afflicting the public; in fact, the economy provided previously rare opportunities to claim credit for popular governance outcomes. As the British noted in a 1975 report about the minimal opposition in Jordan to the monarchy, "A struggling but well-intentioned development machine, fueled by

6.2 Power Sharing and Blame under King Hussein

foreign aid, is slowly transforming a landscape naturally poor. Stability brings its own rewards."

As the theory would predict, the king responded to the reduced likelihood of public dissatisfaction by centering the decision-making process more fully around the palace than had previously been the case, with the British referring to this period as one of "benevolent paternalism" (TNA FCO 93/664). The parliament was dissolved in 1974 as a result of issues related to representation in the West Bank, such that there was no legislative body at all until 1978. In that year, King Hussein finally acted on the advice of his advisers to establish the National Consultative Council, following discontent with the lack of representation in the political process (Rath 1994). However, the body was purely advisory. It lacked legislative powers and was fully appointed by the king, and its clear weakness highlights the extent to which Hussein felt secure in delegating less credibly or not at all on many policy matters. Parliament was finally called back in 1984 because its elderly members were dying and it risked falling below a quorum – controlled elections were held, and the institution was then quickly undermined and co-opted by the government.

During this period, the king asserted himself even more dominantly in foreign policy, and domestic policy also came to be controlled more closely by the palace. While the prime minister and cabinet still played an important role, Hussein empowered his brother Hassan, the crown prince, with handling issues related to "internal affairs, planning, and the economy" (Shlaim 2007, 359). Ashton (2008, 159) notes that, during this period, the king:

...made most of his important decisions closeted in a lunch room at the Royal Diwan with a small cabal of advisers, which almost always included Zeid al-Rifai, Zeid bin Shaker, the current prime minister and the head of the Mukhabarat. The cabinet and the ministries of government lay out-side this close circle of power, and essentially acted as little more than ciphers – implementers of policies already agreed by the King and his close circle.

In the early and mid 1980s, King Hussein appointed two prime ministers with reformist aspirations and the strength of personality to assert their independence from the palace. The first, Abdulhamid Sharaf, died after less than a year in office. The second, Ahmed Obeidat, lasted for one year and three months. Obeidat "was determined

192   *Power Sharing and Blame in Jordan Over Time*

to be his own man," but as a result, "it became progressively clear that the two men [Obeidat and the king] could not easily work together." Indicating that he was "increasingly set in his ways," Hussein fired Obeidat in 1985 and returned the premiership to Zaid al-Rifai, with whom he was particularly close (Robins 2004, 156).

In short, facing no real pressure from the public, King Hussein had little motivation to delegate responsibility credibly to other elites who might then turn on him and challenge the monarchy. As a result, while economic times remained good and the prospects of mass opposition remained slim, he chose to keep control over the policy process concentrated within the royal court.

6.2.3 Period 3: The Return of Popular Politics (1986–1998)

By 1986, Jordan's economic boom had ended. Oil prices were falling, and with it, aid and remittances from the Gulf. These problems were made worse by the lingering Iran–Iraq War, as well as the civil war in Lebanon. Growth faltered, and debt reached unsustainable levels. As these changes took place, King Hussein "virtually switched off from domestic politics," focusing more and more of his time on foreign affairs, and specifically the peace process with Israel (Robins 2004, 157). While the motivations behind this change cannot be known, the shift is consistent with the king attempting to distance himself more credibly from economic decision-making as the potential for popular dissatisfaction increased. It is less consistent with co-optation theory, as there was no compelling need for the king to grant more of this decision-making influence to other elites for the purpose of keeping them loyal. Whatever his intentions, that distancing proved auspicious for the king's political survival, as Jordan slowly but surely headed toward economic disaster.

The government of Zaid al-Rifai initially tried to cover up the extent of their problems, but already by 1987, the prime minister faced mounting criticism of his administration. In a report about Jordanian politics from 1987, the British wrote that "Jordan is passing through one of those not unfamiliar periods of growing dissatisfaction with the country's situation and increasing criticism of the existing government ... At such times Jordanians focus on the performance of the prime minister and his administration." The alleged problem for the prime minister was that he had "very little to show by way

6.2 *Power Sharing and Blame under King Hussein*

of success for his policies," having failed to revitalize the economy, allow more political freedoms, or secure more foreign aid (TNA FCO 93/4895). Al-Rifai's reputation took a further hit following several cases of corruption and an incident in which potentially polluted water was allowed to be pumped into Amman. In addition, the prime minister found himself engaged in a feud with Jordan's Islamists, rooted in the government's increasingly aggressive stance toward the Muslim Brotherhood and their allies. The Islamists, however, continued to profess "complete loyalty to the King," directing their ire at al-Rifai for what they saw as his efforts to disrupt "many years of ... peaceful coexistence" (TNA FCO 93/4895). Given this mounting pressure from several directions, the British had already predicted a year earlier that "Rifai's prospects of surviving till the end of the year as prime minister were not all that bright" (TNA FCO 93/4895).

The government recognized its political problem with the economy and did what it could to remedy it. For example, the government formed a committee of several ministers, government officials, and university professors to propose solutions to the high unemployment rate that was particularly severe for Jordan's many college graduates. Understanding that they not only needed "to create employment" but also "to be seen to be doing so," the government made sure to leak the committee's report and have several articles about its work published in the press (TNA FCO 93/4895).

But Jordan could not outrun fiscal insolvency. By 1988, the country had the highest debt per capita in the world, and its currency was fluctuating dangerously (Robins 2004). Out of options, al-Rifai's government turned to the IMF for help, which agreed to provide more than two hundred million dollars of loans and credit over the following two years. However, this assistance did not come free, and the IMF required Jordan to make significant economic adjustments designed to rein in government expenditures (Ryan 1998). As mentioned in the opening of this chapter, these changes severely shocked the country's economy and resulted in drastic price increases for basic goods.

Mass riots erupted in April 1989 in response to these devastating economic developments. The king appeared to escape the brunt of the public's anger. Instead, Jordanians focused their fury on al-Rifai and his ministers (Ryan 1998), as reflected by the words of a Jordanian farmer that "What made us revolt was the move by your [Hussein's] ministers to deprive us of eggs, onions, potatoes, and tomatoes" (Shlaim 2007,

482). Nevertheless, the king felt exposed to popular pressure with an intensity that he had not confronted since 1970. Hussein responded by firing al-Rifai's government to meet the public's demands for accountability. He also agreed to implement liberalizing reforms that included the lifting of martial law, the return of meaningful parliamentary elections, and stronger parliamentary influence over the policy process. In private, Hussein stated explicitly that his motivation for implementing these reforms was to "let off steam" and "reduce the political pressures" that could challenge the monarchy (Ashton 2008, 254).

This process of liberalization included the formation of a commission to draft a new National Charter that would define the relationship between the people and the monarchy. The charter promised the establishment of a more democratic political system if Jordanians accepted the monarch's legitimate role as Head of State, reflecting attempts to define Jordan as a democratic, constitutional monarchy in which the king reigned rather than ruled. Hussein appointed Ahmed Obeidat to head the commission, since his "relationship with the kind had often been far from smooth," which reinforced the perceived independence of the body in the eyes of the public (Robins 2004, 174). Parliament was also strengthened. The 1989 parliamentary election was allowed to proceed without substantial manipulation, and it brought an array of ideological currents into the legislature, including the Muslim Brotherhood, whose affiliates won almost one-quarter of the seats. Their presence would go on to create complications for both Hussein and his governments. In other words, liberalization promised to increase the credibility of power sharing over policymaking, since the king and the government both would need to contend more actively with the preferences of elected representatives and other constitutional constraints.

Hussein knew that receiving greater responsibility for governance would be a double-edged sword for his elite opponents. After the 1989 elections, he reportedly told his wife that "They had been living on slogans," and "Now they are going to have to deliver results" (Shlaim 2007, 483). Thus, delegating responsibility more credibly to the parliament and other institutions helped to soften the dangers of popular unrest for the monarchy by distancing the king from state policies (Lucas 2005), and it did so at a time when Jordan was likely to be dealing with poor economic performance for years to come. Indeed, other austerity measures occurred throughout the remainder of

6.2 Power Sharing and Blame under King Hussein

Hussein's rule in the 1990s. For instance, subsidies for milk powder, rice, and sugar were reduced in subsequent years (Andoni and Schwedler 1996).

The credibility of delegation soon weakened, however, after Hussein undermined the reforms adopted in 1989. The motivation for this change was a significant divergence over policy matters related to foreign affairs, with the king believing that a peace treaty with Israel was necessary to secure the regime and many of the country's political elites opposing this idea outright. The situation originated with the Persian Gulf War, during which the king had sided with Iraq rather than the American-led coalition. This stance earned the king "desperate, almost intoxicated adulation" from Jordanians, many of whom viewed Saddam Hussein positively (Robins 2004, 179). However, it also damaged the country's relations with its US and Gulf patrons, resulting in aid cuts that cost the already-struggling economy and isolating Hussein from his most important foreign protector. The United States made it clear to the king that he could rehabilitate himself by pursuing peace with Israel (Ryan and Schwedler 2004). As a result, he authorized the government to negotiate a peace treaty and involved himself substantially in those efforts.

However, the role of the elected and empowered parliament in this process now posed a challenge, since many of the MPs – along with most of their constituents – were strongly opposed to a treaty and mobilized against it both publicly and privately. Hussein and the government responded by implementing electoral reforms that weakened the parliament's independence and its ability to influence the policy process (Ryan and Schwedler 2004). By changing the voting system from block voting to the single nontransferable vote, they deliberately encouraged voting along tribal lines. Because these candidates won almost solely on the basis of patronage distribution, they needed government favors to win over their constituents, and thus they were less likely to challenge the government or the palace on major policy decisions. The 1993 elections were the first in which political parties were legally allowed to run since 1956, but the new voting system actually decreased de facto party representation and returned a more pliant parliament. The peace treaty was signed in 1994, despite a campaign by the opposition to stop its passage. Moving forward, Jordan's parliament would continue to shape the policy process more so than it had in previous decades, but its credibility as an independent actor has not since returned to the same level as the years between 1989 and 1993.

Nonetheless, Hussein continued to distance himself from many domestic policy issues throughout the 1990s, leaving decisions to the cabinet and, to a lesser extent, the parliament. As noted by Ryan and Schwedler of this period (2004, 148), "King Hussein allowed the deputies final say over many domestic issues in exchange for support for his foreign-policy programs, notably the peace with Israel and now the close relations with the United States." This delegation appeared to matter for the king's support. His reputation seemed to fluctuate on these foreign policy matters where he involved himself openly: it suffered from his personal push on the peace treaty, but it rebounded somewhat when he became critical of the Netanyahu government – especially following its attempted assassination of the Palestinian Hamas leader Khalid Meshal in Amman in 1997 (Jansen 1996; Robins 2004). On the other hand, his reputation did not seem to be affected greatly by continued economic disruption. For instance, in 1996, the government met the IMF's final requirements for additional financial support by lifting bread subsidies, which many lower-income Jordanians relied upon heavily. This policy change was implemented under the administration of Prime Minister Kabariti, who had become unpopular for "pushing forward the IMF economic reform program despite strong opposition in the elected Lower House of Parliament" (Andoni and Schwedler 1996, 41). The subsequent rise in bread prices led to riots in the city of Karak, where demonstrators set up roadblocks and attacked government buildings. However, anger remained focused on the prime minister, with the protesters calling for his resignation as they chanted "Long live the King, down with Kabariti" (Andoni and Schwedler 1996, 41).

In sum, when confronted by a declining economic situation that was likely to generate grievances and increase the costs of being held responsible by the public for policy outcomes, King Hussein stepped back from his monopolization of decision-making during the 1970s and early 1980s, delegating more credibly to the cabinet and parliament. He then walked back these changes somewhat when parliament's heightened influence threatened his ability to secure a policy he viewed as crucial to the survival of his regime, even if doing so meant that he was blamed more directly for that policy and lost some of his support as a result. These shifts are consistent with the theory's

6.3 Power Sharing and Blame under King Abdullah

argument that autocrats can empower other governing institutions to redirect blame and protect their popularity, while also highlighting how autocrats are more (less) likely to rely on this strategy as blame becomes relatively more (less) central to their survival prospects.

6.3 Power Sharing and Blame under King Abdullah

6.3.1 Period 4: Transitioning to a New King (1999–2009)

King Hussein succumbed to cancer in February 1999, at which point his son Abdullah came to the throne. For several reasons, the new king was less secure than his father in terms of his relations with the country's political elites. First, there had been controversy over the succession. For much of Hussein's reign, his younger brother, Prince Hassan, had been heir to the throne. From his deathbed, Hussein replaced Hassan with Abdullah, his oldest son. While Hassan accepted the decision, many of his loyalists were frustrated (Ryan 1999). Hussein also made it known that he expected his young and openly-favored son Hamzah to be made Abdullah's crown prince. After a few years, Abdullah went back on his promise to his father and changed the succession so that his own son would become the heir. In 2021, Hamzah would be accused of fomenting opposition to the king and the crown prince, as will be discussed further at the end of the chapter (Ryan 2021; Schwedler 2021). In other words, there have been plausible royal challengers to Abdullah in a way that was not the case for Hussein.

Second, Abdullah was a solider like his father, and he had good relations with the military – he had previously led the country's special operations forces. However, he lacked the same effectiveness in terms of his connections with the tribal elites who dominated the political system. Abdullah was half British and had spent much of his time in the West. Famously, he did not speak classical Arabic fluently when he took the throne and needed to take lessons (Sharrock 1999). In addition, Abdullah married a Palestinian woman, Rania, which has been a further source of tension with the East Bank tribes who consider her to be opposed to their interests (Al-Khalidi 2011). As such, Abdullah had reasons to be less confident in his ability to manage the country's most powerful political elites, and he has often struggled to do so (Robins 2004). Indicative of this dynamic, Ryan (2018, 30) quotes a Jordanian analyst who noted that "all his [Abdullah's] choices are contested; his choice of prime minister, his choice of crown prince, his choice of wife. All are contested."

At the same time, Abdullah's early reign was characterized by relatively few serious threats from the public. By the time he took the throne, Jordan's economy had recovered from the crisis of the late 1980s, and it was entering a period of significant growth. The economy was further buoyed by increased foreign aid that followed the Global War on Terror, in which Jordan became a key partner of the United States (Baylouny 2008). Hussein's death had also prompted an outpouring of sympathy for the monarchy, and there were no major opposition groups that sought to overthrow the Hashemites. Since the drafting of the National Charter in 1989, the country's leftist and Islamist parties had accepted the monarchy's right to exist, though they opposed the extent of its powers.

That is not to say the public was irrelevant. Abdullah was not as personally popular as his father (Schwedler 2002), who benefited from a charisma and popular adoration that had accumulated over his many decades on the throne. In addition, major protests erupted in 2000 with the start of the Second Intifada in Palestine, as Jordanians mobilized for the Palestinian cause and against their government's own peace treaty with Israel. These protests were the largest in Jordan since the 1989 uprising, and the regime oscillated between repressing them and signaling their support, with Queen Rania herself joining a solidarity march in 2002 (Schwedler 2003). Abdullah received criticism for other foreign policy initiatives as well. For instance, Jordan's quiet but concrete support for the United States' invasion of Iraq earned the king critics not only among the Islamist opposition but also among tribal groups in the monarchy's base. Just prior to the invasion, a tribal leader openly announced that "If King Abdullah supports a war, we will oppose him to the utmost" (Burns 2003). Yet, the king was not going to cede control over policy matters related to Israel or the United States, given their centrality to the monarchy's security, and widespread opposition to the monarchy did not appear to be a major risk at the time.

In other words, when compared to the late 1980s and 1990s, Abdullah faced a threat environment in which managing political elites had become relatively more important, whereas distancing the king from popular politics and blame seemed less warranted given the strong economy and widespread support for the monarchy. This situation

6.3 *Power Sharing and Blame under King Abdullah* 199

implies that avoiding blame should have become relatively less important to the king, who may have wished to claim credit for economic successes while ensuring that other political elites did not acquire too much influence at his expense. Consistent with the theory, Abdullah's early years on the throne were characterized by less credible delegation and an expanding role for the monarchy in the country's decision-making process.

To facilitate this greater involvement, King Abdullah restructured the country's political institutions to weaken the independence of the cabinet and parliament. As one former deputy prime minister put it, Abdullah moved the country from a "parliamentary, royal system to a semi-presidential system, from the British model to the French model." He pursued this transition through four channels. First, the king greatly expanded the bureaucracy in the royal court, which answers directly to him rather than to the prime minister. These officials produce their own policy plans and conduct oversight of other government institutions, providing an effective behind-the-scenes pressure point on the cabinet and parliament. Second, Abdullah strengthened the domestic role of the intelligence services, which are also closely tied to the monarchy. Their political power had been growing steadily since Black September in 1970, but their influence expanded even more under the new king, and GID officers are known to lean on ministers and members of parliament to ensure they support the palace on particularly sensitive issues. Third, Abdullah was inclined to choose weaker, technocratic prime ministers who lacked their own political base, depended more heavily on the king, and were therefore less willing or able to deviate from the king's interests to pursue their own policy agendas. Fourth, the king dissolved parliament in 2001 and kept it closed for two years, repeatedly delaying elections for the body. During this period, the cabinet governed directly, implementing hundreds of temporary laws favored by the king, which were eventually passed formally when a new parliament was elected in 2003 (Schwedler 2012).

This more direct control from the monarchy was most evident with regards to economic issues (Alissa 2007), where Abdullah abandoned the monarchy's traditional reticence to take responsibility for policy related to the economy. For instance, a former prime minister who expressed the view that King Hussein left internal affairs to the cabinet said that this arrangement "is not so" under the present king.

Robins (2004, 203) observes that, "From the outset, King Abdullah has stated time and time again that the economy is to be his top priority." This dynamic was especially pronounced for reforms aimed at liberalizing the economy along the lines advocated for by the IMF. As Ryan (2018, 25) writes, "Hussein may have started the economic liberalization process ... but his son pursued it even more vigorously, charting a neoliberal course for Jordanian development that would involve extensive privatization measures and emphasis on trade, investment, and development of communications and other infrastructure." During the parliamentary absence from 2001 to 2003, most of the laws passed by the cabinet focused on "economic reforms aimed at expanding foreign trade, encouraging foreign investment, and easing restrictions for business transactions in general" (Schwedler 2012, 264). In November 2009, King Abdullah dissolved the parliament again because it had not been moving quickly enough on his preferred economic reforms; instead, under pressure from their constituents, the MPs "failed to act" on many of the proposals while "amending others beyond recognition" (Schwedler 2010). Following the dissolution, the cabinet proceeded to implement the neoliberal policies advocated for by the palace.

While it is not possible to identify the precise motives behind these changes, the policies allowed Abdullah to funnel resources into his narrower support base in the military (Baylouny 2008), while also securing the continued goodwill of the United States (Moore 2018). For instance, Ryan (2018, 25) notes how this model "endeared it [Jordan] to many key Western powers such as the United States..." In addition, Abdullah used the advancement of these policies to bring in new elites less connected to the tribal elites who had traditionally dominated Jordanian politics, and who often had frosty relations with the new king (Alissa 2007). In sum, with a less secure hold on the country's elites and relatively fewer concerns about the potential for mass opposition to the monarchy, King Abdullah spent his initial years in power centralizing decision-making more heavily in his own hands, pushing forward policies with implications for his ability to manage elite politics, and claiming credit for economic successes. Consistent with the theory, the king became less willing to share decision-making powers credibly at a point when blame avoidance appeared to be less crucial for maintaining the reputation and survival of the monarchy.

6.3 Power Sharing and Blame under King Abdullah

6.3.2 Period 5: Turmoil and Malaise (2010–2020)

By 2010, the potential for public unrest had shifted in a more ominous direction for the monarchy. Problems began with the 2007 financial crisis, which soon became a global recession. Jordan's GDP growth began to slow in 2009 and then fell nearly to zero in 2010, after which the economy entered a prolonged period of stagnation and austerity that was still ongoing when this book was written a decade later. Following and then exacerbating these economic difficulties, the region was rocked by the Arab Spring between 2011 and 2013. The revolutions in Tunisia and Egypt caused alarm in the royal court, while also triggering renewed activism within Jordan. Opposition groups including the Muslim Brotherhood and the Communist Party held weekly demonstrations, and youthful protest movements referred to as the Hirak emerged across the country. Most worryingly for the monarchy, these youth movements were dominated by Jordanians of East Bank descent from tribes that had long been central to the regime's coalition (Yom 2014). Their efforts were reinforced by senior tribal sheikhs who made their own calls for reform. In fact, in 2010, just before the Arab Spring, retired military officers – mostly from these same tribal backgrounds – had begun to advocate publicly against the kingdom's economic reforms and handling of the Palestine issue (Tell 2015). With the region in turmoil, the Hashemite monarchy found itself suddenly facing the potential for revolutionary, mass mobilization, with the threat coming from constituencies that were crucial to the persistence of the regime.

As the economy declined and it became more likely that Jordanians would be looking for someone to blame for the country's economic malaise, the government planned elections for November 2010 that they hoped would "focus attention away from growing economic problems..." (Schwedler 2010). The king also began to step back from his overt interventions in economic affairs. Once the Arab Spring erupted, Abdullah followed his father's playbook from 1989, backing political reforms that promised a measure of democratization, while also strengthening the credibility of his distance from the decision-making process. These changes included the establishment of a constitutional court and an independent election commission to bolster perceptions that parliament was elected freely and fairly. In 2016, the new electoral law – which came closer to resembling the fairer 1989 law – was also acknowledged as a "step in the right direction" by opposition forces, including the Muslim Brotherhood (Ryan 2018). The Brotherhood, which had boycotted the previous parliament, decided to run for elections once again, creating a more ideologically-diverse body with a greater proclivity for opposition. In addition, the reforms involved constitutional amendments that made it more difficult for the king to dissolve parliament indefinitely or rule unilaterally by decree (Ryan 2018). Because a more freely elected and institutionally stronger parliament could prove more capable of constraining the government and palace, these reforms had the potential to increase the perceived credibility of the parliament's influence over decision-making.

Alongside these formal changes, King Abdullah also started to choose some prime ministers who could more credibly demonstrate their independence from the palace. His first choice during the Arab Spring – Marouf al-Bakhit – was a strongman conservative who had already served Abdullah as prime minister once before, and opposition movements reacted poorly. However, nine months later, al-Bakhit was replaced with Awn al-Khasawneh, a respected judge mentioned in Chapter 4 for his fiery resignation. Al-Khasawneh's reformist reputation and willingness to defy the king gave credence to the idea that Abdullah would play less of a role in deciding the state's policies. This arrangement faltered after several months because al-Khasawneh proved more independent than Abdullah wanted. He was replaced for a short time by Fayez al-Tarawneh, another conservative stalwart close to the palace. Al-Tarawneh was then replaced by Abdullah Ensour, a former MP also of reformist leanings who had some credibility as "an independent thinker," "an advocate for ... democratic reform," and "an outspoken critic of corruption" (Ryan 2018, 40). This background should have increased his ability to demonstrate his influence over decision-making alongside the palace.

Ensour went on to serve more than three years in office, until 2016. He was then followed by Hani al-Mulki for two years, another strong personality, though a political figure associated with the royal family. Al-Mulki was replaced in 2018 by Omar al-Razzaz. As discussed in Chapter 5, he was a former World Bank economist and minister of education who had implemented educational reforms and was widely respected by the country's opposition forces (Hartnett 2018). One point indicative of the king's greater willingness to delegate economic

6.3 Power Sharing and Blame under King Abdullah

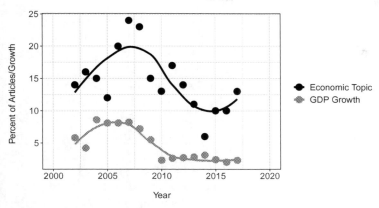

Figure 6.1 Abdullah steps back from economic policymaking
Note: The gray points depict the annual GDP growth percentage in Jordan, and the black points show the percent of articles in each year that were classified as addressing economic issues.

matters can be seen in the sharply different economic approaches taken by the governments of these three prime ministers. Ensour attempted to reduce economic pressures by increasing government spending dramatically, which worked to keep him relatively popular for a time. However, this strategy soon saddled the country with unsustainable debts, and al-Mulki turned to austerity policies instead, including tax increases and subsidy cuts (Sowell 2018). Al-Razzaz largely followed these policies.

Analysis of text data from the official websites of the monarchy, discussed in Chapter 4, reinforces how the king limited his involvement in economic affairs as the expected costs of being held responsible for economic policy increased. In black, Figure 6.1 plots the percentage of articles on the monarchy, by year of Abdullah's reign, that were focused predominantly on his role in shaping economic policy.[1] The figure also shows Jordan's annual GDP growth over that same period in gray. Lowess lines are plotted over the sixteen data points for both variables, illustrating a clear pattern. Early in his reign, GDP growth was relatively strong, and Abdullah was actively engaged in economic matters, with most years during this period showing 15–20 percent

---

[1] The percentage of articles in which the topic model suggested the article featured the king's involvement in economic policy matters.

204   *Power Sharing and Blame in Jordan Over Time*

of the articles classified in the economic topic. However, as GDP growth slowed, the percentage of articles classified in the economic topic dropped as well. By 2013, it was below ten, and it remained there until the data ended in 2017.[2]

The fact that Abdullah was more directly involved in economic policy prior to 2010 does appear to have left him relatively more exposed to public attributions of blame for domestic problems than his father was during similar moments in the 1980s. In particular, some of the youth activists and military veterans who became active in the protest movement launched unprecedented verbal attacks on the king and the royal family during the Arab Spring, most of which referenced privatization policies and their connection to corruption (Ryan 2018; Tell 2015; Yom 2014). For instance, in one particularly infamous incident during the Arab Spring, the king's motorcade was stoned by youth demonstrators during a visit to the impoverished East Bank town of Tafilah. In subsequent protest waves, the king was also, at times, criticized directly. As one Jordanian activist and political analyst noted, "Most people put the monarchy aside ... But you have a good percentage sometimes, who compare ... the era of King Hussein and the current era. Especially East Bank Jordanians, who say ... that they've lost their privileges because of privatization." As the decade of austerity has dragged on, a growing number of Jordanians appear willing to criticize the king publicly for corruption and economic malaise, prompting increasing use of repression by the security forces to silence this dissent (Schwedler 2021).

Nevertheless, even among the more radical protest groups, demonstrators publicly blaming the king have remained a minority (Ryan 2018), and many Jordanians continue to direct their anger toward the country's other institutions. Protests during al-Mulki's premiership illustrate this dynamic well. When al-Mulki became prime minister in 2016, he confronted a daunting economic situation defined by anemic growth and a skyrocketing debt-to-GDP ratio. He responded by pledging to pursue austerity, and in January 2018 his government passed

---

[2] The same caveats apply here as were discussed earlier – it is possible that this press is merely presentational and does not reflect the extent to which the king was actually involved in economic affairs in these years. Yet the manner in which this pattern aligns with the interview evidence suggests it is capturing actual variation in the king's efforts to shape these policies.

6.3 Power Sharing and Blame under King Abdullah

a budget that helped to slow the rising debt by increasing taxes and reducing subsidies (Sowell 2018). Unsurprisingly, these policies proved unpopular, and small but persistent protests plagued the government throughout the first half of the year. When al-Mulki's cabinet proposed further tax hikes in May, the country erupted. Mass protests led by trade unions and opposition activists clogged the streets of Amman and the demonstrators demanded that al-Mulki resign and the government withdraw the bill, which led to the king dismissing the prime minister and replacing him with Omar al-Razzaz. While these protests were large enough to force the prime minister's resignation, however, the vast majority of demonstrators did not direct their fury at the king.

Similarly, as the economic crisis continued during al-Razzaz's tenure, large and persistent demonstrations occurred in 2019 as the teacher's syndicate held the largest public-sector strike in Jordan's history to push for higher wages. Though al-Razzaz and his government eventually conceded on wages, they responded in 2020 by cracking down on the syndicate, spurring additional protests (Safi 2020). Again, however, despite the scale of the movement, the focus remained primarily on the government and not on the king.

Analysis of data from Google Trends suggests that Abdullah's attempts to step back from domestic policymaking following the Arab Spring helped to reduce his exposure to blame during a period of mass discontent with the state's economic performance. As with the Google Trends data from Morocco and Russia in Chapter 3, I collected monthly trends data in Jordan from the start of its availability in 2004 until the end of 2020, comparing search interest for King Abdullah to search interest for the twelve prime ministers who held office in this period.[3] I collapsed the data for the various prime ministers into a single variable based on who was in office at that time, and I then created a ratio of the monthly trend value for the king to the monthly trend value for the prime minister. This ratio is plotted in Figure 6.2, with higher values showing relatively more public attention on the king and vice versa.

[3] Because Google Trends only facilitates five searches at once, I conducted three searches: one for the four prime ministers prior to the Arab Spring, one for the four prime ministers during the Arab Spring, and one for the four prime ministers following the Arab Spring. The data from the Arab Spring were returned weekly due to the shorter time period, so I averaged the scores for each month.

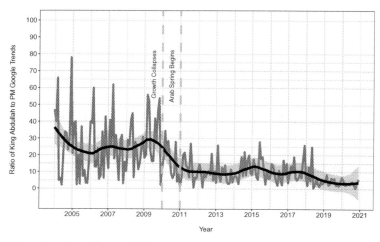

Figure 6.2 Google Trends for King Abdullah and prime ministers in Jordan
Note: Figure displays ratio of Google Trends for King Abdullah to his prime ministers for the period between 2004 and 2020. A higher ratio indicates relatively higher search interest in the king, suggesting greater public attention.

As with Russia and Morocco previously, more credible delegation by the king should result in relatively greater attention being given to the prime ministers. Because this more credible delegation means that the prime ministers become more important for making decisions that affect Jordanians' lives, Jordanians should start to search for more information about them online. It is a plausible assumption that this relatively greater attention should result in more blame directed at these officials – and away from the king – when the public is unhappy with policy outcomes. As shown in Figure 6.2, there is a large decline in the ratio around the time that Jordan began to experience economic difficulties and the pressures of the Arab Spring. This was the period in which the king began to share power over the policy process more credibly, aligning with the visible shift in the text data in Figure 6.1 earlier, as well as the appointment of more independent prime ministers and institutional reforms to increase the monarchy's distance from decision-making. In other words, the decline of the ratio at this moment is consistent with more credible delegation resulting in the king becoming relatively less exposed to the public's attributions at a time when discontent was mounting and the dangers of being blamed were increasing. Additional details for this analysis, including regression models and robustness checks, can be found in the chapter's appendix.

When faced with a declining economic situation and regional turmoil that raised the potential costs of being blamed for public grievances, Abdullah responded as the theory would predict, attempting to distance himself from day-to-day governance by strengthening the credibility of delegation to the cabinet and parliament. Though Abdullah has been more exposed to blame for unpopular policies than his father because of his association with the economic policies he championed directly in the early years of his reign, he appears to have limited his vulnerability by having his governments take the lead on economic matters and keeping a measure of the public's anger away from the monarchy.

6.4 Back to More Direct Royal Rule?

As was just discussed, King Abdullah responded to the pressures of the Arab Spring by stepping back from decision-making and delegating more credibly to the cabinet and parliament. However, some subsequent developments suggest that Abdullah continues to wish for a more active role for the monarchy in the policy process. In 2016, amendments to the constitution gave the king sole responsibility for appointing senior officials in the security apparatus, including the heads of the army, gendarmerie, and the GID. The king had previously gotten his way on such appointments, but formally they had needed to be initiated and approved by the cabinet. While these changes were in line with the monarchy's already-dominant role in foreign policy and national security, the amendments provoked serious opposition from Jordan's liberal reformists (Obeidat 2016). On the one hand, the move was seen as an indicator of the king's growing absolutist tendencies: Several interview subjects expressed the view that the political system was no longer a constitutional monarchy, but was now a "presidential" regime or even a plain old "dictatorship." On the other hand, many of these same figures expressed concerns that the king was provoking instability by placing himself – and the monarchy more generally – in the political firing line. As one opposition-inclined journalist put it, "if it's his sole decision to appoint the head of the army, this will negatively reflect on the king himself..." Another journalist noted that parliamentarians opposed to the amendments had told the king the changes were bad "because the system protected you ... but by doing this, if you appoint a guy who turns out to be bad, you cannot shirk responsibility."

Another set of amendments were pursued by the palace in 2021 and then ratified by parliament in January 2022. The king appointed a ninety-two-member "Royal Committee to Modernize the Political System" in June 2021, which included not only royalist stalwarts but also opposition-leaning political figures tied to the Muslim Brotherhood and leftist parties. Tasked with proposing reforms to democratize Jordan's political system, the committee developed a roadmap that is supposed to lead toward party-dominated parliaments that wield the power to appoint the prime minister. These reforms were approved by parliament and then signed by the king. If implemented fully over the next decade, these reforms could transform Jordan into a constitutional monarchy in which the king remains influential but possesses far more limited powers over decision-making (Yom and Al-Khatib 2022). In theory, this shift would substantially increase the monarchy's ability to avoid blame for poor governance. However, these reforms were passed alongside another set of amendments that strengthened the king's powers in other ways. Similar to those in 2016, these amendments gave the king the direct power to appoint several important officials, including the heads of the police and judiciary, as well as the Grand Mufti. In addition, the amendments created a new national foreign relations and security council headed by the king, which will exercise control over external policies, security issues, and the budget (Ersan 2021). To some extent, these changes merely reinforced the king's de facto (and well known) dominance over foreign policy and national security. Nonetheless, this formalized control makes it even less credible that the king is not directly responsible for decisions in these areas, and they are also likely to undermine the perceived decision-making role of the cabinet more broadly. While the effects of these changes on the credibility of power sharing may be somewhat ambiguous in the longer-term, particularly if the reforms strengthening parliament are adhered to, in the short run they appear to increase the king's relative power and are likely to increase perceptions of the monarchy's responsibility for governance outcomes.

Why might King Abdullah have pursued these changes at this time? The economic situation in Jordan remains dire, and popular pressure

6.5 Conclusion

on the regime continues to be high. Protests are frequent and discontent seems to be on an upward trajectory, which suggests that it will be costly to attract a greater share of the blame. One possibility consistent with the theory is that Abdullah is increasingly concerned about internal political struggles within the regime and is seeking to ward off these threats by formally concentrating greater powers in his own hands. The most visible example of this issue is the aforementioned coup plot that is alleged to have been connected in some way to the former crown prince, Hamzah. While the details remain murky, two important political elites in Jordan, the former royal court chief Bassem Awadallah and the distant royal Sharif Hassan bin Zaid, were convicted of sedition for trying to stir up anger against the king, possibly with the goal of replacing him with Hamzah. There are some insinuations that the plot received support from Saudi Arabia. Whatever the case, Hamzah was informally placed under house arrest and later renounced his royal title, while implicitly criticizing King Abdullah's rule (Ryan 2022). Hamzah remains popular in Jordan and could pose a genuine threat to either Abdullah or Crown Prince Hussein. This maneuvering also occurs at a time when the palace has been giving the crown prince an increasingly prominent role in royal affairs, signaling preparations for the eventual succession. Hussein does not appear to be especially popular in the country, and his Palestinian roots through his mother are allegedly a source of frustration for many of Jordan's East Bank elites. This fragile position may also contribute to Abdullah's attempts to formalize the monarchy's power over national security and foreign policy, for the purposes of protecting both himself and his son from future challenges within the regime.

It remains to be seen whether the king will continue back toward a more direct policymaking role for the monarchy, or whether he will honor the other set of formally-accepted reforms that promise to usher Jordan into an era of more genuinely-constitutional monarchy. As the discussion in this chapter shows, that choice is likely to have significant implications for the monarchy's exposure to popular anger during periods of discontent.

6.5 Conclusion

This chapter has shown that when the potential for popular dissatisfaction has increased in Jordan, the country's kings have typically responded by attempting to delegate more credibly to other political elites in the regime, whether by appointing stronger prime ministers or allowing reforms to increase the independence of the parliament. On the other hand, at times when the economy has boomed and the likelihood of widespread discontent seems low, the kings have been more likely to strengthen their hold over decision-making in a way that should position them to claim credit and reduce the influence of other political elites. These patterns align with the theory's expectations about strategic delegation, suggesting that the kings take the public's attributions into account when evaluating how and when to share power over policymaking.

The evidence presented in this chapter also implies that Jordanians' attributions of responsibility are shaped by the credibility of the monarchy's delegation. When the kings have delegated to more independent cabinets and parliaments, Jordanians have been more likely to direct their anger at these actors. Yet, at time periods where the king has more clearly been the key decision-maker, opposition has focused much more directly on the monarchy. In other words, Jordan's kings are not immune to popular dissatisfaction, and they have been more vulnerable to mass opposition when they have shared decision-making powers less credibly with other political elites. This pattern further supports the claim that autocrats become more vulnerable to blame and the loss of political support when they choose to concentrate powers more directly in their own hands.

One point that reinforces this relationship between delegation and blame attributions is the issues for which Jordan's kings have typically faced the most direct criticism. Throughout the country's history, the monarchy has been more likely to come under attack because of policy decisions and outcomes related to foreign affairs and national security, over which the kings have more consistently wielded direct control. Whether the kingdom's pro-British policies of the 1950s, defeats by Israel in the 1960s, civil war with Palestinian nationalists in the 1970s, attempts to forge a peace agreement with Israel in the 1980s and 1990s, or participation in the War on Terror in the 2000s, the monarchy's influence over these policies has often motivated opposition targeting the king. In contrast, anger at economic developments has historically been less likely to tarnish the king's support. To the extent that this dynamic has changed, it has done so under the reign of Abdullah, who has involved himself much more closely in economic decision-making than his father.

6.5 Conclusion

It is important to note how my discussion of Jordanian political developments and their relationship to my theory differ from the predictions of other important political science theories about authoritarian politics. There are two related but distinct arguments that are relevant here. The first is that the monarchy strengthens the credibility of power sharing to ensure the loyalty of elite allies during moments of discontent by rewarding them with greater influence. However, the greater decision-making influence of these elites has often resulted in them being held accountable and removed from office after they are blamed for governance failures, which would be an odd move for the king to make if the primary goal was to cement their loyalty. Furthermore, even during periods where the king has dominated decision-making the most, elites have still had access to rents that tie them to the regime and facilitate co-optation. Thus, power sharing related to policymaking seems to shift more in response to the monarchy's concerns about being blamed for the public's grievances. The second argument is that delegation is not crucial for protecting the king from blame, but rather that the monarchy is engaging in policy responsiveness by allowing political elites to steer the country's policies in the direction that the people want, which then strengthens support for the monarchy. But in many of the periods of higher delegation, Jordan's governments ended up pursuing deeply unpopular policies that generated mass opposition to the prime minister and their cabinets, suggesting a failure to respond effectively to the public's preferences. While both of these dynamics do occur in Jordan to some extent, neither is likely to account fully for the patterns discussed in the chapter and summarized in the paragraphs earlier.

Yet another alternative explanation could be that the king delegates more credibly to convince the public that Jordan is a democracy, thus satisfying Jordanians' preference to be governed democratically. At certain points, this dynamic likely applies to the king's strategic logic, as I explore in other works. During the riots of 1989 and during the Arab Spring, many demonstrators called for more democracy, and the king responded by strengthening parliament in part to address these demands. However, the kings' own rhetoric around these moments suggests that an important motive for their approach was to grant parliament greater responsibility so that it could redirect pressure from the monarchy, which is consistent with the relevance of blame avoidance. In addition, many of the other maneuverings of the monarchs described in this chapter, such as choosing stronger or weaker prime ministers, seem much less directly related to attempts to convince the public of Jordan's democratic character.

One question is why Jordanians have not learned over time that they are being manipulated in some way by the king's strategy. My argument actually suggests that the public is not just being manipulated (though certainly propaganda and misdirection are used by the regime), but is instead reacting to genuine changes in the balance of power between the king and other political elites. As the king is more involved, he receives more blame or credit; as he backs away credibly, the public attributes less responsibility to him. Just because the strategy appears to reinforce the stability of Jordan's authoritarian regime does not mean that the wool has been completely pulled over the people's eyes about how power operates in the system.

At the same time, there are some indications that Jordanians have become increasingly disgruntled with the political system and that these attitudes may be undermining support for the monarchy. While the cabinet may take the lead in day-to-day governance, it remains the case that the king appoints the prime minister and is assumed to be involved in the selection of the ministers. While they may bear the brunt of the blame for decisions they make directly, the king's reputation may still be affected if he is perceived to repeatedly appoint ineffective officials. Over time, this dynamic may sap support for the monarchy even if power sharing remains relatively credible and continues to help protect the king from absorbing even more of the public's anger.

In the following chapter, I consider how the relationship between power sharing and blame in the Jordanian context has influenced other aspects of the country's governance. I discuss the regime's reliance on relatively limited repression and how this approach – along with access to rents – affects elites' willingness to take the blame. I also show how the monarchy is able to use delegation to provide limited accountability, and I explore why delegation makes it difficult for the opposition to coordinate against the regime.

7 | How Jordan's Blame Games Influence Governance

Samir al-Rifai was first appointed prime minister of Jordan during World War II, while the country was still a British protectorate. Nearly two decades later, he served as prime minister for his sixth and final time in 1963. Throughout his career, al-Rifai developed a reputation as a conservative known for "toughness" and "strongman" politics (Ashton 2008). A young King Hussein appointed him prime minister at several moments of crisis, in which al-Rifai took the blame for using heavy-handed tactics against opponents of his government and the monarchy more generally. Unsurprisingly, this approach earned him relatively few friends. He was unpopular with much of the public, and he clashed often with the king as well. Nonetheless, al-Rifai used his influence to shape the policies of the Jordanian state and acquire significant wealth. Furthermore, even when he was forced to leave office, the king always held out the possibility that he could return to government in the future. After his sixth time as prime minister, al-Rifai became president of the Jordanian senate, and he died in office two years later, in 1965.

In fact, al-Rifai's influence outlasted his death. A decade after his final term as prime minister, his son, Zaid al-Rifai, was appointed to the position in 1973, serving for three years. Zaid then returned to the office for a second term from 1985 to 1989. Like his father, he was generally disliked, and also like his father, he used the office to generate wealth through an extensive array of corrupt activities (Shlaim 2007). As mentioned in the previous chapter, Zaid was ousted by King Hussein in response to the mass protests of the 1989 April Uprising, but like his father, he later became president of the Jordanian senate as well. Furthermore, Zaid's son, named Samir after his grandfather, would also serve as prime minister, taking office in 2009. With history repeating itself, Samir and his government were dismissed as the Arab Spring protests erupted in early 2011, but he continued to remain a fixture of Jordanian politics and was appointed by the king to lead the Political Modernization Committee in 2021.

The al-Rifais' political history illustrates several aspects of governance in Jordan that are shaped by the monarchy's delegation of policymaking responsibility to political elites in the cabinet, parliament, and other institutions. Because the monarchy is less exposed to blame as a result of delegation, it has less need to repress the public, and protests frequently target nonroyal decision-makers such as the al-Rifais without facing significant violence from the security forces. The kings do what they can to reduce the costs experienced by elites for taking the blame, so they rarely punish them for poor performance beyond removing them from office, but rather allow them continued access to rents as well as the chance to return to positions of influence in the future. However, because the king removes these elites from office when public dissatisfaction with their performance becomes pronounced, the political system does provide the public with some degree of accountability. These patterns reflect the theory's expectations about the relationship between more credible power sharing, attributions, and governance outcomes, insofar as Jordan is less repressive than many authoritarian regimes, protests are tolerated since opposition rarely escalates into attacks on the monarch, and accountability is attained through the removal of decision-makers following visible public discontent.

This chapter discusses these dynamics further. To do so, I draw on my interviews with Jordanian political elites, data on Jordanian protests, and an original dataset of Jordanian ministers who have held office from the 1950s until the present. I first draw on the protest data and interviews to discuss the use of repression in Jordan, illustrating how it is rarely used against most citizens or elites but is instead highly targeted to punish specific individuals who openly criticize the king. I then explore how this approach incentivizes loyalist elites to take the blame for the king, while also complicating the ability of the opposition to coordinate effectively against the monarchy. Finally, I turn to my data on ministerial tenures to show that ministers are substantially more likely to be removed from office following major governance failures or visible indicators of popular dissatisfaction.

7.1 Limiting Repression

As the theory would expect given the nature of power sharing in Jordan, repression is less intense under the Hashemite monarchy than

7.1 *Limiting Repression* 215

it is in many other authoritarian regimes. According to V-Dem, Jordan's mean civil liberties score between 1952 and 2020 places it in the top quarter of authoritarian regimes with regard to respect for personal and political freedoms. This relatively limited repression exists for both the public and political elites, as will be discussed in detail below. On many topics, Jordanians are able to not only speak their minds but also to mobilize collectively without fear of punishment; likewise, political elites are rarely targeted with severe sanctions by the regime. That is not to say that repression is absent from the political system, and many Jordanians do face repercussions for voicing their opinions. However, this repression tends to be targeted, focusing on individuals who criticize the king and the monarchy specifically.

This approach to repression reflects the ability of the king to avoid blame for many of the country's problems. Because disgruntled Jordanians typically focus their anger not on the king but on other actors in the political system, the monarchy is less threatened by public expressions of discontent and is therefore less likely to crack down on them. At the same time, limited repression of political elites facilitates the existence of the monarchy's delegation strategy by lowering the costs experienced by elites when they are blamed for the public's grievances. If the monarch routinely punished these elites severely for governance failures, they might be less willing to play the king's blame games. Instead, those who attract the public's anger know that they will most likely maintain their access to economic rents even after they lose office, and many of them are given the chance to return to positions of influence in the future. Thus, many elites calculate that it is in their interest to hold positions with responsibility over the decision-making process because the benefits can be quite high and the costs tend to be relatively low. It is important to note, however, that this system is bolstered by repression of those who challenge the monarchy publicly. The existence of this redline makes it harder for opponents of the monarchy to coordinate effectively and incentivizes many of them to reinforce rather than weaken the king's ability to avoid blame. This section discusses each of these points in turn.

7.1.1 *Permitting Protest, Mostly*

As the previous chapters should have demonstrated, protests have been a frequent occurrence in Jordanian history. Whether the mass protests of 1989 and 2011 or smaller mobilizations of a few dozen individuals focused on specific grievances, collective action has long been a central component of Jordanian politics (Schwedler 2022). For the most part, such protests are tolerated by the regime. Historically, the intensity of repression has waxed and waned, and some groups of Jordanians are more likely to be confronted with repression than others. Focusing on the monarchy is also likely to trigger a response from the security apparatus. Nonetheless, the general approach of the regime is one of permissiveness when it comes to mobilization. The fact that protests rarely express anger against the king likely contributes to this relatively muted response. As has been discussed previously, Jordanians are more likely to direct blame for their grievances at the cabinet, parliament, bureaucracy, or some other political actor because they are perceived by many to bear responsibility for governance outcomes. As a result, the king is less likely to feel threatened by mobilization and often benefits from it, as will be explored at the end of the chapter regarding the provision of accountability in Jordan. Of course, large, sustained protests do have the potential to threaten the monarchy and regime stability, the security forces often do break up protests, and Jordanian history is replete with examples of repression reflecting archetypal images of political contestation in authoritarian regimes. However, the important point is that repression in Jordan is less intensive than in many other cases, in part because the king's approach to power sharing helps to redirect anger away from the monarchy.

To illustrate more systematically how common protests are in Jordan, I draw on data compiled from monitoring of twenty different local news sources.[1] Protest datasets built from local sources tend to provide the most comprehensive coverage of collective action within a country (Clarke 2021); indeed, the dataset records 4,967 protests in Jordan between 2010 and 2019, reflecting an average of 1.4 protest events per day over this time span. Figure 7.1 shows the distribution of these protests by year. Their intensity is highest during the Arab Spring from 2011 to 2013, and they peak again during the 2018 tax protests and the 2019 teacher's union protests, but even from 2014 to 2017 the dataset records close to an average of one protest per day.

---

[1] The data were collected by a team of Arabic-speaking researchers based in the Middle East.

7.1 Limiting Repression

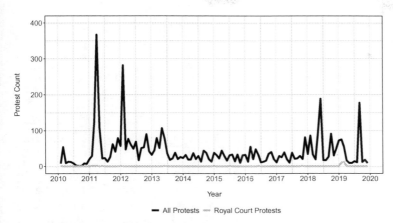

Figure 7.1 Protests in Jordan occur frequently
Note: Figure displays protest counts from 2010 to 2020. Whereas protests are common overall, they are very rare in front of the Royal Court.

The protest dataset also compiles information about where the protests took place. One proxy for protesters focusing on the monarchy is protests that take place in front of the Royal Court. Figure 7.1 also plots the occurrence of these events over time, showing that they take place infrequently. This proxy does not necessarily capture anger against the king, as protesters may see mobilization outside the Royal Court as a strategy for directing the king's attention toward their plight, and demonstrations elsewhere may still attack the king directly. Nonetheless, the rarity of these events helps to illustrate how infrequently Jordanians visibly try to bring the king into their protests, indicating why the monarchy may feel less need to repress collective action. In addition, the dataset codes whether demonstrations focused on political, economic, or social grievances. The majority – 57 percent – were coded as protests motivated primarily by economic grievances. Only 26 percent were predominantly political in nature, and the other 18 percent focused on social grievances. With most demonstrations addressing economic or social issues and most political protests not targeting their anger at the monarchy, the king can afford to avoid harsh crackdowns on public mobilization in most circumstances.

This limited repression is reflected in the protest dataset, which also records whether demonstrators were arrested, wounded, or killed at

218   *How Jordan's Blame Games Influence Governance*

Table 7.1 *Most protests in Jordan are not repressed*

	All protests	Protests by opposition
Protesters arrested (%)	2.3	2.7
Protesters wounded (%)	1.1	2.5
Protesters killed (%)	0.3	0.7

Table shows the percent of protest events in which protesters experienced repression.

each event. The data may undercount these incidents of repression to some extent, since local media may be less capable of acquiring or publishing accurate information about cases of protest that the regime views as more threatening. In general, however, press freedom in Jordan is good enough that such information should be accessible when triangulating information from multiple media sources. Furthermore, even if the dataset undercounts repressive incidents substantially, the numbers are such that it would still be the case that the vast majority of demonstrations in Jordan are not subjected to repression. Table 7.1 shows that protesters were recorded as being arrested at 2.3 percent of protests in the dataset, that protesters were reported wounded in 1.1 percent of protests, and that protesters were found to have been killed in 0.3 percent of protests. The table also lists the percent of protests linked explicitly to opposition movements, including leftists, youth activists, and Islamists. These groups are most likely to organize political protests and are most likely to challenge the monarch openly, though doing so is still relatively rare. The data indicate that these protests are somewhat more likely to experience repression, but even here, the vast majority go forward without harsh crackdowns from the security forces. In other words, Jordanians have significant leeway to mobilize and express their views on political, economic, and social issues. This situation is likely facilitated in part by the ability of the monarchy to avoid bearing the brunt of protesters' anger during periods of discontent.

7.1.2 Incentivizing Elite Loyalty

It is not just the Jordanian public that experiences relatively muted repression compared to the reality of many other authoritarian regimes. Political elites have also been unlikely to face harsh repression

7.1 Limiting Repression

from the monarchy. This restraint by the kings is important for maintaining the loyalty of these individuals. In my interviews, it was the most common answer from elite interview subjects about why the monarchy in Jordan had survived for so long. As one well-connected lawyer stated when trying to explain the stability of the Jordanian system, "there is no bloodshed in our history of the royal family." The fates of those who perhaps came closest to overturning the monarchy during the upheavals of the late 1950s illustrate why this view is widespread among Jordan's political elites. As prime minister, Suleiman al-Nabulsi had confronted and attempted to sideline the monarchy, prompting the 1957 political crisis that triggered an alleged coup attempt by the chief of staff of the Jordanian military, Ali Abu Nuwar. Al-Nabulsi spent several years under house arrest following Hussein's subsequent crackdown, while Abu Nuwar fled into exile. By the early 1960s, however, al-Nabulsi had been pardoned and released, and Abu Nuwar was likewise pardoned a few years later. Both men would eventually hold positions again in the Jordanian state. Forgiveness rather than ferocity has been the primary approach of Jordan's kings when it comes to handling the country's political elites, certainly when speaking from a comparative perspective.

This approach is reflected in how the kings typically deal with elites who attract public anger for their performance in office. While they are frequently removed from office, it is rare for them to be treated harshly. In some cases, leading officials are punished as scapegoats. In 2012, for instance, the former head of the GID, Mohammed al-Dahabi, received a thirteen year prison sentence for corruption during his four year term at the intelligence agency. The charges for which he was found guilty included money laundering, embezzlement, and abuse of power, and he was said to have acquired more than thirty million dollars through these activities, which he was ordered to pay back to the government (Al-Khalidi 2012). Al-Dahabi was an unpopular figure, and his arrest occurred approximately one year after the initial protests of the Arab Spring, as the regime attempted to demonstrate its commitment to rooting out corruption and implementing political reforms. Dozens of former ministers and businessmen were also investigated during this period, though relatively few were brought to court. However, cases such as al-Dahabi's are uncommon: Elites who rise far up in the regime are rarely punished with violence or imprisonment, even if they engage in conduct that generates serious public anger.

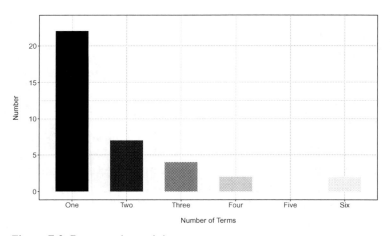

Figure 7.2 Repeat prime ministers
Note: Figure displays the number of terms held by Jordan's prime ministers.

Instead, powerful political elites are often allowed to return to office in the future once the furor over their performance has dissipated. The al-Rifais illustrate this possibility well, as discussed in the opening paragraphs of the chapter, but as Figure 7.2 shows, they are not the only prime ministers to have served multiple terms. Ibrahim Hashem was prime minister six times, while Tawfiq Abu al-Huda and Bahjat al-Talhouni were prime minister four times. Wasfi al-Tell held the position three times, as did Said al-Mufti, Zaid ibn Shaker, and Mudar Badran. The latter's younger brother, Adnan Badran, also served as prime minister, while Hani al-Mulki – the prime minister from 2016 to 2019 – was the son of a prime minister from the early 1950s. Another seven prime ministers were appointed to the office twice. Furthermore, former prime ministers are often called back frequently to participate in other government positions, especially in the senate, which is appointed by the king. Nearly every president of Jordan's senate has been a former prime minister.

It is not just prime ministers who have the chance to return to office in the future: ministers do as well. Using data I collected on ministers who held positions in the cabinet between 1947 and 2018, I find that approximately 40 percent of ministers were appointed more than once, including 20 percent who held office twice and another 17 percent who served as a minister several times. A handful of individuals were appointed six or more times, with a maximum of thirteen terms. Some

7.1 Limiting Repression 221

of these ministers earned repeat appointments in the same ministries in which they developed their expertise; for example, Mohammed al-Shanqiti was minister of education six times. Others circulated through several positions. For instance, Khalid al-Karaki served in the ministries of culture, education, higher education, and youth, while Nasser al-Lawzi was minister of transportation, culture, and public works. Particularly for ministers who perform well and establish relationships across the government, one's first appointment may only be a stepping stone to influence in future governments, even if they are removed from their first position to absorb blame for some outcome that has angered the public.

This relatively benign treatment of political elites who influence decision-making is an important component of the monarchy's ability to delegate successfully, because it lowers the costs of taking the blame. These costs are real for many elites who hold important political positions. As an illustration of these costs, most prime ministers leave office substantially less popular than when they entered, according to the public approval data gathered by the Center for Strategic Studies. For example, in the months before he resigned, following the passage of a deeply unpopular budget, Prime Minister Hani al-Mulki's approval had fallen to just 29 percent of the public. Popular dissatisfaction also hit the government ministers and MPs who had helped to pass al-Mulki's budget. A former minister whom I interviewed at the time shared an anecdote in which "no members of parliament dared to attend" a commemoration for Jordanians killed in the fight against ISIS because nobody knew "how people would react." Likewise, the minister passed on accounts of "signs at the entrances of some diwans [tribal gathering halls]" saying that "no members of parliament are allowed [to enter]." Given the extent to which most MPs depend on tribal support to maintain their positions and are closely embedded in these communities, such anger implies a sharp reduction in social status. More generally, when ministers and members of parliament are perceived to have failed in their duties – whether by performing poorly, being fired quickly, or losing an election – they often come to be "viewed negatively" by their constituents. If these elites needed to worry that they would not only become deeply unpopular but would also be imprisoned or harassed by the state to satiate the public, they would likely be far less willing to take the blame for the king. But while cases such as the imprisonment of al-Dahabi remain rare, and with many elites able to count on returning to political office in the future once the public's anger shifts elsewhere, the monarchy is able to keep the costs of being blamed relatively low.

Elites also receive positive incentives to hold important decision-making positions that may subject them to the public's anger. In particular, holding public office provides opportunities to acquire rents, even after one's term in office ends. Consider how one opposition activist described the motivation of Jordanians running to be MPs:

They [elites] have all done so well in the new order with privatization. A lot of people who are running for parliament are average people trying to get into this system, this alumni association. They're trying to use parliament to parachute into that system. It's well known, it's not something that is hidden though it is not well documented ... They run for self-interest. They run for investment opportunities. They want the ability to rub shoulders with elites and to get contracts for their companies. It's a small country, so it's all about who you know. Political and business elites are quite intertwined.

This idea of the elite "alumni association" that enriches its members is widely held across the country. Others referred to this network as a "club" or "mafia." A former minister noted that many members of parliament are "looking after their own interests," claiming that "you have a good number who are contractors or lawyers and who go in front of courts or lobby for their clients administratively with the government." In other words, they "have business deals with the government" that benefit their bottom lines. Once formed, these networks are sticky and permit elites to continue building their economic portfolios after they no longer hold their positions, even if they leave office reviled by much of the public. Crackdowns on corruption are rare in Jordan; as a result, continued access to rents provides a strong incentive to participate in decision-making and shield the monarchy from blame.

Positions in the government and parliament also provide the ability to steer jobs, services, and other material benefits to one's family and community. For example, one interview subject alleged that a senior MP affiliated with the Muslim Brotherhood – ostensibly an opposition organization – approached ministers in the government almost "daily" to ask that they find jobs for his many children and relatives. Others noted how holding office "gives your tribe prominence and ... gives

7.1 Limiting Repression

you a chance to serve your community," in part because it involves the opportunity to receive benefits like "special medications" for your supporters. Lust-Okar (2006, 2009) and Kao (2015) have documented how members of parliament use their positions to distribute various forms of patronage to their constituencies, many of which are tribal with strong familial connections.

Altogether then, political elites who wield influence over the decision-making process can expect relatively benign treatment by the monarchy, including a low likelihood of being punished for unpopular performance in office and the opportunity to acquire economic rents for one's self and one's community. In addition, they can expect to have some influence over decision-making that may permit them to nudge the country's policies more toward their own preferences, as has been discussed in Chapters 4–6. This combination of incentives encourages elites to bear responsibility for policy outcomes, allowing the kings to delegate in a manner that helps to limit the monarchy's exposure to blame.

7.1.3 Targeting the King's Most Vocal Opponents

As Chapters 5 and 6 made clear, not all Jordanians absolve the monarchy of blame for their grievances. Many believe that the monarchy's powers mean it is to blame for the country's trajectory, even if the king does delegate responsibility for specific policy decisions to elites within the political system. Others believe that delegation is just for show and that the king calls the shots for all major policies. At certain points in the country's history, this anger at the monarchy has been both vocal and visible. Since the Arab Spring, for instance, King Abdullah has faced more direct criticism than was common in previous decades, as activists tied the king to policies he had openly championed (Schwedler 2022). For these Jordanians who dare to speak out against the king, the relatively hands-off approach of the monarchy that has been discussed so far becomes much more heavy-handed. They face harassment from the coercive apparatus as well as potential jail time under the *lèse majeste* law that criminalizes criticism of the monarchy.

Harassment takes many forms. A commonly reported tactic that the GID uses to intimidate the king's critics is to lean on their family members and close acquaintances to pressure them to stop. One activist who had been outspoken against the king described how the

GID would call his family members and his tribal sheikh, asking them to take responsibility and stop his activism. Similarly, one journalist described how their spouse pressured them to quit writing critical stories after they received negative attention from the security apparatus. Another editor working at a critical media outlet left after the GID leaned on a business partner to convince them to leave the company.

The security apparatus will also threaten to block the person or their family from government services and other opportunities. One interview subject claimed that "almost every government document goes to the GID for their approval." If someone who is causing problems needs a new passport, license, or anything else, the GID can reject them until they cooperate. Two editors of opposition-oriented independent media outlets said that they had faced financial difficulties because of pressure on advertisers to avoid doing business with them. I was also told of a case in which an MP voted against the government on an important bill and then found that pressure was being applied on private companies not to hire his son. Such tactics can make life difficult for those who speak out too openly and cross the regime's redlines.

Blaming the king publicly for the country's problems – or even attacking his advisers in the royal court or the GID – is also likely to end the political career of any elite who dares to take this step. They are unofficially disqualified from holding important offices in the state, even if their positions limit the other consequences they experience. As articulated by one former minister, "there is an unspoken rule that if you want to be in politics, you don't challenge these issues [the royal court and GID], and if you do you cannot be in government. It's unwritten but everybody knows it."

While Jordan is not known for murdering or disappearing the king's critics, as occurs in many other authoritarian regimes, the threat of imprisonment is very real for those who challenge the monarchy directly. The *lèse majeste* law dictates penalties of one to three years in prison for insulting the king, queen, or crown prince, and those affiliated with activist circles are likely to know friends and colleagues jailed for speaking out too critically. A number of these cases are prosecuted each year. One example involved a Salafi preacher who wrote a Facebook post called, "Jordan going down the toilet." The post criticized "un-Islamic" phenomenon such as unveiled women, vineyards, and also Jordan's participation in the Charlie Hebdo march. Since the only Jordanian to participate in the march was the king, mentioning the march was enough for the preacher to be jailed. Prominent individuals can also be swept up by the law, though such occurrences are rarer. In 2020, for instance, a former member of parliament known as a long-time critic of the monarchy was arrested on charges that included insulting the king and queen (Younes 2017).

In line with the monarchy's targeted use of repression, imprisonment in these cases is often short. According to one human rights analyst, usually "people get arrested and held for a couple of weeks, and the charges don't really move forward." The king also tries to downplay the perceived importance of the laws to the monarchy. In late 2021, for example, the king pardoned dozens of Jordanians charged for insulting him or undermining the monarchy (IPI 2021). However, the government stated that it had no plans to repeal the law going forward, and other charges are also brought against activists who oppose the monarchy directly. In early 2022, for instance, ten activists were arrested on charges of "broadcasting false news that aims at causing internal strife." The arrests occurred following news reports about King Abdullah's wealth, and they appeared to be motivated by the subsequent spread of criticism of the monarchy online (Ersan 2022). In fact, human rights reporting suggests that such crackdowns have become more common in Jordan since 2019, with the security forces using vague charges of "undermining the regime" to target activists and journalists more aggressively (Human Rights Watch 2019, 2020). While repression in Jordan may be less pervasive and more targeted than in many other authoritarian regimes, the costs of speaking out in ways that challenge the monarchy can be highly detrimental to the lives of individual Jordanians.

7.2 The Failure of Anti-Monarchical Coordination

As discussed in Section 7.1 of this chapter, protests and other forms of political action are common in Jordan, but they rarely escalate into direct challenges against the monarchy. Those protests that do criticize the king or others in the royal court tend to be small and on the fringes of Jordanian politics, and that has now been the case for several decades, even during periods of consistently poor governance. The evidence from previous chapters suggests that this pattern can be explained in part by credible delegation of decision-making responsibilities convincing enough Jordanians that the monarchy is not to blame for their grievances. However, even many of the opposition activists and other political elites who do hold the king at fault typically fail at coordinating against the monarchy, choosing for strategic reasons to publicly absolve the king of guilt by casting blame on the prime minister, cabinet, parliament, or bureaucracy. In doing so, they reinforce the monarchy's reputation and make coordination against the king even less likely to succeed. This section explains how delegation interacts with the targeted repression described above to undermine the ability of anti-royal activists to challenge the monarchy effectively.

Consider the calculation a political activist must make if they personally wish to criticize the king and are deciding whether to organize pubic opposition around this stance. If enough Jordanians privately agree with them that the king is to blame, the activist may be able to act as a first mover who triggers widespread opposition against the monarchy directly. In this case, the concessions gained from the regime are likely to be high, and perhaps regime change itself could be on the table. However, if the activist fails to attract enough public support for their challenge to the monarchy, their small protest is unlikely to achieve any concrete objectives; instead, they are likely to be subjected to the repressive costs discussed previously, including harassment by the coercive apparatus and potentially imprisonment. On the other hand, if the activist hides their true opinions about the king's responsibility, and focuses their anger against other political elites, they are less likely to facilitate transformational change in the political system. But their efforts will likely be tolerated by the regime rather than repressed. In fact, even if they are linked openly to the opposition, they may have the ability to join parliament and perhaps the cabinet, from which they can influence state policies and achieve some of their more modest objectives. Thus, the activists face a choice between challenging the monarchy and risking the regime's targeted repression to achieve their maximalist goals or directing their anger lower for the chance to shape decision-making within the constraints of the royal system.

Among other factors, delegation is likely to affect this calculation. As the king delegates more credibly, fewer Jordanians should hold him responsible for their grievances, which should make it less likely that the activists succeed at mobilizing large enough crowds to challenge the king effectively. Even if they personally believe that the king is at fault, the expectations that not enough people will join them and that

7.2 The Failure of Anti-Monarchical Coordination

they will then face repression from the security forces should provide strong incentives to hide their true beliefs and strategically direct their blame away from the monarchy.

These incentives usually win out in enticing the opposition to play the king's blame games. Many of them believe that much of the public is sincere in attributing blame to actors and institutions other than the king, meaning that they are unlikely to find a receptive audience when they speak out. As one activist noted, "No one has ever gotten anywhere going after the king or monarchy ... in a society where he has overwhelming support." When Hirak activists during the Arab Spring engaged in unprecedented attacks on King Abdullah, they likely hoped to trigger widespread, public displays of anger against the monarchy. But this anger never materialized outside of relatively limited circles, meaning that the security apparatus could effectively punish those activists who did cross the regime's redline. In fact, according to one Jordanian analyst who is close to many of the activists in Hirak and other youth movements, targeting the king was "one of their mistakes," and it actually lost them support with the public. Now, their position is that "you have nothing to do with the king," because "he is responsible, but you cannot tell people that." In response, many of them adjusted their strategy to avoid targeting the king, focusing on blaming other political figures and institutions in an effort to build popular support for their economic and political demands.

This approach also reflects the predominant strategy of the Jordanian Muslim Brotherhood. As the largest and most organized opposition group in the country, they have typically refrained from blaming the king directly, and they have participated in several parliamentary elections since 1989 to establish a degree of input on the policy process (Wiktorowicz 1999). An MP associated with the Muslim Brotherhood's bloc in parliament described this position to me in an interview, noting how the organization tries to maintain a good relationship with the palace while focusing their criticisms on the government and its decisions instead. He stated, "We [the Muslim Brotherhood] lived together under the umbrella of four great kings ... If the government took positive decisions, we would support them, not oppose them automatically. We oppose their bad decisions."

This stance is understandable given the personal costs of repression that come with blaming the king publicly. However, in adopting this strategy, the opposition likely reinforces perceptions among the public

228 *How Jordan's Blame Games Influence Governance*

that the king is not to blame, undermining the likelihood of revolutionary mass mobilization in the process. When Jordanians evaluate who in the political system is responsible for the country's problems, they might expect that organizations and individuals identified with the opposition would be most likely to blame the king. If even the opposition chooses not to do so, it should send a relatively strong signal that blame lies elsewhere, with the officials and institutions to which the king has delegated. As one opposition activist observed:

It is important for the political elite to talk more clearly. I used to talk about policies in general but now I talk about the king on Facebook directly ... When you talk to the people saying the problem is the economy, poverty, etc., then you're not making it clear to the people. It is important to emphasize directly that the problem is with the royal court and the king.

In reinforcing perceptions that the king is not to blame, the opposition facilitates the longer term stability of the king's support. This role, and the way in which it is motivated in part by fear of coercion, helps to explain why delegation need not convince all Jordanians that the king can do no wrong to be effective at protecting the monarchy over time. These dynamics also illustrate how delegation reduces the likelihood that protests escalate to challenge the monarchy.

7.3 Providing Limited Accountability

Thus far, the chapter has discussed the link between delegation, repression, and the escalation of opposition in Jordan. The monarchy's sharing of decision-making powers also has implications for the provision of accountability in the political system. Because blame is less likely to be directed at the king, the regime permits many expressions of popular discontent, and the monarchy is able to evaluate whether officials have lost the support of the public because of their performance in office. When this loss of support occurs, these officials are more likely to lose their positions. Insofar as this removal reflects a form of sanctioning for their role in decision-making, it provides a limited measure of accountability to the public.

The functioning of this system is visible in how the king and his advisers in the palace pay close attention to public approval of the prime minister so that they know when removal may be warranted in

7.3 Providing Limited Accountability 229

response to popular opinion. Since the 1990s, the Center for Strategic Studies at the University of Jordan has conducted regular approval polls of the prime minister and parliament, and these polls are allegedly reviewed closely by the palace. At one point in the late 1990s, a prime minister angered by his low approval ratings forced out the director of the center, in a maneuver designed to reduce its independence. However, the king soon restored the director himself, ratifying the institution's ability to serve as a barometer of public opinion toward the government.

These same dynamics apply to individual cabinet ministers, who are often asked to resign after they are perceived to have performed poorly, or after public pressure in which they are blamed directly for some grievance. As one tragic example, the ministers of tourism and education resigned in November 2018, following an accident in which several schoolgirls were killed by a flash flood while on a field trip near the Dead Sea. After the incident, Prime Minister al-Razzaz faced pressure from citizens, MPs, and the king for those at fault to be removed from their positions, and he conceded that he and his government held "administrative, procedural, and moral responsibility" for what had occurred (Al-Sharif 2018). Pressure on the government included a parliamentary probe that cited the tourism and education ministries for negligence in their emergency preparedness (Al-Khalidi, 2018b), as well as a statement by the king calling for "a report that determines what took place," so as "to identify who should be held accountable" (Al-Sharif 2018). As another example, the interior minister resigned during the COVID-19 pandemic after rioting followed the announcement of election results in November 2020. The minister, Tawfiq al-Halalmeh, said that he had "submitted his resignation out of the concept of moral responsibility," implying that the breakdown in law and order was his fault. The resignation was then "sent to his majesty the king and it was accepted" (The National 2020), completing the provision of accountability for this specific governance failure.

It is possible to test empirically whether Jordanian officials are removed from their positions more frequently during periods of intense pressure on the political system, when the public is clearly frustrated with governance outcomes. To do so, I use data on 964 ministerial tenures between 1947 and 2018 to evaluate whether Jordanian ministers are more likely to be removed from office when the potential for

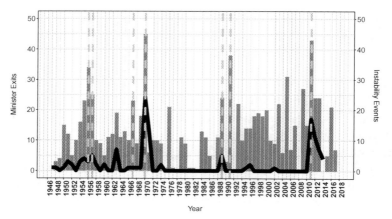

Figure 7.3 Minister exits by year, 1947–2018
Note: Bars indicate the number of ministers removed each year. The black line indicates the number of political instability events recorded by Banks each year. The vertical light grey lines indicate crisis years, from left to right: Challenges from the al-Nabulsi government in 1956 and 1957; the Six Day War with Israel in 1967; the civil war of Black September in 1970; the economic crisis in 1989; the Gulf War in 1991; the Arab Spring in 2011.

public pressure on the regime is high. Each tenure is a single observation, even if the minister had previously held office. I collected this data primarily from the official websites of Jordan's ministries, most of which include timelines of the ministers who have served in them, and data from some missing ministries were compiled from other assorted sources.[2]

Figure 7.3 uses two approaches to demonstrate that removals occur with greater frequency during periods of heightened public discontent, reflecting the argument that ministers are being fired as an accountability mechanism. First, the black line uses data compiled by Banks to plot the number of instability incidents in each year that are indicative of popular pressure on the regime.[3] These count data show that a higher number of incidents typically aligns with a higher number of

---

[2] Data were collected from twenty ministries. Those for which data were incomplete or unavailable included: finance; tourism and antiquities; water and irrigation; agriculture; and information and communications technology.

[3] This measure includes protests, strikes, riots, insurgent attacks, assassinations, crises, and attempted revolutions.

7.3 Providing Limited Accountability

Table 7.2 *Minister removals and public pressure*

	OLS removals (1)	NB removals (2)	OLS removals (3)	NB removals (4)
Instability count			1.30***	0.06**
			(0.26)	(0.02)
Major crises	21.05***	1.07***		
	(2.88)	(0.28)		
Constant	10.95***	2.39***	10.86***	2.42***
	(0.96)	(0.10)	(1.16)	(0.11)
R^2	0.43		0.27	
Obs.	72	72	68	68

*** $p < 0.001$; ** $p < 0.01$; * $p < 0.05$; † $p < 0.10$

minister removals in that year, with the minister removals displayed by the dark gray bars. Second, as a robustness check, the light gray lines mark self-coded political crises confronted by the regime during these seventy years, all of which involved significant public grievances that suggested the potential for a revolutionary uprising.[4] As with the Bank's data, these crises align with especially high ministerial turnover.

Table 7.2 demonstrates this relationship more formally, using OLS and negative binomial regressions. For both the self-coded crisis variable and the count of instability indicators from Banks, the correlation with minister removals is highly significant, both statistically and substantively, regardless of which regression model is used.[5] Each additional instability event was associated with slightly more than one additional minister exit, reflecting nearly a ten percent increase in minister removals from the baseline of years with no instability. A standard deviation increase of these incidents (4.16 per year) indicates a

---

[4] This measure includes unrest surrounding Israel, Great Britain, and the al-Nabulsi government in 1956 and 1957, the loss of the West Bank in 1967, the civil war in 1970, the April Uprising of 1989, the economic crisis in 1991 triggered by the Gulf War, and then the Arab Spring protests in 2011.

[5] The instability count coefficient is robust to including a year time trend to account for potential reporting bias in Banks, with instability indicators increasing as reporting becomes better and more accessible internationally.

50 percent rise in the number of ministers exiting in a given year. In addition, each major crisis was associated with twenty-one more ministers exiting in that year, reflecting an increase over the baseline of nearly 200 percent.

The theory discussed in Chapter 2 also predicts that autocrats will replace officials less frequently when power is more concentrated in their hands. The reduced decision-making role of these elites means that their removal will be less likely to satisfy the public's appetite for accountability, and the autocrat will be more focused on keeping loyalists in their positions to protect their own dominance. While Chapter 3 offers cross-national support for this expectation, the ministerial tenure data from Jordan allow us to test it within a single country over time. Specifically, we can return to the periods of Jordanian history discussed in the previous chapter to examine whether the average number of ministers removed in a given year was lower in periods where the kings were taking a more active decision-making role and sharing power less credibly. Table 7.3 reports the average number of minister removals per year across the five periods, and the pattern generally aligns with the theory's expectation. The average number of removals is lowest from 1972 to 1985, at seven per year. This period perhaps reflects the apotheosis of direct royal rule in Jordan, as King Hussein and a small set of close advisers made nearly all major decisions from the palace. The average was also relatively low at ten per year during the first period of King Abdullah's reign, from 1999 to 2009, as the new king consolidated power, expanded the royal court, and more openly involved the monarchy in the decision-making process. By contrast, during periods where the monarchy has more frequently shared power with relatively strong prime ministers, ministers, and parliaments, the mean number of removals has been higher, ranging from 14 to 18 per year.

Of course, ministers are also cycled in and out of office to fulfill other needs of the monarchy. In particular, the king grants these positions to Jordanians from different tribes and social groups as one part of the monarchy's co-optation strategy, and frequent rotation can ensure that no group feels left out for too long (Ryan 2018). However, this dynamic would suggest a steady pattern of replacements and cannot explain why appointments would peak during periods of public pressure. Rather, the results shown above are consistent with the argument that these officials absorb the public's anger and are then removed from

7.4 Conclusion

Table 7.3 *Minister removals are lowest during periods of less credible delegation*

	Period 1 Hussein 1952– 1971	Period 2 Hussein 1972– 1985	Period 3 Hussein 1986– 1998	Period 4 Abdullah 1999– 2009	Period 5 Abdullah 2010– 2020
Delegation credibility	Medium	Low	High	Low	Medium
Mean yearly removals	16	7	14	10	18

The five periods are drawn from Table 6.1.

office by the king as a mechanism for providing accountability and sustaining support for his rule.

7.4 Conclusion

The delegation of decision-making responsibilities to the cabinet and parliament in Jordan facilitates a system of stable authoritarian rule in which there is less need for repression, opposition is less likely to escalate into demands for regime change, and the public is able to acquire limited accountability. The monarchy tolerates a substantial degree of political activity because it is relatively rare for public anger to target the monarch specifically, allowing the security apparatus to engage in targeted repression against those who do attempt to challenge the royal family. Opposition leaders doubt their ability to mobilize the public against the monarchy, so they avoid criticizing the king to avoid being repressed; in the process, they reinforce the king's perceived blamelessness and make anti-monarchical coordination even less likely to occur. At the same time, because the king can tolerate political activity relatively safely, and because political elites in the cabinet and parliament do wield a degree of influence over decision-making, it is possible for the public to acquire some level of accountability for the performance of political elites in office. When those elites have lost public confidence in their performance, they are removed from their positions. While taking the blame can be costly for these individuals in terms of their reputations and social status, they can also count on the monarchy to minimize the costs by refraining from scapegoating them with harsh punishments and by allowing them to acquire economic rents. As a

234 *How Jordan's Blame Games Influence Governance*

result, most Jordanian elites are willing to partake in the system and absorb blame instead of the monarchy.

This system has served the monarchy well for the decades of royal rule in Jordan. The credibility with which the kings have shared decision-making powers has varied over time in response to changing threat environments, as was discussed in the previous chapter, but with a few short exceptions, the monarchy has generally adhered to this governance approach. However, it is not inevitable that the monarchy will adhere to this system indefinitely. As mentioned previously, there are some indications from recent years that the king and crown prince wish to centralize power much more directly in the hands of the monarchy, and the regime has also become more repressive and less tolerant of political activism in this same time period. It is possible that Jordan could transition into a system where the monarchy depends much more openly on heavy-handed repression than on trying to protect its reputation and popular support. If such a shift occurs, it would not necessarily mean the end of stability in Jordan, but it would likely mean a breakdown in the system's ability to provide limited accountability or tolerate a substantial degree of political activity. It would also leave the monarchy more exposed to blame for the public's grievances, increasing the likelihood of a major explosion of opposition against the king if the regime's capacity to repress ever faltered. The other possibility, of course, is that Jordan moves in the opposite direction, with the king backing institutional reforms that strengthen the credibility of delegation to the cabinet and parliament. In particular, allowing the parliament to choose the prime minister, developing an electoral law that favors political parties over independents, and restricting the size of the royal court would all lead in this direction by making it more difficult and costly for the monarchy to force its preferences onto the decision-making process. Moving down this road could eventually transform Jordan into a genuine parliamentary democracy under the Hashemite monarchy. Looking past the king's rhetoric, however, there has been little indication that the monarchy is interested in this trajectory.

Though the political situation in Jordan is currently defined by less violence and more accountability than what occurs in many other authoritarian regimes, it is important to emphasize that Jordan remains an autocracy in which repression is common and what accountability exists is limited. Ultimately, the political system sustains the power

7.4 Conclusion

of the monarchy first and foremost, and those who attempt to challenge this status quo openly very often see their lives upended by the regime. Would revolution ever be likely under the current system? If it is to occur, it will likely be driven by activists persistently drawing attention to how the king benefits from the system and shapes many of the country's most important policies. Jordan's monarchy may delegate more credibly than many other authoritarian regimes, but the fact remains that the king is immensely powerful and deeply intertwined in the country's governance. The willingness of activists to brave repression and clearly express this reality would be an important factor for persuading many Jordanians to think differently about how to attribute responsibility in the political system. In doing so, they would increase the likelihood of coordinated opposition challenging the monarchy. Certainly since the Arab Spring, some of Jordan's activists have attempted to stick to this strategy despite the costs of repression. It remains to be seen whether their efforts will fall on deaf ears or not. If the king moves increasingly toward more direct rule, however, the country's more radical activists may find the public becoming more open to their message about who should be blamed for the country's problems.

8 | *The Royal Advantage in Power Sharing and Blame Shifting*

The Hashemite monarchy in Jordan is hardly the only authoritarian regime in the Arab world in which the autocrat shares decision-making powers with other political elites, who are then blamed and held accountable for governance failures or unpopular policy decisions. In Morocco, for instance, when Mohammed VI ascended to the throne in 1999 after his father's death, he sought to make amends for the regime's dismal human rights record by blaming and then sacking his father's long-serving minister of the interior, Driss al-Basri. The new king's spokesperson noted that "The last King was a prisoner of the system he [al-Basri] created; the new King will have a better margin of maneuver" because of the firing (Pelham 1999). Al-Basri and dozens of his closest colleagues were then investigated for corruption and human rights abuses.

In Egypt, this approach to blame shifting can be traced through a series of devastating train accidents in the past two decades. In 2002, Transportation Minister Ibrahim al-Demeri resigned after a train fire killed 370 people during the holiday of Eid el-Adha. The opposition claimed that the government's "gross negligence" was to blame for the accident, and the prime minister promised investigations (BBC 2002). Several additional accidents occurred in subsequent years, and in 2009 another transportation minister resigned after eighteen people were killed when two trains collided. According to state news, President Mubarak "accepted the resignation of Transport Minister Mohammed Mansour ... in which he bears the responsibility over the crash" (Reuters 2009). A decade later, the same story repeated itself, when the transportation minister was forced to resign after an accident in Cairo's main metro station killed twenty-five people (AfricaNews 2019).

As unrest erupted during the Arab Spring, Presidents Ben Ali and Mubarak attempted to defend themselves with this strategy, blaming their cabinets for the public's grievances and then firing them. After weeks of persistent demonstrations in which state repression further

The Royal Advantage in Avoiding Blame

inflamed popular anger, Ben Ali fired the interior minister, Rafiq Belhaj Kacem, on January 12, 2011 (Maktabi 2011). A day later, Ben Ali then dismissed the entire government and called for early elections to be held in six months. Likewise, in Egypt, Mubarak fired his government after several days of unrest in late January 2011, blaming the prime minister and cabinet for the upheaval and promising to provide the new cabinet with "very specific goals" that would improve Egyptians' living conditions (Witte et al. 2011). In both countries, however, blaming and changing cabinets failed to satisfy the demonstrators, who held their presidents responsible for their grievances and continued to push for their removal. In contrast, removing ministers seemingly helped the Jordanian and Moroccan monarchs to contain unrest during this period. What explains these different trajectories of opposition in the monarchies and nonmonarchies of the Arab world?

This chapter addresses this question, providing evidence for the argument discussed in Chapter 2 about why monarchs are better positioned than nonroyal autocrats to rely on delegation of decision-making responsibilities as a blame avoidance strategy. The argument identifies two key distinctions between royal and nonroyal autocrats that accounts for this difference. First, sharing decision-making powers with equal credibility should on average be less costly for monarchs, because the rigid rules about who can be king increase the risks for nonroyal political elites when trying to seize power for themselves. Because monarchs can delegate more safely, they should tend to share decision-making powers more credibly when faced by similar threats of popular discontent, and thus the public should be more likely to accept that other elites bear responsibility and less likely to direct blame toward the autocrat. Second, monarchs also benefit from expectations about *how* different ruler types are meant to be involved in the decision-making process. Presidents and other rulers, whose claims to power rest on ideas about popular sovereignty, are supposed to be involved heavily in the policy process, and they are supposed to be held accountable when outcomes do not turn out well. On the other hand, there is no similar expectation that monarchs be involved in and accountable for the policy process, since the claim to their position is rooted in hereditary succession. As a result, when monarchs choose to delegate, it should align more closely with the public's views about how responsibility is supposed to be attributed, making delegation of equal credibility more effective at shifting blame.

In the pages that follow, I offer evidence for these two royal advantages by focusing primarily on the Arab world. As discussed previously, most of the world's ruling monarchies today are in the region, and the uprisings of the Arab Spring provide only the latest example of their stability advantage over their republican counterparts. With the exception of the 1950s, when both monarchies and nonmonarchies in the region struggled with instability, the Arab monarchies have been less likely to confront coups or major unrest (Menaldo 2012). My argument implies that part of this difference may be explained by institutional features of monarchy that enable royal autocrats to protect their reputations more effectively than nonroyal autocrats through power-sharing arrangements that delegate decision-making responsibilities to other political elites. I also leverage global cross-national data to further reinforce my claims.

I first show that monarchs have more stable relations with political elites than other types of autocrats, and I then provide evidence that delegation in the Arab monarchies has been more credible on average than delegation in the Arab republics. In particular, for the past several decades, the region's monarchs have been less likely than their presidential counterparts to stack their cabinets and parliaments with elites holding personal ties – whether partisan or familial – to the autocrat. These personal ties give the autocrat further leverage over these elites, which should reduce the costs of overriding or ignoring their influence on decision-making and therefore weaken the credibility of delegating to them. I also provide evidence that this variation in credibility reflects the perceptions of the Arab publics, using survey data that show citizens of the monarchies see their parliaments as more influential players in the policy process. Finally, I turn to cross-national data to demonstrate that these patterns generalize beyond the Arab world and with a broader timespan, showing that autocratic monarchs are more likely to share power with another executive and less likely to stack their parliaments and cabinets with members of a ruling party.

Second, I explore whether expectations of royal and nonroyal autocrats differ with regards to their involvement in decision-making. Here, I use a survey experiment implemented in Egypt, Tunisia, Jordan, and Morocco to demonstrate that citizens of Arab monarchies and republics believe that presidents more than kings are meant to be part of and accountable for the policy process. I then use cross-national data on constitutions to document that authoritarian republics often

8.1 Variation in the Credibility of Delegation

incorporate provisions to hold nonroyal rulers accountable for their performance, whereas no such provisions exist in monarchies. I argue that this difference reflects divergent expectations about how responsibility is supposed to operate in these political systems.

The chapter concludes with an exploration of mass opposition in royal and nonroyal authoritarian regimes, tracing how the ability of kings to avoid blame more effectively through delegation reduces their exposure to escalating public anger and thus contributes to the stability of their rule.

8.1 Variation in the Credibility of Delegation

Like all autocrats, ruling monarchs can be overthrown by internal challenges, and there are numerous historical cases of such instances occurring at the hands of other family members or their advisers (Kokkonen et al. 2022). Nonetheless, ruling monarchs should have relatively less to fear from elite challengers than other autocrats, particularly with regards to nonroyals with whom they share power. As discussed in Chapter 2, these elites have no legitimate way to become the monarch, since royal blood defines access to the throne. Lacking institutional pathways through which they can become the "rightful" ruler, they will have to seize power by force, which raises the potential costs associated with their plotting. In addition, they will need to not just remove and replace the autocrat but to restructure the country's political system significantly, which may be more likely to trigger backlash. For these reasons, nonroyal elite challengers should on average face higher costs for attempting to seize power for themselves, and these higher costs should make it relatively safer for monarchs to empower nonroyal elites credibly in the decision-making process.

I provide support for this expectation with data on coups and purges in authoritarian regimes, shown in Figure 8.1. The data on coups come from Bjornskov and Rode (2020), who updated Cheibub et al.'s (2010) earlier dataset. Bjornskov and Rode record attempted coups and successful coups by military elites and civilian elites between the years 1950 and 2020. They also use Cheibub et al.'s coding for whether a regime is governed by a monarch, a civilian dictator, or a military dictator. Their data show that royal autocrats are far less likely to face coup attempts from both civilian and military actors. Military coups were attempted in 6 percent of country-years for

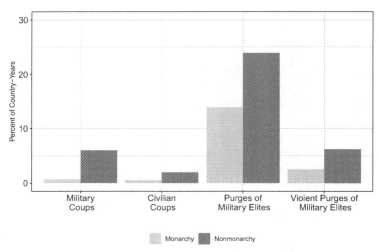

Figure 8.1 Monarchs are less threatened by other political elites
Note: The plot shows that monarchs are much less likely to face coup attempts (successful or failed) from military or civilian elites in a given year. They are also less likely to purge elites with access to military power. All differences are statistically significant at 0.01.

nonroyal authoritarian regimes, but only in 0.7 percent of country-years in the monarchies; likewise, civilian coups were attempted in 2 percent of country-years for nonroyal authoritarian regimes, but only in 0.5 percent of country-years in the monarchies ($p < 0.000$).

The data on purges are taken from the Military Purges in Dictatorships (MPD) dataset (Sudduth 2021), which covers the years 1965 – 2005. Though focused specifically on purges of military officers and civilians associated with the security forces, the dataset provides the most detailed and comprehensive overview of purges in authoritarian regimes. I look at the frequency of these purges overall as well as purges that involved violence against the targeted elites in the royal and nonroyal authoritarian regimes identified by Geddes et al. (2014). Purges occurred in 24 percent of country-years in the nonmonarchies, and they happened in 14 percent of country-years for the monarchies ($p < 0.000$). Likewise, violent purges involving "arresting, jailing or killing" of the targets were recorded in 6 percent of country-years for the nonmonarchies and 3 percent of country-years for the monarchies ($p < 0.01$).

8.1 Variation in the Credibility of Delegation

These same patterns appear when analyzing the occurrence of coups and purges among nonmonarchies and monarchies in the Middle East only. They indicate a more stable and less threatening relationship between political elites and the autocrat in monarchies, with elites less likely to challenge royal autocrats compared to nonroyal autocrats, and with monarchs less likely to repress the elites in their regimes with the most access to coercive power. In other words, there is evidence that monarchs should be able to grant decision-making influence to political elites in ways that may be costly for the monarch to overturn, without needing to worry as much as other autocrats that this delegation will threaten their hold on power. As a result, monarchs should be more willing to delegate credibly, which should leave them less exposed to blame when governance goes poorly.

Is it the case that autocratic monarchs tend to share power over policymaking more credibly than nonroyal autocrats? Furthermore, what does variation look like within the world's monarchies, and does this variation align with the theory? I first consider these questions in the context of the Arab world before turning to cross-national patterns of power sharing across authoritarian regime types.

8.1.1 Arab Monarchies Delegated More Credibly

In the decade prior to the Arab Spring uprisings, the Middle East's authoritarian presidents had more reason than most of their royal counterparts to fear mass unrest. Egypt, Syria, Yemen, and Sudan were very poor (Lofgren and Richards 2003), and though Tunisia, Algeria, and Libya were better off, they continued to struggle with underdevelopment (Abed and Davoodi 2003; Saif 2008). Inequality and unemployment were worsening as liberalizing reforms undermined the welfare states on which the poor and middle class had depended for decades, and people were increasingly angered by perceptions of cronyism and corruption among the political elite. In the monarchies, only Jordan and Morocco suffered from similar economic grievances. In the Persian Gulf, resource wealth allowed the region's other monarchies to continue growing rapidly, while enriching many of their citizens, and prospects for substantial political mobilization seemed slim.

Despite having more to fear from their citizens, presidents in the Arab republics also had to worry more than monarchs about challenges from other political elites, in line with the argument explored

242 *The Royal Advantage in Avoiding Blame*

in Chapter 2 and summarized in the previous section. This difference is visible in how some of these countries' constitutions define how power is attained, with rigid rules regarding hereditary succession in the monarchies compared to institutional pathways relating to popular sovereignty in the republics.

In Morocco and Jordan, for instance, it is established in law that only male heirs of the dynastic line can ascend to the throne. In Jordan, the constitution states that "The Throne of the Hashemite Kingdom of Jordan is hereditary to the dynasty of King Abdullah Bin al-Hussein in a direct line through the male heirs..." Similarly, the Moroccan constitution asserts that "The Crown of Morocco and its constitutional rights are hereditary and are transmitted from father to son through male descendants in direct line and by order of primogeniture." Since independence, kings in both countries have had to face down attempted military coups by officers who had wanted to overthrow the monarchy and establish a republic in its place. Yet, they did not need to worry that a particularly successful prime minister or other government official to whom they had delegated policy responsibility would replace them as the legitimate monarch, reducing the risks of this power sharing. Similarly explicit provisions exist in the region's other monarchies. For example, the basic law of Saudi Arabia limits the throne to the sons of the founding king and their descendants, the Kuwaiti constitution reserves succession for the male descendants of the first Emir Mubarak al-Sabah, and the Bahraini constitution establishes succession for the sons of the al-Khalifa king.

The situation has differed for the presidents. In Tunisia, Ben Ali came to power through a constitutional coup against his predecessor – Habib Bourguiba – in which he had Bourguiba declared medically unfit for the presidency and then took the position legally as his prime minister. In Syria, the al-Asad family acquired the presidency following decades of turmoil in which presidents were frequently unseated and replaced by competing civilian or military elites acting in the name of the "people." Furthermore, in many of the republics, presidents were meant to be chosen by the public through popular elections. In the Egyptian constitution of 1971, the president needed to receive a two-thirds endorsement from the elected parliament, and by 2005 this provision had been changed to direct election for the presidency. In Tunisia's 1959 constitution, the president was supposed to be elected with "an absolute majority of the votes passed," though Bourguiba

8.1 *Variation in the Credibility of Delegation* 243

had made himself president for life. In other words, presidents could face direct competition for their positions from almost anyone with whom they shared power, requiring them to manage potential challengers carefully by ensuring that they could not succeed in building successful electoral coalitions or enough internal support to replace the president legally.

In evaluating the costs and benefits of credibly empowering other elites in the decision-making process, the region's presidents appear to have decided that keeping their elite allies as dependent as possible outweighed the risks of exposing themselves more to blame. As such, they maintained an iron grip on other political institutions. Interviews I conducted in Tunisia illustrate this dynamic by underscoring the extent to which Ben Ali sought to keep his cabinet and parliament in line. Regarding the cabinet, one of Ben Ali's two prime ministers verified to me that "final decisions were with the president," who monitored and reviewed almost all cabinet proposals. According to this prime minister, Ben Ali often adopted the ministers' recommendations, but he would also rely on advice from his closest advisers outside of the cabinet to make sure that his interests were protected. In other words, "All of the laws came from the president." A Tunisian human rights activist who studied the policy process of the Ben Ali regime agreed with this account, arguing that Ben Ali gave ministers some leeway to influence the most technical issues, but involved himself heavily in economic and social policy to protect his political interests. Another activist reinforced this view further, noting that "It was individual rule. All of the decisions were taken by the president ... There was a government and there were advisers to the president. These advisers to Ben Ali carefully monitored the ministers and reported to Ben Ali. So the decisions were taken in Carthage [at the presidential palace]." Likewise, a member of parliament in Tunisia after the revolution noted that under Ben Ali, the prime minister "did not have a big role and all of the powers of the state were in the hands of the president," who maintained direct control of "all kinds of portfolios, including oil, importing cars, etc." The influence of Tunisia's parliament was even less. As the former prime minister told me "The parliament would agree on any of the laws because of the party's dominance ... Once it went through the ministers and the presidency, it was final."

The "party" just mentioned was the Rassemblement Constitutionnel Démocratique (RCD), which was the (renamed) hegemonic party that had controlled Tunisia since its independence in 1956. Such ruling parties were a common feature of the Arab republics, particularly since the 1970s. Fearing the loss of their positions to elite challengers through coups or elections and other constitutional means of removal, the region's presidents created dominant parties that could ensure electoral victories and provide an effective tool through which to tie elites to their political fortunes (Blaydes 2010; Magaloni 2006; Svolik 2012). Members of these parties then controlled nearly all state institutions, including the cabinet, parliament, and bureaucracy. In Tunisia, for example, even the most technocratic ministers were required to join the RCD (Buehler and Ayari 2018).

While parties solved some problems for presidential autocrats, these partisan ties weakened the credibility of delegation from the presidents to other political elites relative to the situation in many of the region's monarchies. When presidents gave decision-making responsibilities to their cabinets or parliaments, they were sharing power with officials who were connected to them directly through partisanship, and whose political careers were heavily dependent on staying in the good graces of the party head. In some cases, dominant parties can constrain autocrats credibly (Magaloni 2006), and in these contexts, they may help autocrats to shift blame. However, many dominant parties are relatively weak institutions that are controlled from the top (Meng 2021), and this was the situation in the Middle East's republics prior to the Arab Spring. Thus, elites were making policy decisions not just as members of the government, but in part through their involvement in a partisan organization controlled closely by the president – a fact that likely reduced how costly it would be for the president to overturn their decisions, and in a manner that would have been highly visible to the people as they decided how to attribute responsibility for their grievances. Research in democratic political systems indicates that citizens are more likely to blame incumbent governments when they are controlled by a single, cohesive party (e.g., Powell and Whitten 1993; Tavits 2007), and it seems likely that attributions would function similarly in authoritarian regimes where autocrats govern alongside and through a dominant party, especially one that they clearly control closely.

The monarchies have looked very different since the kings have had little need for dominant parties. They do not need to win elections, so they do not need an electoral juggernaut to scare off potential elite

8.1 Variation in the Credibility of Delegation

challengers. They also have less reason to be concerned about displacement by other elites who are not royal, and so they have less reason to create an organized party structure through which to bind these elites closely to their own political fortunes. As a result, when the monarchs have delegated decision-making responsibilities to cabinets and parliaments, they have been more likely to empower institutions consisting of independents or multiple, competing parties with fewer direct connections to the throne (Lust-Okar and Jamal 2002).

This dynamic has been particularly apparent in the monarchies of Jordan and Morocco, where the intensity of popular grievances was most similar to that of the republics prior to the Arab Spring. In Morocco, for example, the affiliation of prime ministers has varied and is usually not tied clearly to a royalist party associated strongly with the crown. In fact, several of the country's prime ministers have come from "loyal" opposition parties that accept the monarchy but have a history of arguing for constraints on royal rule. The last prime minister to serve under King Hassan and the first under King Mohammed – Abderrahmane al-Youssoufi (1998–2002) – was a human rights lawyer and a leader in the Socialist Union of Popular Forces, a leftist opposition group that won the largest share of seats in the 1997 parliamentary elections. The next prime minister, Driss Jettou (2002–2007), was an independent, and his successor, Abbas al-Fassi (2007–2012), was from the Istiqlal Party. Following the Arab Spring uprisings, the Moroccan Prime Ministers Abdelilah Benkirane (2012–2017) and Saadeddine al-Othmani (2017–Present) were from the Party of Justice and Development (PJD), an Islamist opposition party that won the largest share of seats in the 2011 and 2016 parliamentary elections. Morocco's cabinets also reflect this diversity of party activity. In early 2019, the PJD-led cabinet of al-Othmani had representation from six parties, and Benkirane's two previous PJD cabinets had representation from four parties and independents. The cabinets of al-Fassi, Jettou, and al-Youssoufi were constructed similarly.

The wealthier Gulf monarchies may seem less different from the republics because members of the ruling family often hold key positions in their countries' cabinets (Herb 1999). As with partisan attachment, family identity should be a clear marker tying political elites to the autocrat in a manner that weakens the credibility of delegation. In Kuwait, for example, the prime minister has always been a member of the al-Sabah family. Saad al-Salim al-Sabah held the position for twenty-five years, from 1978 until 2003. His successors have lasted in the office for much shorter periods of time (less than seven years), in large part because of pressures from parliamentary politics. Of twenty-six ministerial positions in Kuwait in 2010, just prior to the Arab Spring uprisings, twelve were in the hands of the ruling family.[1] These included some of the most important cabinet positions, including two of three deputy prime ministers and the ministers of defense, foreign affairs, oil, and the interior. Nonetheless, several important ministries were led by nonroyals, including the Ministry of Justice, the Ministry of Finance, the Ministry of Commerce and Industry, the Ministry of Education and Higher Education, the Ministry of Public Works, the Ministry of Religious Endowments and Islamic Affairs, and others. The situation has been similar in Bahrain, where the premiership was held by the same royal, Khalifa bin Salman al-Khalifa, for fifty years, from just before independence in 1970 until his death in 2020. Members of the royal family filled approximately half of the cabinet in 2010, with fourteen of twenty-six ministerial positions. While al-Khalifas held some of the most influential ministries, such as defense and foreign affairs, nonroyals controlled several with importance for day-to-day governance, including the Ministry of Oil and Gas. In both countries, the tendency of the royal families to hold onto ministries with implications for coercive power, while giving many of the ministries with responsibility for more controversial economic and social policies to nonroyals, reflects the pattern of cross-issue delegation in Jordan discussed in Chapter 4.

Figure 8.2 highlights the stark differences in cabinet composition between the Arab monarchies and republics in the decade prior to the Arab Spring by plotting the percentage of cabinet ministers who were members of the ruling party or family. Nearly all of the republics, with the exception of Libya, stacked their cabinets with members of the ruling party. By comparison, even the Gulf monarchies, which are known for their family governance, are still less likely to have appointed ministers with visible identifiers connecting them to the autocrat.

This difference repeated itself with parliaments in the monarchies and republics, such that power has in general been shared more credibly with legislatures in the former than the latter. To be sure, not all of

---

[1] Data on ministers come from the WhoGov dataset.

8.1 Variation in the Credibility of Delegation

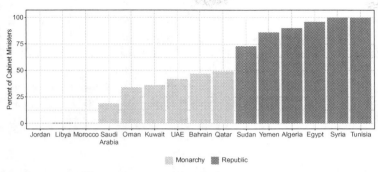

Figure 8.2 Ruling party or family representation in cabinets, 2000–2010
Note: Figure displays the percentage of cabinet ministers in Arab republics and monarchies who were either a member of the ruling party or the ruling family between the years 2000 and 2010. Data are from WhoGov. Note that these results drop ministers with missing data. Only Yemen had a substantial portion of missing data.

the monarchies have legislatures with meaningful influence over the decision-making process. The Consultative Assembly of Saudi Arabia is fully appointed by the monarch and plays an advisory role rather than wielding genuine legislative powers. In this position, it is unlikely that the assembly draws any blame away from the king. The legislatures of the UAE, Oman, and Qatar are also weak and have little relevance to politics or policymaking in their countries, though in all three cases, some members are elected and the bodies are endowed with some legislative prerogatives. Half of the members of the Federal National Council of the United Arab Emirates are elected, but the franchise is restricted to a small part of the citizenry, and the body has relatively little capacity to influence legislation or conduct oversight of the executive. The Omani Shura Council is an elected body that functions alongside an appointed upper house. It acquired more formal powers following the Arab Spring uprisings, including the ability to propose, approve, and amend legislation, as well as some capacity to question ministers; however, these rights were restricted through legislation in 2021, and the cabinet remains entirely dominant in decision-making (Al Talei 2021). The first elections for the Qatari Shura Council were held in 2021. Its formal position is relatively strong among the legislatures of the Gulf monarchies, suggesting it could develop into an influential player in policymaking, but historically it has held little power (Thafer 2021).

Meanwhile, the Moroccan, Jordanian, Kuwaiti, and Bahraini parliaments have, at various points, been active arenas of political competition in which elected elites have acquired policy influence, while making life difficult for their governments and royals. In Kuwait, the parliament has not been shy about exercising its prerogatives and clashing with the government, and it has forced numerous ministerial and even government resignations over the years through its ability to question ministers, publicly criticize and then vote against the government's policies, and set the political agenda (Brown 2001; Herb 2002). Consistent with the book's argument, the parliament's influence makes it a useful scapegoat for the monarchy, which will blame unpopular governance outcomes on obstructionism by the legislature (Westall 2014). Bahrain has a less developed history of parliamentary life, but Hamad bin Isa al-Khalifa came to the throne in 1999 promising political reforms, and an elected parliament was restored three years later. While parliament remained a relatively weak political actor throughout this period, it had a fairly large opposition presence, and the body had some success in pressuring the government to respond to its demands (Khalaf 2008). In 2006, for example, the parliament would not ratify the government's approval of the International Covenant on Civil and Political Rights because of concerns from socially conservative MPs that the covenant would allow religious conversions (Zweiri 2007). However, following the Arab Spring, Bahrain cracked down on its opposition movements, substantially weakening the parliament's influence in the process. The influence of the Jordanian and Moroccan parliaments has been discussed in previous chapters. The ability of these bodies to influence decision-making and push back against the executive reflects power sharing that should be perceived as credible by some of the citizenry in these countries, allowing the monarchs to shift blame onto their legislatures more effectively.

In contrast, the republican legislatures were dominated by their countries' hegemonic parties, and parliamentary influence on decision-making was slim at best. In Tunisia, the RCD always won more than 80 percent of the vote in Tunisian parliamentary elections, while taking between 75 and 100 percent of the legislative seats. The situation was similar in Egypt, where the NDP never won less than 70 percent of the vote and 69 percent of the seats in the People's Assembly. In 2010,

8.1 *Variation in the Credibility of Delegation*

in the last Egyptian election prior to the revolution, the NDP won 80 percent of the vote and 88 percent of the seats, driving out several representatives from the Muslim Brotherhood who had previously given a voice to the opposition within the legislature. These dominant victories ensured that the parties could rewrite constitutional rules to benefit themselves and ensure the president's continued rule, as in other hegemonic party states (Magaloni 2006). They were also influenced heavily by vote buying and other forms of fraudulent activity to maintain this dominance, and elites used their seats more to enrich themselves than to advocate for policy positions (Blaydes 2010). Parties in the other republics operated similarly. In Algeria, where the FLN as the former ruling party was damaged by the civil war in the 1990s, this dynamic was weakest; nevertheless, the FLN and its closest allied party typically controlled 60 percent of seats in the legislature. In Sudan, President Bashir's National Congress Party held more than 70 percent of the seats during this period, and in Yemen, President Saleh's General People's Congress took more than 75 percent of the seats in the 2003 legislative election – the last before he was ousted during the Arab Spring. When legislatures are dominated by a single party controlled by the president, they should be less able or willing to push back against the executive's preferences and more likely to rubber stamp whatever laws the party elites send their way.

These differences suggest that citizens of the Arab republics should have been more likely than those of the Arab monarchies to believe that their autocrats were controlling nearly all major policy decisions through their parties' dominance of the cabinet and parliament. Elites were not their own actors but were merely an extension of the president's will, such that delegation would have been perceived as less credible. This royal advantage should have been especially pronounced for Jordan and Morocco, where royal families had no presence in the cabinet and parliaments were fairly active. These monarchies also happened to be the two that most resembled the republics in the extent to which widespread grievances suggested autocrats had reasons to worry about being blamed and becoming the target of mass unrest.

What explains variation in the credibility of delegation within the region's monarchies? While there are a number of factors that likely explain these differences, it is worth pointing out that it is the monarchies facing a higher likelihood of popular mobilization who have delegated more credibly to cabinets and parliaments, in line with the expectations of the theory. That is not just true of resource poor Jordan and Morocco, but also within the Gulf states. Among these wealthier monarchies, Kuwait and Bahrain have a history of popular mobilization that should incentivize delegation to protect the monarchy from blame. Bahrain experienced an uprising during the 1990s in which opposition forces united to demand an end to emergency rule. Kuwait has a long history of active politics, and Kuwaiti citizens mobilized for the reinstatement of parliament following the Gulf War. Bahrain also faces sectarian divisions between its Sunni monarchy and the approximately two-thirds of the population who are Shia, and this divide has contributed to political conflict and mobilization in the country. In contrast, Shia communities constitute approximately one-tenth of the populations in Saudi Arabia, Qatar, and the UAE, where there is also less experience generally with mass mobilizations by disgruntled citizens. Oman is somewhat of an outlier, insofar as the sultan delegated little despite being less wealthy than its Gulf neighbors and having a pronounced (though not politically salient) religious divide of its own. However, since the regional upheaval of 2011, and especially following the death of Sultan Qaboos in 2020 after fifty years on the throne, some reforms have been implemented to strengthen the decision-making influence of the cabinet and legislature. In other words, Arab monarchs with more reasons to worry about mass politics and how the public attributes responsibility for their grievances have been more likely to delegate credibly to nonroyal political elites.

8.1.2 Arab Citizens Perceive Power Sharing Differently in Monarchies

If it is the case that Arab monarchies have delegated more credibly to their cabinets and legislatures on average, one implication is that citizens of the republics should have been less likely than citizens in the monarchies to believe that political elites other than the autocrat held influence over the decision-making process. While data is not available regarding perceptions of ministers, we can test this implication for parliaments with data from the first and second waves of the Arab Barometer surveys. These surveys include questions about perceptions of parliamentary involvement in the policy process, and they were implemented between 2006 and 2011, just prior to and during the initial uprisings of the Arab Spring.

8.1 Variation in the Credibility of Delegation 251

Consistent with the argument, the surveys show that respondents in the monarchies were more likely than respondents in the republics to perceive their parliaments as meaningful players in the policy process. The barometers asked the following question, already analyzed for Jordan in Chapter 5: "To what extent do you think Parliament has a role in deciding the following policies: economic / social / foreign." This question was asked in Jordan, Morocco, and Bahrain, though not in Kuwait. Of the republics, the question was not asked in Egypt or Tunisia, since neither country was polled prior to the Arab Spring. However, it was asked in the republics of Algeria, Sudan, and Yemen. This set of countries provides a useful comparison of presidential regimes with hegemonic parties versus monarchies that shared power with elected parliaments in the years before the uprisings.

Figure 8.3 plots the percentage of respondents across the three monarchies and the three republics who answered that their parliament played a large or medium role in shaping policy in the respective domains, compared to those who said the parliament played a small role or none at all.[2] Respondents in the monarchies were substantially more likely to view their parliaments as meaningful contributors to the policy process across all three issue domains. On economic policy, 56 percent of respondents in the monarchies reported that parliament played a large or medium role. For social policy, it was 55 percent, and for foreign policy it was 49 percent. By contrast, only 42 percent of respondents in the republics said that parliament played a large or medium role on economic policy, 39 percent said the same for social policy, and 37 percent answered in this way for foreign policy. These responses reflect substantial gaps of 14 percentage points on economic policy, 16 percentage points on social policy, and 12 percentage points on foreign policy. In the chapter appendix, I show that this pattern is consistent when looking at each country individually.

To demonstrate the robustness of the pattern, I implement a multilevel model with individual-level observations and country-wave observations. I use country-waves because these questions were asked in two waves in Jordan and Yemen, and because this expands the number of higher-level observations from 6 to 8. I also created a

---

[2] The question was asked in Jordan, Algeria, and Yemen in both waves 1 and 2. The question was asked in Morocco and Bahrain in wave 1. It was asked in Sudan in wave 2.

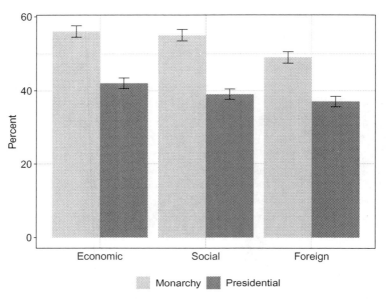

Figure 8.3 Citizens of Arab monarchies perceived parliaments to have more policy influence
Note: Figure displays the percentage of respondents living in monarchies versus presidential republics in waves 1 and 2 of the Arab Barometer who believed that their parliaments had a big or medium role to play in economic, social, and foreign policy.

new dependent variable that aggregates respondents' answers to the three policy domains. I then control for several individual-level covariates that may relate to knowledge of political institutions, including age, gender, education, trust in others, political interest, and internet usage. The results are displayed in Table 8.1. Even with the small number of country-wave observations, they show a statistically significant relationship for the aggregate measure of parliamentary responsibility, and for perceived responsibility for economic and social policies. Note that the weaker relationship for foreign issues is consistent with monarchs retaining more direct control over foreign policy relative to domestic policy, as discussed in detail in the Jordan case, and as is consistent with the theory's expectation about variation across issue domains.

These results are consistent with the expectation that citizens of the region's monarchies were more likely to perceive parliaments as active

8.1 Variation in the Credibility of Delegation

Table 8.1 *Perceptions of parliamentary responsibility*

	All issues	Econ issues	Social issues	Foreign issues
Monarchy	0.422*	0.146*	0.177***	0.103
	(0.183)	(0.067)	(0.055)	(0.074)
Age	0.087**	0.030**	0.031**	0.023*
	(0.030)	(0.012)	(0.012)	(0.012)
Male	−0.121***	−0.053***	−0.036***	−0.031**
	(0.029)	(0.011)	(0.011)	(0.011)
Education	−0.018†	−0.002	−0.005	−0.011***
	(0.009)	(0.004)	(0.004)	(0.004)
Trust	0.327***	0.123***	0.118***	0.090***
	(0.033)	(0.013)	(0.013)	(0.013)
Political interest	−0.089***	−0.029***	−0.027***	−0.034***
	(0.015)	(0.006)	(0.006)	
Internet usage	0.013	0.002	0.018	−0.004
	(0.035)	(0.013)	(0.013)	(0.013)
Constant	1.433***	0.490***	0.452***	0.490***
	(0.144)	(0.054)	(0.046)	(0.058)
Observations	7,793	7,826	7,819	7,812
Units	8	8	8	8
χ^2	161.49	144.98	134.30	99.28

*** $p < 0.001$, ** $p < 0.01$, * $p < 0.05$, † <0.10
Multilevel models with random intercept.

contributors to the policy process in the years before the uprisings of 2011. Such perceptions are consistent with the claim that delegation to legislatures in the monarchies was seen as more credible, and that these parliaments were better positioned to redirect blame from the autocrat as a result.

8.1.3 Cross-National Delegation by Monarchs and Nonmonarchs

The earlier evidence on the credibility of delegation focuses on the Arab world, particularly in the years prior to the Arab Spring uprisings. Do similar patterns extend to different periods of time and geographic regions? To assess generalizability, I first rely on data from Geddes et al. (2018) on the composition of authoritarian legislatures and data

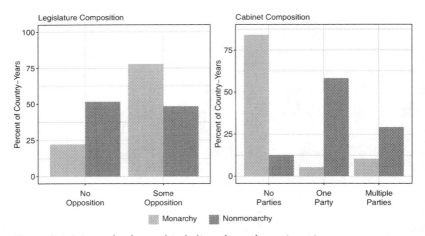

Figure 8.4 Monarchs do not bind elites through partisan ties
Note: The plot on the left shows that monarchies with legislatures are much more likely to include members from the opposition. The plot on the right shows that monarchs' cabinets are dominated by independents, whereas nonmonarchs' cabinets are dominated by a single, ruling party typically controlled by the autocrat.

from Nyrup and Bramwell (2020) on authoritarian cabinets to illustrate how monarchs are more likely than other autocrats to share power with institutions that incorporate elites who are not linked as directly to the autocrat. Both datasets have global coverage and extend back to the 1940s and 1960s respectively. As with the Arab countries, the idea here is that if the autocrat shares decision-making responsibility with a parliament and cabinet, but then excludes opposition and stacks those institutions with members of a political party they control, it should be perceived as less credible by the public that these institutions can exercise some independent influence over policy decisions.

The left plot in Figure 8.4 shows the percent of country-years in the data for monarchies and nonmonarchies in which an existing legislature incorporated independent members of the opposition or members of opposition political parties. The data show that when monarchies share power with a legislature, they are more likely than nonroyal autocracies to allow opposition forces into the body. Whereas opposition members are present in seventy-eight percent of the monarchy

8.1 Variation in the Credibility of Delegation

country-years, they are present in only 48 percent of the nonmonarchy country-years.[3]

The right plot of Figure 8.4 shows whether the autocrat's cabinet includes no parties, one party, or multiple parties. To identify monarchies, this analysis relies on the coding used by Bjornskov and Rode (2020). In 84 percent of the monarchy country-years, no parties are represented in the cabinet, reflecting the frequency at which monarchs and their prime ministers appoint independents to these bodies. Multiple parties are represented in 10 percent of country-years, whereas a single party is represented in 5 percent of country-years. On the other hand, in 58 percent of country-years for the nonmonarchies, cabinets include only a single party, reflecting the tendency of hegemonic parties to monopolize decision-making institutions. Multiple parties are represented in 29 percent of country-years, and no parties in just 13 percent of country-years. For both legislatures and cabinets, these patterns reflect those documented above in the Middle East, suggesting that the differences between monarchies and nonmonarchies are not limited to the region.

Next, I turn to cross-national data on constitutions from the Comparative Constitutions Project (Elkins and Ginsburg 2021), using their data on global constitutions from 1946 to 2010. One feature coded by the authors is whether constitutions include just one executive or multiple executive positions. In cases where there is a unitary executive, it should be less feasible for that executive to distance themselves from important decisions in the political system. By contrast, in political systems where executive power is shared between more than one political actor – for instance, between a king or president and a prime minister – the dominant executive should have more leeway to claim that they are not involved in all decisions, since there may be some costs to them for trying to dominate their subordinate entirely in the policy process. I combine these data on constitutions with the Geddes et al. (2014) regime type data and show the percentage of country-years for monarchies and nonmonarchies in which there was a single executive or multiple executives. Figure 8.5 shows that almost all authoritarian monarchies include multiple executives (91 percent of country-years),

---

[3] Note that monarchies are more likely to have not had a legislature in the first place, as was already discussed with Saudi Arabia. The patterns shown in Figure 8.4 are conditional on the existence of a legislature.

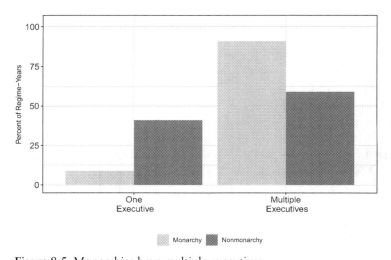

Figure 8.5 Monarchies have multiple executives
Note: The plot shows that nearly all monarchies have multiple executives – typically a prime minister with whom the monarch shares power – whereas many nonmonarchies have a unitary executive.

whereby the king shares executive power with a prime minister. These arrangements are less common in nonroyal authoritarian regimes, occurring in 59 percent of country-years.

Altogether, these patterns support the argument that authoritarian monarchs tend to delegate influence over the decision-making process more credibly than other autocrats. This delegation should help to protect them from blame more effectively when the public becomes dissatisfied.

8.2 Variation in Expectations

As discussed in Chapter 2, kings are not just advantaged in sharing power to avoid blame because their positions enable them to delegate more credibly. They also benefit from popular expectations of their role in the political system, with people less likely to believe that the monarch *should* take responsibility for governance outcomes because of the principles of leader selection that differentiate kings from nonroyal autocrats. Hereditary succession implies nothing about the need for the king to govern effectively to maintain their position, and

8.2 Variation in Expectations

modern-day constitutional monarchies explicitly direct responsibility to the cabinet and parliament. On the other hand, the principle of popular sovereignty that undergirds republican political systems implies that leaders are accountable to the people and should be replaceable when their governance fails to satisfy the public. As a result, autocratic presidents may try to insulate themselves from blame by delegating policy responsibility to subordinate elites, but many citizens may still believe that the president is supposed to be held responsible and should be removed regardless of whether he directly controlled the decisions that produced their grievances. This difference should have implications for the ability of royal and nonroyal autocrats to leverage power-sharing arrangements to avoid blame.

Is it the case that different expectations exist for royal and nonroyal autocrats with regards to their responsibility for governance? As with Section 8.1, I first test this argument by looking within the Arab world. I briefly illustrate different expectations about governance set out by some of the monarchical and republican constitutions in the region, before discussing results from a survey experiment designed to capture beliefs of Arab citizens on the matter. I then turn to cross-national constitutions data to assess generalizability beyond the region.

8.2.1 Experimental Evidence of Expectations in the Arab World

Different expectations about the governance roles of kings and presidents are codified in the constitutions of authoritarian Egypt, Tunisia, Jordan, and Morocco. Put simply, presidents are meant to steer policy and kings are not. In Egypt's pre-Arab Spring constitution from 1971, Section III, which focuses on the executive, states that "The President of the Republic in coordination with the Government shall lay down the general policy of the State and supervise its implementation..." Likewise, in Tunisia, Section I of the 1959 pre-Arab Spring constitution stipulated that "The President of the Republic directs the general policy of the State, defines it basic options, and informs the Chamber of Deputies accordingly." The prime minister and ministers in the cabinet are also given responsibility for contributing to the policy process, but always alongside the president. In the former Tunisian constitution, "The Government makes sure that the general national policy is put into effect in accordance with the orientations ... defined by the President of the Republic," and in the former Egyptian constitution, the cabinet's chief function is to "lay down the general policy of the state, and to control its implementation in collaboration with the President of the Republic and in accordance with the presidential laws and decrees." In other words, to the extent that presidents delegated, it was still expected that they would be active in the policy process, with ultimate responsibility for whatever outcomes the political system produced.

No such expectation was spelled out in the constitutions from Jordan and Morocco. While the constitutions give the kings direct control over their countries' militaries, they are not given explicit control over policy generally. Instead, they are intended to serve a symbolic and politically neutral role. In Morocco, for instance, "The King is Head of State ... Symbol of the unity of the Nation ... Supreme Arbiter between the institutions ...," etc. As discussed previously, the situation is similar in Jordan. Instead, in both countries, responsibility is supposed to be held by the prime minister and his cabinet. In Morocco, the constitution charges the prime minister with developing and implementing a policy agenda, and the Council of Government is given responsibility for deliberating on public policies and the general policies of the state. Similarly, in Jordan, the cabinet is explicitly given "the responsibility for administering all affairs of the State...," rather than the king.

Are these expectations just words on paper in the constitutions of these countries, or do they reflect societal norms about how presidents and kings are meant to interact with their political systems? I provide evidence for this argument with a survey experiment conducted online with YouGov in Egypt ($n = 1,000$), Jordan ($n = 500$), Morocco ($n = 1,000$), and Tunisia ($n = 500$). The samples were constructed from YouGov's preexisting panels for its omnibus surveys in the region, and while not nationally representative, they are diverse and generally reflective of the urban populations in these countries. The experiment was conducted in February 2018, with the goal of understanding how people think about the extent to which presidents and kings are meant to be responsible for the policies of their states.

In the survey, respondents were randomly assigned with equal probability to read a prompt that asked about their general understanding of the roles that either *presidents* or *kings* play in their political systems. The prompt was framed around respondents' broad views

8.2 Variation in Expectations

of these political leader types, and they were explicitly asked to avoid thinking about specific leaders or countries. This language was intended to capture expectations about how these rulers are generally *supposed* to relate to responsibility for decision-making. To that end, after reading the prompt, respondents were asked to rate their level of agreement with two outcome statements written to capture views about whether it is considered normal and acceptable for these leader types to remove themselves from the policy process by delegating responsibility to other actors in the political system.[4] The prompt and outcome statements were as follows:

Please tell us the extent to which you agree or disagree with the following statements about the role of (presidents/kings) in their political systems. We are interested in your understanding about the typical roles of (presidents/kings) around the world, not in your views of specific political leaders or countries.

- (Presidents/Kings) are neutral figures who monitor the political system for problems, not partisan figures who compete to influence the policy making process.
- (Presidents/Kings) are separate from the government and the policy making process, so they should not be blamed for failed policies.

The first statement was meant to reflect the expectation that monarchs do not actively involve themselves in attempts to shape policy but instead sit above the political process as the head of state. The second statement directly connected this separation from the policy process to the question of responsibility and blame for policy failures. Respondents could rate their agreement with the outcome statements on a ten point scale, where ten meant full agreement and one meant full disagreement. Treatment assignment was balanced across several pre-treatment covariates, as shown in the Appendix. For each statement, the average level of agreement should be higher for the king treatment if the results are consistent with the argument that people expect presidents more than kings to take responsibility for the state's policies.

The main effects are reported in Figure 8.6. As expected, respondents were more likely to agree that monarchs are neutral monitors of the political system as opposed to partisan actors attempting to shape

---

[4] The order of these statements was randomized.

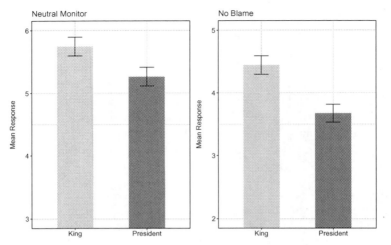

Figure 8.6 Experimental results: Acceptability of delegation
Note: Figure compares results for the King and President treatments with the full sample from the YouGov survey experiment. Higher values indicate higher agreement with the statements.

policies ($p < 0.000$). They were also more likely to agree that monarchs are separate from the government and therefore should not be blamed for poor policy outcomes ($p < 0.000$). The substantive effects of the monarchy treatment on these outcomes were large, with agreement increasing by 20 percent for the first statement and 21 percent for the second statement.

Furthermore, these patterns persist when subsetting the respondents based on the regime type in which they live, as shown in Figure 8.7. Whether respondents lived in the monarchies of Jordan and Morocco or the republics of Egypt and Tunisia, average agreement was higher for the king treatment than the president treatment. This relationship was statistically significant at $p < 0.000$ for both outcomes in the monarchies, and at $p < 0.006$ and $p < 0.003$ in the republics. The treatment effects are substantively smaller in the presidential regimes, reflecting increases of approximately 10 percent for both statements. In the monarchies, the treatment effects were larger, with agreement increasing by approximately 30 percent. The larger effects in the monarchies are unsurprising, because these respondents are repeatedly exposed in their daily lives to the principle of hereditary succession and what it entails about ruler conduct, as shown by the discussion

8.2 Variation in Expectations

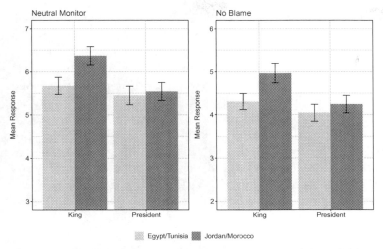

Figure 8.7 Experimental results by regime type: Acceptability of delegation
Note: Figure compares results for the King and President treatments from the YouGov survey experiment, with respondents grouped together based on whether they live in a monarchy or republic. Higher values indicate higher agreement with the statements.

of Jordanian textbooks in Chapter 4. Importantly, however, the fact that these effects also exist among Egyptian and Tunisian respondents, even if substantively smaller, implies that the results reflect general differences in how people expect kings and presidents to relate to the decision-making process. These findings suggest that, all else equal, delegation should help to protect monarchs from blame more effectively than presidents, because delegation aligns more closely with expectations of what these rulers are meant to be doing and the outcomes for which they are meant to take responsibility.

8.2.2 Cross-National Expectations in Royal and Non-Royal Constitutions

I provide more generalizable evidence for this difference in expectations by returning to the constitutional data collected by Elkins and Ginsburg (2021). The dataset includes information about whether constitutions establish popular sovereignty as an important principle of the political system, which has implications for whether officials are meant to be accountable to the public's demands. Specifically, I look at the percentage of country-years for authoritarian monarchies and nonmonarchies in which the constitution mentioned democracy. The dataset also includes information about whether procedures exist for removing the chief executive from their position, beyond elections and term limits. The existence of these procedures is indicative of expectations that the executive is supposed to be subject to accountability for their actions. Here, I compare the percentage of country-years for authoritarian monarchies and nonmonarchies in which these procedures exist, and the percentage of country-years in which the constitutions specify that the autocrat can be removed through these procedures because of public dissatisfaction with their governance, because of crimes and bad conduct in office, and because of constitutional violations.

The comparisons are plotted in Figure 8.8. Whereas constitutions mention democracy in 93 percent of country-years in the authoritarian nonmonarchies, they do so for only 42 percent of country-years in the monarchies. Likewise, royal constitutions include procedures for removing the monarch in just 2 percent of country-years, aligning with the idea that monarchs are not responsible and not meant to be held accountable. On the other hand, constitutions contain such procedures

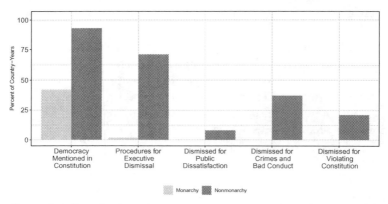

Figure 8.8 Constitutions do not create an expectation of accountability for monarchs
Note: The plot shows the percentage of country-years for authoritarian monarchies and nonmonarchies where constitutions define the country as a democracy, include procedures (other than elections) for removing executives, and specify certain conditions under which such removal is warranted.

8.3 Variation in Escalation of Opposition

in 71 percent of country-years for the nonmonarchies. In addition, a nontrivial number of constitutions mention specific reasons for which the executive can be removed through these procedures: In 8 percent of country-years they can be removed solely because the public is dissatisfied; in 37 percent of country-years they can be removed for crimes and bad conduct; and in twenty-one percent of country-years they can be removed for violating the constitution.

Even in authoritarian regimes, political leaders in nonmonarchies are *supposed* to govern for the people, and they are *supposed* to face accountability when they fail to do so. In contrast, there is little expectation that monarchs participate actively in governance and represent the public; instead, they are usually expected to be distant from decision-making, with responsibility attributed to more representative institutions. This difference suggests that when monarchs delegate credibly, it will align more closely with the public's beliefs about how responsibility *should* operate, which should make that delegation relatively more effective at shifting blame away from the monarch.

8.3 Variation in Escalation of Opposition

Sections 8.1 and 8.2 have provided evidence that monarchs (1) tend to share power more credibly with other political elites and (2) are less expected to govern and be held accountable. These differences imply that ruling monarchs should be more effective than other autocrats at protecting themselves from blame through delegation. Not only do they tend to share decision-making powers more credibly with others, but what delegation does occur should also be more capable of shifting blame because of its alignment with norms about how responsibility should operate in the political systems. If monarchs are better positioned to avoid blame, popular discontent should be less likely to escalate into mass opposition capable of removing the monarch from power. Many citizens will direct their anger against elites other than the monarch, and those citizens who do hold the monarch responsible will find it more difficult to coordinate opposition against the ruler.

This last section of the chapter provides evidence for the ability of monarchs to avoid escalating opposition against their rule. I first return to the Arab Spring, documenting more systematically the royal advantage in avoiding mass opposition and regime change, and

264 *The Royal Advantage in Avoiding Blame*

exploring how dissatisfaction in the nonmonarchies of Egypt and Tunisia contrasted with opposition in Morocco and Jordan by increasingly focusing on the countries' presidents prior to the uprisings. I then turn to cross-national data on regime type, ruler tenures, and protest to show that monarchs are less likely than other autocrats to be overthrown during periods of popular mobilization, consistent with their advantage in avoiding blame and escaping the escalation of opposition to their rule.

8.3.1 Escalation during the Arab Spring

As has been mentioned previously throughout the book, the authoritarian monarchies of the Arab world experienced greater stability than the region's authoritarian republics during the Arab Spring uprisings. Four autocratic presidents were overthrown via processes triggered by mass mobilizations: Husni Mubarak in Egypt, Zine al-Abidine Ben Ali in Tunisia, Muammar al-Qadhafi in Libya, and Ali Abdullah Saleh in Yemen. Mass opposition also came close to toppling Bashar al-Asad in Syria. In the region's other two authoritarian republics during the Arab Spring, Abdelaziz Bouteflika held onto power without facing major opposition in Algeria, and Omar al-Bashir likewise remained in power in Sudan, yet both were overthrown after mass protests several years later. By contrast, none of the Arab world's monarchs fell from power during the Arab Spring or the region's subsequent decade of instability. Bahrain came closest to experiencing an uprising intended to facilitate regime change, with large-scale mobilization occurring early in 2011. Even here, however, most protesters were initially focused on constitutional reforms that would strengthen the legislature and reduce the monarchy's powers rather than demanding that the monarchy be overthrown, suggesting some ability of the king to preserve his reputation (Al-Rawi 2015; Diwan 2020; Mabon 2019; Zunes 2013). It took Saudi intervention, months of sustained repression, and clear attempts to strengthen royal control before a significant portion of the Bahraini opposition began to turn openly against the royal regime (El Gamal 2014; Louer 2012).

Table 8.2 portrays the starkness of this divergence between the region's monarchies and republics. Using Fisher's exact test to assess statistical significance with the small sample, the difference is significant at $p < 0.05$ regardless of whether Algeria and Sudan are treated as

8.3 Variation in Escalation of Opposition

Table 8.2 Regime survival during the Arab uprisings

	Overthrown in initial uprisings	Overthrown later	Survived to present
Republic	Egypt Libya Tunisia Yemen	Algeria Sudan	Syria
Monarchy			Bahrain Jordan Kuwait Morocco Oman Qatar Saudi Arabia UAE

Difference is significant at 0.05 with Fisher's exact test.

survivors or as regimes whose rulers were overthrown in an extension of the Arab Spring uprisings. It should also be noted that the difference is not significant when looking at outcomes among states with and without oil wealth – another argument that is commonly made about regime survival during this period.

The survival of the monarchs was not just about the absence of political discontent. Citizens mobilized to express grievances in several of these countries, often in very large numbers that surpassed protest size in the republics on a per capita basis. Instead, what mattered most was where demonstrators directed their anger, with opposition escalating against presidents in the republics but – for the most part – not against monarchs in the monarchies.

The past several chapters documented how power-sharing arrangements in Jordan – in which substantial decision-making responsibilities were delegated to the cabinet and parliament – helped to protect the king from blame around the time of the uprisings. Chapter 3 also explored dynamics of power sharing and protest in Morocco in the years surrounding the Arab Spring, showing how the king benefited from delegation but also varied its credibility in response to shifting threats from the public and elites. As the two poorest monarchies in

266   *The Royal Advantage in Avoiding Blame*

the region, Jordan and Morocco are most similar to the republics in terms of struggling with persistent political and economic grievances that worsened during the economic crisis of the late 2000s. Yet, even though both countries experienced large and sustained protest movements, the majority of angry Jordanians and Moroccans did not and have not come to focus their discontent on their countries' autocrats.

Did the situation differ in the republics? If my argument about the royal advantage in blame avoidance is correct, it should be observable that presidential autocrats in the region were increasingly attracting blame for their citizens' grievances prior to the Arab Spring in a way that the monarchs did not, as their less credible delegation and less favorable expectations about responsibility meant they increasingly struggled to protect themselves from popular discontent. I probe this idea by reviewing patterns of opposition in Egypt and Tunisia prior to their 2011 revolutions. In both countries, there were visible signs that opposition was escalating to focus more directly on the presidents themselves during this period.

Mubarak and Egypt

In 2004, President Mubarak appointed Ahmed Nazif as prime minister alongside a cabinet of technocrats and businessmen whose goal was to further liberalize Egypt's economy. The government did reduce regulations, cut taxes, and limit tariffs, among other reforms, and their efforts helped Egypt to reach an impressive 7 percent growth rate by 2007 (Peters 2009). Nonetheless, this growth was unevenly distributed, the reforms appeared to facilitate corruption, and the government failed to rein in inflation of basic goods such as bread that so many Egyptians depended on day in and day out. As a result, the government became increasingly unpopular and faced growing contentious mobilizations in subsequent years.

This unpopularity began to hit the president directly at this time. It was also in 2004 that the Kifaya Movement was founded: The group emerged as the first, non-Islamist political organization to blame Mubarak directly for many of the country's problems. The group's name – meaning "Enough" – captured Egyptians' frustrations with government performance, and their straightforward demands were that the Mubarak family must lose power for the country's problems to be solved (Oweidat et al. 2008). Alongside Kifaya's activism, several opposition organizations from different ideological backgrounds,

8.3 Variation in Escalation of Opposition

including the Muslim Brotherhood and the Communist Party, took advantage of "growing public frustration at the continuing domestic economic crisis" to form an alliance demanding that Mubarak no longer run for president in the 2005 election, aiming their opposition explicitly at the president (Shehata 2005). There was little focus on Nazif and his cabinet because there was little sense in which he was responsible for the opposition's grievances. They were subordinate to the president through the party apparatus of the NDP, and it was the president who needed to be held responsible for what was going wrong.

Kifaya and similar groups had been repressed and largely faded away by 2008, but their approach of blaming the president directly was reflected in the increasing mobilization of opposition forces during this period. Motivated by grievances against the government's economic reforms, labor strikes were skyrocketing, with estimates that 2–4 million workers participated in these actions between 1998 and 2010 (Beinin 2012). Most of these mobilizations advocated for company- or industry-specific concessions, without making explicitly political demands (Shehata 2011). Yet, in the larger strikes, workers were becoming increasingly and openly political in their slogans and demands, especially as the government failed to uphold many of its promises. For instance, in 2006, 2007, and 2008, large strikes occurred in the city of el-Mahalla el-Kubra. In 2006, workers negotiated with the minister of labor, eventually accepting a deal. A year later, the strike adopted a more overt challenge to Mubarak, with the organizers holding a demonstration with the wife of jailed presidential candidate Ayman Nour, who had challenged Mubarak in the 2005 election (Clement 2009).

The strike that erupted in the city in 2008 was even more openly political, with long-run implications for the trajectory of opposition to the president. Protesters during the strike chanted "Down, down Mubarak," and their efforts triggered an attempt at a general strike across the country to which the regime responded with force (Slackman 2008). The 2008 strike also spurred the formation of the April 6 Youth Group, which acquired tens of thousands of online followers who were opposed to the president and in some cases willing to participate in protests and other forms of activism challenging his authority (Knickmeyer 2008). These groups also began to promote Mohammed el-Baradei – former head of the International Atomic

Energy Agency – for president, explicitly linking their grievances to the need for Mubarak's replacement (Shehata 2011). Workers continued to target the president as well. In 2010, less than one year prior to the revolution, workers demonstrating in front of the parliament building were repeating this same chant of "Down, down Mubarak" alongside their demands for more equitable policies such as an increased minimum wage. Some more prominent opposition elites blamed Nazif and his cabinet. For instance, the prominent lawyer Khalid Ali stated that "The government represents the marriage between authority and money ... We call for the resignation of Ahmed Nazif's government because it works only for businessmen and ignores social justice" (Beinin 2012). Yet, as the growing protest movements demonstrated, many Egyptians frustrated with the regime were focused squarely on the president in their public activism, because Nazif's policies were seen as an extension of Mubarak's governance.

Mubarak was not just blamed for frustrations with economic malaise and corruption. As discussed at the start of the book, the brutal murder of the young man Khaled Said by Egyptian police officers motivated the formation of another opposition-oriented Facebook page that attracted tens of thousands of followers (Londono 2011). A central demand of this page – which ostensibly focused primarily on police brutality – was the imposition of term limits that would end Mubarak's presidency (Alaimo 2015). Mubarak was responsible for the police who did his bidding, and in the view of many Egyptian activists, removing Mubarak from the presidency was an important part of solving problems like abuse by low-level police officers.

As the 2000s went on, Mubarak appeared to struggle more and more to escape blame for the regime's performance failures, ranging from declining standards of living to abusive security forces and corruption. The prime minister and cabinet often took the lead on implementing state policies, but they were technocratic members of the president's party and tightly tied to his office. Demonstrators who took to the streets prior to the Arab Spring increasingly agreed that Mubarak had to go if they were to achieve their objectives for Egypt. These attributions of responsibility left Mubarak vulnerable to an eruption of mass opposition by the time that Ben Ali's ouster in Tunisia demonstrated that protests could force an Arab autocrat from power.

8.3 Variation in Escalation of Opposition

Ben Ali and Tunisia

Tunisia under Ben Ali was more repressive than Egypt under Mubarak, so public attributions of blame against Ben Ali were rarer in the years leading up to the Arab Spring (Chomiak 2011). Nonetheless, the country experienced similar dynamics to Egypt in this period, with perceived corruption and rising inequality generating increasing anger toward Ben Ali personally. As in Egypt, Tunisia's government had long pursued liberalizing economic reforms in coordination with the IMF and the World Bank, and these reforms generated uneven gains that fostered significant resentment among many working-class Tunisians. As a result, labor unions, including the powerful Union Générale Tunisienne du Travail (UGTT), played an important role in contesting the regime. Throughout the 2000s, the UGTT took several positions indicating that its members held Ben Ali responsible for their grievances, even while the national leadership was largely co-opted by the president. For instance, by 2004, militant activists in the party had become powerful enough to force debate over supporting Ben Ali's fourth presidential term. Though it was unsurprising that they lost the eventual vote, several important regional and industry-specific unions did vote openly against supporting Ben Ali, and some others abstained rather than endorsing him (Beinin 2015). The next year, the union directly criticized Ben Ali for inviting the Israeli prime minister to the country and supported other organizations as they clashed with and were repressed by the president (Beinin 2015).

In 2008, an uprising in the interior town of Gafsa, in which the country's phosphate industry is concentrated, posed the most potent challenge to the regime in decades. Angered by persistently high unemployment, thousands of protesters repeatedly mobilized to push for concessions from the government. While organizers explicitly forbade political slogans for tactical reasons, it was clear that demonstrators considered Ben Ali to be primarily responsible for their grievances (Beinin 2015). Not only were the president's campaign posters disfigured or torn down across the region, but indirect yet pointed messages also made opposition to the president readily apparent. Two years later, the Arab Spring would begin in these same interior regions, motivated by anger at these same economic grievances and the government's failure to address them. When it became clear that the regime could not contain protesters with violence as it had previously, demonstrators did not call for ministers or the prime minister to be fired;

rather, they focused directly on the removal of Ben Ali and the political party he led as the solution to their problems.

As with economic issues, the president also struggled to escape blame for corruption. Rumors circulated frequently about the illicit financial gains of his family, and the US ambassador to Tunisia in 2009 noted that they were "disliked and even hated by some Tunisians" because of their excesses (Raghavan 2011). With the government and parliament viewed as an extension of the president rather than actors with some independent influence over decision-making, policies that encouraged corrupt gains for the wealthy – including Ben Ali's own family – were perceived by the public to be the president's responsibility. As one Tunisian said following the revolution, "Ben Ali stole from his people ... He dominated with an iron fist."

Perceptions of the president's responsibility also helped the country's fragmented opposition groups to overcome their ideological differences and coordinate against Ben Ali. By 2005, several opposition groups, including both Islamists and leftists, formed the October 18 Coalition to challenge the government's policies and advocate for a new president (Nugent 2020). There were few beliefs that changes to the cabinet would solve the country's problems: What was needed was an entirely new presidential administration. While repression kept these organizations weak or in exile, their focus on the president appears to have aligned with the public's beliefs that the president was responsible for their grievances.

When the 2010 protests began, people understood the reality of the political system. They recognized the extent to which Ben Ali dominated decision-making, and they blamed him for the country's problems, especially surrounding the economy, corruption, and the lack of political freedoms. In fact, even many members of the ruling party began to turn on the president in the years prior to the revolution, angered by the fact that he "had gained vast personal powers and progressively marginalized ruling party activists" (Wolf 2023). Conversations in the interviews I conducted reflected this assessment of how Ben Ali's monopolization of power made him a target of popular discontent. For instance, Ben Ali's former prime minister noted two reasons that people mobilized against Ben Ali and not other actors in the political system. First, they understood the president "was the decision-maker." Second, they were well aware of "the corruption of

8.3 Variation in Escalation of Opposition

the family," and that Ben Ali was the "chief of the mafia that did most of the theft." Likewise, an activist during Ben Ali's presidency said that "all the people knew" that "corruption was his family." Another activist observed how repression, corruption, and poor economic performance were linked to the president in the eyes of the public, which undermined his popularity over time. As a result, eventually Tunisians "were all united against the corruption and repression" of Ben Ali.

8.3.2 Cross-National Protest Escalation in Monarchies and Nonmonarchies

Have monarchs generally been less vulnerable to popular mobilizations than other autocrats in the modern period, or is this pattern an artifact of the Arab Spring? To investigate this question, I rely on cross-national data on regime type and mass mobilizations from several datasets. First, I use the Geddes et al. (2014) data on authoritarian regimes to identify authoritarian country-years between 1946 and 2010. I then use their data to identify years in which the autocrat of a given country was removed from power. This indicator of an autocrat's tenure ending provides my dependent variable in the analysis. The authors also classify authoritarian regimes into four types, one of which is ruling monarchy. I use an indicator that a given country-year was governed by a monarchy as one of two primary independent variables.

The second independent variable in which I am interested is an indicator for popular mobilization in the country that year. I rely on two datasets for different measures of mobilization. The first is V-Dem, which codes an ordinal rating for protest frequency. I create an indicator coded as 1 if V-Dem rated the country as experiencing any level of mobilization and 0 if it coded the country as experiencing almost no protest. The second measure is taken from NAVCO, which identifies mass mobilizations sustained by more than 1,000 participants making maximalist goals on the political system. I create a second indicator coded as 1 if NAVCO records a mass mobilization in a given year. This variable reflects a more intense measure of protest than the V-Dem measure, which incorporates mass mobilizations but also smaller, less persistent, and less organized eruptions of collective action.

To assess whether monarchs are less vulnerable than other autocrats to popular mobilization, I analyze whether an interaction exists between the indicator for monarchy and the indicators for protest activity. If monarchs are less vulnerable to periods of opposition protest, we would expect to see a negative interaction term indicating that protests have a smaller relationship with the ouster of an autocrat from power when that autocrat is a monarch. The results are reported in Table 8.3, and they align with this expectation. The first column shows the naive relationship between monarchy, the V-Dem protest measure, their interaction, and the autocrat's ouster. The second column shows the same but with the NAVCO protest measure instead. As expected, nonroyal autocrats are particularly vulnerable to being overthrown in years where protests occur: The V-Dem measure increases the likelihood of removal by 7 percentage points, and the NAVCO measure by 11 percentage points. However, the interaction indicates that this connection between protest and ouster almost disappears when the autocrat is a monarch, dropping by 5 percentage points for the V-Dem variable and 9 percentage points for the NAVCO variable.

Omitted variable bias may contribute to these results, so I incorporate control variables in columns 3 and 4. I control for the occurrence of an economic crisis, the log of GDP per capita, and the log of oil income to account for the possibility that monarchies perform better economically and are less vulnerable to mobilizations for this reason. I also control for the frequency of political killings and the openness of the political system in case variation in repression accounts for these patterns, as well as the area of the country since monarchies tend to be smaller and may benefit from their size. In addition, I include dummies for region and year. With the inclusion of controls, the magnitude of the interaction term increases slightly to a 6 percentage point reduction with the V-Dem measure of protest and an 11 percentage point reduction with the NAVCO measure of mass mobilization, suggesting that protests are less threatening to the ability of monarchs to hold onto power compared to other autocrats.

These results are consistent with monarchs being more capable of shifting blame onto other political elites because of the advantages they possess with regards to delegation, making it less likely that the people direct their anger at the monarch when they take to the streets to express their grievances. Note that the data do not extend past 2010,

8.3 Variation in Escalation of Opposition

Table 8.3 *Autocratic monarchs are less vulnerable to protests*

	Autocrat ousted (1)	Autocrat ousted (2)	Autocrat ousted (3)	Autocrat ousted (4)
Monarchy	0.00	−0.02	0.04	−0.00
	(0.02)	(0.01)	(0.03)	(0.02)
V-Dem protest	0.07***		0.06***	
	(0.01)		(0.02)	
NAVCO protest		0.11***		0.12***
		(0.02)		(0.02)
Monarchy × Protest	−0.05[†]	−0.09*	−0.06[†]	−0.11*
	(0.03)	(0.04)	(0.03)	(0.04)
Economic crisis			0.05**	0.04**
			(0.02)	(0.02)
GDP PC (Log)			0.00	0.00
			(0.01)	(0.01)
Free from killings			0.01	0.01[†]
			(0.01)	(0.01)
Open autocracy			0.03	0.01
			(0.02)	(0.01)
Area			0.00	0.00
			(0.00)	(0.00)
Log oil wealth			−0.00	−0.00
			(0.00)	(0.00)
Constant	0.05***	0.09***	0.15	0.18
	(0.01)	(0.01)	(0.14)	(0.13)
Region dummies			✓	✓
Year dummies			✓	✓
Observations	4,168	4,428	3,582	3,745
Clusters	113	118	107	109

[†]$p < 0.10$; * $p < 0.05$; ** $p < 0.01$; *** $p < 0.001$
OLS models with standard errors clustered by countries.

so the period of the Arab Spring, which would likely strengthen the results, is not included in the analysis. In other words, the fact that monarchs had relatively less to fear from protests during the Arab Spring was not an artifact of that moment but instead reflects a more generalizable trend in the modern period.

8.4 Conclusion

Despite predictions to the contrary, ruling monarchies continue to survive and even thrive. Their numbers are small and are still gradually fading, and it seems unlikely that monarchies will reverse that trend in the foreseeable future given the dominance of ideas about popular sovereignty in the modern world. But for those ruling monarchs that remain, their institutional position appears to be a sound one. Monarchies rival if not surpass even party regimes in terms of their durability and stability, and the competition with other types of authoritarian rule is not even close (Geddes et al. 2014).

Scholars have puzzled over this trend, but there have been few general arguments proposed to explain it. My theory suggests that a royal advantage in protecting the reputation of the king may account for part of the stability of royal rule. Because sharing decision-making powers is less risky for monarchs, they can delegate more credibly with less to fear from potential elite rivals; furthermore, because of expectations about how different ruler types relate to governance and accountability, this delegation should be relatively more effective at shaping the public's attributions. As a result, popular dissatisfaction is less likely to bubble up against the monarch and more likely to target other government officials and political elites, and thus opponents of the monarch who do exist will have a harder time coordinating for regime change. Evidence presented in the chapter demonstrates that monarchs typically do share power more credibly and that monarchs face different expectations about their responsibility for decision-making. It also indicates that monarchs are less likely to be overthrown during periods in which the public is mobilized, even controlling for economic performance, repression, and other factors related to protest outcomes.

Of course, monarchies can be – and indeed have been – overthrown by mass uprisings and popular revolutions. Kings and queens who forego power sharing to dominate their countries' policy processes will also be held responsible by the public for whatever outcomes their governance produces. In Chapter 9, I provide support for this claim and explore whether it contributes to understanding why monarchy survived into the modern period in some countries but not in others.

8.5 Appendix

Parliamentary Responsibility

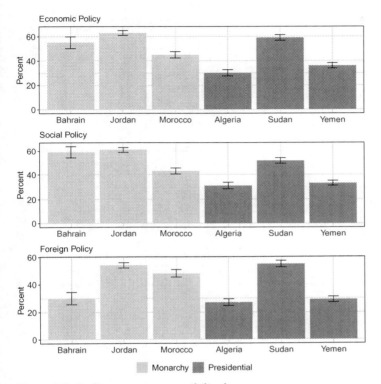

Figure 8.9 Parliamentary responsibility by country

Note: Regarding perceptions of parliamentary policy influence by country, Figure 8.9 shows that survey takers in Morocco were less likely than those in Jordan and Bahrain to view parliament as an important factor in the policy process, whereas survey takers in Sudan were more likely than those in Yemen and Algeria to view the parliament as an important contributor. However, the Morocco results are higher than those in Yemen and Algeria, whereas the Sudan results are lower than those in Jordan and Bahrain, particularly for social policy.

Balance for YouGov Experiment

Table 8.4 *Logit model for balance in YouGov experiment*

	Treatment assignment
Gender	0.022
	(0.077)
Age	−0.004
	(0.028)
Income	−0.009
	(0.021)
Marital status	−0.002
	(0.054)
Employment status	−0.020
	(0.079)
Constant	0.104
	(0.203)
Observations	3,005
Prob. of χ^2	0.996

*** $p < 0.001$, ** $p < 0.01$, * $p < 0.05$, † <0.10

9 | Power Sharing, Blame, and the Collapse of Royal Regimes

Monarchy predominated globally for most of human history. Its decline began at the start of the nineteenth century, following the Napoleonic Wars, but monarchies persisted in a majority of the world's states until approximately 1900 (Gerring et al. 2021). Gradually, however, monarchs were either overthrown or relegated to symbolic status; meanwhile, republican government became the norm, and ruling monarchies held onto power in a relatively small number of states.

A number of factors likely contributed to this transition away from royal rule, ranging from the spread of new ideas (Censer 2019) to new technologies that lowered communication costs (Gerring et al. 2021). However, what explains why some monarchies collapsed in the face of revolutionary challenges while others survived, even if they eventually lost their ability to rule? This chapter argues that the answer to this question rests partially on the extent to which monarchs dominated decision-making in their countries. Where monarchs delegated meaningful decision-making powers to other political elites, they were less likely to become targets of revolutionary anger as the world transitioned toward republicanism, and they may have even succeeded in holding onto significant political influence well into the twentieth century and beyond. On the other hand, in political systems where power was concentrated much more directly in the hands of the monarch, they were more likely to become the principal target of political opposition when the performance of their regimes faltered, and their monarchies were more likely to be swept away entirely.

The traditional comparison of Great Britain and France illustrates this argument well. The Stuart kings of England and Scotland faced multiple rebellions in the 1600s, motivated in part by alleged absolutism at the expense of other political elites in parliament, and the monarchs who ruled after the Glorious Revolution of 1688 increasingly delegated decision-making responsibilities to cabinet ministers and parliamentarians (Cox 2011). This division facilitated acceptance of the idea that the monarch was not responsible for state policies (Bogdanor 1995). While Great Britain experienced political upheaval and revolutionary pressures throughout the nineteenth century (Acemoglu and Robinson 2000), anti-royalist forces never gained significant momentum to challenge the monarchy (Taylor 2013), and political conflict focused primarily on parliament and other nonroyal officials (Tilly 1993). This positioning was not costless for the monarchy, which eventually lost its ability to shape political affairs in any meaningful sense. However, this transition was gradual, lasting at least until the late 1800s if not longer, and the monarchy continues to retain numerous privileges today.

By contrast to its British counterpart, the French monarchy held greater power throughout the eighteenth century, until it was undone during the revolutionary period in 1792. French absolutism should not be overstated, as the French kings also faced meaningful limits to their powers; nonetheless, power sharing was certainly less pronounced in France, where the national parliament was absent for nearly two centuries, the king was sole sovereign, and the monarchy issued all laws and dominated politics (Henshall 2014; Morrill 1978). Louis XVI, for instance, refused to choose a prime minister for most of his reign (1774–1792), because it "contradicted his vision of what constituted the true modus operandi of a French king," by which "he would solicit and receive information from his ministers and then he himself would make the necessary decisions" (Shakibi 2007: 95). Yet, France was increasingly beset by economic and financial challenges during this period, and the cash-strapped monarchy repeatedly sought more resources from the people. The king also involved himself directly in a series of reform proposals whose primary outcome was to alienate various constituencies and drive mounting anger toward the king (Shakibi 2007). When the revolution erupted, popular anger focused on the monarchy as the source of the country's problems, and the king was eventually deposed and then executed.

Monarchy would return to France after the revolutionary period, first under the House of Bourbon (1815–1830), then under the July Monarchy (1830–1848), and finally under the House of Bonaparte (1852–1870). These French monarchies adopted the trappings of constitutional monarchy, with an elected parliament and theoretically responsible ministers, but when compared to the situation in the United Kingdom, power remained firmly in the hands of the kings.

Power Sharing, Blame, and the Collapse of Royal Regimes 279

The Bourbon King Charles X allegedly claimed that parliamentary responsibility "would be an absurdity and an injustice in France. In England ... the ministers govern and should be responsible. In France, the King governs and the ministers cannot be punished for obeying him. It is their duty" (de Wasquerel and Yvert 2002: 411, as quoted in Przeworski et al. 2012). With opposition to the regime increasing in the late 1820s, royalists lost control of the parliament; in response, Charles dissolved it and attempted to rule by decree, triggering a popular revolution.

In the Orleans monarchy that was established after Charles' deposition, the king remained dominant, ensuring parliamentary elections were rigged and ministers were dependent on the throne. As France struggled with economic crisis and worsening corruption during the mid 1840s, the monarchy increasingly became associated with these grievances (Fortescue 2002), and it was overthrown and abolished in the revolutionary upheavals of 1848. A brief republican period followed until President Louis Napoleon Bonaparte had himself declared Emperor Napoleon III in 1852. Napoleon III also dominated the French political system. In part for that reason, he could not escape his greatest governance failure, when he led France into a disastrous war with Prussia in 1870. Having been involved closely in the decision to fight and then leading France's armies himself, his popular support was tied up in the outcome. As the Empress told him, he "could not return without a victory," because "otherwise there would be a revolution on the streets of Paris" (McMillan 1991, 163). Indeed, following his defeat and capture, the masses mobilized in Paris and demanded that a republic be established (McMillan 1991). This experience was France's last with monarchy, following nearly a century of turmoil in which powerful kings dominated decision-making and were undone by popular backlash to their governance.

In the remainder of the chapter, I analyze data on monarchies gathered by Przeworski et al. (2012) and Gerring et al. (2021) to provide more systematic support for the claim that monarchies which monopolized decision-making powers more fully were less likely to survive into the twentieth century. I then consider my argument's relevance to the failure of ruling monarchies in the modern period by exploring the only two cases in which these regimes were clearly toppled by mass mobilization. Previous chapters have illustrated how autocratic monarchs in Jordan, Morocco, and other countries have

280 *Power Sharing, Blame, and the Collapse of Royal Regimes*

shared power to protect their reputations and limit the likelihood that discontent escalates against them personally; here, I examine whether modern monarchs who did succumb to popular uprisings were less likely to take advantage of this delegation strategy. I review the revolution that toppled the Iranian monarchy in 1979, showing how the shah's tendency to dominate decision-making exposed him to blame and undermined his popular support prior to the revolution. I also briefly consider the trajectory of the Nepali monarchy – the only other case of a ruling monarchy that was overthrown by mass opposition since 1950. Consistent with the broader theory of the book, these cases suggest that monarchs who forego credible power sharing are more at risk of attracting popular anger, and thus more vulnerable to governance outcomes that produce widespread grievances in their societies. While monarchs' advantages in delegating to avoid blame can help to explain their durability in the modern world, whether or not monarchs chose to share power historically can help us understand why some survived while others were overthrown.

9.1 Which Monarchies Survived into the Modern World?

The collapse of monarchy was not inevitable. Even as republicanism became the dominant form of government in the nineteenth and twentieth centuries, many monarchs held onto their positions for decades before fading into symbolic sovereigns, whereas others continue to rule in authoritarian regimes today. Does the divergence between the British and French experience reflect a more general trend regarding the survival of monarchy into the modern world? This section draws on two sources of data about monarchies in the nineteenth and twentieth century to test more systematically whether the monarchies that held onto their thrones – whether as rulers or eventually as ceremonial figureheads – were those where royals delegated more decision-making responsibility to nonroyal political elites.

First, Przeworski et al. (2012) compiled information on all constitutional monarchies that have existed since the nineteenth century and the extent to which they ever allowed for parliamentary responsibility to become the norm in the political system. Here, parliamentary responsibility is defined as the "collective political responsibility of governments to the parliament," such that cabinets were beholden to the elected parliament rather than an autocratic monarch. The

9.1 Which Monarchies Survived

monarchies considered by the authors include Albania, Austria, Belgium, Brazil, Bulgaria, Denmark, Egypt, France, Germany, Greece, Hungary, Iran, Iraq, Italy, Japan, Jordan, Kuwait, Lesotho, Morocco, Nepal, the Netherlands, Norway, the Ottoman Empire, Portugal, Romania, Russia, Serbia, Spain, Swaziland, Sweden, Thailand, the United Kingdom, and Yugoslavia.

What is particularly useful for our purpose is that Przeworski et al. categorize these monarchies based on their experience with parliamentary responsibility, and specifically whether they contended with a parliament powerful enough to act as an important governance institution with influence over decision-making independent of the monarchy's power. The first category of constitutional monarchies is those in which the principle of parliamentary responsibility was never tested, because the monarch was always able to ensure that royalist forces dominated the parliament. In some cases, this dominance was achieved by consistently successful electoral manipulation combined with royal patronage, or because the monarch rotated control of the government between factions that accepted royal supremacy. In other words, these were constitutional monarchies in which the monarch shared some limited power with parliament but never allowed them to take the lead in governance. The second category includes monarchies in which opposition forces succeeded in winning a parliamentary majority at some point in time, attempted to form a government, and were subsequently repressed by the monarch through the dissolution of the parliament and possibly the establishment of a royal dictatorship. These cases reflect instances in which parliament acquired enough influence to challenge the monarch's preeminent decision-making role and the monarchy responded by fighting back. The third and final category also includes monarchies in which opposition forces won a parliamentary majority, but where the monarch eventually yielded in allowing this majority to dictate the government and assume more significant influence over decision-making.

Table 9.1 lists each constitutional monarchy within these categories, along with whether the monarchy has survived or was overthrown. A clear pattern emerges from the table. Monarchs who consistently dominated the parliament were all eventually deposed, with the exception of Japan. Likewise, only a handful of monarchs survived who reacted to an opposition-controlled parliament by suppressing its ability to choose the government and thus substantially reduce the

282 *Power Sharing, Blame, and the Collapse of Royal Regimes*

Table 9.1 *Royal survival and parliamentary responsibility*

	Never challenged by parliament	Suppressed parliament	Yielded to parliament
Deposed	Albania	Austria	Italy
	France (1852–1870)	Bulgaria (1878–1886)	
	France (1830–1848)	Bulgaria (1918–1946)	
	Germany	Egypt	
	Iraq	France (1815–1830)	
	Brazil	Greece	
	Bulgaria (1887–1918)	Hungary	
	Portugal	Iran	
	Spain*	Lesotho	
		Nepal	
		Ottoman	
		Romania	
		Russia	
		Serbia	
		Yugoslavia	
Survived	Japan	Jordan	Belgium
		Kuwait	Denmark
		Morocco	Netherlands
		Swaziland	Norway
			Sweden
			Thailand
			United Kingdom

* Monarchy abolished (1931) but later restored (1978) as ceremonial monarchy.

monarchy's influence over decision-making. On the other hand, those monarchs who ceded responsibility to parliament almost all survived. Of these, only the Italian monarchy was abolished.

In other words, constitutional monarchs who remained the predominant political actor in their political systems were much more likely to have been deposed at some point during the past two centuries, compared to those who allowed parliament to assume genuine responsibility for governance. Many of these deposed monarchies exercised political power for decades before they were ousted, successfully surviving major political challenges by maintaining sufficient popular and elite support. These monarchs often delegated political influence to powerful prime ministers and cabinets, while also granting a degree of

9.1 *Which Monarchies Survived* 283

influence to their subordinate parliaments, as in Jordan, Kuwait, and Morocco today. Nonetheless, at some point, nearly all of them confronted a crisis that they could not manage effectively, whether defeat in war or economic disruption. Their centrality to the political system attracted enough opposition during these moments to result in their deposition. By contrast, monarchs who stepped back from decision-making more fully were much more likely to survive these moments, consistent with their ability to avoid blame for the public's grievances. Of course, those monarchies that yielded to parliamentary responsibility eventually became ceremonial leaders, losing their political power almost entirely. However, it is worth emphasizing again that this process could take decades or even centuries, as in the United Kingdom, Sweden, or Thailand, such that monarchs often retained substantial political influence even as parliament exercised formal responsibility.

As a second test of this argument, I draw on a dataset of monarchies from Gerring et al. (2021) and V-Dem's historic data about legislative constraints on the executive, which extend back to 1800. I analyze whether monarchies with stronger legislatures were less likely to experience regime changes between 1800 and 1940.[1] This pattern would also be consistent with less credible delegation of responsibility from the monarch to the parliament resulting in more exposure to blame, greater instability and vulnerability to mass opposition, and less likelihood of survival into the modern period. The combined monarchy and V-Dem data include monarchies from thirty-one countries.

I use OLS regression to analyze the correlation between legislative constraints on the executive and the occurrence of regime change in a country-year, with standard errors clustered by country. The results are presented in Table 9.2. As the independent variable, I use V-Dem's continuous measure of legislative constraints, which ranges between 0 and 1, in addition to a dummy variable for whether monarchies were above or below the mean of legislative constraints in a given country-year. Columns 1 and 2 show the bivariate relationship between the legislative constraint variables and regime change; columns 3 and 4 add dummy variables for region and year; columns 5 and 6 lag the legislative constraint variable by one year; and columns 7 and 8 add control variables for log GDP per capita, log population, and regime duration.

---

[1] I choose this cutoff to explore this relationship prior to World War II and the emergence of the period on which most datasets of modern authoritarian regimes focus.

Table 9.2 *More constrained monarchies experienced fewer regime changes, 1800–1940*

	(1)	(2)	(3)	(4)	(5)	(6)	(7)	(8)
Legislative constraints	−0.11**		−0.10***		−0.10***		−0.10†	
(Continuous)	(0.03)		(0.02)		(0.02)		(0.05)	
Legislative constraints		−0.04**		−0.04***		−0.04**		−0.03
(Binary)		(0.01)		(0.01)		(0.01)		(0.02)
Constant	0.14***	0.10***	0.08***	0.06*	0.07**	0.05*	0.50†	0.54†
	(0.02)	(0.01)	(0.02)	(0.02)	(0.02)	(0.02)	(0.29)	(0.30)
Region dummies			✓	✓	✓	✓	✓	✓
Year dummies			✓	✓	✓	✓	✓	✓
Lagged constraint variable					✓	✓		
Control variables							✓	✓
Clusters	31	31	31	31	30	30	29	29
Observations	1,614	1,614	1,614	1,614	1,507	1,503	1,259	1,259

*** $p < 0.001$, ** $p < 0.01$, * $p < 0.05$, † $ < 0.10$
Standard Errors clustered by country.

9.2 The Collapse of Modern Monarchies

The results show a correlation between the strength of legislative constraints on the royal executive and the likelihood of a regime change incident. The coefficient for the binary constraints variable suggests that a legislature above the mean in its ability to constrain the monarch was associated with a four percentage point decrease in the probability of regime change each year. With regime change occurring in approximately eight percent of country-years for monarchies between 1800 and 1940, a four percentage point decrease indicates a meaningful reduction of risk to the monarch.

This pattern suggests that monarchs who reigned between 1800 and 1940, during a period in which the world was transitioning toward norms of democratic, republican government, were more stable and less likely to be deposed when they shared greater powers with parliament. The analysis does not establish why this difference is observed, and it is possible that the greater stability of these monarchies can be explained at least partially by more effective co-optation of parliamentary elites, strengthened democratic legitimacy, and other mechanisms. The analysis is also not intended to dismiss other factors that likely explain why some monarchies survived into the modern period, whereas others did not, including political culture, the strength of democratic, socialist, and other ideologies, foreign intervention, and even chance. Nonetheless, the pattern is consistent with the argument that monarchs who delegated more credibly to their parliaments benefited from better positioning to avoid blame for popular discontent and were more likely to survive crises as a result.

9.2 The Collapse of Modern Monarchies

As discussed previously, monarchies in the modern era have been exceptionally durable on average compared to other authoritarian regimes; furthermore, monarchs tend to experience more stable relations with other political elites and are less likely to confront mass opposition to their rule, particularly during periods of discontent in which grievances with political and economic outcomes are widespread. Despite these advantages, monarchies still lose power and a number have been overthrown since 1950.

If monarchs are advantaged in avoiding blame and thus minimizing mass opposition as this book has argued, one implication is that relatively few modern monarchs should have lost power to mass uprisings compared to other autocracies. Another implication is that monarchs who did lose power in this way should be those who eschewed delegating credibly and instead prioritized controlling the decision-making process closely; in addition, there should be evidence that this approach to governance left the monarch exposed to blame for many of the grievances that motivated the uprisings that overthrew them.

Regarding the first point, it is the case that ruling monarchies have been less likely than other autocracies to lose power to challenges from the masses, with these regime changes occurring in 1.3 percent of years for nonmonarchies and 0.7 percent of years for monarchies between 1946 and 2010 (Geddes et al. 2014). Most of the monarchies that experienced regime change during this period lost power instead to military coups, including those in Afghanistan, Burundi, Cambodia, Egypt, Iraq, Libya, and Yemen. In addition, the Sultan of the Maldives was deposed via a parliamentary vote in favor of establishing a republic, and the monarchs of Bhutan and Tonga ceded powers to elected legislatures, though in both cases the monarchs continue to wield substantial political influence today. Only in two cases – Iran and Nepal – have revolutionary mobilizations clearly resulted in the end of ruling monarchies. The regime change that ended the Ethiopian monarchy in 1974 is an ambiguous case that has been coded as a popular uprising (e.g., Geddes et al. 2014), but where the Emperor was ultimately deposed by a military council. While the coup was preceded by mass mobilizations, popular anger appeared to be aimed primarily at government elites and feudal lords other than the monarch (Zewde 2001), and it is possible that the Ethiopian monarchy would have survived the unrest had the military not taken advantage of the disruptions to depose the emperor. In fact, fearing popular discontent over the abolition of the monarchy, the military council named the incapacitated crown prince as King of Ethiopia after deposing Emperor Selassie. Only five months later did they finally move to end Ethiopia's status as a monarchy.

Did the Iranian and Nepali monarchs govern in such a way as to leave themselves relatively exposed to popular discontent, and if so, did this style of governance contribute to their loss of power? In what follows, I explore the theory's relevance to regime change in these countries. I focus first on Iran, whose revolution has received substantial scholarly attention due to its wide-ranging repercussions

9.2 The Collapse of Modern Monarchies

for global politics (e.g., Arjomand 1988; Bashiriyeh 1984; Kurzman 1996, 2005; Moaddel 1993; Parsa 1989; Rasler 1996; Yom 2015). I then consider Nepal more briefly. In both countries, kings who chose to monopolize decision-making found themselves vulnerable to mass opposition during periods of political and economic crisis.

9.2.1 Revolution in Iran

Mohammad Reza Shah governed Iran from 1941 until he was overthrown in the Iranian Revolution of 1979. During his early years in power, Iran remained an authoritarian political system, but the shah did not dominate its decision-making processes to the extent that he would in later decades. Instead, he was constrained significantly by other political actors, including landed elites in the parliament and cabinet. These notables used their wealth to cultivate extensive patronage networks, which they relied upon to mobilize peasants and tribesmen at the polls for parliamentary elections. With access to reliable voter bases independent from the palace, the notables were able to assert themselves actively in the political system, relative to the shah. In fact, whereas the previous shah had customarily appointed his own prime minister and influenced the formation of the cabinet, Mohammad Reza lost this power to parliament, whose leading members were much more involved in the selection process (Abrahamian 2008). Though the monarch continued to possess substantial political influence, the notables dominated decision-making for many policy domains through their influence over the cabinet. The one exception was the military, where the shah made sure to protect his prerogatives.

This arrangement may have helped to protect the shah's reputation during the political and economic turmoil of the 1940s, as when the Tudeh Party mobilized against the cabinet for refusing to sign an oil agreement with the Soviet Union (Abrahamian 1968). However, it also meant that the monarch was vulnerable to internal challenges from other political elites. A particularly threatening challenge emerged from the nationalist politician Dr. Mohammad Mossadeq, whose agenda included eliminating the shah's political power and perhaps establishing a republic. By early 1951, Mossadeq had acquired enough influence to secure the premiership, and he was soon taking actions that greatly undermined the shah's ability to control the military

288 *Power Sharing, Blame, and the Collapse of Royal Regimes*

and shape other political matters. The shah was only able to reassert himself after a coup backed by the US and British governments forced Mossadeq out of office.

Historians note that the Mossadeq episode taught the shah a lesson he would never forget. He was now "determined never to allow a Mossadeq type of situation to recur," which meant following in his father's footsteps by "ignoring the main thrust of the 1906–1907 constitution, which had ... reserved few powers for the shah" (Keddie 2003, 135). Thus, the shah responded by working to monopolize power, with the goal of protecting the monarchy from elite threats "such as military coups d'etat and strong political rivals..." (Fatemi 1982). These efforts began even before Mossadeq was overthrown. The shah refused to go along with the CIA-backed coup plan until its leading general – Zahedi – agreed to sign his own predated resignation letter from the premiership. In other words, "The shah had no desire to replace Mossadeq with some potentially dangerous general" (Abrahamian 2008, 121). Powers of decision-making would now be concentrated in his hands.

The shah accomplished this transformation in a number of ways. First, he continued to foster special attention on the military, strengthening his control over the institution even further. This emphasis involved personal interventions on matters of "training, maneuvers, barracks, and the general well-being of the officers," on whom he showered "generous salaries, pensions, and fringe benefits" (Abrahamian 2008, 125). He also pursued the creation of SAVAK, a secret police force run by a close friend who reported directly to the royal court.

The constitution was changed as well so that the shah had full authority to appoint prime ministers. Zahedi, the general who ousted Mossadeq, was himself forced out of the premiership in only twenty months after the shah spread rumors that he had embezzled large sums of money (Abrahamian 2008). Of the other seven prime ministers who held office prior to the beginning of the revolution in 1977, six were the shah's personal choice, and they were "mostly young European-educated civil servants from prominent families that had hitched their careers to the Pahlavi dynasty" (Abrahamian 2008, 128). Given their dependency on the palace, these prime ministers had little leeway to influence policymaking themselves. The shah personally presided over

9.2 The Collapse of Modern Monarchies

weekly cabinet meetings, demonstrating clearly who was in charge of most policy decisions.

Landowning notables in the parliament did manage to wield a degree of influence over the policy process throughout the 1950s. For instance, they blocked major land reforms pursued by the shah during this decade (Keddie 2003). Their obstruction frustrated the monarch, who maneuvered to undercut the conservatives' power by eroding their local bases of independent support and weakening the independence of the legislature (Westwood 1961). First, administrative boundaries were changed to fragment notables' patronage networks in their localities, and selection processes for local officials were revamped to give the central government control over appointments to these positions (Abrahamian 2008). Second, by 1960, the shah conspired with his prime minister at the time, Manoucher Eqbal, to reduce the dominance of the notables in parliament (Bashiriyeh 1984). These changes were disguised as liberalizing reforms, with the government permitting "free" elections where Iranians would be able to choose between two competing parties ostensibly defined by different positions. However, these parties were led by two close associates of the shah, who personally assigned deputies to the respective parties in coordination with SAVAK (Abrahamian 2008; Westwood 1961). Landowning notables were replaced by young professionals or civil servants with no power base outside of the palace. The public soon referred to these organizations derogatorily as the "yes," "yes, sir," and "yes, of course" parties, given their visibly dependent status (Abrahamian 2008, 130).

During this period, the shah used other political institutions as scapegoats for governance problems, and he occasionally delegated more credibly as the potential for popular anger increased. In 1960, for example, the Iranian economy was weakening, which resulted in growing opposition to the prime minister, and even the shah directly (Keddie 2003). Combined with elite and public anger at the rigging of the parliamentary election that year, the shah felt increasingly insecure, and he replaced the prime minister in 1961 with a prominent member of the independent opposition, Ali Amini. As conditions for accepting the position, Amini insisted to the shah that the unfairly elected parliament be dissolved and that the monarch give him a clear statement of support to make decisions as he saw fit. The fact that he had "imposed terms on the shah" enhanced his reputation with the public

290 *Power Sharing, Blame, and the Collapse of Royal Regimes*

(Keddie 2003). Thus, with a more independent prime minister in charge of the government, the shah's concentrated power was diminished, but this change positioned him to ride out the poor economy more effectively by appointing a prime minister who could help him to "recoup" some of his popular support (Keddie 2003, 143).

The biggest challenge confronting Amini was the state's deteriorating finances, and he pushed for all ministries to cut their budgets in response. However, the shah refused to allow him to cut funding for the military as a cornerstone of his royal power. As a result, by 1962, Amini had resigned. He was replaced by another old friend of the shah (Bashiriyeh 1984). According to Keddie (2003, 145), this replacement illustrates how "Clearly the shah would allow powerful and partially independent ministers to exist only so long as the alternative appeared even more dangerous to his own power." In other words, the shah weighed the risk of exposing himself to popular anger against the threat of empowering other elite actors. No longer wanting to risk the dangers of an independent prime minister, the shah unleashed SAVAK on the opposition to end the public unrest. By 1963, the situation in the country had stabilized significantly, and the shah continued to increase his domination of decision-making within the political system.

The shah used these heightened powers to push major policy reforms during the 1960s and 1970s. These reforms became known as the White Revolution, but also as "The Revolution of the Shah and the People," clearly identifying who owned these momentous changes (Arjomand 1988; Keddie 2003). The shah hoped that his agenda would legitimate his rule by providing the regime with important policy successes that would tie new social classes to the political system (Ansari 2001). This revolution involved six initial policy programs: land reform; nationalization of forests and pastures; liberalization of state-owned factories; profit sharing for industry; reforming electoral laws to include women; and a literacy corps to improve literacy rates. These were then followed by six more: a health corps; a reconstruction and development corps; the establishment of rural courts, nationalization of waterways; national reconstruction of infrastructure; and an educational and administrative revolution (Bill 1970). The shah had every intention of transforming the country's society in fundamental ways.

The revolution placed its greatest emphasis on land reform. Approximately 1,638,000 peasant families were given land that had previously

9.2 The Collapse of Modern Monarchies

been owned by the local notables (Abrahamian 1980). Land ownership remained unequal, and many families did not receive enough to be self-sufficient commercial farmers. Furthermore, in 1963 the shah forced the resignation of the effective and energetic Agricultural Minister, Arsanjani, demonstrating once again that he "never allowed another man to become too popular and pose a potential threat to his autocracy" (Keddie 2003, 152). In the years that followed, the reforms would be implemented in a more conservative fashion by a competing group of ministries and government agencies (Bill 1970; Keddie 2003). Nevertheless, the reforms did have a substantial social impact by expanding peasant landowning and stripping the landlord notables of much of their power in the process (Abrahamian 2008).

Beyond land reform, the shah's revolution made strides on many of its other objectives as well. Three five-years plans occurred between 1962 and 1978, and these plans spurred substantial growth in the country's GDP per capita and imports (Abrahamian 1980; Razi 1987). Industrial growth rates were among the highest in the world (Keddie 2003). Education rates rose rapidly (Arjomand 1988), with the literacy corps alone teaching nearly 700,000 students in village schools (Abrahamian 1980). There were improvements to ports, roads, factories, dams, and other forms of infrastructure, and the healthcare system improved quickly as well with the opening of several new hospitals (Abrahamian 2008). Many of these rapid changes were fueled by a dramatic increase in the state's oil revenues during this period. Between 1963 and 1973, revenues increased from twenty-nine billion rials to 182 billion rials, enabling the shah to go on a massive spending spree (Bashiriyeh 1984). This oil windfall suggests the shah had good reason to expect positive economic outcomes during this period, which may have tempered his concerns about being blamed by an angry public if he centralized power too much.

Nonetheless, less positive developments also occurred as a result of the shah's policies. The monarch had a "mania" for spending on new and mostly useless weapons systems (Keddie 2003, 162). The government's heavy hand in the economy resulted in favorable treatment of large, Western-style industries at the expense of smaller merchants and companies (Keddie 2003). Income inequality increased as a result of these policies, and persistently high rates of illiteracy and infant mortality in the countryside further indicated the uneven distribution of the country's gains (Razi 1987). This combination of rapid growth for some but high expectations for all led to rising social tensions that ultimately contributed to the revolution (Fatemi 1982).

In 1975, the shah consolidated his control over the country's political elites even more decisively. Dissatisfied with the performance of the controlled two-party system, he dissolved both parties and replaced them with a single organization called the Resurgence Party (Bashiriyeh 1984). Membership in the party was required of MPs, as well as most state employees in the bureaucracy and universities (Keddie 2003). The organization pushed a number of controversial reforms. On economic policy, it forced small merchants to pay minimum wages, provide health insurance, and pay taxes. On social policy, it pushed liberalizing reforms that included opening birth control clinics, permitting abortions, and attacking the religious establishment (Abrahamian 2008). The shah tied himself closely to this party and its agenda. In fact, he boasted at the time that "No other nation has given its ruler such a carte-blanche" (Abrahamian 2008, 150).

By the mid 1970s, the shah's regime had alienated almost every important social and political faction in the country (Yom 2015). The notables, who might have formed a conservative bulwark in favor of the monarchy, were instead pushed away by the land reforms that had stripped them of their status (Abrahamian 2008). The clergy were angered by the shah's culturally liberal policies regarding religious issues and women's rights (Keddie 2003), and nationalists were upset by his close relations with the United States and the United Kingdom (Abrahamian 2008). Middle-class merchants and business owners were distraught over economic policies pursued by the Resurgence Party in the mid 1970s (Arjomand 1988; Parsa 1989), and the lower classes had often failed to receive the benefits of Iran's rapid economic growth (Kurzman 2003; Parsa 1989). Even the bureaucracy was dissatisfied, as the establishment of the Resurgence Party had created disruptions to the governance system that left many feeling betrayed (Zonis 1983). Furthermore, by the mid 1970s, the economic boom of the preceding decade had dissipated, and the regime was faced by a worsening economy that further increased the public's anger (Bashiriyeh 1984).

All of these grievances were linked directly to policies that the shah had pushed onto the country through the royal court. As was just discussed, land reform was the principal objective of the White Revolution, of which the monarchy was the leading institution. The shah

9.2 *The Collapse of Modern Monarchies* 293

personally advocated for the social policies that alienated the country's religious conservatives, and he tied himself closely to the establishment of the Resurgence Party and its policies during the mid to late 1970s. As a result, when these grievances began to drive mass unrest in 1977, there was little question of who was to blame. All of the country's problems were perceived to be the responsibility of the monarch, and it was anger against him personally – rather than a positive vision of what the future state would look like – that motivated so many to join the uprising (Arjomand 1988). According to Razi (1987), "only two centers of allegiance and active support for the Shah were left in a nation of thirty-five million people during the period of revolution: The SAVAK and the so-called Javidans (Immortals) of the Imperial Guard." Fed up with their ruler's policies, the rest of Iran's people had abandoned him.

Scholars of the revolution have noted the extent to which the shah had concentrated power in his hands, as well as the risks associated with this approach. For instance, Arjomand (1985) wrote that "The Shah had constructed the state machine around his person. There can be no doubt that the collapse of the man preceded the collapse of the machine." Zonis (1983) observed how "the visions and needs of the day were his [the shah's] visions and his needs. He imposed his set of reforms from above ... and made little effort to explain why his visions and needs were appropriate." As a result, over time, "an infinite number of actions [by the shah] suggested to the Iranian people that the rule of the Shah was an insult to them." Parsa (1989) writes that "To strengthen his position, the Shah attempted to make himself indispensable by centralizing power as much as possible." However, in pursuing "manipulation of economic and social processes," his control over the political system "unleashed forces contradictory to centralized rule." In fact, this risk of centralized power had even been recognized before it resulted in the monarch's downfall. Writing back in 1961, a US government official assessing the country's Iran policy noted that the shah's "unwillingness to share power" was partly responsible for driving his isolation from much of the country's population (Zonis 1983).

As economic problems worsened in 1976, protests began to occur across the country. Initially, the shah responded by trying to pass blame onto his prime minister, Hoveyda, who was removed from office in July 1977. However, firing a weak and dependent prime minister had

294   *Power Sharing, Blame, and the Collapse of Royal Regimes*

little effect on the public. Furthermore, the new prime minister, Amuzegar, was just as dependent on the palace – he was a technocrat with repeated experience at high levels of the shah's government and he was a leading member of the Resurgence Party (Keddie 2003). His elevation did little to slow the discontent building against the shah even as he attempted to leverage his economic expertise to address the crisis. In August 1978, the shah again replaced the prime minister, this time appointing the opposition-leaning politician Sharif-Emami who had held the position briefly during the unrest of the early 1960s. However, fearful as ever of other powerful political elites, the shah "did not trust him and would allow him very little latitude in dealing with the crisis" (Arjomand 1985).

While Emami attempted to use his office to offer major concessions to the opposition, the shah responded by ramping up repression, and he declared martial law in September, just one month into Emami's premiership (Rasler 1996). On September 8, protests turned into clashes with the security forces that killed hundreds. This day came to be known as "Black Friday," and it was a decisive turning point that indicated the shah would only outlast the upheaval by relying on massive repression (Zonis 1983). By November, the shah appointed General Gholam Reza Azhari as the prime minister of a new military-led government, and he attempted to fight his way out (Keddie 2003). Yet, his resolve to use force wavered throughout the crisis, and the shah eventually fled in 1979. As it were, thousands died at the hands of the security forces during the revolution (Rasler 1996; Zonis 1983). With such widespread anger against his regime, the shah likely would have needed to order the deaths of many thousands more to have any chance of holding onto his dictatorship.

The shah's tendency to centralize power and dominate decision-making, and the subsequent trajectory of opposition to his regime, is consistent with the argument that monarchs who forgo credible delegation to other political elites risk making themselves vulnerable to mass opposition. Ironically, the revolutionary religious regime that replaced the shah developed new political institutions that more closely resembled a constitutional monarchy – albeit one with a powerful, autocratic monarch – as the Supreme Leader shares significant power with an elected president and parliament (Abrahamian 2008; Keddie 2003). This revolutionary regime has proven resilient in the face of numerous crises and frequent mass discontent in the past four decades.

9.2.2 Abolishing Monarchy in Nepal

The Nepali monarchy that survived until 2008 was established in the mid 1700s by the Shah dynasty. Its long-term survival is consistent with the ability of ruling monarchs to retain popular support by distancing themselves from decision-making, and its ultimate collapse also illustrates the risks of concentrating too much power in royal hands. The Shah dynasty's early kings governed as powerful Hindu monarchs, but they were relegated to ceremonial status in the mid 1800s by a powerful military leader Jung Bahadur Rana, who installed himself as prime minister and made the position hereditary to his family. The Ranas would dominate the political system for the next century as pseudo-monarchs themselves, though the Shah kings retained their symbolic power as a source of legitimacy for the Ranas (Ganguly and Shoup 2005). In 1950, however, King Tribhuvan opportunistically played into growing discontent with the Ranas by challenging their power and then fleeing to India, which sparked a popular revolt against them.

In the aftermath of the uprising, the king's position was enhanced, and the emerging political system was defined by a tussle between a restored monarchy and the Nepali Congress Party, which had significant popular support and strong ties with the Indian government. The king dispensed with direct administration of the country, allowing Congress to form a single-party government, but he also refused to appoint B. P. Koirala, the party leader with the strongest popular support, choosing instead another party elite with more sympathy for royal authority (Whelpton 2005). This move simultaneously provided the king with some distance from decision-making, while also dividing the Congress Party, which struggled to address internal strife. When the king died in 1955, he was succeeded by his son Mahendra, who had ambitions to govern more directly and pushed to delay elections, while appointing royalists to the cabinet. After a public pressure campaign in 1957, Mahendra agreed to parliamentary elections, which were held in 1959 and won resoundingly by Congress. B. P. Koirala was finally appointed as prime minister, but his power was to be short-lived. Unwilling to cede too much influence to a powerful prime minister with party-backing in the legislature, Mahendra cited an alleged decline in law and order to dismiss the government and then had the prime minister and his cabinet arrested by the army in 1960.

296   *Power Sharing, Blame, and the Collapse of Royal Regimes*

The coup faced little opposition, with a majority of Congress MPs endorsing the king's actions, and Mahendra proceeded by designing his own constitution, promulgated in 1962 (Whelpton 2005). The "panchayat democracy" he established was effective in protecting royal autocracy, but it did so by creating several layers of nominally-representative institutions with responsibility for day-to-day decision-making. The system banned political parties, but it established elected village assemblies to oversee local issues, along with indirectly-elected district assemblies and an indirectly-elected national assembly. Elites with backgrounds in a number of the country's political parties competed for the positions (Rose 1964). The king created a National Guidance Council to coordinate and gather information from the panchas, and the monarchy also retained the ability to appoint a prime minister and advise on the selection of cabinet ministers (Khadka 1986). In other words, though significant powers were held by the king, responsibility was also delegated credibly to a broad array of actors across the political system.

This structure remained largely stable for two decades, preserving power but also popular support for the king and his son, Birendra, who succeeded to the throne following his father's death in 1972. Nonetheless, opposition continued to simmer, with dissidents conducting sporadic attacks and demonstrations, and by the late 1970s Nepal's mounting social and economic problems resulted in a level of popular pressure on the regime that the king could not ignore (Ganguly and Shoup 2005). In 1979, Birendra held a referendum allowing voters to choose between the status quo and multiparty democracy, and though the panchayat status quo won, it did so only narrowly. In response, the king pursued reforms that gave more power to the country's nonroyal political institutions, distancing the monarchy more credibly from decision-making. Specifically, the national council became directly elected and was given the power to select the prime minister and cabinet, who could remain in their positions if they retained the confidence of the council. The king still had the ability to get his way with appointing the prime minister, though in 1983 Prime Minister Surya Bahadur Thapa refused a private request to resign and insisted that a vote of no confidence be held. As described by Whelpton (2005, 110), "Somewhat in the manner employed by George III of Great Britain in the eighteenth century, the palace was getting its way through the use of patronage and manipulation rather than by

9.2 The Collapse of Modern Monarchies

directly overruling the legislature. However, also as in the British case, there was clearly the possibility of something like a two-party system evolving within the legislature, based on the divisions between the 'ins' and the 'outs.'" In line with this interpretation, factions within the council criticized each other fiercely, while competing over the direction of economic and social policy to be carried out by the government (Baral 1987).

The panchayat system survived for another decade, but the 1980s continued to spawn mounting economic problems that the regime struggled to address, and anger at perceived corruption – even within the palace – was growing (Baral 1987; Whelpton 2005). With activists emboldened by the uprisings in the Soviet Union, a trade dispute with India that resulted in a semi-blockade and then an economic crisis proved too much for the system to bear (Whelpton 2005). Mass protests erupted in 1990, and a change in government and promised reforms failed to quell them (Baral 1994). In response to intensifying public pressure for multiparty democracy, the king relented, legalizing parties and appointing an interim cabinet to govern the country until the promulgation of a new constitution. Despite the mobilizations, support for the monarchy remained high enough that the king's hold on the throne was not directly threatened. This dynamic is illustrated by the approach of the parties to the monarchy. Whereas some wanted to preserve its constitutional status, others – namely the more radical Communist factions – wanted it abolished (Murthy 2003). To paper over these differences and avoid alienating the monarch's genuine supporters, the parties agreed to strategically direct their anger at the panchas and not the king. For instance, the United Left Front, a union of Communist Parties, stated publicly at the time that "We are not prepared to accept the evil activities of Panchas aimed at undermining the glory of the Crown" (Murthy 2003, 3). Thus, despite the revolutionary changes in Nepal at the time, the monarchy did not become the focal point of opposition, and it survived in the new political order. This result is consistent with the monarchy's approach to power sharing helping to mute anger directed at the king, while also incentivizing opposition to coordinate their demands against nonroyal members of the regime instead.

Though the king retained his throne, Nepal's 1990 constitution also moved the country toward the status of a democratic, constitutional monarchy. The king was positioned as a constitutional figurehead, and his formal powers were significantly diminished in favor of the elected parliament and cabinet (Parajulee 2010; Whelpton 2005). Still, royal influence was not stripped entirely from the constitution, and the monarchy was not purely ceremonial. The king had the right to "offer suggestions or encouragements to or alert the Council of Ministers on matters of national importance," and the king kept his title as supreme commander of the army (Baral 1994). Though the continuation of the monarchy contributed to the emergence of a Maoist insurgency in the mid 1990s (Murthy 2003), King Birendra accepted his new constitutional position and largely refrained from attempting to assert influence over decision-making. With this greater distance from governance, his popularity increased during this period (Parajulee 2010).

In the three decades from the royal coup in 1960 to the democratic transition in 1990, Nepal's trajectory reflected a gradual decrease in the monarchy's decision-making powers as the kings sought to distance themselves from governance to ward off growing popular discontent. Had Nepal continued on this path, it seems plausible that the country would have come to resemble neighboring Bhutan, where the powerful monarch has been effective at protecting his reputation and popular support for the monarchy by choosing to delegate genuine power to popular institutions.

Instead, after a decade of unstable civilian politics throughout the 1990s, the Nepali monarchy attempted to reassert its full dominance over the political system. This effort followed a bloody incident in the palace in 2001 when the crown prince murdered King Birendra, eight other members of the royal family, and then himself, and the throne passed to Birendra's brother, Gyanendra. In 2002, the king took advantage of instability surrounding elections to dismiss the parliament and assume executive authority, after which he governed through royalist prime ministers (Ganguly and Shoup 2005). In 2005, Gyanendra went even further, abandoning cabinet government to exercise power directly. The coup had some initial popular support because of continued instability in the country related to the Maoist insurgency (Hutt 2005), but its ultimate impact was to unite Nepal's divided political parties against the monarchy, which formed the Seven Parties Alliance (SPA) to reinstall democracy. The SPA even made common cause with the Maoists, with whom its leading members had recently been in conflict, agreeing in a November meeting in India that "autocratic

9.3 Conclusion

monarchy" was Nepal's primary problem and would be confronted jointly (Gellner 2007). Mass protests erupted in early 2006, during which popular support increasingly drained away from the king. Gyanendra recalled parliament in April, and power was stripped from the king. Then, in December 2007, a new constituent assembly abolished the Nepali monarchy. While opposition to Gyanendra was motivated by a number of factors, the king's decision to concentrate political power entirely in his hands made the monarchy the focus of all other political factions and their grievances, contributing to the abolition of Nepali monarchy.

9.3 Conclusion

Over the past two centuries, monarchy moved from the most common form of government to one that persists in a minority of countries. Despite the importance of this shift, few social scientists have attempted to study it systematically. The findings in this chapter provide support for one argument about why some monarchies survived and others did not. Where monarchs shared power widely, they were less likely to attract blame and thus opposition, and they were more likely to hang onto their thrones even if they eventually became ceremonial figureheads. Alternatively, where monarchs centralized decision-making powers in their own hands and dominated the political system, they were more likely to become the targets of revolutionary fervor and were more at risk of being overthrown as a result. In other words, the politics of blame can help us to understand not only why ruling monarchies tend to be longer-lived on average than other types of authoritarian regimes, but also why some monarchs fell to revolution and others persisted into the democratic age.

This argument does not weaken the case for other explanations about which monarchies were more likely to hold onto their thrones. Indeed, the quantitative evidence provided in this chapter could be consistent with other dynamics, such as more centralizing monarchs being less capable of dealing with the political pressures unleashed by modernization (Huntington 1968) or less effective at co-opting other political elites (Gandhi 2008). To the extent that the transition from monarchy to republicanism was a core political transformation of the past two centuries, these patterns deserve greater attention from social science researchers as well.

This chapter also sheds light on two important royal failures of the past several decades. Among the monarchies that survived past World War II, few were overthrown by mass uprisings. However, the two monarchs whose dynasties did collapse directly from popular opposition – the Iranian shah and the Nepali king – had been centralizing autocrats who sought to concentrate all political power in their hands. In general, monarchs may be better positioned than other autocrats to avoid blame for poor governance and unpopular policy decisions, but when they structure political institutions in a manner that places them at the center of the political maelstrom, they are still vulnerable like any other political leader to the public's anger.

10 | *Conclusion*

This book has argued that understanding the connection between how autocrats share power and how the public attributes responsibility can produce a number of insights into how popular politics shapes authoritarian governance. Blame games are a key feature of politics almost everywhere (Hood 2011), and their importance is applicable to authoritarian regimes as well. People tend to want accountability, and acquiring it requires identifying who is at fault when outcomes turn out poorly. As a result, political leaders are frequently concerned about how to mitigate the risks of becoming a magnet for blame when the public becomes disgruntled. Even powerful autocrats have reasons to be worried about exposing themselves to blame in a manner that facilitates mass opposition against their rule.

In attempting to address this risk, one strategy autocrats can use is to limit their own influence over the decision-making process, empowering other elites to set policies and therefore positioning these elites to absorb the public's attributions of responsibility. Despite their great powers, if autocrats can share decision-making responsibilities in ways that would be costly for them to overturn, the public will be more likely to perceive this delegation as credible and less likely to believe the autocrat is primarily at fault for what goes wrong in the political system. These beliefs should complicate coordination against the autocrat, because even individuals who personally blame the autocrat may refrain from saying so publicly if they believe that too few of their country's citizens will agree with them. Strategically, autocrats should be more likely to pursue these blame avoidance benefits by delegating in contexts where they have more reasons to be worried that their regime's governance will fail to satisfy the public's preferences. And with this better protection from blame, these autocrats should indeed be less vulnerable to mass protests that may arise from the public's anger. At the same time, they should also be less likely to repress expressions of discontent, which are more likely to be directed at other

301

302   *Conclusion*

political elites, and they should be better positioned to provide a measure of accountability by removing these elites when people become dissatisfied with their performance in office.

The book draws on a variety of data sources to provide evidence of these patterns both within and across countries. Internet search data from Google Trends show that people living in authoritarian regimes pay relatively more or less attention to the autocrat as the credibility of power sharing shifts, implying that the public observes and recognizes variation in delegation. Survey responses from dozens of countries indicate that disapproval of the autocrat is correlated more strongly with perceptions of negative economic performance among individuals who also perceive the autocrat to share less power with elites in other institutions, consistent with delegation affecting autocrats' exposure to blame. Furthermore, interviews and survey responses from Jordan highlight how people living in authoritarian regimes often hold other institutions responsible for their grievances. The detailed assessment of politics in Jordan, as well as shorter case studies of Russia and Morocco, also suggest that autocrats respond strategically to changing threat environments, delegating more credibly as the risks of popular discontent rise, and reining in power sharing over decision-making as they become relatively more concerned about internal challenges from other elites. Cross-national evidence sheds light on the broader implications of these relationships for governance and politics under autocracy, demonstrating that autocrats are less repressive, less likely to face mass opposition targeting them personally, and more likely to rotate elites out of office when they delegate decision-making more credibly.

The book has also argued that some autocrats are more likely to benefit from this strategy than others. Sharing decision-making powers comes with risks for autocrats, since it can strengthen elites who may wish to challenge their dominance, and autocrats are more likely to rely on delegation as a blame avoidance strategy when these baseline risks are relatively lower. In addition, norms typically exist about how responsibility should be attributed in the political system, and delegating influence to other elites may prove less effective as a blame avoidance strategy in contexts where the autocrat is expected by much of the public to be held responsible and face accountability for governance outcomes.

Taking these two factors into account, autocratic monarchs should be better positioned than other types of autocrats in the modern period

10.1 *Popular Politics in Autocracies*

to benefit from delegation as a blame avoidance strategy. This advantage stems from differences between hereditary succession and popular sovereignty, the principles that inform leader selection in monarchies and nonmonarchies respectively. Because hereditary succession creates rigid rules about who can be the monarch, it should be costlier on average for nonroyal elites to attempt a coup in a monarchy, which should make it relatively safer for monarchs to delegate credibly to these elites. Furthermore, because hereditary succession does not create expectations for the monarch to govern and be held accountable, whereas popular sovereignty does, delegation in monarchies should be less likely to contravene the public's expectations about how responsibility should be attributed, making it relatively more effective at shifting blame. Because of these delegation advantages, monarchs are better positioned than other autocrats to protect their popular support and thus stabilize their rule over time. The book provides evidence for these arguments from contemporary authoritarian monarchies and nonmonarchies in the Arab world, as well as the universe of authoritarian regimes since the 1950s. Analysis of data on political elites suggests that monarchs have more stable relationships with regime elites and are more likely to share power over decision-making; experimental findings highlight divergent expectations for how monarchs and presidents should be involved in the policy process; and monarchs are less likely to become the targets of mass opposition during periods of popular discontent in their regimes.

In the remainder of this concluding chapter, I expand on the book's contributions to our understanding of authoritarian politics. I first discuss how the argument extends research on the link between popular politics and authoritarian institutions, while also considering possible extensions. I then consider the book's implications for conceptualizing differences and similarities between autocracies and democracies, and for understanding the likelihood of transitions from autocratic to democratic rule.

10.1 Popular Politics in Autocracies

Though the standard view of autocracy leaves little room for popular politics, the reality is that how everyday people think about governance often has significant implications for the political trajectories of these regimes. The public holds opinions about political and economic affairs; they frequently find avenues for expressing these views through social media, voting, or protests; and political elites will commonly develop close ties to different social groups as they jockey for influence within the regime. These factors can affect the stability of the political system, how autocrats seek to manage various threats to their power, and the types of governance outcomes produced by these regimes. As such, understanding popular politics in greater depth represents an important avenue for expanding knowledge of authoritarian political systems. In a global context in which powerful authoritarian states are resurgent internationally and autocratization has been occurring in a number of countries, this knowledge will remain highly relevant to global politics.

Two key points from the book are worth emphasizing. The first is that how power is shared between the autocrat and other elites in the political system can shape the public's perceptions of how they are being governed, which in turn can influence the autocrat's incentives to share power in the first place. The second is that people think differently about different types of autocratic rule, such that autocrats face varying expectations from the public about how they should govern and for what they should be held accountable. These expectations then affect the contexts in which autocrats are more or less likely to face mass opposition. Subsections 10.1.1 and 10.1.2 expand on these points and consider extensions to the arguments and empirics discussed so far in the book.

10.1.1 Popular Politics, Elites, and Institutions under Autocracy

The study of how the public relates to political elites and institutions in authoritarian regimes has typically focused on distributive politics, exploring how elites use institutions – whether legislatures, parties, or elections – to give people material incentives to remain loyal or at least quiescent. While this body of work is clearly important for our understanding of authoritarianism, there is more to the story of how everyday people interact with and influence politics in these contexts. As reflected in the focus of this book, for instance, the public observes how the dictator engages with other elites, including who wields power over policymaking as well as the institutional processes through which these decisions are made. These observations

10.1 Popular Politics in Autocracies

subsequently shape how people attribute responsibility for their grievances, impacting their attitudes toward the autocrat and the likelihood that they take to the streets to challenge their rule. Knowing this, autocrats respond strategically by structuring power sharing in part to manage potential threats from the public. In other words, we can better understand why autocrats empower other institutions and tie their own hands in the decision-making process by studying how regular people think about responsibility in these political systems. This insight points to a number of additional questions worth probing in future studies.

For one, this book has focused primarily on how autocrats try to avoid blame strategically, with elites incentivized to accept decision-making responsibilities because they can shape policy and acquire rents, even if it means becoming the target of the public's anger. But authoritarian elites also possess agency to play blame games, even in the more controlled environments of these political systems. Different elite factions may attempt to blame each other for poor policy outcomes as they seek to preserve their reputation both with the autocrat and the public, and these claims may be more or less effective depending on which faction more visibly wields decision-making influence at that moment in time. In Jordan, for instance, proponents of different visions for foreign and domestic policy will publicly accuse each other through the press and political speeches of worsening the country's situation and weakening the monarchy.

At times, elites may also try to signal their dependency on the autocrat to minimize their own exposure to popular anger. This maneuvering can also be observed in Jordan. One columnist, for instance, accused high-level political elites of undermining the monarchy by trying to "spread among the public, in clever ways, that they are not advisors to the King, but rather recipients of his orders," for the purpose of implying that "every failure that occurs in their work, and every mistake related to their decisions ... is not of their making ... but is imposed on them from above" (Adwan 2018). To the extent that the autocrat remains the most powerful figure in the political system, these attempts could plausibly mute the benefits of delegation for the autocrat. Studying how elites try to disperse blame among themselves or back onto the autocrat, and the contexts in which such attempts are more likely to occur and more effective at shaping public opinion, would be a useful avenue for further exploration.

Another blame game that is common in authoritarian regimes is to argue that foreign powers are responsible for poor outcomes that occur in one's country. Whether it is the Russian regime attributing poor economic performance to external conditions (Rozenas and Stukal 2019) or the Syrian regime blaming violence and instability on a foreign conspiracy (Alrababa'h and Blaydes 2021), autocracies frequently claim their countries were the victims of outside factors they could not control. One possibility is that autocrats are more likely to rely on these narratives when they concentrate power in their own hands, because they know that citizens are less likely to believe claims that domestic political elites other than the autocrat are responsible for governance outcomes. Thus, understanding how people attribute responsibility in authoritarian regimes may shed light on the types of propaganda strategies that autocrats choose to emphasize.

At the same time, autocrats may feel less pressure to share power with other elites if they have a credible foreign actor on whom they can blame their country's problems. If it is plausible that foreign economic and political policies are damaging the country's interests, the public may be less likely to believe the autocrat is at fault even if they do monopolize power, in which case there is less incentive for the autocrat to delegate. Certainly in the Middle East, where foreign states have caused or contributed to problematic policy outcomes, many people appear to believe that external rather than internal factors should be blamed for their countries' problems. In the second wave of the Arab Barometer, which was implemented around the time of the Arab Spring, respondents were asked if they blamed the lack of development in the region primarily on internal factors, primarily on external factors, or on both equally. In all ten of the countries surveyed, a plurality of respondents held both factors equally responsible. If foreign dynamics mean that domestic political elites are not needed as much to shield the autocrat from blame, the autocrat may be less willing to grant them genuine influence over decision-making.

It is also important to reiterate a point made in Chapter 2, which is that people do not attribute responsibility based solely on their straightforward evaluations of how much control was exercised by the various actors involved in the decision-making process. These evaluations are often biased by ideological factors, with individuals motivated to cast blame toward a certain person or institution. In democracies, these biases often appear to be rooted in partisan

10.1 Popular Politics in Autocracies

motivated reasoning (e.g., Bisgaard 2015), as individuals find ways to blame the opposing party for their grievances regardless of how much power that party wields over governance at the time. In many authoritarian regimes, partisan politics are less pronounced, as party systems tend to be weak and ideological consistency across parties may be low. Nonetheless, ideological factors likely do play a role. For example, individuals committed to stability above all else may be motivated to blame someone other than the autocrat for their grievances, because they do not want to accept the instability that may follow mass opposition against the autocrat. This dynamic is also visible in Jordan, with the monarch benefiting from the sense that the collapse of the monarchy would unleash destructive conflict such as that witnessed in Syria's civil war. Identifying how institutional aspects of blame avoidance interact with psychological biases would further contribute to our understanding of when public pressure is more likely to incentivize power sharing in authoritarian regimes.

How the public attributes blame and credit is not the only set of perceptions autocrats may wish to influence through the sharing of power with other political elites. Many autocrats go to great lengths to persuade their citizens that they govern democratically (Williamson 2021). And though propaganda certainly can play a role here, the public will also evaluate whether the regime is democratic based on their assessment of how the regime governs. Sharing power more broadly with other political elites through elections and institutions such as the legislature and cabinet can affect whether people living in the country believe that the regime is at least somewhat democratic (Chu and Williamson 2024). Thus, to the extent that autocrats believe that the public cares about democracy, they may have incentives to reduce their own control over the political system. It is possible that other ideological beliefs or social norms among the public could create similar dynamics. The point, then, is that our understanding of why and when autocrats share power with other political elites can benefit from the study of mass politics and how people living under authoritarianism perceive the ways in which they are being governed.

10.1.2 Thinking Differently about Different Autocrats

Another contribution of the book regarding popular politics and institutions in authoritarian regimes is to highlight that people think differently about different types of autocratic rulers. Scholars have developed a number of categorizations for autocracies, and they have explored how these various types of autocracy differ from each other in terms of their internal politics, but the focus has been primarily on how these regimes create different incentives for political elites (e.g., Geddes 1999). To date, there has been little consideration of how people may perceive regime and ruler types differently, with implications for the contexts in which they are more or less likely to challenge or support the authorities. Along these lines, this book has focused on how monarchs and presidents face divergent expectations from the public about their responsibility for governance, with people much more likely to expect presidents rather than monarchs to take an active role in – and be held accountable for – their country's decision-making process. As a result, when monarchs share power more credibly with elites in the cabinet or legislature, it is more likely to align with norms about how responsibility should be attributed, and the public is more likely to accept that they are not to blame for what goes wrong.

Militaries constitute another institution that may be able to benefit from this strategy. Militaries are heavily involved in the politics of many authoritarian regimes (Meng and Paine 2022), and this involvement takes different forms. In many cases, the military receives special perks and privileges but remains relatively apolitical and distant from governance. In others, however, the officers wield substantial political power and are a key part – if not the most important part – of the regime. A number of scholars classify these cases as military regimes, though their form can differ substantially. At times, the senior officers govern directly through the military; in other cases, a single officer seizes power and may govern as a strongman president; and in still others, the military is closely intertwined and shares power with a civilian political party or elite network (Geddes et al. 2014b).

In thinking through the relationship between militaries and power sharing, it seems plausible that militaries would benefit from similar advantages held by monarchies. First, military rulers who delegate to civilian officials may find it less costly to delegate credibly, since they control the coercive apparatus and therefore should be relatively less threatened by these civilian elites with whom they are sharing power. Indeed, civilian autocrats usually have to worry about a "guardianship dilemma" in which the military's coercive power makes it risky to delegate too much power to the institution, since it can turn its

10.1 Popular Politics in Autocracies

weapons on the autocrat more easily than almost any other actor in the regime (Greitens 2016; Paine 2022; Svolik 2012). Second, there is a strong norm in global politics against the military governing directly. For instance, in survey data from a number of countries, citizens overwhelmingly oppose the idea of the military ruling, and this opposition is usually higher than opposition to other forms of authoritarian governance. This norm poses a problem for militaries that choose to govern openly because it can strengthen mass opposition to these regimes; indeed, it may help to account for the empirical pattern whereby direct military rule is on average the shortest-lived authoritarian regime type in the modern world. On the other hand, because this norm implies that militaries *should* be removed from politics, the public is unlikely to expect the military to be blamed and held accountable for governance in cases where they delegate somewhat credibly to civilian leadership. In other words, delegation by the military would align with rather than contradict expectations about how responsibility should operate.

For these reasons, militaries that dominate the political system but share power regarding day-to-day decision-making may also be particularly capable of avoiding blame for poor governance, allowing the officers to perpetuate their influence, while civilian politicians are rotated in and out of their positions in response to public anger. In fact, such a system defines the politics of many authoritarian regimes, as well as some countries that occasionally cycle between authoritarianism and democracy. For example, Cook (2007) described the roles of politically powerful militaries in Algeria, Egypt, and Turkey as "ruling but not governing." For decades in all three countries, militaries were the most influential institution within the political system, which allowed them to reap many material perks, while also steering the overall direction of their countries. However, civilian presidents exercised direct policymaking responsibility, alongside parliaments and in some cases powerful political parties. These actors accrued much of the blame for poor governance, and the militaries maintained not only their influence but also substantial popular support.

This pattern was visible in the Arab Spring in Egypt, where Mubarak and his National Democratic Party were overthrown while many Egyptians cheered for the military to step in and lead the country. Of course, once the Egyptian military did so, governing for more than a year through the Supreme Council of the Armed Forces, its reputation with the public weakened as it came to be seen as a political actor

310   *Conclusion*

deserving of blame for the rocky transition. This damage to the military's reputation was especially visible after it intervened to remove Egypt's first elected civilian president, Mohammed Morsi, in July 2013 (Pew 2014). In Algeria, likewise, the military evaded much of the anger that resulted in the overthrow of President Bouteflika in 2019, and it continues to constitute a key actor under the reestablished authoritarian regime of President Tebboune (Ottaway 2021).

Similar examples abound. In Pakistan, for instance, the military has consistently wielded substantial political influence, while also sharing significant decision-making powers with civilian leaders. These civilians, rather than the military, have tended to absorb the public's anger, resulting in them falling victim either to popular politics or "housecleaning" coups by the armed forces. Though Pakistan has at times resembled an imperfect democracy, the military's influence has demonstrated substantial staying power. In Myanmar, the military attempted to pursue this model after decades of direct rule, when it forged a power-sharing agreement with the opposition party that would preserve the military's significant influence, while allowing civilians to take on responsibility for decision-making in many domains. Over time, however, the military became increasingly threatened by the durable popularity of the civilian leadership, and they seized direct power again, triggering a cycle of mass opposition and severe repression (Maizland 2022). In many Latin American countries, militaries cycled through periods of more direct or indirect rule, and their influence often proved difficult to reduce even after democratic transitions had occurred.

In fact, authoritarian regimes in which militaries play a key role but also share substantial powers with civilians may, like monarchy, constitute one of the most durable versions of authoritarianism. Geddes (2004) finds that a small number of regimes combining elements of military, party, and personalist rule were some of the longest-lived in the post-World War II period. Indeed, examples that were just mentioned, such as Egypt and Algeria, reflect some of the cases in which authoritarianism has flourished the longest and democracy has found little purchase, in large part because militaries have proved effective at retaining political influence even if they allow civilians to take the lead in governance.

Of course, military rule is also frequently characterized by a single military strongman or a small clique of officers seizing power and then

10.2 Autocracy and Democracy

concentrating as much influence as possible in their hands (Geddes et al. 2014b). In these cases, the public has a clear target to blame, mass opposition often occurs relatively quickly, and the autocrat tends to respond with extreme violence, as the book's theory would predict. In short, thinking about what the public expects of different types of authoritarian rulers and regimes can help us understand patterns of opposition both across and within these variations of autocratic rule.

10.2 Autocracy and Democracy

Much of the research on authoritarianism in political science has long been motivated by questions about, and understandings of, democracy. Scholars and practitioners alike are interested in understanding when autocracies are more or less likely to collapse, and when they are more or less likely to transition to democracy. And with democratic political systems treated as the norm, autocracies became a hodgepodge of everything else, defined primarily by the absence of a few key features shared by democracies. The book concludes by speaking to both of these dynamics. I first consider the theory's implications for democratization, and I then discuss ways in which autocracies and democracies can function similarly despite their important underlying differences.

10.2.1 Transitioning from Autocracy to Democracy

Throughout the book, the costs of delegation for autocrats have been discussed in terms of the potential for increasing their coup risk. By sharing power, autocrats may strengthen rivals within the regime who are looking for an opportunity to move against them. Another possibility, however, is that autocrats gradually cede so much decision-making power that they no longer wield influence at all, even if they are permitted to remain in their position. This possibility is reflected in the trajectory of many of the world's remaining monarchies that shared power with nonroyal political elites. Though they were not overthrown in popular revolutions or military coups, and though they continue in many cases to receive substantial wealth due to their positions, they did eventually lose all meaningful power and their countries transitioned to democracy.

What does this route to democratization, interpreted through the lens of my argument, tell us about transitions from authoritarian to

312   *Conclusion*

democratic rule? To the extent that kings willingly ceded their powers over time in part *because* they wanted to be more protected from the vagaries of governance and its impact on their reputations, it would align with theories about how democratization can occur in response to pressures from below (e.g., Acemoglu and Robinson 2000). In particular, autocrats may be more willing to let elites take the lead in governance, cycling them in and out of official positions partly in response to popular politics, when they worry about their own ability to satisfy the public and to avoid being blamed for widely-held grievances.

Is a similar scenario likely to play out in some of the world's ruling monarchies that remain? Jordan, Morocco, and Kuwait seem like contenders where such an outcome *could* manifest, as Michael Herb (2004) noted two decades ago. If governance problems persist and popular politics remains highly contentious, monarchs may increasingly feel that their interests are best served by withdrawing further from politics and allowing civilian elites to exercise more credible influence over decision-making. However, two points are worth noting here. First, this process is certainly not inevitable and will depend on how monarchs choose to confront threats to their rule. Doubling down on repression and direct rule may prove alluring and even effective in the shorter-term, though it could increase the likelihood of a revolutionary uprising in the longer-term that sweeps away the monarchy for good. Second, historical examples suggest that monarchies often transitioned to democracy quite suddenly, at a moment of immense crisis such as the aftermath of World War I. Facing severe public pressure, monarchs ceded what decision-making powers they still wielded to become ceremonial figures. Thus, while these transitions may appear gradual because the monarch slowly stepped back from governance over a long period of time, the gradual nature of these earlier changes likely reflected strategic attempts by the monarchies to retain their power and the actual transition to democracy occurred relatively quickly (Stepan et al. 2014).

In the Middle East, then, it may be another period of pronounced economic shock and political unrest, as in the Arab Spring, that prompts some of the region's monarchs to truly democratize, rather than tinkering with reforms that marginally adjust the credibility of power sharing within the regime. As implied by the discussion of Nepal in Chapter 9, however, the important point to take away from the

10.2 Autocracy and Democracy

theory is that more credible delegation in the period prior to such a transition should increase the likelihood that the monarchy persists through democratization, rather than being abolished by popular demand. If many people do not believe the monarch is principally responsible for the ills afflicting the country, the monarchy should be less likely to be swept away.

This idea of gradually-increasing delegation resulting in democratization could also be relevant to understanding cases of democratization from authoritarian regimes in which the military plays a dominant role, as discussed earlier. Military elites often care a lot about sustaining the reputation of the armed forces, and this priority can influence their political calculations (Geddes 1999). If the officers feel that the armed forces' reputation is being harmed by their close involvement in politics, they may gradually grant more and more power to civilian elites over time. If these civilian elites are selected through reasonably free and fair elections, the regime may reach a stage in which institutions still grant too much protection to military interests to qualify as a healthy democracy, but democratically-elected civilians are the key decision-makers in almost all domains. Such arrangements can go wrong if the military backtracks, as with the example of Myanmar mentioned previously. However, though imperfect, they can also produce durable constitutions and eventually fully-fledged democracies (Albertus and Menaldo 2014).

10.2.2 Where Autocracies and Democracies Overlap

As was discussed in the book's introduction, autocracies are typically treated as a residual category by political scientists. They are defined principally by the absence of what democracies possess, which is the use of competitive elections for the selection of key political leaders in the executive and legislative branches. This approach means that autocracy as a category encompasses a wide range of political systems. Nonetheless, without the regularized and widely accepted use of elections to select leaders, autocratic politics are said to be defined by an ever-present current of violence and unpredictability (Svolik 2012). A substantial body of scholarly work is devoted to understanding how these features of authoritarianism lead to divergent political incentives and governance outcomes from democracies.

There is little doubt that autocracies and democracies differ substantially in ways that matter for the quality of life of their citizens. Democratic governments are more likely to respect human rights (Davenport 2007), their economies tend to grow more quickly (Knutsen 2021), and on average they are less corrupt, more effective at promoting health and human development, and less belligerent in the international system (Gerring et al. 2022; Ray 1998). Yet, in terms of understanding how autocracies function and when they are more or less likely to produce malignant political outcomes, there is a risk that key insights could be lost if their fundamental differences with democracies are overstated. Researchers have considered the extent to which political institutions such as legislatures fulfill similar functions in democracies and autocracies (Gandhi et al. 2020), and I would argue that exploring more deliberately how politics can sometimes be similar in authoritarian and democratic settings may help to improve our knowledge about the former by allowing us to draw on the much more substantial literature on the latter. Two examples from the book illustrate this point.

First, for several decades now, a number of political scientists studying democratic politics have explored why delegation occurs. One of these explanations has emphasized the blame avoidance advantages associated with delegation (e.g., Alesina and Tabellini 2005; Bartling and Fischbacher 2012). For example, the US Congress may choose to delegate to the bureaucracy in part to protect its members from blame (e.g., Fiorina 1982). This book has built from this framework to develop an argument that furthers understanding of the contexts in which autocratic political leaders are more likely to share power with other political elites: Fear of being blamed by the masses may motivate even dictators to cede some decision-making control to other actors. Research on power sharing in autocracies may benefit from other insights about delegation in democracies, including the extent to which delegation decisions can also be driven by concerns about expertise and time. Understanding when autocrats choose to share power to help manage the complexities of day-to-day governance, and how they approach this problem, would deepen understanding of decision-making processes in these regimes.

Second, there is much less focus on accountability in autocracies, because the absence of elections is thought to reduce the ability of these regimes to provide it. Certainly, competitive elections have important

10.3 In Conclusion

implications for accountability since the public can vote out politicians who fail to perform effectively (Healy and Malhotra 2013). But the absence of competitive elections as the means of selecting the most important political leaders does not necessarily mean that accountability cannot be provided in authoritarian political systems. This book suggests that when an autocrat delegates meaningful decision-making responsibility to other political elites, a modicum of accountability can be present if the autocrat removes these elites from their positions when they contribute to decisions the public dislikes. Sitting above the realm of day-to-day politics, a kingly autocrat can respond to the public's demands, shuffling out of power those officials whom many in the public consider to be responsible for their grievances. This accountability may then facilitate continued popular support for the autocrat and the broader political system they control. In some aspects, this dynamic reflects the occurrence of accountability in democracies as well: The public's perceptions and votes influence (imperfectly) which political elites are removed from office, the public's loyalty to the overall democratic system remains or is perhaps reinforced when these elites are held accountable, but even so, not all officials involved in the decision-making process are turned out of their positions in response to failures or grievances. Recognizing how some autocracies may be able to establish a system of accountability that reflects aspects of democratic politics, and how such a system may contribute to stability by bolstering public confidence in the regime, can provide insights into both elite decision-making and popular politics in authoritarian settings.

Clearly, autocracies and democracies differ in important ways. But everyday people, regardless of where they live, tend to care about similar processes and outcomes when they make political judgments – such as who may be to blame for something they dislike. And in some cases, autocrats and political elites in their regimes may face political incentives that resemble those in democracies. There may still be much to learn about authoritarian politics by exploring more fully where and when these similarities apply.

10.3 In Conclusion

Authoritarian politics can be opaque, violent, and dominated by a coterie of scheming elites who sit well above the everyday people over whom they rule. Yet even when these descriptors hold true, the public can still matter greatly for political outcome in autocracies. Many people in these political systems hold preferences over policy outcomes and pay attention to political developments where possible. When the political system fails to produce outcomes that satisfy these preferences, instability and escalating opposition can be the result. Some autocrats may be confident they can wield enough coercive capacity to suppress such challenges. Others may believe they can meet the public's demands consistently enough to mitigate the risks of revolution. But many autocrats, despite their significant powers and controlled political systems, are not in this position; instead, they must worry much more about popular anger. For those who do face this concern, an important strategy documented in this book is to delegate decision-making responsibilities in such a way that they can more easily redirect blame toward the elites with whom they share power. When the public does become dissatisfied, these autocrats are better positioned to preserve their reputations and avoid mass opposition that targets them personally.

Though their prevalence has gradually faded over time, ruling monarchs are particularly effective at using this strategy in our modern, democratic age. With credible delegation both safer and more in line with the public's expectations about how responsibility is meant to be attributed in monarchies, royal autocrats can protect their popular support by placing themselves beyond the bounds of accountability, while also sharing power meaningfully with nonroyal elites in cabinets and parliaments. And with their reputations more secured, modern monarchs have been some of the most durable authoritarian rulers of the past several decades.

References

Abdel Ghafar, Adel. 2021. "The Arrest of Maati Monjib and the Continued Retreat of Human Rights in Morocco." *Brookings Institution*. March 9.

Abed, George T. and Hamid R. Davoodi. 2003. "Challenges of Growth and Globalization in the Middle East and North Africa." *International Monetary Fund*.

Abouzzohour, Yasmina. 2020. "Progress and Missed Opportunities: Morocco Enters Its Third Decade under King Mohammed VI." *Brookings Institution*. July 29.

Abrahamian, Ervand. 1968. "The Crowd in Iranian Politics 1905–1953." *Past & Present* 41: 184–210.

Abrahamian, Ervand. 1980. "Structural Causes of the Iranian Revolution." *MERIP Reports* 87: 21–26.

Abrahamian, Ervand. 2008. *A History of Modern Iran*. Cambridge University Press.

Acemoglu, Daron and James A. Robinson. 2000. "Why Did the West Extend the Franchise? Democracy, Inequality, and Growth in Historical Perspective." *The Quarterly Journal of Economics* 115 (4): 1167–1199.

Adena, Maja, Ruben Enikolopov, Maria Petrova, Vernoica Santarosa, and Ekaterina Zhuravskaya. 2015. "Radio and the Rise of the Nazis in Prewar Germany." *Quarterly Journal of Economics* 130 (4): 1885–1939.

Adwan, Tahir. 2018. "Men of the King: A Blessing or Curse for Him?" *Al-Maqar*. March 3. [Translated from Arabic by Author].

AfricaNews. 2019. "Egypt Transport Minister Resigns after Train Crash Kills 25." February 27.

Alaimo, Kara. 2015. "How the Facebook Arabic Page "We Are All Khaled Said" Helped Promote the Egyptian Revolution." *Social Media and Society* 1 (2).

Albertus, Michael and Victor Menaldo. 2012. "Coercive Capacity and the Prospects for Democratization." *Comparative Politics* 44 (2): 151–169.

Albertus, Michael and Victor Menaldo. 2014. "Why Egypt's New Constitution May Not Turn Out as Badly as You Think." *The Washington Post*. January 16.

Alesina, Alberto and Guido Tabellini. 2005. "Why Do Politicians Delegate?" NBER Working Paper Series. Working Paper 11531.

Alicke, Mark D. 2000. "Culpable Control and the Psychology of Blame." *Psychological Bulletin* 126 (4): 556–574.

Alissa, Sufyan. 2007. "Rethinking Economic Reform in Jordan: Confronting Socioeconomic Realities." *Carnegie Endowment for International Peace*, 4.

Alon, Yoav. 2009. *The Making of Jordan: Tribes, Colonialism and the Modern State*. IB Tauris & Company.

Alrababa'h, Ala' and Lisa Blaydes. 2021. "Authoritarian Media and Diversionary Threats: Lessons from 30 Years of Syrian State Discourse." *Political Science Research and Methods* 9 (4): 693–708.

Alshoubaki, Wa'ed and Michael Harris. 2021. "Jordan's Public Policy Response to COVID-19 Pandemic: Insight and Policy Analysis." *Public Organization Review* 21 (4): 687–706.

Anderson, Christopher J. 2007. "The End of Economic Voting? Contingency Dilemmas and the Limits of Democratic Accountability." *Annual Review of Political Science* 10: 271–296.

Anderson, Lisa. 1991. "Absolutism and the Resilience of Monarchy in the Middle East." *Political Science Quarterly* 106 (1): 1–15.

Anderson, Lisa. 2000. "Dynasts and Nationalists: Why Monarchies Survive." In *Middle East Monarchies: The Challenge of Modernity*. Ed. Joseph Kostiner. Lynee Rienner Publishers.

Andoni, Lamis and Jillian Schwedler. 1996. "Bread Riots in Jordan." *Middle East Report* 201: 40–42.

Ansari, Ali M. 2001. "The Myth of the White Revolution: Mohammad Reza Shah, 'Modernization' and the Consolidation of Power." *Middle Eastern Studies* 37 (3): 1–24.

Arceneaux, Kevin. 2006. "The Federal Face of Voting: Are Elected Officials Held Accountable for the Functions Relevant to Their Office?" *Political Psychology* 27 (5): 731–754.

Arceneaux, Kevin and Robert M. Stein. 2006. "Who Is Held Responsible When Disaster Strikes? The Attribution of Responsibility for a Natural Disaster in an Urban Election." *Journal of Urban Affairs* 28 (1): 43–53.

Arjomand, Said Amir. 1988. *The Turban for the Crown: The Islamic Revolution in Iran*. Oxford University Press.

Arjomand, Said Amir. 1985. "The Causes and Significance of the Iranian Revolution." *State, Culture, and Society* 1 (3): 41–66.

Armstrong, David, Ora John Reuter, and Graeme B. Robertson. 2020. "Getting the Opposition Together: Protest Coordination in Authoritarian Regimes." *Post-Soviet Affairs* 36 (1): 1–19.

Ashton, Nigel. 2008. *King Hussein of Jordan: A Political Life*. Yale University Press.

References

Aytaç, Selim Erdem. 2021. "Effectiveness of Incumbent's Strategic Communication during Economic Crisis under Electoral Authoritarianism: Evidence from Turkey." *American Political Science Review* 115 (4): 1517–1523.

Baekkeskov, Erik and Olivier Rubin. 2016. "Information Dilemmas and Blame Avoidance Strategies: From Secrecy to Lighting Rods in Chinese Health Crises." *Governance* 30 (3): 425–443.

Bank, Andre, Thomas Richter, and Anna Sunik. 2015. "Long-Term Monarchical Survival in the Middle East: A Configurational Comparison, 1945–2012." *Democratization* 22 (1): 179–200.

Bank, Andre and Oliver Schlumberger. 2004. "Jordan: Between Regime Survival and Economic Reform." In *Arab Elites: Negotiating the Politics of Change*. Ed. Volker Perthes. Lynne Rienner Publishers.

Baral, Lok Raj. 1987. "Nepal in 1986: Problem of Political Management." *Asian Survey* 27 (2): 173–180.

Baral, Lok Raj. 1994. "The Return of Party Politics in Nepal." *Journal of Democracy* 5 (1): 121–133.

Bartling, Bjorn, and Urs Fischbacher. 2012. "Shifting the Blame: On Delegation and Responsibility." *The Review of Economic Studies* 79 (1): 67–87.

Bashiriyeh, Hossein. 1984. *The State and Revolution in Iran*. St. Martin's Press.

Baylouny, Anne Marie. 2008. "Militarizing Welfare: Neo-liberalism and Jordanian Policy." *Middle East Journal* 62 (2): 277–303.

BBC. 2002. "Minister Resigns over Egypt Train Fire." February 22.

Beazer, Quintin H. and Ora John Reuter. 2019. "Who's to Blame? Political Centralization and Electoral Punishment under Authoritarianism." *The Journal of Politics* 81 (2): 648–662.

Beinin, Joel. 2012. "The Rise of Egypt's Workers." *Carnegie Endowment for International Peace*. June 28.

Beinin, Joel. 2015. *Workers and Thieves*. Stanford University Press.

Beissinger, Mark, Amaney Jamal, and Kevin Mazur. 2015. "Explaining Divergent Revolutionary Coalitions: Regime Strategies and the Structuring of Participation in the Tunisian and Egyptian Revolutions." *Journal of Comparative Politics* 48 (1): 1–24.

Beliakova, Polina. 2020. "COVID-19 and the Limits of Putin's Power." *War on the Rocks*. May 13.

Bellin, Eva. 2004. "The Robustness of Authoritarianism in the Middle East: Exceptionalism in Comparative Perspective." *Comparative Politics* 36 (2): 139–157.

Bendix, Reinhard. 1978. *Kings or People: Power and the Mandate to Rule*. University of California Press.

Bill, James A. 1970. "Modernization and Reform from Above: The Case of Iran." *Journal of Politics* 32 (1): 19–40.

Bisgaard, Martin. 2015. "Bias Will Find a Way: Economic Perceptions, Attributions of Blame, and Partisan-Motivated Reasoning during Crisis." *The Journal of Politics* 77 (3): 849–860.

Bjornskov, Christian and Martin Rode. 2020. "Regime Types and Regime Change: A New Dataset on Democracy, Coups, and Political Institutions." *Review of International Organizations* 15: 531–551.

Black, Ian. 2012. "Jordan's Prime Minister Quits Suddenly." *The Guardian*. April 26.

Blair, Graeme, Alexander Coppock, and Margaret Moor. 2020. "When to Worry about Sensitivity Bias: A Social Reference Theory and Evidence from 30 Years of List Experiments." *American Political Science Review* 114 (4): 1297–1315.

Blaydes, Lisa. 2010. *Elections and Distributive Politics in Mubarak's Egypt*. Cambridge University Press.

Blaydes, Lisa. 2018. *State of Repression: Iraq under Saddam Hussein*. Princeton University Press.

Blaydes, Lisa and Eric Chaney. 2013. "The Feudal Revolution and Europe's Rise: Political Divergence of the Christian West and the Muslim World before 1500 CE." *American Political Science Review* 107 (1): 16–34.

Boeker, Warren. 1992. "Power and Managerial Dismissal: Scapegoating at the Top." *Administrative Science Quarterly* 37 (3): 400–421.

Bogdanor, Vernon. 1995. *The Monarchy and the Constitution*. Clarendon Press.

Boix, Carles and Milan Svolik. 2013. "The Foundations of Limited Authoritarian Government: Institutions, Commitment, and Power-Sharing in Dictatorships." *Journal of Politics* 75 (2): 300–316.

Boyne, George A., Oliver James, Peter John, and Nicolai Petrovsky. 2008. "Executive Succession in English Local Government." *Public Money and Management* 28 (5): 267–274.

Brand, Laurie. 1995. *Jordan's Inter-Arab Relations: The Political Economy of Alliance-Making*. Columbia University Press.

Brand, Laurie. 2014. *Official Stories: Politics and National Narratives in Egypt and Algeria*. Stanford University Press.

Bratton, Michael and Nicholas van de Walle. 1997. *Democratic Experiments in Africa: Regime Transitions in Comparative Perspective*. Cambridge University Press.

Brown, Nathan J. 2001. "Mechanisms of Accountability in Arab Governance: The Present and Future of Judiciaries and Parliaments in the Arab World." *United Nations Development Programme*.

References

Brown, Nathan. 2017. "Official Islam in the Arab World: The Contest for Religious Authority." *Carnegie Endowment for International Peace*. May 11.

Brownlee, Jason. 2007. "Hereditary Succession in Modern Autocracies." *World Politics* 59 (4): 595–628.

Brownlee, Jason, Tarek Masoud, and Anthony Reynolds. 2015. *The Arab Spring: Pathways of Repression and Reform*. Oxford University Press.

Buckley, Noah, Kyle L. Marquardt, Ora John Reuter, and Katerina Tertytchnaya. 2022. "How Popular Is Putin, really?" *The Washington Post*. April 13.

Buehler, Matt and Mehdi Ayari. 2018. "The Autocrat's Advisors: Opening the Black Box of Ruling Coalitions in Tunisia's Authoritarian Regime." *Political Research Quarterly* 71 (2): 330–346.

Bueno de Mesquita, Bruce, Alastair Smith, Randolph M. Siverson, and James D. Morrow. 2003. *The Logic of Political Survival*. MIT Press.

Burgess, Glenn. 1996. *Absolute Monarchy and the Stuart Constitution*. Yale University Press.

Burns, John F. 2003. "Threats and Responses: Allies; Jordan's King, in Gamble, Lends Hand to the U.S." *New York Times*. March 9.

Cai, Yongshun. 2008. "Power Structure and Regime Resilience: Contentious Politics in China." *British Journal of Political Science* 38 (3): 411–432.

Cantoni, Davide, Yuyu Chen, David Y. Yang, Noam Yuchtman, and Y. Jane Zhang. 2017. "Curriculum and Ideology." *Journal of Political Economy* 125 (2): 338–392.

Carter, Erin Baggott and Brett L. Carter. 2023. *Propaganda in Autocracies: Institutions, Information, and the Politics of Belief*. Cambridge University Press.

Casper, Brett Allen and Scott A. Tyson. 2014. "Popular Protest and Elite Coordination in a Coup d'etat." *Journal of Politics* 76 (2): 548–564.

Censer, Jack R. 2019. "Intellectual History and the Causes of the French Revolution." *Journal of Social History* 52 (3): 545–554.

Cheibub, Jose Antonio, Jennifer Gandhi, and James Raymond Vreeland. 2010. "Democracy and Dictatorship Revisited." *Public Choice* 143 (2–1): 67–101.

Chomiak, Laryssa. 2011. "The Making of a Revolution in Tunisia." *Middle East Law and Governance* 3 (68): 68–83.

Christensen, Darin and Francisco Garfias. 2018. "Can You Hear Me Now? How Communication Technology Affects Protest and Repression." *Quarterly Journal of Political Science* 13 (1): 89–117.

Christophersen, Mona. 2013. "Protest and Reform in Jordan: Popular Demand and Government Response 2011 to 2012." *Fafo-report* 50.

Chu, Jonathan and Scott Williamson. 2024. "Respect the Process: The Public Cost of Unilateral Action in Comparative Perspective." *Journal of Politics*.

Chwe, Michael Suk-Young. 2001. *Rational Ritual: Culture, Coordination, and Common Knowledge*. Princeton University Press.

Clarke, Killian. 2021. "Which Protests Count? Coverage Bias in Middle East Event Datasets." *Mediterranean Politics* 28 (2): 302–328.

Clement, Francoise. 2009. "Worker Protests under Economic Liberalization in Egypt." In *Political and Social Protest in Egypt*. Ed. Nicholas S. Hopkins. American University in Cairo Press.

Cohen, Amnon. 1980. *Political Parties in the West Bank under the Jordanian Regime, 1949–1979*. Cornell University Press.

Cook, Steven A. 2007. *Ruling but Not Governing: The Military and Political Development in Egypt, Algeria, and Turkey*. Johns Hopkins University Press.

Cox, Gary W. 2011. "War, Moral Hazard, and Ministerial Responsibility: England after the Glorious Revolution." *The Journal of Economic History* 71 (1): 133–161.

Cunha, Raphael, Paul Schuler, and Scott Williamson. 2022. "Signal Received? Authoritarian Elections and the Salience of Autocrats." *Electoral Studies* 76 (102441).

Daadaoui, Mohamed. 2011. *Moroccan Monarchy and the Islamist Challenge: Maintaining Makhzen Power*. Palgrave Macmillan.

Dabashi, Hamid. 2013. "What Happened to the Green Movement in Iran?" *Al-Jazeera*. June 12.

Daragahi, Borzou. 2019. "A Decade after Iran's Green Movement, Some Lessons." *The Atlantic Council*. June 12.

Davenport, Christian. 2007. "State Repression and Political Order." *Annual Review of Political Science* 10: 1–23.

Davies, Sarah. 1997. *Popular Opinion in Stalin's Russia: Terror, Propaganda, and Dissent, 1934–1941*. Cambridge University Press.

De Vries, Catherine E., Erica E. Edwards, and Erik R. Tillman. 2011. "Clarity of Responsibility Beyond the Pocketbook: How Political Institutions Condition EU Issue Voting." *Comparative Political Studies* 44 (3): 339–363.

Diwan, Kristin. 2020. "Shifting State Strategies toward Sectarian Politics in Bahrain." *Mediterranean Politics* 26 (4): 505–510.

Drhimeur, Amina. 2018. "The Party of Justice and Development's Pragmatic Politics." *Baker Institute for Public Policy*. May 31.

Driffill, John and Zeno Rotondi. 2006. "Credibility of Optimal Monetary Delegation: Comment." *The American Economic Review* 96 (4): 1361–1366.

References

Duch, Raymond M. and Randolph T. Stevenson. 2008. *The Economic Vote: How Political and Economic Institutions Condition Election Results.* Cambridge University Press.

Ellis, Richard J. 1994. *Presidential Lightning Rods: The Politics of Blame Avoidance.* Lawrence: University Press of Kansas.

Elkins, Zachary and Tom Ginsburg. 2021. "Characteristics of National Constitutions, Version 3.0." *Comparative Constitutions Project.* Last modified May 20, 2021.

Elkins, Zachary and James Melton. 2014. "The Content of Authoritarian Constitutions." In *Constitutions in Authoritarian Regimes.* Eds. Tom Ginsburg and Alberto Simpser. Cambridge University Press.

Ersan, Mohammad. 2021. "Jordan's King Accused of Expanding Powers through Constitutional Amendments." *Middle East Eye.* December 3.

Ersan, Mohammad. 2022. "Arrests in Jordan Spark Fury and Rare Public Rebukes of the King." *Middle East Eye.* February 18.

Fakir, Intissar. 2016. "The King and Us." *Carnegie Endowment for International Peace.* May 10.

Fatemi, Khosrow. 1982. "Leadership by Distrust: The Shah's Modus Operandi." *Middle East Journal* 36 (1): 48–61.

Fiorina, Morris. 1982. "Legislative Choice of Regulatory Forms: Legal Process or Administrative Process?" *Public Choice* 39 (1): 33–66.

Fokht, Elizaveta. 2019. "Russia and Putin: Is President's Popularity in Decline?" *BBC.* June 20.

Fortescue, William. 2002. "Morality and Monarchy: Corruption and the Fall of the Regime of Louis-Philippe in 1848." *French History* 16 (1): 83–100.

Fox, Justin and Stuart V. Jordan. 2011. "Delegation and Accountability." *The Journal of Politics* 73 (3): 831–844.

Frantz, Erica, Andrea Kendall-Taylor, Joseph Wright, and Xu Xu. 2020. "Personalization of Power and Repression in Dictatorships." *The Journal of Politics* 82 (1): 372–377.

Freedman, Amy L. 2005. "Economic Crises and Political Change: Indonesia, South Korea, and Malaysia." *Asian Affairs: An American Review* 31 (4): 232–249.

Frye, Timothy, Scott Gehlbach, Kyle L. Marquardt, and Ora Jon Reuter. 2017. "Is Putin's Popularity Real?" *Post-Soviet Affairs* 33 (1): 1–15.

El Gamal, Rania. 2014. "Bahraini Shi'ite Youth Risk Radicalization as Political Talks Stall." *Reuters.* May 4.

Gandhi, Jennifer. 2008. *Political Institutions under Dictatorship.* Cambridge University Press.

Gandhi, Jennifer and Ellen Lust. 2009. "Elections under Authoritarianism." *Annual Review of Political Science* 12: 403–422.

Gandhi, Jennifer and Adam Przeworski. 2007. "Authoritarian Institutions and the Survival of Autocrats." *Comparative Political Studies* 40 (11): 1279–1301.

Gandhi, Jennifer, Ben Noble, and Milan Svolik. 2020. "Legislatures and Legislative Politics without Democracy." *Comparative Political Studies* 53 (9): 1359–1379.

Ganguly, Sumit and Brian Shoup. 2005. "Nepal: Between Dictatorship and Anarchy." *Journal of Democracy* 16 (4): 129–143.

Gause, Gregory. 1994. *Oil Monarchies: Domestic and Security Challenges in the Arab Gulf States.* Council on Foreign Relations Press.

Gause, Gregory. 2013. "Kings for All Seasons: How the Middle East's Monarchies Survived the Arab Spring." *Brookings Doha Center.* Analysis Paper 8.

Gause, Gregory and Sean Yom. 2012. "Resilient Royals: How Arab Monarchies Hang On." *Journal of Democracy* 23 (4): 74–88.

Geddes, Barbara. 1999. "What Do We Know about Democratization after Twenty Years?" *Annual Review of Political Science* 2: 115–144.

Geddes, Barbara. 2004. "Authoritarian Breakdown." Working Paper.

Geddes, Barbara, Joseph Wright, and Erica Frantz. 2014. "Autocratic Breakdown and Regime Transitions: A New Data Set." *Perspectives on Politics* 12 (2): 313–331.

Geddes, Barbara, Erica Frantz, and Joseph Wright. 2014b. "Military Rule." *Annual Review of Political Science* 17: 147–162.

Geddes, Barbara, Joseph Wright, and Erica Frantz. 2018. *How Dictatorships Work.* Cambridge University Press.

Gellner, David N. 2007. "Nepal and Bhutan in 2006: A Year of Revolution." *Asian Survey* 47 (1): 80–86.

Gerring, John, Carl Henrik Knutsen, and Jonas Berge. 2022. "Does Democracy Matter?" *Annual Review of Political Science* 25: 357–375.

Gerring, John, Tore Wig, Wouter Veenendaal, Daniel Weitzel, Jan Teorell, and Kyosuke Kikuta. 2021. "Why Monarchy? The Rise and Demise of a Regime Type." *Comparative Political Studies* 54 (3–4): 585–622.

Goldman, Stuart D. 2008. "Russia's 2008 Presidential Succession." *Congressional Research Service.*

Greitens, Sheena. 2016. *Dictators and Their Secret Police: Coercive Institutions and State Violence.* Cambridge University Press.

Grewal, Sharan and Yasser Kureshi. 2019. "How to Sell a Coup: Elections as Coup Legitimation." *Journal of Conflict Resolution* 63 (4): 1001–1031.

References

Grimmer, Justin and Brandon M. Stewart. 2013. "Text as Data: The Promise and Pitfalls of Automatic Content Analysis Methods for Political Texts." *Political Analysis* 21 (3): 267–297.

Grossman, Guy and Tara Slough. 2022. "Government Responsiveness in Developing Countries." *Annual Review of Political Science* 25: 131–153.

Guadalupe, Patricia. 2007. "Many Russians Unhappy with Their National Government." *Gallup News*. October 30.

Gueorguiev, Dimitar and Paul Schuler. 2016. "Keeping Your Head Down: Public Profiles and Promotion under Autocracy." *Journal of East Asian Studies* 16 (1): 87–116.

Gulzar, Saad and Benjamin J. Pasquale. 2017. "Politicians, Bureaucrats, and Development: Evidence from India." *American Political Science Review* 111 (1): 162–183.

Guo, Gang. 2007. "Retrospective Economic Accountability under Authoritarianism: Evidence from China." *Political Research Quarterly* 60 (3): 378–390.

Guriev, Sergei and Daniel Treisman. 2020. "A Theory of Informational Autocracy." *Journal of Public Economics* 186: 104158.

Guriev, Sergei and Daniel Treisman. 2020b. "The Popularity of Authoritarian Leaders." *World Politics* 72 (4): 601–638.

Guriev, Sergei and Daniel Treisman. 2022. *Spin Dictators: The Changing Face of Tyranny in the 21st Century*. Princeton University Press.

Haber, Stephen. 2008. "Authoritarian Government." In *The Oxford Handbook of Political Economy*. Eds. Donald A. Wittman and Barry R. Weingast. Oxford University Press.

Hahn, Erich. 1977. "Ministerial Responsibility and Impeachment in Prussia 1848–63." *Central European History* 10 (1): 3–27.

Hale, Henry E. and Timothy J. Colton. 2010. "Russians and the Putin-Medvedev "Tandemocracy": A Survey-Based Portrait of the 2007–2008 Election Season." *Problems of Post-Communism* 57 (2): 3–20.

Hamzawy, Amr and Nathan J. Brown. 2020. "How Much Will the Pandemic Change Egyptian Governance and for How Long?" *Carnegie Endowment for International Peace*. July 23.

Hanson, Stephen E. 2011. "Plebiscitarian Patrimonialism in Putin's Russia: Legitimating Authoritarianism in a Postideological Era." *The ANNALS of the American Academy of Political and Social Sciences* 636 (1): 32–48.

Harrigan, Jane, Hamed El-Said, and Ghengang Wang. 2006. "The IMF and the World Bank in Jordan: A Case of over Optimism and Elusive Growth." *Review of International Organizations* 1 (3): 263–292.

Hartnett, Allison Spencer. 2018. "Can Jordan's New Prime Minister Reform the Government?" *The Washington Post*. June 13.

Al-Hayat Center. 2018. "Yearly Report on the Performance of the Eighteenth House of Representatives." [Translated from Arabic].

Healy, Andrew and Neil Malhotra. 2013. "Retrospective Voting Reconsidered." *Annual Review of Political Science* 16: 285–306.

Hedlun, Stefan. 2008. "Rents, Rights, and Service: Boyar Economics and the Putin Transition." *Problems of Post-Communism* 55 (4): 29–41.

Henshall, Nicholas. 2014. *The Myth of Absolutism: Change & Continuity in Early Modern European Monarchy*. Routledge.

Herb, Michael. 1999. *All in the Family: Absolutism, Revolution, and Democracy in the Middle Eastern Monarchies*. SUNY University Press.

Herb, Michael. 2002. "Democratization in the Arab World? Emirs and Parliaments in the Gulf." *Journal of Democracy* 13 (4): 41–47.

Herb, Michael. 2004. "Princes and Parliaments in the Arab World." *Middle East Journal* 58 (3): 367–384.

Hewison, Kevin. 1997. "The Monarchy and Democratization." In *Political Change in Thailand*. Ed. Kevin Hewison. Routledge.

Hobolt, Sara, James Tilley, and Susan Banducci. 2012. "Clarity of Responsibility: How Government Cohesion Conditions Performance Voting." *European Journal of Political Research* 52 (2): 164–187.

Hood, Christopher. 2011. *The Blame Game: Spin, Bureaucracy, and Self-Preservation in Government*. Princeton University Press.

Hood, Christopher. 2014. "Accountability and Blame-Avoidance." In *The Oxford Handbook of Public Accountability*. Eds. Mark Bovens, Robert E. Goodin, and Thomas Schillemans. Oxford University Press.

Howard, Marc Morje and Philip G. Roessler. 2006. "Liberalizing Electoral Outcomes in Competitive Authoritarian Regimes." *American Journal of Political Science* 50 (2): 365–381.

Huang, Haifeng. 2015. "Propaganda as Signaling." *Comparative Politics* 47 (4): 419–437.

Huang, Haifeng and Nicholas Cruz. 2021. "Propaganda, Presumed Influence, and Collective Protest." *Political Behavior* 44: 1789–1812.

Huang, Haifeng, Chanita Intawan, and Stephen P. Nicholson. 2022. "In Government We Trust: Implicit Political Trust and Regime Support in China." *Perspectives on Politics* 21 (4): 1357–1375.

Human Rights Watch. 2019. "Jordan: Crackdown on Political Activists." June 4.

Human Rights Watch. 2020. "Jordan: Stepped Up Arrests of Activists, Protesters." January 14.

Huntington, Samuel P. 1968. *Political Order in Changing Societies*. Yale University Press.

References

Al-Hussein, Abdullah bin. 2013. "Each Playing Our Part in a New Democracy."

Al-Hussein, Abdullah bin. 2018. "Letter of Designation to Omar Razzaz."

Hutt, Michael. 2005. "King Gyanendra's Coup and Its Implications for Nepal's Future." *The Brown Journal of World Affairs* 12 (1): 111–123.

Hyde, Susan D. and Nikolay Marinov. 2012. "Which Elections Can Be Lost?" *Political Analysis* 20 (2): 191–210.

International Press Institute. 2021. "Jordan: Lese-majeste Pardons Stir Calls for Decriminalizing Free Expression." October 22.

Al-Isawe, Hiba. 2012. "Jordan's Prime Minister Khasawneh Resigns." *Reuters*. April 26.

Jamal, Amaney A. 2013. *Of Empires and Citizens: Pro-American Democracy or No Democracy at All?* Princeton University Press.

Jansen, Michael. 1996. "Hussein Bridges Dangerous Gap between People and the Palace." *Irish Times*. November 15.

Javeline, Debra. 2003a. "The Role of Blame in Collective Action: Evidence from Russia." *American Political Science Review* 97 (1): 107–121.

Javeline, Debra. 2003b. *Protest and the Politics of Blame*. University of Michigan Press.

Al-Jazeera. 2011. "Mubarak Dismisses Government." January 29.

Johnson, Jaclyn and Clayton L. Thyne. 2018. "Squeaky Wheels and Troop Loyalty: How Domestic Protests Influence Coups d'etat, 1951–2005." *Journal of Conflict Resolution* 62 (3): 597–625.

Jost, John T. 2018. "A Quarter Century of System Justification Theory: Questions, Answers, Criticisms, and Societal Applications." *British Journal of Social Psychology* 58 (2): 263–314.

Jost, John T., Mahzarin R. Banaji, and Brian A. Nosek. 2004. "A Decade of System Justification Theory: Accumulated Evidence of Conscious and Unconscious Bolstering of the Status Quo." *Political Psychology* 25 (6): 881–919.

Jugl, Marlene. 2020. "Country Size and the Survival of Authoritarian Monarchies: Developing a New Argument." *Democratization* 27 (2): 283–301.

Kao, Kristen. 2015. "Ethnicity, Electoral Institutions, and Clientelism: Authoritarianism in Jordan." PhD thesis, UCLA.

Karmel, E. J. 2021. "Designing Decentralization in Jordan: Locating the Policy among the Politics." *Middle East Law and Governance*.

Kayyali, Abdul-Wahab and Dina Al-Wakeel. 2015. "Mubadarah: The Politics of the Possible." *Venture Magazine*. April 12.

Keddie, Nikki R. 2003. *Modern Iran: Roots and Results of Revolution*. Yale University Press.

Keefer, Philip and David Stasavage. 2003. "The Limits of Delegation: Veto Players, Central Bank Independence, and the Credibility of Monetary Policy." *American Political Science Review* 97 (3): 407–423.

Kendall-Taylor, Andrea and Erica Frantz. 2014. "How Autocracies Fall." *The Washington Quarterly* 37 (1): 35–47.

Khadka, Narayan. 1986. "Crisis in Nepal's Partyless Panchayat System: The Case for More Democracy." *Pacific Affairs* 59 (3): 429–454.

Khalaf, Abdulhadi. 2008. "Bahrain's Parliament: The Quest for a Role." *Carnegie Endowment for International Peace*. August 22.

Al-Khalidi, Suleiman. 2011. "Jordan's Tribes Criticize Queen's Role." *Reuters*. February 8.

Al-Khalidi, Suleiman. 2012. "Jordan Sentences Ex-spy Chief to 13 Years Jail over Graft." *Reuters*. November 11.

Al-Khalidi, Suleiman. 2018. "Jordan Pushes New IMF-backed Tax Bill to Parliament." *Reuters*. September 25.

Al-Khalidi, Suleiman. 2018b. "Jordan Ministers Resign over Dead Sea Flood Deaths." *Reuters*. November 1, 2018.

Khlevniuk, Oleg V. 2016. *Stalin: New Biography of a Dictator*. Yale University Press.

Khurshudyan, Isabelle. 2020. "As Russian Coronavirus Cases Rise, Putin Delegates Tough Action to Moscow Mayor." *The Washington Post*. March 30.

Knickmeyer, Ellen. 2008. "Fledgling Rebellion on Facebook Is Struck Down by Force in Egypt." *The Washington Post*. May 18.

Knight, Amy. 2008. "The Truth about Putin and Medvedev." *The New York Review of Books*. May 15.

Knobloch-Westerwick, Silvia and Laramie D. Taylor. 2008. "The Blame Game: Elements of Causal Attribution and Its Impact on Siding with Agents in the News." *Communication Research* 35 (6): 723–744.

Knutsen, Carl Henrik. 2021. "A Business Case for Democracy: Regime Type, Growth, and Growth Volatility." *Democratization* 28 (8): 1505–1524.

Knutsen, Carl Henrik and Janne Fjelde. 2013. "Property Rights in Dictatorships: Kings Protect Property Better than Generals or Party Bosses." *Contemporary Politics* 19 (1): 94–114.

Koehler-Derrick, Gabriel. 2013. "Quantifying Anecdotes: Google Search Data and Political Developments in Egypt." *PS: Political Science and Politics* 46 (2): 291–298.

Kokkonen, Andrej, Suthan Krishnarajan, Jorgen Moller, and Anders Sundell. 2021. "Blood Is Thicker than Water: Family Size and Leader Deposition in Medieval and Early Modern Europe." *The Journal of Politics*: 1246–1259.

References

Kokkonen, Andrej, Jorgen Moller, and Anders Sundell. 2022. *The Politics of Succession: Forging Stable Monarchies in Europe, AD 1000–1800.* Oxford University Press.

Kull, Steven, Clay Ramsay, Stephen Weber, and Evan Lewis. 2010. "An Analysis of Multiple Polls of the Iranian Public." *World Public Opinion.* February 3.

Kuran, Timur. 1991. "Now Out of Never: The Element of Surprise in the East European Revolution of 1989." *World Politics* 44 (1): 7–48.

Kurzman, Charles. 1996. "Structural Opportunity and Perceived Opportunity in Social-Movement Theory: The Iranian Revolution of 1979." *American Sociological Review* 61 (1): 153–170.

Kurzman, Charles. 2003. "The Qum Protests and the Coming of the Iranian Revolution, 1975 and 1978." *Social Science History* 27 (3): 287–325.

Kurzman, Charles. 2005. *The Unthinkable Revolution in Iran.* Harvard University Press.

Kurzman, Charles. 2012. "The Arab Spring: Ideals of the Iranian Green Movement, Methods of the Iranian Revolution." *International Journal of Middle East Studies* 44: 162–165.

Lawrence, Adria. 2014. "Kings in a Democratic Age: Collective Protest and the Institutional Promise of Monarchy." Working Paper.

Leber, Andrew and Christopher Carothers. 2017. "Is the Saudi Purge Really about Corruption?" *Foreign Affairs.* November 15.

Levitsky, Steven and Lucan A. Way. 2010. *Competitive Authoritarianism.* Cambridge University Press.

Lewis, Bernard. 2000. "Monarchy in the Middle East." In *Middle East Monarchies: The Challenge of Modernity.* Ed. Joseph Kostiner, 15–22. Lynne Rienner.

Lewis-Beck, Michael S. and Mary Stegmaier. 2000. "Economic Determinants of Electoral Outcomes." *Annual Review of Political Science* 3(1): 183–219.

Lofgren, Hans and Alan Richards. 2003. "Food Security, Poverty, and Economic Policy in the Middle East and North Africa." *International Food Policy Research Institute.*

Londono, Ernesto. 2011. "Egyptian Man's Death Becomes Symbol of Callous State." *Washington Post.* February 8.

Lorentzen, Peter L. 2013. "Regularizing Rioting: Permitting Public Protest in an Authoritarian Regime." *Quarterly Journal of Political Science* 8 (2): 127–158.

Louer, Laurence. 2012. "Houses Divided: The Splintering of Bahrain's Political Camps." *Carnegie Endowment for International Peace.* April 4.

Lu, Xiaobo. 2014. "Social Policy and Regime Legitimacy: The Effects of Education Reform in China." *American Political Science Review* 108 (2): 423–437.

Lü, Xiaobo, Mingxing Liu, and Feiyue Li. 2020. "Policy Coalition Building in an Authoritarian Legislature: Evidence from China's National Assemblies." *Comparative Political Studies* 53 (9): 1380–1416.

Lucardi, Adrian. 2019. "Strength in Expectation: Elections, Economic Performance, and Authoritarian Breakdown." *The Journal of Politics* 81 (2): 552–570.

Lucas, Russell E. 2003. "Deliberalization in Jordan." *Journal of Democracy* 14 (1): 137–144.

Lucas, Russell E. 2005. *Institutions and the Politics of Survival in Jordan.* SUNY Press.

Luciani, Giacomo. 1987. "Allocation vs. Production State." In *The Rentier State.* Ed. Hazem Beblawi and Giacomo Luciani, 63–84. London: Croom Helm.

Lueders, Hans. 2022. "Electoral Responsiveness in Closed Autocracies: Evidence from Petitions in the Former German Democratic Republic." *American Political Science Review* 116 (3): 827–842.

Luhrmann, Anna et al. 2020. "Autocratization Surges – Resistance Grows." *Varieties of Democracy.*

Lust, Ellen. 2009. "Democratization by Elections? Competitive Clientelism in the Middle East." *Journal of Democracy* 20 (3): 122–135.

Lust, Ellen and Sami Hourani. 2011. "Jordan Votes: Election or Selection?" *Journal of Democracy* 22 (2): 119–129.

Lust-Okar, Ellen. 2001. "The Decline of Jordanian Political Parties: Myth or Reality?" *International Journal of Middle East Studies* 33: 545–569.

Lust-Okar, Ellen. 2006. "Elections under Authoritarianism: Preliminary Lessons from Jordan." *Democratization* 13 (3): 456–471.

Lust-Okar, Ellen and Amaney Jamal. 2002. "Rulers and Rules: Reassessing the Influence of Regime Type on Electoral Law Formation." *Comparative Political Studies* 35 (3): 337–366.

Mabon, Simon. 2019. "The End of the Battle for Bahrain and the Securitization of Bahraini Shi'a." *Middle East Journal* 73 (1): 29–50.

Mackinnon, Amy and Reid Standish. 2019. "Russians Begin to Consider Life without Putin." *Foreign Policy Magazine.* September 3.

Madani, Mohamed, Driss Maghraoui, and Salona Zerhouni. 2012. "The 2011 Moroccan Constitution: A Critical Analysis." *International Institute for Democracy and Electoral Assistance.*

Magaloni, Beatriz. 2006. *Voting for Autocracy: Hegemonic Party Survival and Its Demise in Mexico.* Cambridge University Press.

References

Magaloni, Beatriz. 2008. "Credible Power-Sharing and the Longevity of Authoritarian Rule." *Comparative Political Studies*. 41 (4–5): 715–741.

Magaloni, Beatriz and Jeremy Wallace. 2008. "Citizen Loyalty, Mass Protest and Authoritarian Survival." Working Paper.

Magaloni, Beatriz, Jonathan Chu, and Eric Min. 2013. *Autocracies of the World, 1950–2012*. Stanford University.

Maghraoui, Driss. 2018. "Working under Constraints: The PJD in the Aftermath of the 2016 Elections." *Baker Institute for Public Policy*. May 29.

Magid, Aaron. 2016. "The King and the Islamists: Jordan Cracks Down on the Muslim Brotherhood." *Foreign Affairs*. May 3.

Maizland, Lindsay. 2022. "Myanmar's Troubled History: Coups, Military Rule, and Ethnic Conflict." *Council on Foreign Relations*. January 31.

Majd, Hooman. 2010. "Think Again: Iran's Green Movement." *Foreign Policy Magazine*. January 6.

Maktabi, Rima. 2011. "Tunisia Fires Minister after Fatal Riots." *CNN*. January 13.

Malesky, Edmund and Paul Schuler. 2011. "The Single-Party Dictator's Dilemma: Information in Elections without Opposition." *Legislative Studies Quarterly* 36 (4): 491–530.

Malhotra, Neil and Alexander G. Kuo. 2008. "Attributing Blame: The Public's Response to Hurricane Katrina." *The Journal of Politics* 70 (1): 120–135.

Maloney, Suzanne. 2015. *Iran's Political Economy since the Revolution*. Cambridge University Press.

Manin, Bernard, Adam Przeworski, and Susan C. Stokes. 1999. "Introduction." In *Democracy, Accountability, and Representation*. Eds. Adam Przeworski, Susan C. Stokes, and Bernard Manin. Cambridge University Press.

Martin, Lucy and Pia J. Raffler. 2021. "Fault Lines: The Effects of Bureaucratic Power on Electoral Accountability." *American Journal of Political Science* 65 (1): 210–224.

Masbah, Mohammed. 2013. "The PJD's Balancing Act." *Sada, Carnegie Endowment for International Peace*. May 1.

Mayhew, David R. 1974. *Congress: The Electoral Connection*. Yale University Press.

McCubbins, Matthew D. and Thomas Schwartz. 1984. "Congressional Oversight Overlooked: Police Patrols versus Fire Alarms." *American Journal of Political Science* 28 (1): 165–179.

McMillan, James F. 1991. *Napoleon III*. Longman.

Mebtoul, Taha. 2020. "Interior Minister: Some Moroccans Don't Want to Help Fight COVID-19." *Morocco World News*. November 5.

Mellon, Jonathan. 2013. "Where and When Can We Use Google Trends to Measure Issue Salience?" *PS: Political Science & Politics*. 46 (2): 280–290.

Menaldo, Victor. 2012. "The Middle East and North Africa's Resilient Monarchs." *The Journal of Politics* 74 (3): 707–722.

Meng, Anne. 2020. *Constraining Dictatorship: From Personalized Rule to Institutionalized Regimes*. Cambridge University Press.

Meng Anne. 2021. "Ruling Parties in Authoritarian Regimes: Rethinking Institutional Strength." *British Journal of Political Science* 51(2): 526–540.

Meng, Anne and Jack Paine. 2022. "Power Sharing and Authoritarian Stability: How Rebel Regimes Solve the Guardianship Dilemma." *American Political Science Review* 116 (4): 1208–1225.

Meng, Anne, Jack Paine, and Robert Powell. 2023. "Authoritarian Power-Sharing: Concepts, Mechanisms, and Strategies." *Annual Review of Political Science* 26: 153–173.

Milani, Abbas. 2010. "The Green Movement." *US Institute for Peace*. October 6.

Moaddel, Mansoor. 1993. *Class, Politics, and Ideology in the Iranian Revolution*. Columbia University Press.

Monjib, Maati. 2012. "All the King's Islamists." *Sada, Carnegie Endowment for International Peace*. September 20.

Monjib, Maati. 2013. "Constitutionally Imbalanced." *Sada, Carnegie Endowment for International Peace*. August 8.

Monjib, Maati. 2014. "The Islamists Ahead in Morocco." *Sada, Carnegie Endowment for International Peace*. July 29.

Monjib, Maati. 2016. "Record Gains for Morocco's Islamist Party." *Sada, Carnegie Endowment for International Peace*. October 27.

Monjib, Maati. 2017. "Lopsided Struggle for Power in Morocco." *Sada, Carnegie Endowment for International Peace*. January 25.

Monod, Paul Kleber. 2001. *The Power of Kings: Monarchy and Religion in Europe, 1589–1715*. Yale University Press.

Montinola, Gabriella R. and Robert W. Jackman. 2002. "Sources of Corruption: A Cross-Country Study." *British Journal of Political Science* 32 (1): 147–170.

Moore, Henry Clement. 1970. *Politics in North Africa: Algeria, Morocco, and Tunisia*. Little, Brown and Company.

Moore, Pete. 2018. "The Fiscal Politics of Rebellious Jordan." *Middle East Report Online*. June 21.

Morrill, J. S. 1978. "French Absolutism as Limited Monarchy." *The Historical Journal* 21 (4): 961–972.

Moustafa, Tamir. 2014. "Law and Courts in Authoritarian Regimes." *Annual Review of Law and Social Science* 10: 281–299.

References

El Muhtaseb, Lamis. 2013. "Jordan's East Banker-Palestinian Schism." Norwegian Peacebuilding Resource Centre.

Murphy, A. M. Dima. 2022. "Popular Sovereignty." Max Planck Encyclopedia of Comparative Constitutional Law. Last Updated May 2022.

Murthy, Padmaja. 2003. "Understanding Nepal Maoists' Demands: Revisiting Events of 1990." *Strategic Analysis* 27 (1): 41–55.

Nadeau, Richard and Michael S. Lewis-Beck. 2001. "National Economic Voting in U.S. Presidential Elections." *The Journal of Politics* 63 (1): 159–181.

Nadrelli, Alberto, Jennifer Rankin, and George Arnett. 2015. "Vladimir Putin's Approval Rating at Record Levels." *The Guardian.* July 23.

Nadzri, Muhamad M. N. 2018. "The 14th General Election, the Fall of Barisan Nasional, and Political Development in Malaysia, 1957–2018." *Journal of Current Southeast Asian Affairs* 37 (3): 139–171.

Nielsen, Richard A. 2017. *Deadly Clerics: Blocked Ambition and the Paths to Jihad.* Cambridge University Press.

Noble, Ben. 2020. "Authoritarian Amendments: Legislative Institutions as Intraexecutive Constraints in Post-Soviet Russia." *Comparative Political Studies* 53 (9): 1417–1454.

North, Douglass C. and Barry R. Weingast. 1989. "Constitutions and Commitment: The Evolution of Institutions Governing Public Choice in Seventeenth-Century England." *The Journal of Economic History* 49 (4): 803–832.

Nugent, Elizabeth R. 2020. "The Psychology of Repression and Polarization." *World Politics* 72 (2): 291–334.

Nyrup, Jacob and Stuart Bramwell. 2020. "Who Governs? A New Global Dataset on Members of Cabinets." *American Political Science Review* 114 (4): 1366–1374.

Obeidat, Sufian. 2014. "Security Sector Oversight, Protecting Democratic Consolidation from Partisan Abuse: The Case of Jordan."

Obeidat, Sufian. 2016. "Jordan's 2016 Constitutional Amendments: A Return to Absolute Monarchy?" *ConstitutionNet.* May 27.

O'Connell, Jack. 2011. *King's Counsel: A Memoir of War, Espionage, and Diplomacy in the Middle East.* W.W. Norton and Company.

O'Donnell, Guillermo. 2007. "The Perpetual Crises of Democracy." *Journal of Democracy* 18 (1): 5–11.

Opalo, Ken Ochieng'. 2020. "Constrained Presidential Power in Africa? Legislative Independence and Executive Rule Making in Kenya, 1963–2013." *British Journal of Political Science* 50 (4): 1341–1358.

Ottaway, Marina. 2011. "The New Moroccan Constitution: Real Change or More of the Same?" *Carnegie Endowment for International Peace.* June 20.

Ottaway, Marina. 2021. "Algeria: The Enduring Failure of Politics." *The Wilson Center*. October 13.

Oweidat, Nadia, Cheryl Benard, Dale Stahl, Walid Kildani, Edward O'Connell, and Audra K. Grant. 2008. "The Kefaya Movement: A Case Study of a Grassroots Reform Initiative." Rand Corporation.

Owen, Roger. 2012. *The Rise and Fall of Arab Presidents for Life*. Cambridge: Harvard University Press.

Paine, Jack. 2021. "The Dictator's Power Sharing Dilemma: Countering Dual Outsider Threats." *American Journal of Political Science* 65 (2): 510–527.

Paine, Jack. 2022. "Strategic Power Sharing: Commitment, Capability, and Authoritarian Survival." *The Journal of Politics* 84 (2): 1226–1232.

Parajulee, Ramjee. 2010. "An Experiment with a Hybrid Regime in Nepal (1990–2006)." *Journal of Asian and African Studies* 45 (1): 87–112.

Parsa, Misagh. 1989. *Social Origins of the Iranian Revolution*. Rutgers University Press.

Pelham, Nick. 1999. "King Humbles Morocco's Man of Iron." *The Guardian*. November 20.

Peters, Anne Mariel. 2009. "Whither Egypt's Economic Reform?" *Sada, Carnegie Endowment for International Peace*. July 7.

Pew Research Center. 2014. "One Year after Morsi's Ouster, Divides Persist on El-Sisi, Muslim Brotherhood." May 22.

Pisch, Anita. 2016. *The Personality Cult of Stalin in Soviet Posters, 1929–1953: Archetypes, Inventions, and Fabrications*. Australian National University Press.

Powell, Jonathan M. and Clayton L. Thyne. 2011. "Global Instances of Coups from 1950 to 2010: A New Dataset." *Journal of Peace Research* 48 (2): 249–259.

Powell, Bingham G. and Guy Whitten. 1993. "A Cross-National Analysis of Economic Voting: Taking Account of the Political Context." *American Journal of Political Science* 37 (2): 391–414.

Przeworski, Adam. 2023. "Formal Models of Authoritarian Regimes: A Critique." *Perspectives on Politics* 21 (3): 979–988.

Przeworski, Adam, Tamar Adadurian, and Anjali Thomas Bohlken. 2012. "The Origins of Parliamentary Responsibility." In *Comparative Constitutional Design*. Ed. Tom Ginsburg. Cambridge University Press.

Radi, Abdelaziz. 2017. "Protest Movements and Social Media: Morocco's February 20 Movement." *Africa Development* 42 (2): 31–55.

Raghavan, Sudarsan. 2011. "In Tunisia, Luxurious Lifestyles of a Corrupt Government." *Washington Post*. January 28.

Rasler, Karen. 1996. "Concessions, Repression, and Political Protest in the Iranian Revolution." *American Sociological Review* 61 (1): 132–152.

References

Rath, Kathrine. 1994. "The Process of Democratization in Jordan." *Middle Eastern Studies* 30 (3): 530–557.

Al-Rawi, Ahmed K. 2015. "Sectarianism and the Arab Spring: Framing the Popular Protests in Bahrain." *Global Media and Communication* 11 (1): 25–42.

Ray, James Lee. 1998. "Does Democracy Cause Peace?" *Annual Review of Political Science* 1: 27–46.

Razi, Hossein. 1987. "The Nexus of Legitimacy and Performance: The Lessons of the Iranian Revolution." *Comparative Politics* 19 (4): 453–469.

Reiter, Yitzhak. 2004. "The Palestinian-Transjordanian Rift: Economic Might and Political Power in Jordan." *Middle East Journal* 58 (1): 72–92.

Reuter, Ora John and Jennifer Gandhi. 2011. "Economic Performance and Elite Defection from Hegemonic Parties." *British Journal of Political Science* 41 (1): 83–110.

Reuter, Ora John and Graeme B. Robertson. 2015. "Subnational Appointments in Authoritarian Regimes: Evidence from Russian Gubernatorial Appointments." *The Journal of Politics* 74 (4): 1023–1037.

Reuters. 2009. "Egypt Transport Minister Resigns over Train Crash." October 27.

Roberts, Margaret E., Brandon M. Stewart, and Dustin Tingley. 2019. "stm: An R Package for Structural Topic Models." *Journal of Statistical Software* 91 (2): 1–40.

Robins, Philip. 2004. *A History of Jordan*. Cambridge University Press.

Robinson, Darrel and Marcus Tannenberg. 2019. "Self-censorship of Regime Support in Authoritarian States: Evidence from List Experiments in China." *Research & Politics* 6 (3).

Roessler, Philip. 2011. "The Enemy Within: Personal Rule, Coups, and Civil War in Africa." *World Politics* 63 (2): 300–346.

Roessler, Philip. 2016. *Ethnic Politics and State Power in Africa*. Cambridge University Press.

Rose, Leo E. 1964. "Nepal: The Quiet Monarchy." *Asian Survey* 4 (2): 723–728.

Rosenfeld, Bryn. 2018. "The Popularity Costs of Economic Crisis under Electoral Authoritarianism: Evidence from Russia." *American Journal of Political Science* 62 (2): 382–397.

Ross, Michael L. 2001. "Does Oil Hinder Democracy?" *World Politics* 53 (3): 325–361.

Rozenas, Arturas and Denis Stukal. 2019. "How Autocrats Manipulate Economic News: Evidence from Russia's State-Controlled Television." *The Journal of Politics* 81 (3): 982–996.

Ryabov, Andrei. 2008. "Tandemocracy in Today's Russia." *Russian Analytical Digest* 49: 2–6.

Ryan, Curtis. 1998. "Peace, Bread and Riots: Jordan and the International Monetary Fund." *Middle East Policy* 6 (2): 54–66.

Ryan, Curtis. 1999. "Jordan after King Hussein: A Troubled Inheritance." *Strategic Comments* 5 (2): 1–2.

Ryan, Curtis. 2018. *Jordan and the Arab Uprisings.* Columbia University Press.

Ryan, Curtis R. 2021. "Family Matters: Plots and Accusations in Jordan's Hashemite Monarchy." *Arab Center Washington DC.* April 8.

Ryan, Curtis. 2022. "Royal Rifts and Other Challenges in Jordan." *Arab Center Washington DC.* April 14.

Ryan, Curtis R. and Jillian Schwedler. 2004. "Return to Democratization or New Hybrid Regime?: The 2003 Elections in Jordan." *Middle East Policy* 11 (2): 138–151.

Safi, Michael. 2020. "Jordan Arrests 1,000 Teachers in Crackdown on Union." *The Guardian.* August 19.

Saif, Ibrahim. 2008. "The Food Price Crisis in the Arab Countries: Short Term Responses to a Lasting Challenge." *Carnegie Endowment for International Peace.*

Sater, James N. 2011. "Morocco's 'Arab' Spring." *Middle East Institute.* October 1.

Scheitle, Christopher P. 2011. "Google's Insights for Search: A Note Evaluating the Use of Search Engine Data in Social Research." *Social Science Quarterly* 92 (1): 285–295.

Schuler, Paul. 2020. "Position Taking or Position Ducking? A Theory of Public Debate in Single-Party Legislatures." *Comparative Political Studies* 53 (9): 1493–1524.

Schwedler, Jillian. 2002. "Don't Blink." *Middle East Report Online.* July 3.

Schwedler, Jillian. 2003. "More Than a Mob: The Dynamics of Political Demonstrations in Jordan." *Middle East Report* 226: 18–23.

Schwedler, Jillian. 2010. "Jordan's Risky Business as Usual." *Middle East Report Online.* June 30.

Schwedler, Jillian. 2012. "The Political Geography of Protest in Neoliberal Jordan." *Middle East Critique* 21 (3): 259–270.

Schwedler, Jillian. 2021. "Jordan Detained a Prince. The Government's Determined to Squash Political Dissent." *The Washington Post.* April 5.

Schwedler, Jillian. 2022. *Protesting Jordan.* Stanford University Press.

Seawright, Jason and John Gerring. 2008. "Case Selection Techniques in Case Study Research: A Menu of Qualitative and Quantitative Options." *Political Research Quarterly* 61 (2): 294–308.

References 337

Shakibi, Zhand. 2007. *Revolutions and the Collapse of Monarchies*. I.B. Tauris & Company.

Shalaby, Marwa and Scott Williamson. 2023. "Executive Compliance with Parliamentary Powers under Authoritarianism: Evidence from Jordan." *Governance*.

Sharabi, Hisham. 1988. *Neopatriarchy: A Theory of Distorted Change in Arab Society*. Oxford University Press.

Al-Sharif, Osama. 2018. "Who's to Blame for Deaths in Jordan Flood?" *Al-Monitor*. November 1.

Sharrock, David. 1999. "Crown Prince with an English Accent." *The Guardian*. January 28.

Shehata, Dina. 2011. "The Fall of the Pharaoh: How Hosni Mubarak's Reign Came to an End." *Foreign Affairs*.

Shehata, Samer. 2005. "Opposition Politics in Egypt: A Fleeting Moment of Opportunity?" *Sada, Carnegie Endowment for International Peace*. August 20.

Shen, Xiaoxiao and Rory Truex. 2021. "In Search of Self-Censorship." *British Journal of Political Science* 51 (4): 1672–1684.

Shlaim, Avi. 2007. *Lion of Jordan*. Knopf Doubleday Publishing Group.

Slackman, Michael. 2008. "Day of Angry Protest Stuns Egypt." *New York Times*. April 6.

Sowell, Kirk. 2018. "Slowing Jordan's Slide into Debt." *Sada, Carnegie Endowment for International Peace*. March 22.

Spinks, B. Todd, Emile Sahliyeh, and Brian Calfano. 2008. "The Status of Democracy and Human Rights in the Middle East: Does Regime Type Make a Difference?" *Democratization* 15 (2): 321–341.

Stepan, Alfred, Juan J. Linz and Juli F. Minoves. 2014. "Democratic Parliamentary Monarchies." *Journal of Democracy* 25 (2): 35–51.

Stockemer, Daniel and Steffan Kailitz. 2020. "Economic Development: How Does It Influence the Survival of Different Types of Autocracy?" *International Political Science Review* 41 (5): 711–727.

Stockmann, Daniela. 2013. *Media Commercialization and Authoritarian Rule in China*. Cambridge University Press.

Sudduth, Jun Koga. 2021. "Purging Militaries: Introducing the Military Purges in Dictatorships (MPD) Dataset." *Journal of Peace Research* 58 (4): 870–880.

Susser, Asher. 1994. *On Both Banks of the Jordan: A Political Biography of Wasfi al-Tall*. Routledge.

Svolik, Milan. 2012. *The Politics of Authoritarian Rule*. Cambridge University Press.

Tal, Lawrence. 1995. "Britain and the Jordan Crisis of 1958." *Middle Eastern Studies* 31 (1): 39–57.

338   *References*

Al Talei, Rafiah. 2021. "Regressing Council Powers in Oman: From Constitutional Rights to Codification." *Carnegie Endowment for International Peace*. April 12.

Tavits, Margit. 2007. "Clarity of Responsibility and Corruption." *American Journal of Political Science* 51 (1): 218–229.

Taylor, Antony. 2013. *Down with the Crown: British Anti-Monarchism and Debates about Royalty since 1790*. London: Reaktion Books.

Tell, Tariq. 2015. "Early Spring in Jordan: The Revolt of the Military Veterans." *Carnegie Endowment for International Peace*. November 4.

Tell, Tariq. 2013. *The Social and Economic Origins of Monarchy in Jordan*. Palgrave Macmillan.

Thafer, Dania. 2021. "Qatar's First Elected Parliament May Have More Power than Other Persian Gulf Legislatures. Here's Why." *Washington Post*. October 14.

The National. 2020. "Jordan Interior Minister Resigns as Thousands Break Covid Rules after Elections." November 12.

The National Archives of the United Kingdom (TNA). FCO 93/664. "Internal Politics of Jordan in 1975."

The National Archives of the United Kingdom (TNA). FCO 93/4895. "Internal Political Affairs in Jordan 1987–8."

The National Archives of the United Kingdom (TNA). FO 371–127876. "Jordan: Annual Political Review for 1956."

The National Archives of the United Kingdom (TNA). FO 371–134006. "Jordan: Annual Political Review for 1957."

The National Archives of the United Kingdom (TNA). FO 371–151040. "Jordan: Annual Political Review for 1959."

The National Archives of the United Kingdom (TNA). FO 437–10. "Jordan: Annual Review for 1960."

The National Archives of the United Kingdom (TNA). FO 371–164080. "Annual Political Review for Jordan 1961."

The National Archives of the United Kingdom (TNA). FO 371–170263. "Annual Political Review for Jordan 1962."

The National Archives of the United Kingdom (TNA). FO 371–180728. "Jordan: Annual Political Review for 1964."

The National Archives of the United Kingdom (TNA). FO 371–186547. "Jordan: Annual Review for 1965."

The National Archives of the United Kingdom (TNA). FO 437–10. "Jordan: Annual Review for 1967."

The National Archives of the United Kingdom (TNA). FO 437–12. "Correspondence Respecting Jordan and Arab Palestine."

References

Thyne, Clayton L. 2010. "Supporter of Stability or Agent of Agitation? The Effect of US Foreign Policy on Coups in Latin America, 1960–99." *Journal of Peace Research* 47 (4): 449–461.

Tilly, Charles. 1993. "Contentious Repertoires in Great Britain, 1758–1834." *Social Science History* 17 (2): 253–280.

Tompson, William J. 1991. "The Fall of Nikita Khrushchev." *Soviet Studies* 43 (6): 1101–1121.

Treisman, Daniel. 2014. "Putin's Popularity since 2010: Why Did Support for the Kremlin Plunge, then Stabilize?" *Post-Soviet Affairs* 30 (5): 370–388.

Truex, Rory. 2014. "The Returns to Office in a 'Rubber Stamp' Parliament." *American Political Science Review* 108 (2): 235–251.

Truex, Rory. 2016. *Making Autocracy Work*. Cambridge University Press.

Truex, Rory. 2020. "Authoritarian Gridlock? Understanding Delay in the Chinese Legislative System." *Comparative Political Studies* 53(9): 1455–1492.

Tsai, Lily. 2007. "Solidary Groups, Informal Accountability, and Local Public Goods Provision in Rural China." *American Political Science Review* 101 (2): 355–372.

Tullock, Gordon. 1987. *Autocracy*. Kluwer Academic Publishers.

Volkov, Denis. 2015. "How Authentic Is Putin's Approval Rating?" *Carnegie Endowment for International Peace*. July 27.

Wahman, Michael, Jan Teorell, and Axel Hadenius. 2013. "Authoritarian Regime Types Revisited: Updated Data in Comparative Perspective." *Contemporary Politics* 19 (1): 19–34.

Wallace, Jeremy L. 2014. "Juking the Stats? Authoritarian Information Problems in China." *British Journal of Political Science* 46 (1): 11–29.

Wasquerel de, Emmanuel and Benoit Yvert. 2002. *Histoire de la Restauration 1814–1830*. Perrin.

Weaver, Kent R. 1986. "The Politics of Blame Avoidance." *Journal of Public Policy* 6 (4): 371–398.

Weeks, Jessica L. 2012. "Strongmen and Straw Men: Authoritarian Regimes and the Initiation of International Conflict." *American Political Science Review* 106 (2): 326–347.

Weeks, Brian E. and Brian Southwell. 2010. "The Symbiosis of News Coverage and Aggregate Online Search Behavior: Obama, Rumors, and Presidential Politics." *Mass Communication & Society* 13 (4): 341–360.

Weiner, Bernard. 1985. "An Attributional Theory of Achievement Motivation and Emotion." *Psychological Review* 92 (4): 26.

Weingast, Barry R. 1997. "The Political Foundations of Democracy and the Rule of the Law." *American Political Science Review* 91 (2): 245–263.

Westall, Sylvia. 2014. "Frustrated Kuwaitis Ask, Why Is Kuwait Falling Behind?" *Reuters*. April 2.

Westwood, Andrew F. 1961. "Elections and Politics in Iran." *Middle East Journal* 15 (2): 153–164.

Whelpton, John. 2005. *A History of Nepal*. Cambridge University Press.

Wiktorowicz, Quintan. 1999. "Islamists, the State, and Cooperation in Jordan." *Arab Studies Quarterly* 21 (4): 1–17.

Williamson, Scott. 2021. "Elections, Legitimacy, and Compliance in Authoritarian Regimes: Evidence from the Arab World." *Democratization* 28 (8): 1483–1504.

Williamson, Scott. 2024. "Do Proxies Provide Plausible Deniability? Evidence from Experiments on Three Surveys." *Journal of Conflict Resolution* 68 (2–3): 322–347.

Williamson, Scott and Beatriz Magaloni. 2020. "Legislatures and Policy Making in Authoritarian Regimes." *Comparative Political Studies* 53 (9): 1525–1543.

Williamson, Scott and Mashail Malik. 2021. "Contesting Narratives of Repression: Experimental Evidence from Sisi's Egypt." *Journal of Peace Research* 58 (5): 1018–1033.

Wintrobe, Ronald. 1998. *The Political Economy of Dictatorship*. Cambridge University Press.

Witte, Griff, Janine Zacharia, and William Branigin. 2011. "Mubarak Addresses Nation, Calls on Government to Resign but Vows to Remain in Power Himself." *The Washington Post*. January 27.

Wolf, Anne. 2023. *Ben Ali's Tunisia: Power and Contention in an Authoritarian Regime*. Oxford University Press.

Wright, Joseph. 2008. "Do Authoritarian Political Institutions Constrain? How Legislatures Affect Economic Growth and Investment." *American Journal of Political Science* 52 (2): 322–343.

Wright, Joseph, Erica Frantz, and Barbara Geddes. 2015. "Oil and Autocratic Regime Survival." *British Journal of Political Science* 45 (2): 287–306.

Yom, Sean. 2014. "Tribal Politics in Contemporary Jordan: The Case of the Hirak Movement." *The Middle East Journal* 68 (2): 229–247.

Yom, Sean. 2015. *From Resilience to Revolution: How Foreign Interventions Destabilize the Middle East*. Columbia University Press.

Yom, Sean and Wael Al-Khatib. 2022. "Democratic Reform in Jordan: Breaking the Impasse." *Project on Middle East Democracy*. February.

References 341

Younes, Ali. 2017. "Jordan Cracks Down on Activists over Social Media Posts." *Al-Jazeera*. January 18.

Zewde, Bahru. 2001. *A History of Modern Ethiopia, 1855–1991*. James Currey, Ohio University Press, and Addis Ababa University Press and Research and Publications Office.

Zhao, Dingxin. 2009. "The Mandate of Heaven and Performance Legitimation in Historical and Contemporary China." *American Behavioral Scientist* 53 (3): 416–433.

Zonis, Marvin. 1983. "Iran: A Theory of Revolution from Accounts of the Revolution." *World Politics* 35 (4): 586–606.

Zunes, Stephen. 2013. "Bahrain's Arrested Revolution." *Arab Studies Quarterly* 35 (2): 149–164.

Zweiri, Mohammed Zahid Mahjoob. 2007. "The Victory of Al Wefaq: The Rise of Shiite Politics in Bahrain." *Research Institute for European and American Studies*. April.

Index

Abdullah bin al-Hussein, *see* Abdullah
    II (king)
Abdullah II (king), 1, 2, 117, 122, 133,
    138
  back to royal rule, 208–210
  essays, 115, 135
  marriage, 198
  transitioning to a new king
    (1999–2009), 179, 198–201
  turmoil and malaise (2010–2020),
    179, 202–208
Abdullah, Emir (king), 117
Abu Nuwar, Ali, 183, 220
accountability, 17, 63
  authoritarian regimes, 76, 264
  autocrats, 110–113, 315
  citizens, 53, 56, 215
  kings, 37, 137
  limited, 27, 34, 229–234
  monarchs, 70
Afro Barometer, 98
Ahmadinejad, Mahmoud, 79
Akhannouch, Aziz, 97
al-Asad, Bishar, 265
al-Asads, 7, 243
al-Bakhit, Marouf, 203
al-Bashir, Omar, 43, 265
al-Basri, Driss, 237
al-Dahabi, Mohammed, 220, 222
al-Demeri, Ibrahim, 237
al-Fassi, Abbas, 246
al-Halalmeh, Tawfiq, 230
Al-Hayat Center, 128
al-Huda, Tawfiq Abu, 221
al-Karaki, Khalid, 222
al-Khalifa (king), 243
al-Khalifa, Hamad bin Isa , 249
al-Khalifa, Khalifa bin Salman, 247
al-Khasawneh, Awn, 129, 203
al-Lawzi, Nasser, 222

al-Majali, Hazza, 181, 185
al-Masri, Taher, 126
al-Mufti, Said, 182, 221
al-Mulki, Fawzi, 180
al-Mulki, Hani, 147, 164, 203, 205,
    221, 222
al-Nabulsi, Suleiman, 183, 220
al-Othmani, Saadeddine, 40, 97, 246
al-Qadhafi, Muammar, 42, 265
al-Ragheb, Ali Abu, 127
al-Razzaz, Omar, 125, 147, 165, 167,
    203, 206, 230
al-Rifai, Abdelmounim, 189
al-Rifai, Samir, 127, 181, 184, 214
al-Rifai, Samir (grandson), 214
al-Rifai, Zaid, 193, 214
al-Sabah, Mubarak, 243
al-Sabah, Saad al-Salim, 246
al-Shanqiti, Mohammed, 222
al-Talhouni, Bahjat, 186, 188, 189,
    221
al-Tarawneh, Fayez, 203
al-Tell, Wasfi, 126, 186, 188, 221
al-Youssoufi, Abderrahmane, 246
Algeria, 3, 43, 250, 265, 311
Amini, Ali, 290
Amman
  bombings, 140
  British embassy, 139, 176
  polluted water, 194
  protests, 147, 206
Amuzegar (prime minister), 295
Anderson, Lisa, 19
April Uprising, 174, 214, 232
Arab Barometer survey, 148, 151,
    158–162, 251
Arab monarchies, 239, 251
  delegation credibility, 242–251
Arab nationalism, 180, 184, 191
Arab republics, 3, 239, 242, 245, 250

Index

343

Arab Spring, 1, 3, 9, 38, 179, 214,
232, 237, 242, 246, 248, 254,
265–267
across Middle East, 2, 115, 313
avoiding mass opposition, 264
criticisms for King Abdullah, 206,
208, 224, 228
Egypt, 310
Arab-Israeli conflict, 140
Arsanjani (minister), 292
Asian Barometer, 98
attributions of responsibility, 4, 10, 50,
60, 74, 82, 98, 102, 175, 187,
302, *see also* Jordanians,
attributions of responsibility
and autocrats, 41–43, 74
and decision-making, 45–50
and delegation, 74
and power sharing, 51–64
under authoritarianism, 12–17
authoritarianism
attributions of responsibility, 12–17
defined, 7
governance, 6
politics, 7, 11, 23, 34, 42, 51, 114
elections, 57, 67
regimes, 3
citizens, 53
governance and public in, 6–12
militaries, 309–312
public's role, 42
autocracy, 23–29
and democracy, 312–316
political elites and politics under,
305–308
popular politics, 304
understanding of monarchies, 29–33
autocrats, 4, 8, 51
accountability, 110–113
and attributions, 74
attributions, 102
blame avoidance, 14
credible delegation and ruler
stability, 62
decision-making, 11
escalated discontent, 107
low credibility delegation and ruler
stability, 60
potential credible delegation and
ruler instability, 61

power-sharing, 16, 98, 102
repression, 103
royal advantage, 64
Awadallah,Bassem, 210
Azhari, Gholam Reza, 295

Badran, Adnan, 221
Badran, Mudar, 221
Baghdad Pact, 182
Bahrain, 3, 243, 247, 249, 251, 265
Ben Ali, Zine al-Abidine, 21, 237, 243,
265, 270–272
benevolent paternalism, 192
Benkirane, Abdelilah, 95, 246
Bhumibol Adulyadej (king), 71
Bhutan, 287
Birendra (king), 297
Black Friday, 295
Black September, 190, 200
blame avoidance, 44, 212
and decision-making, 201, 238
and delegation, 17, 21, 28, 65, 76,
100, 138, 151, 302, 315
and power-sharing, 23, 69, 308
benefits of, 132
discontent, 43
Hashemite kings, 37
intentional, 133–134
Jordanian monarchy, 133
royal advantage in, 267
Bourbon King Charles X, 279
Bourguiba, Habib, 21, 243
Bouteflika, Abdelaziz, 43, 265, 311
British, 21, 30, 117, 139, 176

cabinet and parliament, 35, 93, 125,
177, 234, 258
Ben Ali, 244
empowering, 129, 183, 197
King Abdullah, 200
monarchy blame avoidance, 132
responsibility, 137, 152
Spain, 18
Center for Strategic Studies (CSS), 164,
167
Charlie Hebdo march, 225
China, 7, 23, 27, 52, 57
closed autocracies, 82
COVID-19, 40
economy, 75

344 *Index*

Chun Doo-hwan, 42
civilian elites, 240, 243, 309, 313
civilian leadership, 310, 311
Cleander (Commodus adviser), 57
co-optive strategies, 3
Colour Revolutions, 9
Commodus (emperor), 57
competitive elections, 8, 314, 315
constitutional monarchs, 19, 71, 136,
    208, 279, 281
  ministerial responsibility, 21
  modern-day, 258
constitutions, 258
  and democracy, 263
coordination problems, 57
Council of Ministers, 122
coup attempts, 20, 43, 62, 66, 106,
    176, 287, 311
  against Hussein, 140
  Ali Abu Nuwar, 183, 220
  Nepal, 297
  replacing autocrats through, 9, 53,
    55
  Syria, 7
COVID-19 pandemic, 40, 176, 230
credibility of delegation, 16, 48, 57,
    74, 129–132, 174, 235
  across issue domains, 158
  Arab citizens, 251–254
  Arab monarchs, 242–251
  autocrats credit/blame, 58, 82
  in Jordan's history, 170
  in Russia, 34
  institutional and political factors, 49
  Jordan's history, 177
  King Abdullah, 208
  King Hussein, 185, 196
  monarchs and non-monorchs,
    254–257
  Putin, 92
  variation, 240–242

decentralization, 23
decision-making, 15
  and attributions, 45–50
  and blame avoidance, 201, 238
  in Jordan, 122
delegation, 132
  affecting governance, 76
  and attributions, 15, 74

and autocrats, 54
and monarchs, 65–69
as blame avoidance strategy, 17, 21,
    28, 65, 76, 100, 138, 151, 302,
    315
in Jordan, 122
democracy
  and constitution, 263
  autocracy and, 312–316
dictator, *see* autocrats
direct rule, 313
  by king, 159, 236
  militaries, 311
distributive politics, 119, 305

East Bank, 119
economic crisis, 53, 104, 120, 206,
    232, 267
  France, 280
  mass mobilizations, 107
economic voting, 81
Egypt, 21, 127, 140, 180, 185, 249,
    265, 311
  constitution, 258
  Kifaya Movement, 267
  killing of Khaled Said, 1
  train accidents, 237
el-Baradei, Mohammed, 268
elite politics, 14, 26, 31, 201
Emami, Sharif, 295
English monarchs, 70
Ensour, Abdullah, 203
Eqbal, Manoucher, 290
Erdogan (president), 12
Ethiopia, 287

Facebook Ad experiment, 162
Faisal II (king), 66, 184
February 20 Movement, 93
foreign affairs, 115, 132, 138, 140,
    148, 182, 193, 196, 211,
    247
foreign policy, 75, 94, 141, 152, 161,
    208
free elections, 3, 9
French monarchy, 278

General Intelligence Directorate (GID),
    124, 128, 149, 224
Ghonim, Wael, 2

Index

345

Glorious Revolution, 71, 278
Google Trends, 82, 83, 98, 303
Great Britain, 232, 278, 297
Great Purge, 41
Green Movement, 79
Gulf monarchies, 30
Gulf War, 196, 232, 251
Gyanendra (king), 299

Hamarneh, Mustafa, 128
Hamzah (prince), 198, 210
Hashem, Ibrahim, 184, 221
Hassan (Moroccan king), 246
Hassan (prince), 192, 198
Herb, Michael, 313
hereditary succession, 5, 18, 20, 31,
    65, 243, 257, 304
Hirak protest, 202, 228
House of Bonaparte, 279
House of Bourbon, 279
Hoveyda (prime minister), 294
Huntington, Samuel, 19
Hussein (crown prince), 210
Hussein (king), 118, 122, 130, 134,
    136, 138
  as secure king (1972–1985), 177,
    190–193
  balancing act (1952–1971), 177,
    179–190
  cancer, 198
  martial law, 184, 195
  return of popular politics
    (1986–1998), 179
Hussein, Saddam, 6, 61, 196

ibn Shaker, Zaid, 221
IMF, 153, 165, 174, 194, 197, 270
imprisonment, 225
indirect democracy, 137
Indonesia, 81
institutionalization, 5
Iran, 32, 79–80
Iran–Iraq War, 7
Iranian monarchy, 281, 288
Iranian Revolution (1979), 80
Iraq, 184
Islam, 31, 120, 131, 139, 194, 271
Islamic Republic of Iran, 79
Israel, 130, 140, 153, 191, 193, 196,
    232

Jordan wars, 119
West Bank, 180, 188
Israeli-Palestinian conflict, 141, 160

Jettou, Driss, 246
Jordan
  foreign support, 120
  Hashemite Kingdom, 1, 25, 33, 34,
    36, 114, 175, 180, 185, 237
    background, 117–122
    blame avoidance, 37
    repression, 215
  IMF-backed austerity reforms
    (1989), 174
  Israel wars, 119
  oil crisis (1973), 191
  peace treaty with Israel, 130
  policymaking process, 122
  political system in education, 135
  power-sharing functions in political
    system, 35
Jordan governance
  failure of anti-monarchical
    coordination, 226–229
  incentivizing elite loyalty, 219–224
  limited accountability, 229–234
  limiting repression, 215–216
  opposition, 224–226
  permitting protest, 216–219
Jordanian elites, 35, 124, 148, 235
Jordanian monarchy
  balancing act (1952–1971),
    179–190
  constitutional provisions
    surrounding decision-making,
    122–124
  costs and credibility of delegation,
    129–132
  decision-making in practice,
    124–129
  delegation across issue domains,
    138–142
  expectations of responsibility,
    134–138
  Hashemite kingdom background,
    117–122
  intentional blame avoidance,
    133–134
  transitioning to a new king
    (1999–2009), 198–201

346

Jordanian monarchy (cont.)
  turmoil and malaise (2010–2020),
    202–208
Jordanians, attributions of
    responsibility, 211
  Arab Barometer survey, 158–162
  elites and activists, 148–151
  Facebook Ad experiment, 162–170
  public opinion, 151–162
  YouGov survey, 152–158
July Monarchy, 279
Justice and Charity, 93
Justice and Development Party (PJD),
    95

Kabariti, Abdul Karim, 127, 197
Kacem, Rafiq Belhaj, 238
Khamenei, Ali, 79
Khrushchev, Nikita, 68
Kifaya Movement, 267
Koirala, B.P., 296
Kuwait, 243, 246, 251
  invasion by Iraq, 7
Kuwaiti monarchy , 7

Lampedusa formula, 134
Libya, 42, 265
Linz, Juan, 29
loss aversion, 44

Machiavelli, N., 45
Mahendra (king), 296
Malaysia, 67
Maldives, 287
Mansour, Mohammed, 237
martial law
  Hussein, 184, 195
  Iranian shah, 295
mass grievances, 75, 180
mass mobilizations, 81, 107–110, 265
mass opposition, 31, 50, 265
media, 12
Medvedev, Dmitry
  and Putin, 87, 89–93
Meshal, Khalid, 197
militaries, 43, 259, 309
  direct rule, 311
military elites, 190, 240, 243, 314
Military Purges in Dictatorships
    (MPD) dataset, 241

ministerial responsibility, 21, 71
Mohammed Bin Salman, 32
Mohammed VI, 40, 93–98, 237, 246
monarchs, 64
  and delegation, 65–69
  collapse of modern, 286–288
  delegation advantage, 77
  governance and accountability,
    69–73
  in modern world, 281–286
  opposition, 264
  protests, 272
  religion and divinity, 70
  understanding of, 29
  understanding of(, 33
Morocco, 34, 40, 87, 93–98, 237
  constitution, 259
  prime ministers, 246
Morsi, Mohammed, 311
Mossadeq, Mohammad, 288
Mubarak, Husni, 2, 4, 13, 52, 81, 237,
    265, 267–269, 310
Muslims, 139, 194, 195, 202, 209,
    223, 228, 250, 268, see also
    Islam

Napoleon III, 280
Napoleonic Wars, 278
Nasser, Gamal Abdel, 127, 140, 180,
    184, 187, 191
National Archives of the United
    Kingdom, 176
National Charter in 1989, 199
National Politics Council (NPC), 124
national security, 75, 94, 115, 132,
    138, 140, 148, 152, 161, 182,
    208, 211
NAVCO, 107, 272
Nazif, Ahmed, 267, 269
Nepali monarchy, 281, 296–300
Netanyahu government, 197
non-monarchs, 30, 65, 241, 254, 264
  opposition, 264
  popular sovereignty, 66
  protests, 272
North Korea, 18
Nuri al-Said, 66

Obeidat, Ahmed, 192, 195
oil crisis, 191

Index

347

Oman, 3, 32, 248, 251
Omani Shura Council, 248
opinion polling, 164
opposition elites, 36, 37, 59, 148, 269
Orleans monarchy, 280

Pakistan, 311
Palestine, 119
  assassination of Hamas leader, 197
  fedayeen movements, 188
  Israel conflict, 141, 160
panchayat democracy, 297
parliamentary responsibility, 137, 253,
    279, 281
Pasha, Glubb, 182
political elites, 219–224
  under autocracy, 305
popular mobilization, 60, 76, 250,
    265, 272
popular sovereignty, 19, 20, 28, 32, 65,
    66, 69, 70, 238, 258, 304
power-sharing, 5, 25
  and attributions, 51–64
  and autocrats, 98
  and blame avoidance, 23, 69, 308
  citizens' response to credibility
    changes, 82–83
  different threats and divergent,
    176–179
  King Hussein, 179–198
  of autocrats, 54
preference falsification, 14, 24, 44
presidents
  Abdelaziz Bouteflika, 311
  Abdelmadjid Tebboune, 311
  Ali Abdullah Saleh, 51, 250, 265
  Dmitry Medvedev, 87, 90
  Erdogan, 12
  Gamal Abdel Nasser, 140, 187
  Habib Bourguiba, 21
  Harry Truman, 17
  Husni Mubarak, 2, 4, 13, 52, 81,
    237, 265, 267, 310
  Mahmoud Ahmadinejad, 79
  Mohammed Morsi, 311
  Muammar al-Qadhafi, 265
  Omar al-Bashir, 43, 250, 265
  Vladimir Putin, 7, 12, 14, 24, 40, 73,
    87, 89
  Zine al-Abidine Ben Ali, 265

PRI regime, 8
prime ministers, 71, 177, 229, 289
  Abbas al-Fassi, 246
  Abdelilah Benkirane, 95, 246
  Abdelmounim al-Rifai, 189
  Abdulhamid Sharaf, 192
  Abdullah Ensour, 203
  Adnan Badran, 221
  Ahmed Nazif, 267
  Ahmed Obeidat, 192
  al-Salim al-Sabah, 246
  Amuzegar, 295
  and autocrats, 50, 55
  Awn al-Khasawneh, 129, 203
  Bahjat al-Talhouni, 186, 188
  Ben Ali, 244
  decision-making, 15, 133
  dismissal of, 4, 37, 123
  Dmitry Medvedev, 91
  Driss Jettou, 246
  Fawzi al-Mulki, 180
  Fayez al-Tarawneh, 203
  Gholam Reza Azhari, 295
  Habib Bourguiba, 243
  Hani al-Mulki, 147, 203, 221, 222
  Hazza al-Majali, 185
  Hoveyda, 294
  Ibrahim Hashem, 221
  influence of Jordan, 126
  Jung Bahadur Rana, 296
  Kabariti, 197
  kings appointing, 131
  Koirala, 296
  Malaysia, 67
  Marouf al-Bakhit, 203
  Morocco, 87
  Mudar Badran, 221
  Nuri al-Said, 66
  Omar al-Razzaz, 125, 203, 206, 230
  Saadeddine al-Othmani, 40, 97,
    246
  Said al-Mufti, 182, 221
  Samir al-Rifai, 214
  Suleiman al-Nabulsi, 183, 220
  Surya Bahadur Thapa, 297
  Tawfiq Abu al-Huda, 221
  Vladimir Putin, 88
  Wasfi al-Tell, 186, 221
  Zaid al-Rifai, 214
  Zaid ibn Shaker, 221

348   *Index*

principal components analysis (PCA),
    157
propaganda, 12, 23, 74, 307
protests, 2, 4, 15, 26, 57, 76, 165, 181,
    199, 202, 214
  Amman, 147
  during al-Mulki, 205
  Iran, 79
  Jordan, 1, 174
  Morocco, 93
  Moscow City Council Elections, 93
  permission for, 37, 216–219
Prussia, 71, 280
public opinion, 24, 34, 36, 42, 151,
    167, 170, 185, 190, 306
purges, 68, 184, 241
  Great Purge, 41
Putin, Vladimir, 24, 73
  and Dmitry Medvedev, 87, 89–93
  during COVID-19, 40
  regime in Russia, 7, 12, 14

Qaboos, Sultan, 251
Qatar, 32, 66, 248
Qatari Shura Council, 248

Rana, Jung Bahadur, 296
Rania (queen), 198
Rassemblement Constitutionnel
    Démocratique (RCD), 244, 249
repression, 10, 14, 41, 103–106, 184
  Hashemite monarchy, 215
republic, 5, 250, 267
  Arab republics, 3, 239, 242, 245,
    247, 250, 251
  Iran, 79
  Syria, 62
  United Arab Republic, 184
Rosenfeld, Bryn, 23
royal resiliency, 29
ruling monarchies, 18
Russia, 34, 87
  Putin and Medvedev, 88–93
  Putin's regime in, 7, 14
  War in Ukraine, 88

Said, Khaled, murder of, 1, 269
Saleh, Ali Abdullah, 51, 250, 265
Saudi Arabia, 57, 191, 210, 243
Saudi monarchy, 32

SAVAK (police force), 289
Second Intifada in Palestine, 199
Selassie (emperor), 287
Shah, Mohammad Reza, 38, 80, 281,
    288–295, 301
Sharaf, Abdulhamid, 192
social mobilization, 1
South Korea, 42
Soviet Union, 41, 61, 68, 88
Stalin, 41, 47, 61
strategic delegation, 76, 132, 143, 211
strikes, 1, 206, 268, *see also* protests
Stuart kings, 278
Stuart monarch Charles I, 70
Sudan, 3, 43, 250, 265
Syria, 7, 18, 62, 117, 184, 243, 265,
    308

Talal (Hussein's father), 117, 179
tandemocracy, 89
Tebboune, Abdelmadjid, 311
Thailand, 19, 71
Thapa, Surya Bahadur, 297
Tonga, 287
Tribhuvan (king), 296
Truman, Harry, 17
Tunisia, 2, 21, 243, 249, 258, 265,
    270
Turkey, 12

Ukraine, 88
  invasion 2022, 14
Union Générale Tunisienne du Travail
    (UGTT), 270
United Arab Emirates (UAE), 19, 248
United Arab Republic, 184
United Kingdom, 117, 279
United States, 119, 124, 160, 196, 199
  financial assistance for Jordan, 120,
    140
  invasion of Iraq, 7
unpopular policy, 4, 93, 130, 133, 153,
    156, 157, 169, 184, 208, 237,
    301

Varieties of Democracy (V-Dem), 80,
    84, 85, 104, 107, 111, 216,
    272, 284
  civil liberties index, 103
Vietnam, 23

Index

West Bank, 119, 180
White Revolution, 291
WhoGov, 111
William, Frederick, 72
World Bank, 270

Yemen, 250, 265
YouGov survey, 148, 151, 152

Zaid, Sharif Hassan bin, 210
Zein (queen), 185

Printed in the United States
by Baker & Taylor Publisher Services